A NAVAL CAREER

H. C. Guernsey,
Commander RN (Retired)

ARTHUR H. STOCKWELL LTD.
Elms Court   Ilfracombe   Devon
Established 1898

ISBN 0 7223 2586-X

Printed in Great Britain by
Arthur H. Stockwell Ltd.
Elms Court   Ilfracombe
Devon

Contents

Illustrations between pp.96—97

Chapter 1

The Little Boy

In one of Noel Coward's songs he portrays a wealthy widow who sets off adventurously for foreign parts and fetches up one evening at "a Bar on the Piccolo Marina" on Capri. Two sailors in search of a free drink picked her up and suddenly in their happy company she discovered that "life was for living".

Hugh had reached the same conclusion by the time he was fourteen and proceeded, in his deliberate way, to pursue each avenue of adventure as it opened up to him. He had found out that what he most enjoyed in life was a happening.

The only son, preceded by four daughters, and followed by a fifth, he had been hopelessly swamped by the sheer weight of exhuberant femininity, for in addition to all these sisters, there was a quiet, sensible, but commanding governess in the home, at least in his earlier days, and beyond her his mother, a beautiful and determined woman who lived in a whirlwind often constructed out of fantasy. His father, an equally strong character, was not often seen after Hugh's tenth year, for he, too, seemed to find the excess of femininity somewhat inhibiting. Father had taken himself off to the South African war — during which Hugh was born — and then, shortly after his return, sailed for Canada on a big game shooting trip which included some weeks of gold panning during the Klondike rush.

No sooner had Father returned to the family, happily settled in a particularly lovely Cornish home, than he decided to return to Canada, where he bought a ranch in the mountainous interior of British Columbia, so that the family found themselves in August 1904 travelling the long fifteen days sea and rail journey to Kamloops. Hugh was four, and this exciting experience planted firmly in his young mind an insatiable desire to see the world — all of it. Blowing whales and fantastic blue-green icebergs gliding past the ship as she steamed through the Belle Isle Strait on her way to Quebec, convinced him once and for all that there was much in this life which was worth seeing — and doing.

The following six years on a cattle ranch developed in this young mind a deep love of nature, especially for wild animal life and flowers. He saw coyotes, and an occasional mountain wolf driven down in winter time by heavy snowfall from the higher levels; gophers sitting up on their haunches with hands folded across their breasts and ready to dive into their holes; squirrels building their winter nests inside hollow trees and furnishing themselves with a store of pine-tree nuts; an occasional magnificently antlered deer, and he learned to recognise many of their tracks in the deep snow of winter. In autumn geese flew across the valley two or three thousand feet above his head honking musically to one another as they kept their tight arrowhead formation pointing southwards. Never once did he see a bear, though they were common enough in that region. Still, once out riding in the winter, his father pointed out to him the shimmering air which emerged from an old hollowed-out tree, betraying the presence of a winter hibernator.

Blue and brown grouse appeared in the fall of the year and Father usually went out and shot a few for the table. Duck, teal and widgeon were plentiful in a swampy area a couple of miles down the river from the ranch house. And he never forgot one day finding small fingerling trout frozen in the river ice which had to be broken in order to provide a winter drinking pool for the cattle. Salmon came up the river to spawn most years in August, and on one notable occasion he waded out into a shallow riffle where a large fin could be seen slowly weaving its way amongst the stones. He seized the fish by its tail and dragged it ashore. It was nearly as long as he was himself, and very much the worse for wear, for it had been battling its way for four hundred miles since it left the Pacific Ocean.

There were also muskrats, and a few beaver, very shy people who disappeared into their beehive watery huts while one was still tantalisingly far off. One year someone shot a golden eagle, and his mother made the enormous outstretched wings into a tall firescreen. Passing trappers sometimes came to the house to sell their furs and the ladies wore beaver, musquash, fisher and even ermine. Hugh slew two of these latter high-smelling little creatures himself, having accidentally disturbed them in a hollow log in an old snake fence. His mother's ermine stole and muff made up in

London were truly magnificent, for they were composed of carefully chosen skins showing the greenish line along the backbone which so much enhances the appearance — if only expensive furriers would not dye it out of existence. A very large black bear skin was brought in one winter by a trapper and was made into a handsome rug which adorned the dining-room floor for many years to come.

A Chinese was always employed as cook at the ranch house, and his long pigtail, neatly coiled at the back of his head, was a source of unending interest, and from time to time the children would surprise the man as he combed out his black shiny hair which reached his waist. He was the most efficient, tireless and neatest worker in the whole establishment, and impeccably clean.

At least once every year a motley band of perhaps twenty Nicola Indians passed through the valley on their way from Douglas Lake to pick fruit in the Okanagan orchards, and Father gave them a permanent campsite on the river bank a mile upstream from the house. Here they erected their tall tepees with half a dozen fifteen-foot saplings set up in the shape of a cone covered with old bits of canvas and tanned deer hides. One tepee was used as a sauna, a log fire being lit in a hollow dug out on the floor upon which water was thrown in order to produce the steam. When the men could no longer stand the heat and the sweat they would run out naked and jump into the ice-cold river. The women apparently took their sauna only after dark.

Very early in life Hugh thus learned from these people that there were other races than the British, other customs than those of his English middle-class upbringing, and that the various coloured peoples had skills and virtues at least equal to any he had so far found amongst white people. This was at variance with the almost universal idea of those times that a coloured person was the intellectual inferior of the white. Hugh could never bring himself to look down upon those of a different race, and all through his life he sought out foreigners, feeling sure that they had something new, or interesting and worthwhile, to show to him.

When the boy was ten his parents decided that it was high time he should go to school, and accordingly he was taken home to Hastings on the south coast of England to enter a small preparatory school where the two sons of an old family friend, an Irish doctor, were among the pupils. Hastings was a fishing port and also a summer seaside resort, and as unlike a ranch isolated in the mountains as could possibly be imagined.

The eight-day sea passage from Montreal to Liverpool was awesome indeed, for they ran into an exceptionally severe Atlantic gale, with thirty-foot waves recorded, and the ship hove-to for a couple of days. Each day the deck steward took the children up to a sheltered part on the bridge deck where a dozen chairs were wedged in athwart-ships and firmly lashed to suitable stanchions. Each passenger was then firmly roped into his deck-chair, but on one occasion a lashing gave way and the whole row of chairs broke loose and everyone was thrown violently into the scuppers amidst broken woodwork. A few people suffered minor injuries, and thereafter nobody was allowed on deck again until the storm moderated. This remained for Hugh the worst weather he ever experienced in a long life at sea — for his fate was to be a sailor.

Never before Hastings had Hugh ever had even one boy to play with. All the companions of his own age had been girls. He had never seen a football nor a cricket bat, nor had he ever walked on a cement pavement. Getting to school in a tramcar, with a change to be made at the clock tower in the middle of the town, was simply terrifying. Had he dropped the three pennies for his fare? or the little luncheon packet of sandwiches? or had he remembered to put all of those homework exercise books in the satchel slung over his shoulders? The hour-long daily journey was an anxious time for him.

Two things in particular drove him frantic. The weekly drill hour of the school military cadet corps was preceded by dressing up in the scarlet tunic and blue serge trousers which composed the smart and attractive uniform. But there were shiny black leather gaiters to be laced up — how? There was an excruciatingly hard leather belt carrying the bayonet and a similar bandolier with its ammunition pouch, and then the shiny new rifle, all knobs and excrescences, which on every drill day rubbed the skin off the left collar-bone; and the peaked cap which would get knocked off when the sergeant ordered "Slope Arms!" — unless, of course, one stuffed cardboard round the inside rim and fairly jammed it down almost over the ears, which hurt all through that drill hour. Field days came about twice a year. The cadet corps travelled by train four miles to a Territorial Army rifle-range beyond Bexhill, and there the few who were skilled marksmen fell out and spent the day on their stomachs blazing away at the long-range targets, while the rest of the corps captured or defended a hill. Fighting stopped at lunch-time (hot pea soup and ham sandwiches) and then the remaining unskilled marksmen had a short period of target practice and also learned how to mark in the target butts. At 3 p.m. the corps fell in and started the five-mile march back to the school. The stiff army boots stamping along the paved roadway soon wore away toes and heels and the last mile of bursting blisters was a torturing experience. Thus it was that Hugh, seeing the shining sun, played truant on the next field day, spending it morosely watching ducks being fed breadcrumbs by kind ladies in Hastings park while he himself was foodless and feeling increasingly envious of the plump waterfowl. That evening he had to lie to Mother about his field day experiences, and again on the following morning to the headmaster, who wanted to know why he had not been with the corps - - "It was such a lovely sunny day and we all enjoyed ourselves so much!" said the head, who had himself travelled both ways comfortably by train. Hugh was in a dilemma; he hated lies and he hated blistered feet, but he couldn't make up his mind which was the worse.

He really enjoyed lessons if and when he could understand what was taught. But he was a slow learner and eventually piled up fifty-eight "impots" — lessons unlearned and ordered to be redone. The headmaster sent for him and gave him two weeks in which to clear up the backlog, which of course he failed to do, and then again summoned him into his study and gave him twelve cuts with the cane across the buttocks. He howled, but later experienced an enormous feeling of relief that the "impots" had been wiped out. Thereafter he worked much better than he had ever done before. The Bible, which knows so many things, has words of wisdom about chastisement, and seems, in this case at any rate, to be confirmed in its viewpoint.

Latin or Greek, French or German, had to be chosen in this school, and after a very slow start Hugh found at the end of two years' study that he actually could ask about the pen of his aunt in accurate if not melodious French, while the adventures of Julius Caesar in *De Bello Gallico*, Book One, had begun to unfold with increasing comprehension and whetted interest. He said in later years that the most useful tuition he ever received in his life was his firm foundation in Latin, a language, he claimed, which opened up to his understanding a great part of European civilisation. He also began dimly to comprehend that a Frenchman does not describe in words a given happening in precisely the same way as does an English observer, and that this variation in viewpoint, or interpretation, is the underlying cause of a great part of the friction that arises between nations. Remarkably few people appear to have noticed this divergence, which in fact has such great political effects in international affairs.

It was at the age of about eleven that this boy was told that next term he was to be moved up from the youngsters' dormitory to a room occupied by five intermediate scholars, all a little older than himself. Several of his friends warned him not to move. They told him:

"Those big boys do terrible things to the younger ones when they move in there; you'll just hate it!"

Nobody explained what the terrible things were, but he told his mother about it and urged her to petition the head not to move him. Since he did not know himself what was wrong about that room, she was unable to give the head a definite reason for the request which she immediately made, though she may have had her suspicions. The head questioned him about his objection at length, but of course got no enlightenment, for when he was pressed, Hugh could only answer:

"But I don't know what it is that they do. I've simply been told that it is just awful!"

He was obviously frightened of some unknown bogey, and the head rather angrily decided that he should not be moved, and of course made probing enquiries which led nowhere. Presumably the changes of puberty were being explored as they occurred. The whole thing was unfortunate, and laid a foundation of profound fear of the sexual part of life. His governess had already noticed more than five years earlier that he was "a nervous little boy" and that he suffered from terrors of a number of things he did not understand, or which were not considered suitable for children to be told about. There was a lot of Victorian repression woven into the upbringing of children in those days.

Then, in time for Christmas 1911, he was rather suddenly whipped back to Canada again, this time to St. John, New Brunswick, where his father had invested heavily in commercial property, believing that the Canadian Pacific Railway was about to develop the port as its principal winter outlet on the Atlantic seaboard while the St. Lawrence River was icebound for the usual several months each winter. The Company's decision, if it had in reality ever been made, was reversed a year later and Father suffered fairly heavy monetary losses.

The children were all delighted to return to Canada, and Father promised to get passage on the new liner *Titanic*, which was due to make her maiden voyage shortly. As he walked along Cockspur Street, from which one can see Nelson's Pillar in Trafalgar Square, apprehension seized him. He told them later that he suddenly thought that a new untried ship, and the largest one in the world, might perhaps run into unforseen troubles, and with his wife and all six children on board, any sort of misadventure might turn out to be disastrous for the family. He stopped dead in his tracks and found that he was in front of the Allen Line office door, walked in there and learned that their ship *Victorian* would sail only a day later than *Titanic*, and he bought tickets for the whole family on that ship instead. When he got back to St. Margaret's Bay he ran into loud protests on all sides, but was not to be persuaded to change his mind.

The westbound crossing was duly made only a day behind that of the ill-fated *Titanic*, steaming at about twenty knots in spite of the fog, and she was sunk by an iceberg with the loss of about 1500 lives. *Victorian* was trapped in the same ice-floe as the *Titanic*.

The children were already asleep in their cabins when their father suddenly appeared, got them up, warmly dressed, and into their lifebelts and then shepherded them up to the boat-deck where they were mustered by the ship's officer in charge of their boat, which was turned out, lowered to deck level and then rehoisted to the davit-head; after that they were sent back to their cabins where Father carefully inspected everyone's lifebelt to ensure that it was properly adjusted. Later they were allowed to undress and go back to bed. While on deck they saw nothing but the thick fog and an occasional gleam as the bright lights of the ship were reflected from a nearby iceberg. The tinkling of trash ice could be heard from time to time when small pieces scraped the hull as the ship crept dead slow ahead.

Next day they reached the scene of the disaster, steaming slowly through a mass of jetsam floating on the surface — deck-chairs, stewards' wooden trays, pieces of ship equipment and so on — and Father told them that an old friend, who was one of the ship's officers, had quietly informed him that a signal had been received that *Titanic* had been holed by an iceberg, so that was why he woke up the family even before "lifeboat stations" was ordered. Later at St. John Railway Station the boy watched the loading of about sixty flower-decked coffins containing the recovered bodies of *Titanic* victims.

The whole incident impressed upon him a vivid appreciation of the reality of the peril of the seas.

In the New Year he went off to nearby Rothesay to a preparatory school run by an elderly English clergyman, and gained much from his experiences there. Almost half the boys were Americans from the New England states, and, being out in the country, the life was much more free and open than at his English "prep" school, for they were sited on the edge of a vast uninhabited woodland area where deer, moose or an occasional black bear might be encountered. The masters were, too, of much superior calibre to those he had encountered at Hastings.

Yet here once again he ran into alarming mystery. Everyone over the age of twelve had, according to unwritten schoolboy tradition, to be "initiated" — whatever that might mean — and he was warned to be ready to present himself before a kind of court of senior boys who would muster at a clearing in the woods a few days hence. He had made friends with an older boy, a fine type of young American, an accomplished athlete and an outstanding prefect in the school. Hugh went off to consult his friend in much trepidation.

"Do you know how babies get to be born?" asked Cy.

"No. I never thought about it," Hugh replied.

"Well, you say you were brought up on a cattle ranch. You must have seen what the bull does with a cow, surely?"

"Yes, I have. What's that got to do with it?"

"Didn't your Pa or your Ma ever tell you anything about it at all?" demanded the dumbfounded Cy.

"No; not really. Dad just said I'd find out all about that when I got a bit older later on."

"Well," said Cy, "I'm going to tell them to put off your initiation this time. You're too young for that just yet, I can see."

And that was the last he heard about the "initiation ", and the whole subject slipped away out of his mind for some time to come.

A year later the family moved to the provincial capital of BC, Victoria on Vancouver Island, and he entered his third school, University College just below Mount Tolmie, and began to think of himself as a Canadian.

When Hugh was still a baby in arms the family had gone to Salcombe in South Devon for some months to stay at Trinick's

Hotel while searching for a new home in the West Country. There they became close friends with Captain Chapple and his family, the captain serving at that time in the Royal Yacht which seldom put to sea. Mother was a great admirer of sailors, and Captain Chapple arranged for a ship's tailor at nearby Plymouth to make little sailor suits for the boy almost as soon as he could walk, and a miniature sailor's wide-brimmed straw hat was also procured for him. The outfit was much admired by the family and several local ladies, which caused the child to suffer agonies of embarrassment when they offered extravagant praises about his appearance. Thus thoughts of the sea were introduced to him as soon as active comprehension was reached, and from that time forward his mother planned a naval career for her son.

Social life in Victoria was much connected with the British naval base at Esquimalt which was the station home port of two ancient converted sailing sloops, the *Algerine* and the *Shearwater*, and the senior captain, Corbett of the *Algerine*, became a close friend of the family together with his first lieutenant, Chalmers. It was a memorable day for Hugh when Lieutenant Chalmers invited him on board and showed him all over the spotlessly clean little ship. There was even a gleaming white canvas sail furled on a highly varnished boom, and moreover, it was still in use to stabilise the ship in rough weather.

The older members of the family passed their time in a tightly packed social whirl, the three eldest girls becoming officially engaged, and later married, all within six months. So busy were the grown-ups with social events that it came as a shock when Captain Corbett, turning to Mother at a tea party one day, said:

"If you want Hugh to go into the Navy you will have to put in your application almost at once! They've just altered the regulations," and he promised to write to the Admiralty for the new rules, which, when they arrived, revealed that it was already two months too late for the last chance of entry. Consternation prevailed; every sort of wire was pulled. A close friend, the former Army Chaplain to the Duke of Connaught — now Governor General of Canada — promised to write to His Royal Highness asking him to intervene. A political friend, Martin Burell, a minister in the Cabinet at Ottawa, was asked to get the Prime Minister, Sir Robert Borden, to write to Mr Winston Churchill, First Lord of the Admiralty; and someone else petitioned Prince Louis of Battenberg, the First Sea Lord, while Captain Corbett sent off a couple of notes to senior officers he knew in the Admiralty.

Their Lordships of the Admiralty must have been quite impressed by this storm of appeals (organised by Mother), for they tactfully decided that the slow mail service to the distant west coast of Canada had been responsible for the lateness of the application — not the negligence of the parents; and anyhow each Governor General in the Empire had the privilege of nominating annually one cadet into the Royal Navy, and it was the king's brother who was in fact now exercising this privilege — so Hugh was accepted, subject of course to medical and scholastic examinations. The family doctor performed the first and the Lieutenant Governor's ADC, Captain Muskett, supervised the second in his office in the Parliament Buildings as soon as the necessary papers arrived, and Hugh duly passed his exams.

Having travelled alone from Victoria, Hugh somewhat breathlessly arrived at the Royal Naval College, Osborne, in the Isle of Wight, brass buttoned for the first time in his dark blue serge uniform which Messrs Gieve, Matthews and Seagrove of South Molton Street, London W.1, had tailored for him in just twenty-four hours. He was ten days late for the summer term 1914. Authority at the college, in the shape of a much beribboned commander, was not pleased with this unorthodoxy, but since the Admiralty had permitted it, he saw no reason for reprimand. Indeed, he was genuinely surprised when he learned from the new cadet that he had travelled six thousand miles all on his own to reach Osborne.

World War I broke out on 4th August, and every mind was bent upon making his or her personal contribution to uphold the cause of England. The Osborne Cadets had been sent to the ships of the Home Fleet anchored at Spithead a few days previously; Hugh, together with eleven others in his term, being allocated to *Iron Duke*, the Fleet Flagship of Admiral Sir George Callaghan. King George V had come on board on 29th July to spend the night and go to sea in the Fleet flagship on the following day to witness exercises. After breakfast he came running up the ladder from the Admiral's flat, laughing cheerfully as he stepped out onto the quarterdeck to inspect the ship's company "mustered by Open List" — that is, as they marched past in single file, saluting when they reached the inspecting officer. Then after that was over, the Admiral spoke to His Majesty, who nodded his head evidently in assent, and quickly walked across the quarterdeck to where the cadets were drawn up in single rank to witness the ceremonies. They had been ordered to look His Majesty directly in the eye and stand strictly to attention. The king slowly walked down the line, turning for a moment to look each cadet straight in the face, and Hugh noticed that His Majesty had very bright blue eyes — also a somewhat high colour about the nose and cheeks where they were not hidden behind a neat beard and moustache. It was all over inside of three minutes.

Then, a few minutes later, while they were waiting for the order to "fall out", it seemed as if all pandemonium was suddenly breaking loose. You could see streams of signal flags being hoisted and then hauled down from the foremast yards. Signal flashing lamps were blinking and chattering their shutters in every direction; semaphore arms were twitching jerkily at full speed on the signal deck. The Royal barge from the Royal Yacht *Victoria and Albert* drew alongside the starboard after ladder as the king shook hands with Admiral Callaghan, both of them with grave, no longer smiling, faces. The ceremonial side party, consisting of the botswain, the chief botswain's mate, eight quartermasters, the Royal Marine bugler and half a dozen seamen boy messengers, drawn up in two ranks by the ladder head, piped their sovereign over the side and the Royal Marine Guard of Honour presented arms as the king saluted and then quickly disappeared down the accommodation ladder and out of view.

Presently the lieutenant in charge of the cadets returned and told them that the fleet had been ordered to proceed to war stations and that cadets were to go immediately to their quarters in a six-inch gun casemate, pack their bags as quickly as possible, and muster at the port forward ladder. A boat would convey them to East Cowes about three miles distant where they would disembark, collect their belongings from the college, draw their railway travel warrants, and proceed on summer leave to their homes.

What an anticlimax this was! Everybody else in *Iron Duke* was going away to battle with the German Fleet, while the cadets were to slope off and take a summer holiday. They hung their heads and almost prayed that the war would go on long enough for them to get to sea before it ended. It did, of course, and it claimed the lives of about one-third of that particular dozen.

Chapter 2

The Naval Cadet

There is something about a uniform that confers upon its wearer a sense of responsibility, and upon the public that surrounds him a feeling of trust. They expect him to be dependable; and these almost automatic reactions are greatly enhanced in time of war. Hugh found himself at his fourteenth birthday with but three months' training behind him, now regarded for the first time in his life as a person of consequence, and although he did not grow up to manhood overnight, he did experience a sense of having suddenly advanced in age to a stature beyond that of merely a little boy. He found that he was suddenly treated with a consideration, almost with a respect that was an entirely new experience for him. He was not puffed up by this, but rather felt a weight of responsibility settling upon his shoulders, and obligation to be whatever it was that people now seemed to be expecting of him — and this was, of course, a genuine step in onward growth.

His parents and the three youngest children were to spend the summer holidays at Trinick's Hotel at Salcombe in South Devon, where they had last visited when Hugh was six months old, and there they found Sir Alfred Yarrow, the Clydeside shipbuilder, and one of Mother's oldest friends. The old gentleman had gone to this peaceful spot to plan the vast wartime expansion of his shipyard, and a steady stream of senior men in the company came and went from his upstairs sitting-room where the clatter of his secretary's typewriter could be heard far into the night.

Within a day or two after his arrival at the hotel he invited Hugh to his room where large-scale drawings of the famous Yarrow marine boiler, and of the ships in which it was installed, were laid out on a long table. He spent some time discoursing on the engineering features with which he was concerned, though Hugh had only the vaguest understanding of what he was being told.

These visits were repeated several times each week, and he finally presented the young cadet with a comprehensive set of engineering drawings of the new destroyer *Broke* which he had built, and which was the fastest warship in the world. He seemed to take to the boy and spared no pains to answer whatever questions he was asked, and Hugh was much flattered by these attentions from a man who had almost overnight become one of the really important people in England.

Back again at Osborne in September, ideas of active engagement in warfare sank rapidly into oblivion. You doubled — never walked — everywhere inside the college buildings. You gave way to all other cadets in terms senior to your own. As soon as the cadet captain rang the ship's bell in the morning at his end of the dormitory, you jumped out of bed, ran to the plunge tank at the end of the dormitory, jumped into the cold water, and rather faster jumped out again, cleaned your teeth, ran back to strip your bed, dressed in two minutes, folded pyjamas, closed your sea-chest, and stood at attention beside it. The last cadet to complete was apt to get two strokes of the switch. Then you doubled to your classroom for an hour's early prep work, and then ran to the dining-hall where the Blake Term had its own two long scrubbed deal mess tables. Food was good, plain, and always available for second helpings. Marine waiters were expert and swift in serving the various courses. One night a cadet in the term ate thirty-one fish balls; Hugh counted them. The Marine waiters gathered around awestruck. The boy suffered no harm whatever.

You ran out of the dining-hall and had about ten minutes available for your own private affairs. The day was filled with class work on a general educational timetable. After lunch three hours were devoted to games in which some degree of personal selection was allowed. There was a period of evening study, followed by cocoa and ship's biscuits, after which you ran off to bed.

Sunday afternoon was free, and most cadets went for long walks in the large surrounding grounds of Queen Victoria's Osborne House estate. Life was apt to be enlivened out of doors by a very large kangaroo — an Australian gift to the king — which repeatedly jumped out of its wire enclosure and raced round the playing fields at breakneck speed.

The surrounding world was out of bounds, and special permission had to be obtained to go beyond the set boundaries. The ordinary school terms and holiday periods were observed.

Life was organised and regulated to the last detail, and any infraction of rules was dealt with severely.

The lieutenant in charge of the term had disappeared when the cadets returned in September, and they were dismayed when they heard that since he had gone to sea, a schoolmaster would take charge. Hugh had liked and admired Lieutenant Willoughby — who was lost with his ship *Gloucester* at the Battle of Coronel — and found that, although the master was pleasant to deal with, he really didn't care for him very much, and so, in the event, had almost no dealings or contact with him at all.

Within a few weeks four cruisers on patrol in the English Channel were lost by submarine torpedo. When the first one was hit the next in line stopped to lower boats and pick up survivors and was herself torpedoed; likewise the third, and finally the fourth in line, in exactly the same way. The cadets at Osborne knew many of the young men who had been hurriedly sent to reinforce the manning of the reserve ships called back into service and who had gone to sea as cadets without completing their training and before being rated midshipmen. The loss made a profound impression in the college. They felt that the price of the future glory,which was much in their minds, was going to turn out to be a high one.

Six months later Hugh found he was not feeling well. During gym everything momentarily went black and he wondered if he would fall flat on his face. Somehow he recovered himself and staggered through the remaining few minutes of the class. Then he began to feel sick and to experience a dull pain in the abdomen. Finally he went to sick-bay and quickly got better. But whatever the trouble was it recurred again and again. At last he was sent to Haslar Naval Hospital just across the Solent from the Isle of Wight, and was told that he had appendicitis. His mother arrived at the hospital an hour after he got there, and almost immediately a tall lean middle-aged man wearing the uniform of a surgeon rear-admiral came into the room accompanied by a bevy of lesser doctors, the hospital matron and a couple of nurses in their smart Queen Alexandra's Royal Naval Nursing Service uniforms. This was Sir Lenthal Cheatle, the leading London surgeon who had joined the Navy for the duration of the war. He shook hands with Mother and then sat down on the bed and began to explore the seat of the pain with the most wonderfully gentle hands, chatting to Hugh while he examined him.

"Well, young man; we'll have to take away this troublesome appendix that's been bothering you. It really isn't at all bad, you know, but if you were in a ship at sea and it began to blow up you could find yourself in serious trouble, and I don't want that to happen. I'll fix you up tomorrow morning." And off he went chatting to Mother.

She came back a little later looking strained and subdued. She had found out that the surgeon was a distant cousin of her Scots son-in-law, and that he was the greatest living surgeon in England at that time, so there was absolutely nothing to worry about, she said, and she would come back again tomorrow afternoon, by which time it would be "all over", and Hugh would be coming round out of the anaesthetic. What would he most like her to bring him for tea?

A little later an orderly shaved him and painted his stomach bright green.

"Mr Cheatle's green stuff they call it, Sir. He brought it down from London this morning special for you, he did!"

That was at least some assuagement of the surprise and panic which had surged over him. But no supper came; nothing but a glass of water, then a pill and blessed dreamless sleep.

At eight o'clock — still almost dark in late November — a nurse bustled in, stabbed his arm with a needle, and hurried out again with the cryptic statement:

"They'll be in for you in ten minutes' time!"

The door opened and in came a white trolley followed by several acolytes in white overalls with face masks and hoods over their hair, and mercifully the young Irish doctor who had dealt with him at Osborne and whom he regarded as a friend. They put a white backless gown on him, told him to get on to the trolley and lie down and then clapped a mask over his nose, one strong man on each side holding his arms firmly still, and he beagn to inhale the sickening stench of ether. He seemed to need a lot of it, for he heard one saying to another:

"Surely he is out, isn't he?"

"No; I don't think so. Now breathe away, boy. Take big deep breaths."

Then he woke up to a dimmed light, and was sick, again, and again, and again. Later a cup was held to his lips and he started to drink, queer though the taste was.

"No, no! This is mouthwash, spit it out."

But the voice was too late, he had swallowed most of what was in the cup. The light seemed to grow brighter and the vomiting went on, and on, and his whole body began to have feeling spreading through it once more, a feeling as if it had been cruelly battered and beaten, and a sharp pain emerged beneath a multi-tailed bandage that squeezed him tightly from the hips up to the breast.

"Can't you stop this vomiting? You haven't stopped for sixteen hours and you'll burst all your stitches if you go on like this. Try to control yourself!"

He had no idea who spoke, nor did he care. He wanted to ask if he was dying but couldn't form the words.

His mother's face appeared with a mechanical sort of a smile painfully stretched across it, but he couldn't follow whatever it was she was trying to say to him, and at last oblivion came; and then it was tomorrow, or perhaps the day after that. The sun shone through the window. He felt weak and battered but the pain was now bearable and he no longer felt sick. He fell asleep. Two or three days passed unmarked, unrecognised. Scraps of food came and went, somebody washed his face, his hands; the orderly provided bottles and bedpans. It seemed a long, long time later that he began to feel human again, to have a second pillow at his head, to be able to take in what was said to him and to recognise who it was that spoke; and his mother said that she really ought to be getting home tomorrow, and he must write and let her know if there was anything he needed.

Was all of this worth a second thought, or recording? Not of course in itself; but the shock effect stayed with him for many years and certainly added materially to his innately nervous temperament. He had to fight against fear, especially fear of the unknown, the unpredictable, for the whole of the rest of his life.

This illness had seriously interrupted Hugh's training and the college authorities were considering putting him back one term, his tutor told him one day. He passed this on to his mother, who arrived hot foot at Osborne immediately she got the letter. She first went to see the tutor — retired instructor, Commander Broadbent, who was a real friend to Hugh — to find out the facts. He took her to Headmaster Godfrey who, no doubt after tactful pressure, thought the boy might catch up if he went to a special tutor during the forthcoming five weeks of the Christmas holidays. While there she received a message inviting her to lunch with the captain — that very fine officer Rudolf Bentinck — and his family, where, no doubt, she exercised still more of her powers of gentle persuasion, for, when she left, Captain Bentinck assured her that if the headmaster could recommend a suitable tutor, he himself would approve of the plan. Hugh was quite bright and was placed tenth out of forty-seven in the Blake Term, and ought to be able to catch up on the time he had lost.

So it was that the boy found himself stepping out of the train at Harrow-on-the-Hill Station, and then slowly climbing in a cab up the winding road to the top of the hill behind a wheezing old horse that seemed unfit to draw any cab even on level ground. He was received by Mr Siddons, one of the school housemasters, and his wife. There were two or three small children in the family, and several schoolboys under special tuition. The Siddons were welcoming and kind, and in every possible way did their best to make his stay not only rewarding but happy. He found he made astonishing progress under Mr Siddons' experienced instruction, and after Christmas went up to seventh place in his term which, of course, pleased everyone concerned.

He explored Harrow school buildings and discovered the records of many famous names on desks and walls, and he also met the head, Dr Ford, and was fortunate in still being at Harrow for a few days of the next term there, and so saw the school both at work and at play. Later on he stayed once or twice for a few days with the Siddonses both at Harrow, and also for one whole summer holiday at the cottage they had built at Alum Bay in the Isle of Wight, and the friendship endured for several years to come.

Sports Day at Osborne towards the end of his first term was a gala occasion to which he invited his mother and his sister, who was only two years older than himself. They joined the flock of parents gathered about the rows of seats where Captain Bentinck spotted them and brought them forward to the front row just next to half a dozen chairs marked "Reserved". The various races and contests had already begun when the captain came forward conducting a tall spare man in a brown suit and bowler hat, beside whom Cadet Battenberg was walking; and behind them came the Commander-in-Chief, Portsmouth, Admiral Sir Hedworth Meux with three ladies. The brown bowler was the First Sea Lord, Chief of the Naval Staff, Admiral Prince Louis of Battenberg, whom the captain led along the front row, presenting half a dozen people, all the ladies curtseying to the serene highness. The prince soon thought that enough was enough and turned back to the central chair reserved for him with just one lady before he would have reached Mother. Hugh, watching from a distance, was as disappointed as she was.

"Of course he couldn't have shaken hands with all that crowd of people. He had to stop somewhere!" Anyhow the day was a great success and his sister had looked quite charming as several of his friends to whom he had introduced "his people" assured him.

Schoolboys are acutely anxious that "their people" should look right, create a favourable impression, and in this manner his mother never failed Hugh, and she always succeeded in turning out her girls looking well groomed and attractive.

After only five instead of the prescribed six terms at Osborne, Blake Term — each term bore the name of a famous admiral — moved on to Dartmouth where normally they would have spent two years — that is six terms — but now war losses demanded a shortening of the training period, and the Blakes had done only four terms at this senior college when they were sent to sea as midshipmen in January 1917.

A midshipman is an officer. The ratings salute him and address him as "Sir", but they don't really take him too seriously. They know he is a beginner and they take a keen interest in his progress, but still, when it comes to the point, they obey his order. They also give him much sound instruction and advice. His first "command" is a picket boat — and in those days it was a 47-foot wooden steamboat built to stand rough weather. The midshipman took the wheel and gave the orders, but the petty officer coxswain stood beside him, and would even grab the wheel in moments of stress, to avoid a collision, for example. The service skated over the anomalous position and referred to him as a "young officer", "the young gentleman", and it worked out remarkably well in practice. "Snotty" was the colloquial name he bore; or, during his first year or so, just "wart", an excrescence, which was not intended to be flattering. None of it bothered Hugh in the least; his mind was obsessed, not with status or dignity, but with learning his job as soon as possible.

Today the midshipman has vanished from the Navy List. Young men, mostly from a university with quite impressive scientific degrees, arrive on board their first ship, and it is not yet too clear just how they learn to be officers — for that is a quality, not a qualification.

Life at Dartmouth was almost a replica of that at Osborne, only more so. Here, practical work was in the ascendant. Extensive engineering workshops down on the estuary shore entailed quite a long climb up and down steps, which gave a welcome break out of doors in the day's programme. There was a large swimming-pool, though not much opportunity to use it. Non-swimmers under instruction occupied most of the available time. A benevolent lady had willed a provision of Devonshire cream for tea on one or two days each week — and that was quite a notable item in the life of a sixteen-year-old. Each Saturday night the College Royal Marine Band provided music for an hour or two of dancing on the parquet-floored "Quarterdeck", a very large and handsomely designed indoor parade hall off which opened most of the classrooms. A large number of small boats to row or sail were available on weekends, and Hugh, at least in the summer, was often on the water, for he was a keen, and already quite experienced, small boat sailor.

There was a college pack of beagles, and hunting on foot was a winter sport followed by a small group of devotees. Here there was more freedom than at Osborne to roam the countryside, though the little town at the mouth of the estuary was out of bounds. Many of the farms and cottages in the district provided enormous teas with home-made cakes at an incredibly low price, and they were the goal of small parties of walkers on Saturday and Sunday afternoons all the year round. At half-term a whole holiday gave time enough for a motor boat trip up the river as far as Totnes, or a bus ride out to Slapton Sands and its long lagoon sanctuary for water birds. Cadets were being encouraged to behave like young men, though at the time they did not know it.

The term produced some outstanding athletes, Harry Stevenson among them, who became an Irish Rugby international three-quarter back, and Own Tudor, also a three-quarter, whose defective eyesight unhappily led to his being invalided out of the Service. Hugh was never any use at ball games — just a rabbit — which was the cause of abiding distress to him throughout his early life. Oddly enough though he thoroughly enjoyed playing whatever game was in season: tennis and cricket in summer, and then rugger, soccer, and hockey in the winter months. Swimming and gymnastics were his favourites, but he never shone at them.

Down on the River Dart the ageing wooden sailing line of battle-ship *Britannia* was permanently moored, giving her name to the college — for all Naval establishments ashore are named as though they were ships. The cadets were encouraged to go on board and wander about, but there was not much to see since masts and rigging had long since decayed and been removed. The copper-sheathed hull was still as sound as it had ever been. Several decks down, in the bowels of the ship, a couple of coal-burning steam boilers had been installed, so the cadets could learn and practise the heavy work of a stoker, and they all did a short period of training there, shovelling coal into the blazing furnaces.

School classes occupied the larger part of the time spent in college. A Belgian refugee professor, speaking only very halting English, was the French master, and the Blake Term provided him with what must have been the hardest experiences of his professional life. One particular boy, Seeley, developed to a high art the business of tormenting the professor during his classes.

The peak was reached one day when Cadet Seeley had organised his French class-mates into a band which collected little frogs from a pond, brought them into class in concealed jars, and then at a signal given when the professor's back was turned while writing on the blackboard, released the little creatures. The short-sighted professor couldn't quite identify what was the source of the movement of which he became increasingly conscious until one or two little frogs hopped onto his platform, one even leaping onto his desk. He went purple and stormed out of the room spluttering furious French threats — but the bell marking the end of the hour rang out at that very moment and the class dispersed at the double to their next lessons. A day or two passed in somewhat tremulous expectation of the fall of vengeance, but nothing happened; in due course it became apparent that the misdemeanor had not been reported by the professor. Had his sense of humour — and he did possess that virtue — overtaken him? or what? No one ever knew. And then little by little they began to feel ashamed. After all, they whispered to one another, he was an old man and had been a distinguished figure at university before the Germans overran Belgium, which was still fighting gallantly under the heroic leadership of King Albert, who refused to leave even for one day the remnant of his army still clinging to the last few square miles of his country. And the professor was, too, a refugee, and such people had a claim on England's kindness and goodwill.

So they were tamed. Seeley was commanded to stop his tricks, and the whole class suddenly became studious and a model of good behaviour, and got excellent marks at the end-of-term examinations in French. The professor had won the battle after all.

But the real "character" amongst the staff was Mr Harrison, a very dry, bitter-tongued mathematics master. He knew exactly how to goad the slowest learner into frantic exertion, and nobody dared to be slack in his class. He rather enjoyed baiting Harry Stevenson, whose quick Irish temper insistently showed in his scarlet face and stuttering tongue. One day under the Harrison treatment Harry sprang up from his desk with fists clenched, glaring furiously at the master. The shadow of a smile flitted across Mr Harrison's colourless face as he took up the stance of a boxer on the defensive and said:

"Aha, Stevenson! What you don't know is that I was once the lightweight runner-up for the British Amateur Boxing Championship. I'm quite ready to take you on if you wish!"

The class burst into a roar of laughter and Harry slumped back into his seat, smiling sheepishly, and said nothing.

Their time at Dartmouth passed very quickly and, much as they all longed to get to sea, these last days were registered with feelings of regret and nostalgia. It had, they felt, been a wonderful year of rewarding experience that terminated with three weeks' leave over Christmas 1916.

As soon as he reached London, Hugh hurried off to Gieves to get his uniform converted to midshipman's rank — indicated by a white patch on the coat collar, replacing a small strip of white cord — and to acquire such things as sea-boots, sou'wester and oilskins. He was accompanied by a sister whose husband had come from British Columbia with the 48th Battalion of the Canadian Army, and was now wounded in hospital in London.

He did not have to identify himself at the Naval tailor's; as a senior assistant stepped forward instantly, greeted him by name and announced:

"We heard yesterday, Sir, that you are appointed to the *Colossus*. She is in the Grand Fleet at Scapa."

Hugh asked how they had penetrated war secrets, and Mr Abbot smiled sweetly:

"Well, Sir, we have known most of the officers at the Admiralty for a long time, and they are good enough to help us prepare for the rush which takes place as each term goes to sea. The young gentlemen might otherwise have difficulty in equipping themselves in the short time available.''

The services which this firm rendered to the Navy through the years, while entirely unofficial, were enormous. They were, too, thoroughly appreciated — especially when you ran out of ready money and ''Mr Gieve'' kindly, and invariably, cashed your possibly dubious cheque.

The whole training college period had passed with one half of their minds absorbed by the war, particularly with the naval involvement. A very early naval incident became known through Winston Churchill's action (as First Lord of the Admiralty) in hurriedly sending a naval brigade in an attempt to delay the loss of Antwerp, an unsuccessful expedition severely criticised in Parliament and the Press. Shortly after that, news came that a large calibre heavy naval gun, or perhaps battery of guns, was operating in what little remained of Belgium, and cadets imagined themselves plodding through mud in sea-boots close up to the German armies. During a holiday spent near Folkstone on the English Channel, Hugh could hear the guns booming day after day. The battle of the Dogger Bank was no more than a short brush between Admiral Beatty's battle-cruiser squadron and the inferior division of German battle-cruisers who prudently escaped behind a series of minefields, but it had revealed the extent of damage that can be caused by a heavy shell on a lightly armoured ship and, in particular, anxiety amongst seamen was aroused about the danger of magazine penetration in battle-cruisers. Then came the long-drawn-out agony of the Dardanelles, and defeat which the final withdrawal signalled. Jutland was, and remained, an enigma of the North Sea mists in the mind of the public. How had the well-trusted Jellicoe missed bringing the German fleet to action, they wanted to know? The signal that might have won a victory had gone astray on a dark night, but this did not become public knowledge for many a long day. Admiral Sturdee's victory over Von Spee at the Battle of the Falkland Islands was a clear-cut decision such as the Navy had been wont to achieve in past wars, but it was a very long way away, and although it was a tremendous help to British shipping it had virtually no effect upon the heartland of Germany. Slowly the country began to apprehend that the decisive war at sea was being waged not in great ship battles but under the waters of the whole North Atlantic Ocean around each and every convoy that sailed that stormy region. It was a slow grinding little-by-little contest that nothing but endurance would ever win.

Not since Napoleon's days had British seamen had to fight as they now did, unremittingly for days, extending into years. Resolution and endurance supplied the only keys to victory — and if there was to be one, it would be won at sea, and chiefly by merchant seamen. Where the fate of British trade was at stake, the fleetmen knew exactly where they stood in this contest.

Chapter 3

They Went To Sea

Father had tried unsuccessfully to get into the Army almost from the day that war broke out, but at forty-eight he was over age, and nothing that he attempted to do effectively concealed that truth. So, early in 1915 he went back once again to Canada "to grow food", as he put it. He bought a small cattle ranch in British Columbia, and, as soon as he had found a suitable house, Mother and the two younger girls joined him. From then on Hugh spent his leaves with relations or friends and, having been given a hundred pounds by his father before he went to Canada, opened a bank account and thereafter was in effect completely independent of any further parental control. They simply supposed that he knew how to manage his own affairs, and he very quickly learned how to do just that, even before his fifteenth birthday.

When he left Dartmouth in December 1916, he took himself off to London to spend his fortnight's leave with the Warwick family, and it was they who saw him off from Euston Station on a damp raw winter's evening in January 1917, bound for Scotland he had told them; but the actual destination, Scapa Flow in the Orkney Islands a few miles off the north coast, which was the Grand Fleet base, was secret, and he did not name it.

Colossus, to which he had been appointed, was the flagship of Rear-Admiral Ernest Gaunt, Commander of the 2nd Division of the Fourth Battle Squadron — slower and older coal-burning battleships with eight 12-inch guns. Vice-Admiral Sir Doveton Sturdee, the victor of the Falkland Islands Battle, flying his flag in *Hercules*, was the Commander of the First Division, and also of the whole of the Fourth Battle Squadron.

What this actually implied was a complete mystery to the new midshipmen, but the excitement of going to sea was a breathtaking moment for him and it marked a change from boyhood to

31

manhood as far as he was concerned, young though he was. Now he stood alone; the last props, even of friendships, had been removed, and his naval career and the world lay open to him. Perhaps most young animals when they leave their parents feel much the same as he did: excited, and uncertain, with moments of panic deep down inside.

The rail journey to Thurso on the north coast of Scotland was long and tedious. The train snorts out of Euston Station in late afternoon in a cloud of white steam and black cinder-laden smoke, and rumbles away through the coal-grimed darkness of midland industrial England. The train always stopped at Crewe where the platforms were deserted. But on this particular night, since half a dozen "old Blakes" (as they had now become) were aboard, the journey was a lively one. In the next compartment two ladies in Service uniforms were also travelling north; one turned out to be the famous beauty, Lady Diana Manners, and her companion was Baroness Burton. They immediately made friends with the whole batch of new midshipmen, and a boisterous evening quite unexpectedly blew up.

A dark and bleak early arrival at Inverness gave time for an unheard-of unrationed breakfast at the Station Hotel — and, rather sadly, the two ladies vanished into the pervading fog. Through the whole day they crept laboriously across empty Scottish moorlands, stopping at some of the smallest stations on earth, and then at last it was Thurso and dusk. The antique little Orkney Ferry *King Orrey* lay at the fish-smelling jetty and rumbled slowly across the smooth but heaving twenty miles of the Pentland Firth, and the flat bald Orkney Islands ahead to the north were unseen in the darkness. The ferry passed through a narrow entrance protected by anti-submarine nets supported from a line of buoys, the nets being lowered from two trawlers' winches at either side of the passageway as the ship approached. She berthed alongside the high-sided converted merchantman *Greenwich*, the reception depot ship, and the young gentlemen and their luggage — sea-chest, green canvas-covered trunk, and suitcase — were quickly transported to the steam picket boat with its white lifebuoy lashed to the cabin canopy. There Hugh saw for the first time the majestic name *Colossus* gleaming in bold gilded lettering — and away they sped towards the Fleet anchorage in The Flow — a huge expanse of deep sea eleven miles wide from east to west and nine miles long from south to north, surrounded by several low heather-covered boggy islands with but one solitary little wooded glen full of horizontally bent oak-trees. There is a little hamlet, Scrabster, at the north-western corner and a small fishing township, Kirkwall, invisible from The Flow, at its eastern end. A few tiny scattered farms and whitewashed cottages are dotted about the landscape, and one's first season of the tremendous winter gales to be experienced there explains why the sparse buildings are so low-built and seek to hide themselves in the small depressions on the islands. Only on Hoy to the west and South Ronaldsay to the north are there hills rising to about eight hundred feet.

But all this and much else was invisible in the darkness as the picket boat threaded its way through the unseen anchored fleet of over thirty capital ships. Any that were close could be guessed at from the voice of the sentry who haled every passing boat which must identify itself or risk becoming the target for a .303 bullet, for the white wake rising from the propellor could be easily seen from a battleship's upper deck.

As they came alongside the port after accommodation ladder a screened dim blue light was switched on, and others around the upper deck gave just enough illumination to enable the batch of three new midshipmen to follow the "snotty" of the watch to the gunroom which was to be their home for the next two years.

The old hands looked them up and down as they blinked somewhat dazzled by the bright light in the mess. Only the sub-lieutenant spoke: "What's your name? Where do you come from? Duty Wart, show this new lot where the chest flat and the bathroom are" — and out they filed. Sea-chests and luggage were already being dumped in the chest flat by a working party of seamen, and the Royal Marine servant, allocated to each new officer, took charge of him there and then. He pushed the sea-chest into whatever small space was as yet unoccupied, unpacked the green trunk and suitcase, putting nearly all their contents into the sea-chest, and then took his officer to draw his hammock, mattress, blankets, and pillow from the bedding store, and showed him how to fit the rope lashings and sling the hammock from hooks on the overhead steel beams. The whole was finished off with a pair of sheets and a pillowcase taken from the sea-chest. Then the marine vanished. They were too late for dinner, but a hot meal had been kept for them, and they sat in a silent little group at the end of the long white linen-covered table, and a steward

c

demanded the production of a napkin ring so that each could identify his own table-linen. They all hurried off to the chest flat to dig this article out of their scanty possessions.

The boatswain's shrill pipe preceded the call "Pipedown" at ten o'clock, and the sub-lieutenant's voice from behind *La Vie Parisienne* bellowed out:

"Come on; Pipe down," and the gunroom cleared at the double.

They followed others to the nearby bathroom to clean their teeth, then somewhat nervously knelt down by their chests to say their prayers as had been the routine at Osborne and Dartmouth, but instantly became aware that the other midshipmen did not do so. Nobody had forseen how extremely difficult it is to get into a hammock slung six feet above the deck and only a couple of feet from the steel beams above. The gymnasts swung away with a will and overturned their hammocks, spilling out all the bedding onto the deck below. The athletic rabbits crept in at one side and fell out of the other. It was a full half-hour before all the "new boys" were not only in their hammocks but also had bedding in there too, even if sometimes the mattress was on top and the pillow at the foot. Whatever errors had occurred were almost immediately corrected by blessed sleep. Two of them fell out during the night and learned how unforgiving a steel deck can be, even when covered with its thin carpeting of brown "corticene", a heavy naval linoleum.

At six a.m. — which seemed to have arrived far too soon — the Royal Marine sentry on the flat shook each hammock vigorously and woke the dozen or so midshipmen. They fell out of their hammocks, slipped on a sweater and a pair of old grey flannel trousers over their pyjamas, put on a pair of gym shoes, and tore up several iron ladders to the quarterdeck where the hands were rigging hoses for the daily "scrub and wash decks". A senior midshipmen, or sometimes the PTI (physical training instructor petty officer), took the midshipmen at "physical jerks" — most of which was running round the deck in search of a part that was not yet awash with sea water. Night watchmen and those who had been on late trips in their boats were excused. After twenty minutes they tore down to the bathroom to shave, wash, and if there was still time, to take a bath in a large round shallow tin tub. There was a long white bath, but it was reserved by the sub-lieutenant in charge of the gunroom for his exclusive use.

Breakfast followed, and its character did not vary for the next thirty-four years. Fruit, which was an "extra" and not always available in wartime, consisted of stewed prunes, apricots, or perhaps figs. Porridge followed, with the alternative of cornflakes — you got your own packet from the messman and wrote your name on it. Sugar, severely rationed in wartime, was economically stowed in a screw-top jam jar, and again you wrote your name on that as well. The main dish — usually a concoction of egg powder in those days, sometimes with bacon, or an occasional sausage, and — very rarely indeed — kippers, smoked haddock, fresh herring or kedgeree. The tendency was for the same thing to repeat itself for a month on end and then a loudly welcomed variant would suddenly appear. Tea, bread, strictly rationed butter, and marmalade or jam served to fill whatever holes might be evident at the end. There was always enough bulk; variety and quality were the deficient ingredients in the menu. Meat and rather elderly vegetables were always served at lunch and dinner; and there was also afternoon tea shortly after "evening quarters" at four o'clock (the last muster of hands in the day); although only a bread and jam snack with infrequent and somewhat dubious cake was provided. This meal was seldom missed by anybody. The fact was that the Fleet fed better than their families ashore, and if the food was dull, it was also sufficient for the active life of a sailor. At the age of sixteen and four months, when he went to sea, Hugh and his peers thought a good deal about their meals, especially Hugh, because he found that what was provided did not agree with him; his stomach seemed to be upset very frequently, though he never suffered from seasickness.

Two days after arrival on board a shattering anticlimax developed. The ship sailed for Rosyth Dockyard in the Firth of Forth to undergo a month of periodical refit. It was only a night journey at high speed, and since there was not time to instruct the new midshipmen, they were merely detailed as second midshipman of the watch on the navigating bridge. The chief duty required there was to learn how to regulate a temperamental electric water heater so that a constant supply of good, hot, thick cocoa could be kept ready for instant supply. The captain, Dudley Pound, was up on the bridge watching the intricate passage through invisible protective minefields all through the dark hours, and wanted several cups of cocoa and knew exactly how he liked it. The navigator (and Commander Armstrong was a superb specialist) also had precise ideas about the brewing. There were two officers of the watch, and two more in charge of Defence Stations, one for the guns and the other for searchlights; and of course an old and a new midshipman, so that the cookery department was kept constantly on the alert.

Service cocoa deserved an ode composed by a poet laureate. It came in stout tins a pound or two in weight. Brown sugar, condensed milk, and above all, boiling water were the lesser partners. Everybody had his own method — to boil, or not to boil, when to put in the milk, and how much of it; and sugar, without which it was just nothing. These fine points were fought over for ever and ever, amen. A midshipman who was not able to make a good cup of cocoa was held to be unlikely to go far in the Service.

All the midshipmen were sent off on leave as soon as the ship berthed alongside the Rosyth dockyard wall in the Firth of Forth, and later from Edinburgh, Hugh telegraphed to his friends the Warwicks in London to ask if he might come back to them and that he was due to arrive next morning. Some of them met him, and gave the warmest welcome, albeit surprised. They had said goodbye for a year, or perhaps more, and had no idea what a periodic refit could mean, for nautical technicalities were beyond their experience, and they had never heard of Scapa Flow. He had a glorious time, a second rousing goodbye, and found himself all too soon walking over the filthy dockyard gangway, carrying his green suitcase with difficulty through a milling crowd of hurrying dockyard "maties" (workmen). The ship was in a state of chaotic dirt and absolutely nothing seemed to be in working order anywhere. Twenty-four hours later they left for Scapa and spent most of the passage shovelling debris over the side and cleaning up the ship as fast as they could.

Arrived in the Flow the new midshipmen at once began formal — and informal — instruction in their varied duties. Each one was assigned his action station and took his place with one of the four Divisions into which the upper deck hands (seamen) were divided, namely: fo'c'sle, foretop, maintop, and quarterdeck, corresponding to the different parts of the upper deck. The seamen messed together as near as practical to their own "part of ship". The ship's twelve boats, three of them powered, were divided amongst the Divisions. Below decks each Division was responsible for the watertight bulkhead doors, ship's side scuttles, ventilation openings, and the access hatches from one deck to another that were in their "part of ship". There were two thousand or more apertures in each area through which sea water might possibly flood into the ship if she were damaged, the ventilation trunks and their inlets and exhaust outlets being the most numerous and also the most tricky to control. It was vital that every officer should know the watertight system of his part of ship in complete detail.

But "action stations" was rightly held to be the most important of all the duties in wartime that had to be quickly learned. Hugh was, in a way, the most fortunate in his batch in being allocated to the Transmitting Station, the small heavily protected compartment five decks down in the bowels of the ship to which all relevant factors affecting control of gun-fire were fed, there to be analysed and passed to the turret guns as range and deflection, this latter being the allowance made for wind, enemy course and speed, and certain other variable influences on the projectile during its flight towards the target. The information sent out from the Transmitting Station was never very much better than an intelligent estimate — and it was therefore all the more important that the guess should be carefully considered. Schoolmaster Lieutenant Bowman was in charge of the little crew of eleven and Hugh felt, of course, not only important but very pleased to be the second-in-command.

At a later date Captain Pound (eventually First Sea Lord and Chief of Naval Staff during most of the Second World War) ordained that in a practice at sea the "Second Eleven" should, at least once, take over each relevant duty so that the day came when Instructor Bowman said to Hugh:

"Well, Snottie, do you think you know all about it down here now? Could you take over the job of every one of the other ten of your crew?"

"Yes, Sir, I think I can."

"Very well. Next full calibre firing you will take charge. I shall stand beside you but I shan't open my mouth unless it is necessary to avoid an accident."

Hugh was down in the Transmitting Station almost every day until the 4th Battle Squadron put to sea for their next practice firing. Several ships had completed their firing before *Colossus'* turn came, and her personnel had made good use of the time to assess the conditions. It was a sunny day with maximum visibility and almost no wind. Hugh was very tense and alert, but well aware of the appraising glances of the seamen who only too evidently felt that this seventeen-year-old was more than likely to turn out to be a juvenile disaster.

"Action Stations" was sounded on the bridge and everybody ran to "close up" at their allotted post. The watertight hatch slammed down as the last man climbed down the ladder into the Transmitting Station and he checked the clips that locked the door above him in position, carefully watched by Hugh. Very shortly the polished brass mouthpiece of the speaking tube to the bridge bellowed out with the captain's voice:

"Target in sight bearing red three-o!"

Range-finder dials began to tick, the spotting top (sixty feet up the foremast) voice-pipe reported on wind, barometric pressure and other details. The paper slowly rolled across the iron table where each detail was plotted either mechanically (in the case of the ship's own course) or by hand. The ranges being received were widely different until, at the very last moment when the order "Stand by to open fire" was relayed, three succeeding ranges from "A" turret's very fancy new range-finder flicked across the dial in rapid succession and Hugh "tuned" to the range so indicated and all guns adjusted to his order.

"Open Fire!" It came so quickly that he wondered if the gun-layers could have actually had time to follow their range dials before the fire gong rang. The ship shivered as one gun from each turret fired, and then again twenty seconds later as the second salvo was released.

"Straddle" came down from the spotting officer, and everyone held their breath for twenty interminable seconds. A couple of new ranges came in and were plotted.

"Hit! I think the target is sinking," came through on a triumphant note.

The "Cease Fire" bell screamed all over the ship and both the captain's voice-pipe from the bridge and gunnery officer's from the spotting top could be heard in stoccato jumble of words; then a minute or two later "Guns' " whiplash voice penetrated throughout the Transmitting Station:

"Bowman, is that you? The target has been smashed up and there's going to be hell to pay. The whole squadron programme has been upset and we're returning to harbour. The captain has ordered an immediate inquiry . I want to see you in the gunnery office as soon as we fall out from action stations. I suppose you had that BF snottie in charge down there, didn't you?"

"Yes Sir, I did."

"Well you're responsible for this just the same!"

"He got in three good ranges from the new "A" turret range-finder at the very last moment and took the correct action."

"I'll go into all that later. There's the 'Disperse'. Get along to the gunnery office at once."

The crew sat very quietly, each man gazing steadfastly at his dial or instrument with a smug expression on his face. Lieutenant Bowman fled up the ladder and out of sight at full speed. The senior petty officer relaxed and with a broad smile turned towards the dismayed Hugh:

"Well Sir, I must congratulate you! It's near three years since *Colossus* last hit a target!"

Hugh was somewhat consoled, but still very apprehensive about whatever proceedings might follow the destruction of a target, something he had never heard of.

"Thank you, Ryder. Everyone did his job correctly and our business is to produce hits. Do you think there will be an awful lot of trouble about that target?"

"Lor' bless you Sir, not a bit of it! You mark my words; when the captain 'ears 'ow it 'appened 'e won't be complainin'."

And so, of course, it fell out. Nobody sent for him, and the turret's crews were all delighted with their day's work.

Rear-Admiral Gaunt had been in the habit of inviting one or two midshipmen to lunch in his cabin on Sundays when the ship was in harbour, and a day or so later an invitation conveyed by Flag Lieutenant Angus Cunningham Graham came to Hugh (who was much too junior for it). He carefully brushed his number one suit and polished his shoes and duly presented himself somewhat nervously at the admiral's cabin door. The Royal Marine sentry kindly spoke up:

"Just knock and then go in, Sir. The admiral is waiting for you. He said to send you in as soon as you came."

A moment later a glass of sherry was in Hugh's hand and the admiral was discoursing on the remarkable variety of sea-birds to be seen in the Orkney Islands. Hugh came to the conclusion that the hitting of the target was, after all, approved.

Perhaps coaling ship was the most onerous duty that ever fell to a crew. *Colossus* stowed about 2,000 tons of coal, and on return from every trip at sea a collier came alongside as soon as the anchor was down. Already stokers had brought up on deck great heaps of stout rope-edged coal-sacks made by convicts, and the main derrick, as soon as it had hoisted out the two picket boats and the admiral's steam barge, was rigged for coaling ship. Canvas hoods were placed over nearly all the ventilation inlets on the upper deck level, and any movable gear that could be stowed away was attended to. Hatches were closed and the atmosphere between decks smelt and tasted of coal-dust and was hot and steamy. The collier was fitted with derricks to each of its several holds and had well-worn winches for working the hoists. There would be four groups of seamen loading coal bags in the four corners of each hold and a shower of shovels and bags would be thrown down to them as they climbed down the access ladders. A stoker petty officer worked the steam-driven winch and a chief stoker was in general supervisory charge at each hold, with a lieutenant in command of operations and a midshipman at each hoist to give the actual orders. As soon as a group of seamen had filled about ten bags, the leading hand in charge of them would weave a stout rope sling through the hand grips of all the bags, hook it on to the dangling hoist wire and raise his hand as a signal to the midshipman on the collier's deck above that all was ready to hoist away. This was the moment of danger. There might be a seaman standing with his back to the hoist which was apt to swing heavily and unpredictably; or sometimes a bag had not been harnessed and was carried by pressure a short way into the air before falling with a crash; or again, a bag hand grip might tear out, or the sacking might be worn and split so that heavy lumps of coal could crash back into the hold. Each bag contained about 200 pounds of coal. In the early part of the day everybody was aware of such dangers and alert to avoid them, but late at night when exhaustion was setting in, accidents did occur, and some of these resulted in serious injuries. The worst of all was when a hoist wire broke. The heavy sacks would fall back into the hold and the wire would violently flick back on deck, decimating whatever or whomever it struck. Such mishaps were rare, and only once did Hugh see a hoist wire break. The lieutanant in charge at the hold was held responsible, as he should have noticed when the wire had begun to fray.

This whole operation was conducted as a competitive evolution in the squadron, and ships hoisted a flag signal at the end of each hour indicating the tonnage embarked. On deck the stokers were emptying bags down large round holes as hard as they could go, and the very strongest men were detailed for this task in which they justifiably took great pride. There was an endless contest in progress in which the seamen shovelling in the collier's hold tried to send up more bags than the stowing party of stokers were able to keep pace with on *Colossus*' upper deck.

In the battleship's coal-bunkers, five decks below, each shaft was showering down an intermittent cascade of coal. The bunkers were watertight compartments ranged along the sides of the ship immediately adjacent to the boiler rooms, and had small openings directly onto the boiler room flooring, large enough for a man to crawl through. Here ventilators had to be kept open as several stokers were inside the bunker shovelling the coal out to the farthest corners. The eventual thick wall of coal that grew up in this way was regarded not merely as indispensable fuel, but also as a main part of the armoured protection of the machinery. The men in the bunker had the toughest job of all, and midshipmen took a turn of duty there so that they could learn exactly what was involved, though their own efforts were almost useless, for they were not yet sufficiently grown to handle the heavy shovelling, most of it done kneeling or crouching close to the coal itself. At sea, of course, there were stokers perpetually working inside whichever bunkers were in use, shovelling out of the narrow entrance holes onto the boiler room floor a steady stream of coal which other men fed into the furnace.

The whole scene down there was satanic, lit as it was by the opening of furnace doors from which a tremendous scorching heat could be felt. The stokers were streaming with sweat which made strange runnels down their blackened faces. Fannys (deep tin buckets with strong handles) of cold water, or perhaps lime juice, were hung about the boiler room so that the men on watch could get a drink immediately they required one. They kept a four-hour watch during which the petty officer stoker in charge would frequently move men from one job to another so that everyone got his turn at the easy work.

It is noteworthy that no one on board was excused "coal ship". Certain specialists — for example a sick berth attendant, a wireless operator, a signalman on the flag deck — had, of course, to continue with their normal duties. The "rig of the day" was a matter of choice, and the stokers who worked on deck were always noticeable for the exotic outfits they achieved. Old brightly-coloured football shirts, in one case a dilapidated straw hat, and even once a brown bowler hat appeared. Hugh always wore a bath towel wrapped round his neck and a white duck uniform cap cover on his head in an entirely vain effort to keep the coal dust out. Vaseline was often smeared round the eyes, which made it a little easier to clean them at the end of the day.

The captain occasionally appeared on deck to look round, and wisely kept to the windward side where, of course, not much coal dust was likely to be found. He hadn't very much to do that day; his young paymaster secretary was working down in the collier's hold. But there was always some dust everywhere, and eventually every square inch of the upper works had to be hosed down, and much of it washed off by hand. Between decks things were a little better; a fine black powder would be found to have settled on every exposed surface. Immediately the last hoist was in, the whole ship's company above and below decks set to with feverish goodwill to clean up the mess. It was not very often that much was left to be completed on the morrow. On Christmas Day 1917 *Colossus* and her division returned from a sweep at sea and commenced coaling at about 9 a.m. in a howling gale with snow flurries which slowed down the work somewhat; moreover it was to be the largest intake they ever had, and the work ended at 11 p.m. Scrubbing down and Christmas dinner were postponed to Boxing Day.

Not long before Hugh went to sea, an old cruiser, the *Natal*, anchored in Invergordon Harbour, had been giving a Christmas party for wives and children, when, after they had left, the ship blew up, leaving some remnants of the shattered hull sticking up out of the water. The mysterious circumstances were exhaustively investigated, and although no cause was ever established, the official conclusion was that some of the cordite ammunition could have deteriorated and finally detonated of its own accord — something that had never happened before and was always considered to be highly improbable because cordite by its nature was actually difficult to explode — it required a substantial charge of a much higher explosive, and even in the case of fire it ordinarily did no more than burn with a hot flame.

Some months after Hugh reached Scapa Flow, a ship's concert party was giving a show — a musical revue — on board the *Borodino*, a small cargo ship fitted out to be entertainment and canteen supply centre for the whole fleet. Since the ship could seat an audience of several hundred men in her largest hold, which was equipped as a theatre with a sizeable stage, an invitation had been sent out to all ships present for the several evening performances. On one of these evenings Hugh had arranged to go with a friend serving in the battleship *Vanguard* which was anchored in the next berth to *Colossus*. At the last moment some unexpected duty detained Hugh, and as he finished his job too late to go to the show, he went off early to bed.

He awoke an hour later to the noise of a tremendous roar and *Colossus* rolled violently. He jumped out of his hammock and ran up on deck with a duffel coat over his pyjamas to see ships' searchlights from all directions lighting up an oily patch of water covered with scattered debris to which several ships' boats were hurrying. The *Vanguard* had blown up. One of her turrets with its two twelve-inch guns had flown between *Colossus*' two masts and several large slabs of metal had fallen on the nearby island of Flotta. The stench of burnt oil was sickening, and a little of it could be seen burning on the surface for a few minutes. Only two men were picked up alive, one unhurt who had been sleeping in his hammock directly below an open hatch, and the other a signalman on the flag deck who was badly injured, and later died. It was fortunate that some fifty officers and men were in the *Borodino* enjoying the show. The three *Vanguard* midshipmen who had been there were brought to *Colossus* and fitted up by the gunroom, with the necessary clothing and so forth, as soon as they came aboard.

Here again no cause of the explosion was ever fully established, sabotage being ruled out, although it was obvious that a magazine must have blown up to cause such mighty destruction. Next morning all ships that had cordite on board of the same batch numbers as that held in *Vanguard* hurriedly hoisted it up on deck, and it was sent ashore as quickly as possible.

Perhaps the most responsible, certainly the most difficult and also sought-after duty of a midshipman was his "first command", to be in charge of a steam picket boat. These were very stout wooden boats fifty-four feet long with a beam of about ten feet. They were hoisted out at six a.m. when the hands turned to, and taken inboard again in the evening. Occasionally in fine weather they were moored up overnight at the boat boom, or astern. They were built to stand up to rough weather and keep communications open in harbour. Scapa Flow, with its frequent violent storms, sometimes with winds up to 80 miles an hour, supplied the maximum test to which these boats stood up; none were lost due to heavy weather. Each midshipman took a month's turn — sometimes longer — in charge of a picket boat, and was assisted, and also instructed, by a seasoned petty officer coxswain — but the midshipman took the wheel when the boat was in the water, and he was, of course, free of all other harbour duties.

To bring these heavy boats alongside a ship's gangway in rough weather, when the ship herself would be yawing to and fro quite rapidly, required expert experience and good judgement. It was a splendid kindergarten for future ship handlers, and in a surprisingly short time most midshipmen became skilful. There is a solid satisfaction to be found in bringing a boat alongside without a crash in difficult weather conditions, and the art once learned, is never wholly forgotten.

Saturday was "make and mend" afternoon when no work was done and, theoretically, the ship's company washed and mended their clothing. Electric washing-machines were almost forty years ahead. There was no excuse for being dirty or ragged on board. The paymaster had a clothing store from which all requirements, other than a complete uniform (which was always tailor-made), could be purchased at a figure far below shop prices and of a quality tough enough to stand up to life at sea. Indeed, the Royal Navy was at all points careful to supply the daily needs of its crews and to meet the rugged conditions in which they lived.

That weekly afternoon off was the signal to go ashore, and boats were run to suitable near-by islands. There was an officer-made golf-course on Flotta, several football and hockey fields, and in fine weather a trip to the north shore on South Ronaldsay Island, with the objective, after a long walk over the heather, of a superb Scots tea at the schoolmaster's house in a little glen, where the only trees that one could see in the Orkneys managed to grow a little taller than a man. Hugh never forgot the nine dishes of different varieties of breads, and cakes, and buns that the lady of the house provided for her customers, who, after a four-mile walk through deep heather, were well able to do justice to her wonderful provision. The Scots always knew how to supplement the rations, being an independent-minded, mostly rural people who could still grind their own corn and make their own butter no matter what government regulations were in force. There were also expeditions to the partly ruined St. Magnus ninth-century abbey at Kirkwall, the only little town, where the pubs outnumbered the shops, and the most wonderfully gossamer-light tweeds were spun from the herd of miniature South Ronaldsay sheep, possibly the most ancient breed in the world. Hugh very nearly fell from the rotten wood flooring of the clerestory fifty feet above the flagged stone floor of this ancient abbey. Just to see the little town was a tonic, and also a reassurance that ordinary life still went on in a wartime world.

Friday night in the gunroom was the normal guest night when the messman put on a rather more elaborate, but not necessarily better, dinner than usual — perhaps an extra course would be added. The port was passed and the sub-lieutenant who was in charge of the mess would detail a junior midshipman to make a speech. He had no idea what to say, he was embarrassed beyond measure, and the whole thing was invariably a disaster. The several junior midshipmen had already spent an hour or two "clearing up the mess", which meant that the brass ship's side scuttles, the brass fire fender and fire irons had to be polished, the newspapers neatly folded and placed in their rack, all the books and magazines lying about put on their proper shelves in an orderly manner, the one or two rugs on the floor taken up and well brushed, and everything dusted and swept, so that the place would look well in the eyes of the guests.

After dinner the guests might be invited to play bridge or some other card game in a borrowed cabin, but much more often, after the port, the sub-lieutenant would bellow out:

"Warts clear the mess!" which was the signal for the junior group of midshipmen to bolt out the door at full speed, the last one out being recalled to receive half a dozen cuts across the breeches for being "slack in obeying an order". Next the group would be sent for in order to make sport for the entertainment of the guests and "gunroom games" would begin. There was a wide variety of these. One was to blindfold two contestants with scarves, seat them on the deck and arm each with a rod of tightly rolled-up newspapers or magazines with which they swiped at each other until the weapon disintegrated, calling out: "Are you there, Moriarty?" which gave an indication of the position of the caller. Another was to climb through the scuttle and thence up the ship's side on to the upper deck; many were too broad in the beam to make this possible, and whatever limbs were still left inside the gunroom were belaboured with a stick to encourage greater efforts; successful participants would be given a glass of port at the sub-lieutenant's expense — at a cost of fourpence, which was then quite a lot of money. Still another game was to clear the long polished dinner-table, button up the "torpedoes" in their monkey jackets back to front and launch them along this slippery surface with a tremendous swing, hoping that they would shoot into the padded sofa seat along the bulkhead at the far end. Oddly enough nobody ever suffered a broken neck. Still other games were para-gymnastics such as leap-frog, climbing through the back of a chair, standing or walking on the hands, and that familiar Russian dance performed crouching close to the floor and shooting out the feet on alternate sides. A quite popular one was an obstacle-race combining several of these and perhaps adding the collection of half a dozen disparate objects — a lifebuoy, a roll of toilet-paper, a hammer, a sea-boot, and so on. Songs, always bawdy, interspersed the vigorous games, everybody joined in and participated, if not in all the events, at least in some of them, and often enough some really skilful performance would be witnessed. Ten o'clock came round quickly enough, and that was "pipe down" for the midshipmen, and the guests' boats would call for them about then.

What was it all in aid of? It was rough; there was some risk of physical injury; there was some bullying of the younger members; there could be brutality and drunkeness — but, although the entertainment verged at one time or another on all of these, it did serve to build up physical toughness, to sharpen the wits and develop alertness; and those who look back on the experience will agree that it did no harm, and moreover there was an element of real enjoyment in the contest that ran through it all. It is a wonder that people of all ages (and only one in *Colossus*' gunroom had reached twenty) can and do find humour and enjoyment in dirty songs and stories, and continue to entertain themselves with these things. Gunroom songs were always bawdy, and many were sung on guest nights.

The harbour routine at Scapa was fairly stereotyped. Every day some unit of the armament was exercised at drill — guns, searchlights, torpedoes. There were always some new men to be trained at their particular station. Then too, about twice a week the ship would sail out from the anchorage to the large expanse of the Flow and carry out subcalibre firing practice. A small gun was mounted inside the 12-inch guns and fired at a towed target so that all the drill of working a turret could be practised. The secondary armament of twelve 4-inch guns was similarly exercised. It was a most useful and economical way of training up an efficient organisation while the ship was in complete safety in water protected from submarine attack. At least once a week searchlights and night battle organisation were exercised, after dark, using the ship's power boats as a moving target while the ship usually remained at anchor.

Roughly one half of a midshipman's day was devoted to formal instruction. The instructor lieutenant took them in mathematics and navigation. The departmental heads — or their deputies — took them in engineering, torpedo, and gunnery. One of the upper deck officers took them in seamanship and he was assisted by the boatswain who was the official expert in ropes, anchor work and boats. In the *Colossus* he was a very senior commissioned boatswain of the old school who had done some time in the last of the sailing frigates as a "boy second class" when he first entered the Service. He was the most popular instructor they had, for he could invariably be led off within a few minutes to spin a yarn about his early days. In his store in a locked drawer he kept a cat-o'-nine-tails which, though long since out of official use, had somehow continued to appear on this particular ship's inventory of stores. It ought to have been returned to the dockyard a decade ago, but one way or another successive boatswains had managed to evade the order and it had now become the ship's prize exhibit. Moreover the boatswain could expound in graphic detail how he had seen it used on the victims' bare back as he received his punishment.

The Grand Fleet, or at any rate some part of it, at the start under Admiral Jellicoe and towards the end under Admiral Beatty, was wont to proceed to sea at least once a month to exercise manoeuvres or perhaps carry out a sweep towards Heligoland or the Norwegian coast, where a movement of major German units was sometimes detected, and where often enough a raider was attempting to break out into the North Atlantic, or perhaps return to its home port. The 700-mile sea gap between Scotland and Iceland was too great to be effectively covered by surface ships alone, and the only real chance of an interception would occur somewhere near the German coastline which could never be closely approached on account of minefields. We shall see this problem tackled again under the different conditions prevailing in World War II. The midshipmen, however, knew next to nothing of this strategic situation and the signal to raise steam came as an exciting prospect of possible action against the German battle fleet every time it was hoisted at the *Iron Duke*'s yardarm, for when it came from the commander-in-chief it had special significance.

Late in 1917, the 4th BS was allotted the task of acting as a heavy covering force for the convoys which were running from Leith on the Firth of Forth to Bergen on the Norwegian coast about every second week. Some fifty slow merchantmen would sail at a speed of eight knots, and as the winter weather was appalling, it took them a week to make the passage, and seldom did they arrive in an organised group, the incessant gales splitting them up. They would have been easy meat for any German surface force but were never attacked perhaps because the Germans realised that they were a very scattered target and therefore not very rewarding; and moreover the risk of accidentally running into a battleship covering force was formidable.

These Bergen convoy trips were times of tense discomfort. The *Colossus* was a good ship in a seaway, but rolled and pitched heavily in the short steep seas she met in that area. It was bitterly cold and a lot of casual water seemed always to penetrate below decks, slopping about in unexpected places and making life exceedingly uncomfortable.

On one particularly dark night on Bergen convoy duty a report was received that a fast German force might possibly be out, and the division of four battleships immediately proceeded at high speed (18 knots) towards the most suitable protective position. At the turn of the watch, the new night-duty battle crews were exercised at their stations, and in the case of the searchlights, the light was actually switched on behind a closed shutter by remote control from the bridge. Hugh was the midshipman in charge of that particular switch and as he proceeded to exercise the drill in the usual way one of the after searchlights suddenly exposed its beam. Either he had pressed the wrong button or there was an electrical fault in the control circuit, or the seaman operating the light had misunderstood the order. The squadron's position was given away and a major blow-up immediately took place. The admiral was understandably furious and the captain a good deal more so. In the complete darkness nobody ever did find out exactly what had occurred though it seemed that an inexperienced seaman at the searchlight was at fault. Had a German force been at hand the whole squadron might have been torpedoed without warning. They quickly jammed their helms over and steadied on a different course to counter that risk, but for an hour nerves were very taut indeed. Nothing happened, but the midshipman in charge lived under a cloud for some little while to come.

In January 1918, the midshipmen of Hugh's batch were sent off to gain a month's experience in destroyers, and Hugh found himself boarding the *Restless* at the destroyer anchorage in Gutter Sound protected by the small island of Cava, and close to a rough little landing stage on Hoy Island. The captain was Commander Jock Whitworth, leader of the second division of the 8th Flotilla, later to lead a force into a northern Norwegian fjord to destroy a whole flotilla of German destroyers during World War II. By now our young man had acquired some small measure of experience in sea affairs, and was becoming modestly competent in the minor duties that ordinarily occupied a junior midshipman. He was welcomed warmly by all the officers, for they were short-handed and badly needed another watchkeeper. Whitworth proceeded to find out just how far he was safe and to be trusted on the bridge, and had him under his eye there whenever anything of moment was taking place. He taught the boy how to keep the ship in station in the line at sea, how to anchor her in her correct berth in harbour, and a great deal of small ship sea-law besides, and generally developed and expanded his self-reliance and knowledge of seamanship in all directions. It was the first time he had been actively helped and encouraged and he benefited enormously from the five months he spent in destroyers. At the end of the first month, when he was officially due to return to *Colossus*, Commander Whitworth asked him if he wanted to go back just then. A trip at sea was in view in a few days' time, and he said:

"Oh, no Sir. I should hate to miss our next trip. I wish I could stay on for much longer."

"Well if that's how you feel about it I'll see what can be done. We need another watchkeeper and I won't let you go anyway till we get back here again next week."

No sooner had they returned, and while Hugh was ashore with the sub-lieutenant walking over the heather-covered moors of Hoy in search of gulls' eggs (which they laid right out in the open ground there), when a signal came from Commodore "D" (the senior officer in charge of all the Grand Fleet flotillas) ordering Hugh to be discharged forthwith to the destroyer *Orestes* which was proceeding to sea that night. As Hugh came up the ladder on to *Relentless'* deck the signal was handed to him and his seaman servant was standing there with his two suitcases already packed. The ship's boat waited alongside while he dashed down to his cabin to change into uniform, and a quarter of an hour later he was saluting the quarterdeck on board *Orestes*, where the ship's company were busily securing the ship for sea, rigging lifelines along the upper deck, and closing down ventilators and hatches and the ship's side scuttles. They were off westwards an hour later to form part of the destroyer anti-submarine screen of a division of battleships sailing into the Atlantic to cover an important incoming troop convoy from Canada.

The *Orestes* was commanded by a seasoned lieutenant commander who had transferred from the Merchant Service to the Royal Navy on the outbreak of war — a kindly humorous man named Raw, whom Hugh liked and got on with very well. It was a very happy ship and things went smoothly without any sign of stress and the crew trusted their captain, who was a superb ship handler. Authority seemed to forget all about Hugh and it was not until midsummer that a plaintive signal from *Colossus* called to mind that he should have been sent back to his ship three months ago.

Orestes found herself on several Bergen convoys; all were broken up by bad weather and on only one occasion did the destroyer escort actually find a group of five out of the fifty merchantmen who had set out from Leith. The remainder made port later on in ones and twos, unescorted. On one occasion they had been six days at sea without any star or sun sight to check their navigation and Raw knew that the Norwegian coast must be close ahead. A very heavy stern sea was running and the upper deck was cleared — even of the armament crews — and every ventilator and hatch except the boiler room air intakes high up around the funnels was closed. At a moment when the position of the next following wave seemed favourable, the helm was put over to turn the ship, but the drag of the previous one held her for a long time, and, when at last she began to swing, the following wave swept right over the decks for half the length of the ship, and there she hung half submerged for perhaps a minute. The four or five people on the bridge gazed apprehensively at a situation of the gravest danger about which nothing could be done — and then at last she lifted herself and the water cascaded away from both sides, and so completed her turn. It had been a very ugly moment, for the little ship was only of about three thousand tons burden. A few minutes later the fog lifted for a brief moment, and there, directly astern of them and only a mile away, was Marsten Lighthouse standing out whitely on its little tree -clad conical-shaped island which marks the entrance to Bergen fjiord.

A very similar encounter with Marsten Lighthouse, but concerning fleet aircraft twenty-three years later, led to the destruction of the great German battleship *Bismarck*, an action in which Hugh was to take some part during World War II.

In the early days of the year, on one of the Bergen convoy outings the temperature fell below zero and the heaviest gale they ever encountered blew up. Hugh had gone aft to the wardroom for breakfast at eight o'clock, just after daylight, when he had finished the morning watch on the bridge. They lashed themselves into their seats round the table, and after that found that washing or shaving was impossible — water could not be kept in a basin. He had the afternoon watch, commencing at half-past twelve, and put on every available piece of clothing before starting out for the bridge. Heavy seas were breaking over the slippery iron decks and he had to wait until the green water ran off over the ship's side and then make a dash for some two hundred feet to gain the shelter of the break of the fo'c'sle which led on forward into the messdecks. There was a rope lifeline along the upper deck and he caught hold of it firmly and started to run, but he chose the wrong moment. A big green wave swept inboard, lifted him several feet above the deck and tore his hand away from the lifeline. As the wave swept on aft he suddenly felt something pressing on his forearm and seized on to it, but continued to be swept along until his feet touched solid material, and as the wave broke up and washed away overboard he found himself holding on to the wire jackstay above the torpedo tubes, upon which his feet were now standing. That wire was twelve feet above the upper deck. He gazed for a moment at the boiling green wake and reflected upon his amazing good luck. Men were not infrequently lost overboard in such weather conditions as prevailed that day. No boat could possibly be lowered and their heavy clothing would make rescue nearly impossible.

There wasn't much time for reflection. He made a second run for the break of the fo'c'sle and gained sanctuary before he realised that his sea-boots were full of water. He took them off and emptied them out, and as he did so, a seaman came up:

"Here you are, Sir. Take these; you'll need 'em. They're warm. Me grannie knitted 'em for me." It was a pair of dry heavy sea-boot stockings. He was already late for his watch by a minute or two and there was no time to say more than a quick: "Thank you," which didn't really express half the gratitude he felt.

His misfortune had been seen from the bridge, and the captain who was up there asked if he was not wet to the skin. The boy had not had time to think of that yet and said he thought he was quite dry and that anyhow he had changed his sea-boot stockings. The violently lurching ship demanded everybody's full attention and they quickly forgot about him.

About two hours later, the young seaman helmsman at the wheel suddenly collapsed on the deck, his hands being frozen to the spokes of the wheel. They got him detached from it and carried him below, and Hugh took over the steering. The officer of the watch ordered half-hour tricks only at the wheel, and when later a seaman had come up to relieve him Hugh found that his right hand was quite stiff. He could not get the index finger to move for a long time and realised that it was frozen. It took a couple of weeks to heal and then finished up being bent and remained that way for the rest of his life. Although the temperature was about fifteen degrees Fahrenheit below zero, very little ice formed on the upper works of the ship, probably because the seas constantly breaking over her did not give time for its formation.

In the early summer there was increasing activity in the battle fleet. There were signs that Germany was failing, and it was thought — and hoped — that their fleet would make a do-or-die sortie, the kind of dramatic thing that seemed to be in accord with the theatrical nature of Kaiser Wilhelm. The Grand Fleet was much more frequently out on sweeps in the North Sea. On one such sweep, *Orestes* formed part of the screen of the Fleet flagship's division of *Iron Duke* class battleships. They sailed from Scapa in fog and rain, and when dark closed in, it became increasingly difficult to see the dim blue light exhibited close to the waterline at the stern of all ships. There was a pitching motion which kept those lights often below water, and possibly one might be extinguished without anyone on board being aware of it. *Orestes* lost sight of the destroyer next ahead during a change of course in the dark, and saw nothing until daylight, several hours later. The captain guessed that the battleships might be going to Rosyth, and decided to head in that direction. An hour or so later a division of destroyers was sighted, and after the challenge of identification had been satisfactorily completed, he asked the leader where, oh where, had the battle fleet gone? The reply "Follow me" was flashed back, and *Orestes* tacked on to their tail.

An hour later they sighted battleships ahead in patchy fog, and saw one or two flashes from guns and heard their roar and immediately went to battle stations, supposing that contact had been made with the enemy in the difficult conditions of low visibility. However, later on they were ordered to screen the battleship *Royal Oak* which came in sight, and just after they took up station the fog lifted and the sun came out and there was the mass of forty-one battleships of the Grand Fleet turning into single line ahead, *Royal Oak* being the rear ship of that nine-mile long line of floating steel wall — a sight never seen before and never to be seen again. The target was far too tempting for a submarine and almost at once they moved off in different directions. *Orestes* asked the destroyer ahead what the gun-fire had been about, to which he replied that floating mines had been sighted and a free-for-all effort to sink them had developed. Later they learned that they were going in to Rosyth where they arrived late that evening.

A destroyer on screen did not get a great deal of consideration from a capital ship at sea in wartime in those days. They were small ships and could not stand up to the heavy seas through which a capital ship could easily maintain the speed of the fleet, and it was left to the destroyers to reduce speed to avoid damage as and when they thought advisable. In such conditions a submarine would have serious difficulty in attacking, and so the destroyer screen was not so urgently necessary. Once you had lost sight of the heavy ship you were supposed to be screening there was little hope of regaining contact and often enough the screen was not informed of the sortie, and indeed probably only the senior officer on the screen knew, and it was only too easy to lose sight of him in bad weather.

At the end of his extended five months in destroyers Hugh was at last sent back to *Colossus* when they berthed at Rosyth, and there the Fleet remained during the last three critical months of the war in order to be as close as possible to the German bases at Kiel and Heligoland. Presently the dreadful septic "Spanish influenza" epidemic broke-out and virtually every ship in the fleet was put out of action at one time or another. At her worst moment *Colossus* had 700 men down out of a crew of 1500 and many ships were far worse off than that.

The war was drawing rapidly to its close and there was initially some fear that the German Fleet might, if ordered to surrender, disobey and make a last ditch attack, but the theory proved to be unfounded.

The Grand Fleet, now concentrated at Rosyth, kept at four hours notice for steam, but shore leave was given and arrangements made for rapid recall of liberty men if an emergency should arise. The day before the Armistice was due to be signed was a tense one — nobody could settle down to any steady task. On 11th November, the morning newspapers — and they were on the breakfast-table at eight o'clock in the Firth of Forth — stated that the Armistice would be signed at 11 a.m., and as soon as word was received from General Foch's headquarters in Northern France, the government would order the ringing of all church bells. It was only a few minutes after eleven that those on board *Colossus*, which was moored some miles above the Forth Bridge opposite Campbelltown, heard the distant tinkle of the little village church bell, and at almost the same moment a signal from the Commander-in-Chief Admiral Beatty, informed the Fleet that the signing had taken place.

That afternoon, Hugh, in company with almost everyone on board who was not required for duty, went ashore, and walked, bussed, or trained the six miles into Edinburgh. Flags were hoisted on every building and paper streamers shot out of windows. It seemed as if the whole population was bent on getting into Princes Street below the castle, which soon became jammed so that the trams moved at a snail's pace and finally stopped altogether, and the one or two cars visible were edging away down some side-street. Several of the midshipmen met for tea at Crawford's shortbread shop, by which time life outside had become boisterous. As dark closed in a little later, crowds of sailors, many with Wrens or other girls mounted on their shoulders, were seen charging into groups of soldiers who had similarly hoisted up Waacs, and the melee was indesribable. Bagpipes were playing, kilted men with their girls were dancing reels in the roadway, and a few inebriated songsters were giving tongue to every sort of ditty under heaven. But that was only the beginning of it, and all that Hugh saw, for he had the first watch and must catch the six o'clock boat from South Queensferry back to his ship.

Chapter 4

World War One is Over

About ten days later the Grand Fleet put to sea — with guns trained and ready to load — to escort the surrendering German battle fleet of some forty major ships to an anchorage off Leith in the Firth of Forth. There was a feeling in the air that the Germans might attempt a sudden last hope attack, and ships had been continuously kept at short notice for steam. Somehow they looked woebegone, unpainted, dishevelled, as they came in sight through a thin mist veiling a weak sunshine, but it was a great day in the history of the Royal Navy when they watched the vast mass of the German High Seas Fleet haul down their ensigns for the last time at sunset on the 19th November 1918. Their Fleet Flagship *Bayern* was quite close to *Colossus* at that dramatic moment.

Nobody yet knew the extent of the collapse of German morale. An extract from *The Times* of 21st December quotes the *Kölnische Volkszeitung* thus:

"Until November 9th we had believed that the moral power of our people . . . could not be broken, and that therefore we should be able to raise ourselves after a couple of decades out of the misfortune that the conditions of the Armistice and the coming peace would bring . . . Is it really possible that German, even "red", sailors have sold for 500 marks the last poor remnant of honour of an undying hero? A British admiral renounces the handing over of (Weddingen's submarine which torpedoed three English cruisers) U-9, which, as victor, he wishes with a noble gesture to bestow upon the vanquished, as one is accustomed to leave his sword to the brave commander of a conquered fortress. Revolutionaries in German naval uniform, we are told, would not renounce the 500 marks to be paid to each crewman manning this vessel on her last voyage of surrender to the British."

Hugh was to recall this story almost twenty years later during the Spanish Civil War, when he discovered that a single bomb hit had shattered the morale of a German pocket battleship.

This evening, while fallen in on the upper deck for entering harbour with his seaman division, just as they passed under the Forth Bridge, Hugh fell flat on his face unconscious and had to be carried below. He was put in a cabin and felt very ill and the doctors supposed he was going down with the "Spanish flu". However, next morning a little group of high-up medical men, including a distinguished specialist from London, came in to examine him and were puzzled about some spots that had developed overnight, and they were inclined to believe that he had contracted a new disease attributed to unsatisfactory wartime food and wrongly at that time named "botulism", which was rampant in this ship. As the tail of the line of medicos disappeared out of the cabin door the young Irish ship's surgeon lieutenant, who had tended Hugh the day before, suddenly piped up in his broad brogue:

"Begorra if it isn't chicken-pox I'll eat my hat!"

The experts hurried away looking shocked and tut-tutting. By evening the young doctor was proved to be right and Hugh was quickly hoisted out of the ship in a stretcher and sent to the Edinburgh Fever Hospital where he was placed in a little isolation room at the end of a very long line of 80 beds given up to "Spanish influenza" patients. They looked after him splendidly — a naval man was regarded as a war hero, and the Fleet had always been popular in Edinburgh. Sailors could keep pace at a bar with any Scot who was prepared to pay for the drinks.

Hugh felt very ill for the first day or two, but could get almost no sleep at night. There was a continual trundling noise outside his door. At last he spoke about it to the ward sister who rather hesitantly told him that about twenty patients died every night and the noise was that of the trolleys taking bodies away. She, desperately worn and tired, burst into tears:

"It is just dreadful, and we can't do anything for them. They simply choke to death. I've never seen anything like this in my life before; three-quarters of my patients are going to die."

In spite of it all the nurses never came into Hugh's room without a smile and time for a joke, and in the end they always took their night snacks and cups of tea at his bedside. He fell in love with one or two of the younger ones — which no doubt helped them a little through their very distressing days, but the ward sister changed their duties each time she saw what was happening. Three weeks he spent there in great comfort, and with these delightful companions it was a great contrast to gunroom life at sea in wartime and he was almost sorry to have to return to his ship. On the way through Edinburgh by taxi he stopped at a florist's to send the nurses as many flowers as his small purse would allow.

Just before Christmas the midshipmen were sent on leave to await appointment elsewhere, for *Colossus* was to be paid off and sent to the shipbreaker's yard. Hugh went to stay with relations and a day or two after Christmas an invitation reached him from the Warwicks to join them at the Beau Site Hotel at Cannes. Mama provided a twenty-pound cheque, which, added to his own savings, enabled him to take a three-week holiday in the South of France. The party consisted of the two parents, their two daughters, a son, and the chauffeur who drove their large Daimler car. They all had a splendid time, drove in heavy snow along the hazardous narrow upper Corniche road beyond Mentone to the Italian border; inspected a perfume factory laid out in the middle of acres of lavender and roses, the flowers being used, of course, in the manufacture. Some played golf, others tennis, and everybody edged in towards the court where Suzanne Lenglen and the King of Sweden were to be seen on any sunny day taking on a number of well-known players. They went to lunch with the famous author W. J. Locke at his villa and found themselves seated beside the editor of the *Times* and Colonel House, the American President's personal envoy to several European governments. And of course they went to gamble at the Casino at Monte Carlo where Hugh was rejected because he was not yet twenty and looked much younger. He took himself off to the wide semi-circular driveway in front of the main entrance with its border of shrubs and flowers, where many seats were occupied by raddled, decaying persons dressed in musty finery busily writing in little notebooks. When he sat down the elderly English woman at the other end of the seat at once started a conversation and revealed to him the mysteries of the system she was working out and which must soon make her fortune, for she had been following it for the last four winter seasons.

"Indeed, it must come this month, for I reach the end of my resources at the end of January!" And as she turned back to her pencil and notebook he noticed that her shoes were cracked and almost completely worn away at the heels. The incident cured him of gambling for the rest of his life.

The Beau Site ballroom, where they danced almost every night, was approached by wide steps descending from a terrace and no lady could face that without a new dress. Paul Poiret, surrounded by several lovely girls and a fat black-clad duenna appeared one week, the girls displaying a different gown each evening. He was, he assured everybody, taking a much-needed holiday away from the rigours of winter-time Paris; but no one was deceived, for he was the "grand couturier" of the era, exceeded only by Molyneux, who was so expensive that he had no need to advertise.

Mrs Aitken, the wife of the famous newspaperman Max, was accompanied by daughters, and as the Warwicks knew her, they sometimes joined forces for parties. Each week the Casino at Cannes arranged a "gala night" and a table had to be booked well in advance because it was always an occasion for the appearance of celebrities. There was great excitement one night when a small rather oriental-looking woman sitting at the next table to the Warwicks, dressed in a brown lace dress with, the ladies were convinced, nothing underneath, began quietly to sing to the music being played by the orchestra. The chef d'orchestre quickly spotted her and quietened down the sound until her very lovely voice could be heard throughout the great room and people began to crowd in from elsewhere, and then her friends made her stand up and she sang on and on for almost an hour. She was Kouizenoff, a world-famous opera star. It was the first time Hugh had heard operatic singing, and for the rest of his life thereafter he made every effort to hear whatever opera was being performed within his reach.

The Maharani of Kapurthala came to stay for a few days at the Beau Site. It was said that she was a Spanish lady and everybody had read about her in the papers. She only appeared in transit, walking slowly and majestically, surrounded by three or four nondescript elderly men, perhaps detectives or bodyguards, for she invariably wore one or two magnificent jewels the like of which one had never seen before, and was unlikely to see again. Prince Philipe de Bourbon-Parme, a tired uninterested-looking man, with his tall and handsome blonde wife were always at everything, and one evening Hugh found himself being presented to the Princess. He felt very hung up, not knowing whether he should kiss her hand or not, but she quickly got up and said in perfect English

"Let's dance!" — and off they went. It wasn't a success, for she was so very much larger than he that he couldn't get his arm anywhere near half-way around her waist and couldn't manage to control her movements, though he was quickly able to follow them. However, she didn't want to dance the encore, so it was no more than the briefest of encounters, though he was delighted, for he had never before met a princess, much less danced with one.

The Warwicks decided to go back to London before the month was over, and Hugh, still having some money left — for they had paid practically all his expenses beyond the hotel room — decided to stay on alone for another week, for he had made several friends and wanted to join them for a forthcoming tennis tournament. Mrs Locke volunteered firmly to look after him, and with her six-foot guardsman's figure and splendid red hair was not a person easily to be denied. Her daughter seemed to Hugh to become more attractive day by day. Mrs Locke announced that she had proposed him for membership at the Cercle Nautique at Cannes, at that time the apex of the social ladder. They would go there tomorrow afternoon, and he wondered if he would be able to pay the membership fee, and said something about that to Mrs Locke.

"Oh, no! You don't have to think about that; as a naval officer you automatically become an honorary member." When they met there Hugh found it to be a relatively small building, and after signing the register and being introduced to "Monsieur, le Président" and other officials, they swept on into the ballroom where a tea-dance was in progress. Mrs Locke pointed out various people, all of whom seemed to have distinguished names, and then a little later she was summoned to a table set apart in an alcove at the other side of the room, and Hugh saw her make a curtsey as she reached it. A minute or two later she returned.

"I am going to present you to the Grand Duke Cyril of Russia and the Grand Duchess. You know he will be Czar if ever the Romanoffs are restored."

Hugh had never before met royalty and had no idea what the procedure should be. However, he achieved a deferential sort of bow to the future Czar and managed to kiss the rather wizened little hand of the sad-faced Grand Duchess, who at once asked him if he played bridge, and would he like to join them and a few friends tomorrow evening and they would play at home. He gasped. The only bridge he knew had been played in the gunroom at Scapa Flow and he wasn't much good at it. He quickly thought of an excuse and said, "But Ma'am, I am so sorry, I'm afraid I shan't be able to. I have to catch the evening train to Paris as my leave is up." She looked him in the eye and frowned in displeasure and then turned away and said no more. Later he was told by a friend that they made a living by playing at cards, but it was probably merely unkind gossip, for Mrs Locke would never have led him into that sort of a trap.

Mrs Locke burst out: "I'd no idea you were leaving us so soon!" And neither had Hugh, but he felt he must stick to what he had said, though he would have liked to spend a few more days at Cannes. The journey home was a nightmare, for he found he had even less money left than expected. No sleeper on the train, of course, and only one croissant and a cup of coffee for breakfast, an apple at Dieppe, and on the second night, the roughest crossing to Newhaven during which he was thrown out of his bunk. While awaiting departure of the boat-train to London he counted up his remaining money. There was fivepence. He bought a twopenny orange, and quietly prayed that Ellen Warwick would meet him on arrival in London, as he had sent her a telegram. Never again in his life was a face so welcome when he got out at Victoria Station, for the threepence that remained to him was insufficient for a telephone call, and he was dreading the possibility of a long walk with a heavy suitcase to the Warwick's house in Hyde Park Square on the far side of Hyde Park. He kissed her warmly on both cheeks, something he had never done before.

Hugh and some other *Colossus* midshipmen were appointed on 11th February 1919 to the *Royal Oak*, a 15-inch gun battleship then lying at Rosyth in the Firth of Forth in Scotland. This turned out to be the only ship in which he ever served that he thoroughly disliked. There may have been a general slackening of effort at this time, and too, a thought that nothing mattered much now that the war was over; there certainly was a great deal of disgruntlement in the ship's company about demobilisation, which proceeded very slowly. There was indeed at one moment a degree of insubordination very nearly amounting to mutiny, when a small band of reservists led by a fiery red-headed marine corporal, marched aft and demanded to see the captain, and when they did, they treated him with scant respect, demanding rather more than requesting that he should hasten the discharge to which they believed they were entitled. The matter was expeditiously settled, but it left a very nasty taste. Nobody in the Royal Navy had seen anything like this during the past century, and the new sort of society which was at that time in the process of being born was felt to be something shocking that ought to be suppressed, though nobody in authority could see how this was to be done, and fortunately for England nobody attempted suppression. New ideas, new values were emerging everywhere; it was a period of history full of uncertainties.

Hugh and all the other "old Blakes" were swept up into this. Had the war gone on for just one more month they would have been promoted to sub-lieutenant in March and they were all anxiously waiting to see whether or not they would get this promotion. They did not, and had to serve another year as midshipmen, and through this circumstance were later placed at a disadvantage for promotion on account of their age; only one of them reached Flag rank, and he turned over to the engineering branch.

That summer a national coal strike, the first in Britain's history, broke out, and public services came to a halt. Submarines were moved to Leith and other ports round the coast to supply electric power from their generators in order to maintain a few emergency services. From *Royal Oak* a party of forty was sent to pump out a coal-mine in Durham. Some large trees were cut to block the road from South Queensferry to Edinburgh and a few men returning from leave to their ships got out of their buses to help local people who were cutting up the trunks and rolling them off the roadway. As soon as the strike was settled, the 1st Battle Squadron of "R" class battleships, of which *Royal Oak* was one, sailed for Scapa Flow where the German Fleet had been moved in small groups for internment while their future disposal was being debated at the Versailles' peace conference, all but a minimum number of essential shipkeepers being sent back to Germany. All surplus fuel was disembarked at the same time in order to ensure that no attempt at escape would be possible. Their magazines had been emptied before they left Germany.

The duty of guard-ship was not an inspiring one, but that summer the Orkneys experienced a rare spell of lovely weather, and a walk ashore through carpets of wild flowers, especially the heather after July, was a rewarding exercise. Gunroom sailing picnics were a regular Sunday afternoon expedition and large teas were consumed, including fried sausages which were thought indispensable to any gunroom picnic. A few heroes tried swimming in moorland pools, but found them icy cold.

One afternoon Hugh, at work on the Flotta golf-course draining ditches, happened to come upon a dry gravelly outcrop extending for a couple of hundred yards amongst the prevailing heather. As he walked across this he became aware of the high-pitched shrieks of numerous arctic terns, one of the most beautiful of all sea-birds, and suddenly they commenced diving towards him, getting even closer one actually pecking at his cap. As he looked down on the ground he saw that he was standing in the midst of many eggs laid in pairs on the rough gravel in little depressions that were hardly to be described as nests, and he carefully and quickly picked his way out of this situation. Another day he came upon the newly-hatched brood of a corncrake who darted away from their broken eggshells into the herbage. Close above the sea-shore in thick grass he twice stepped on an eider duck sitting close on her clutch of brown eggs. On the southern side of Flotta, far from any habitation or pathway, there was a flat rocky outcrop stretching away into the sea, and upon this on any fine day could be counted up to forty seals and their pups, some of them brown ones, basking in the sunshine. Hugh would sing to them and then they would halt in their alarmed scurry to the water with heads raised to catch the sound of the music.

The widely scattered farms were this year able to harvest their crops of thin oats, something that they could only count upon every third season. One of the farmers told Hugh that it had taken his father before him and then himself fifty years to build up sufficient fertility on the universal sandstone surface which they had gradually broken down to a depth of about six inches. Their most rewarding crop was eggs, and the Orkneys exported large quantites to the mainland. Most farmers were fisherman too, and their broad-beamed double-ended boats could be seen at all seasons out in the Pentland Firth engaged in line fishing or tending their lobster-pots. One very rainy day Hugh and another midshipman went to get lobsters with no success. On the way home they passed a tiny black cottage crouched under a roof composed of an old upturned fishing boat, and decided to try once more, since lobster-pots could be seen piled outside the rough wooden door. A very old woman in a black shawl and short black skirt and with bare feet, opened to their knocking and invited them inside out of the teeming rain. Yes, she had a couple of lobsters, and would five shillings each be too much to ask? They knew that three and sixpence was the usual price, but guests were coming to dinner that night and they found that between them they could just muster nine shillings and sixpence, which the old dame did not refuse. While she was stuffing her lobsters into a rumpled paper bag they looked around them and realised that the floor was on quite a sharp slope with two small rivulets streaming across the bare earthen surface in the middle of which a peat fire smouldered among half a dozen stones. A black iron pot stood upon two of the stones, and the crone lifted the lid to show them the bread she was baking; the smoke drifted up and escaped out of a hole in the upturned boat. There was a heap of potatoes lying in a corner and a pile of miscellaneous-coloured blankets and men's homespun coats stacked on a wooden bench along one wall which seemed to do duty for a bed. There were no drips from the roofing just there, but elsewhere it could be seen to be far from watertight. There were two rough stools but no chair in sight. The low drystone walling below the upturned boat had many small gaps through which daylight glimmered. There was no sign of any sort of the usual kitchen equipment, nor of a larder. Perhaps stowage was arranged outside, for there were two or three weather-worn packing cases near the doorway. It seemed to be the very poorest hovel.

Harbour drills, an occasional practice firing at sea, and a lot of formal schoolroom study, chiefly mathematics and navigation, kept the midshipmen fully occupied, but there was an uneasy kind of atmosphere about that ship. There was a continuous air of apprehension that the Germans would attempt some sort of dramatic escape, or perhaps scuttle themselves while the great powers wrangled as to who should get what. The arguments were heated, and few statesmen appreciated that a warship with no spare parts and no ammunition was likely to be an expensive burden rather than an asset.

Then an unexpected bombshell fell upon Europe. The four ships of the 1st Battle Squadron weighed anchor at nine a.m. on 21st June, and in company with several destroyers went fifty miles out to sea to do practice torpedo firing exercises. There remained inside Scapa Flow two destroyers and a dozen patrol trawlers, several of the latter keeping up a continuous patrol through the lines of over seventy German warships moored there.

At noon a wireless signal reached the fleet at sea reporting that a "Kaiser" class battleship was sinking, and then a couple of minutes later another signal reported that the whole German fleet had hoisted their ensigns and were sinking.

The battle squadron returned at full speed to harbour and, as *Royal Oak* entered, and in a letter from Hugh to his mother next day he records:

There were two battleships and five light cruisers still afloat. One light cruiser, the *Karlsruhe*, went down soon after we anchored at 3:45 p.m., and stood on her beam ends with her bow sticking up vertically into the air for two or three minutes before submerging. Two other light cruisers were seen to be ashore, having been towed into shallow water by the guard destroyers. Another was in the process of being towed ashore, and yet another one while being towed suddenly slipped backwards and went down almost instantly stern first. The battleship *Markgraf* in tow of a tug was very low down in the water and slowly sank before she could be beached. The battleship *Baden* was the only vessel out of about seventy that was saved intact. A patrol trawler went alongside her and the officer in command got hold of the German captain and ordered him to shut the sea-cocks. He refused and was shot dead where he stood. Then they shut the sea-cocks.

I heard from one of the patrol trawlers' skippers that when some boatloads of Germans attempted to land on the north shore (on South Ronaldsay Island) the island contingent of the Local Defence Volunteers received them with loaded rifles and persuaded them with two or three shots over their heads to get back into their boats and steer across the Flow towards the returning guard battleships. When these farmers had joined the Army five years ago they meant to fight off any German invasion of the Orkney Islands, and apparently no Armistice could dampen their determination!

Can you picture this extraordinary scene? A few ships visibly sinking, and two or three beached and lying perched at odd angles while the whole face of the calm water was dotted with rafts and wooden boxes and huge upturned bottoms, masts, propellors or funnels. The German sailors had taken to their boats, which were collected into groups and then towed alongside the battle squadron, where they were searched on deck and placed under armed guard and then put down below for the night.

As soon as we had anchored I went with a party of fifty

men and some engineer officers to try to salvage the light cruiser *Nuremberg* which had been precariously beached on the rocky shore of Carva Island. She was fairly full up when we got to her and we quickly closed the watertight doors and scuttles which were all open. We worked away till 9 p.m., by which time she had heeled over 40 degrees and we did not dare to stay longer, for if she filled any more she was certain to slip off the rocks into deep water, and the plunge, if it came, would be a sudden one.

The German crews had been ordered to pile all their possessions in one heap between decks so that everything could be properly searched for possible explosives, and during the night a number of our sailors slipped into the compartment to look for "souvenirs", and in the morning it was discovered that this hunt had amounted to a massive theft. An order was immediately broadcast that all articles taken were to be returned forthwith to the dump from which they had come and that after 9 a.m. any man found in possession of stolen German property would be charged with theft, and punished accordingly. So the procession reversed course and a surprisingly large number were seen streaming back in the direction of the dump. Perhaps some disobeyed the order, but it was impossible to track them down amongst a crew of over 1,500 men.

At six o'clock next morning the squadron weighed and proceeded to Invergordon, the *Resolution* being left behind to continue the work of salvage, and Hugh's letter to his mother continues:

Each ship had about 300 Germans on board. As soon as we anchored off Cromarty, tugs and drifters came alongside to take the prisoners ashore. On board the flagship *Revenge* we could see the German Rear-Admiral Muller waving his arms about as he heatedly harangued Vice-Admiral Sir Sidney Fremantle who had upbraided the Germans in no measured terms for breaking the Armistice agreement. Rear-Admiral Muller said that he had ordered the destruction of the German High Seas Fleet entirely on his own responsibility and had received no order from Germany, and he also complained bitterly of the theft of private property on board during the night. At about that point the officer of the guard could be seen hustling the whole contingent down into the waiting transport craft.

E

None of us can gauge the results yet. Will the Allies say that we have betrayed their trust, and that we allowed this to happen because we didn't want anyone else to have ships as good as our own? It may mean a great deal to our country, or on the other hand, be accepted as a heaven-sent solution to a very knotty problem.

A few days later, back again at Scapa Flow, the *Royal Oak* took the German destroyer *V126* alongside, it having not quite sunk. She was pumped out and steam was raised in two boilers and she was towed away. After several hard days of renewed work on board the *Nuremberg* she was towed off the beach at high tide, partially pumped out and then brought alongside *Royal Oak* with only an eight degree list. Further pumping reduced the list to only four degrees, and when steam was raised in two boilers she was towed away to anchor elsewhere.

A Scots firm, Cox and Danks, was given a contract to clear the anchorage of the wrecks and an amazing operation lasting for ten years ensued. The battle-cruiser *Seydlitz*, which had capsized, was eventually raised and towed bottom up to the ship-breaker's yard on the Firth of Forth, and most of the other salvaged craft went to the same destination. Most of the ships were raised by sinking large tanks alongside and passing wires beneath the hull and then pumping out the tanks. As the ship rose above the water all apertures were closed, and air was pumped into the hull, divers continuing the work of closing every opening. It was the biggest salvage operation known to history.

The big event of 1919 was the seven-mile march of the Armed Forces through the streets of London, 5,500 men from the Army, 4,500 from the Royal Navy and small representative contingents from the Allies (Italy, Belgium, France, USA, Japan, Poland, Portugal, Roumania, Serbia, Greece, and Slovakia) took part. Avenues on the route were decorated with flags and bunting and huge tented camps crowded the central London parks. The Fleet (already reduced from forty-seven to fifteen battleships), as well as the Navy's first real carrier, the *Furious*, and five destroyer flotillas, four submarine flotillas, four depot ships, and a host of small patrol craft anchored off Southend in the Thames estuary in several long lines extending over five miles. A small liner conveyed official guests on a tour each day and most ships were opened to visitors from noon onwards. A steady stream of trains left Charing Cross Station for Southend each afternoon.

The Mayors of Chatham, Rochester and Gillingham, naval ports for 400 years past, paid an official visit to *Royal Oak*, and after their ceremonial reception by the captain, were taken by Hugh on a long tour around the ship; there were probably two or three hundred other visitors on board at the same time, so that some of the narrower spaces became crowded. After their inspection of a boiler room the three mayors and their guide stepped into the lift which would take them up to daylight once more, but they had ascended no more than half-way when the lift unaccountably stopped. The "start" button produced no motion. The "alarm" button rang no bell, and the heat from below rapidly increased while all four occupants started to stream with perspiration. They all yelled together, and then tried again one at a time, but elicited no response. One stout little mayor in a straw boater began to lose his head and rampage around, but his two colleagues seized him by the arms and held him fast while Hugh assured him that the forenoon watchkeepers below were due to be relieved in ten minutes' time and it was certain that the petty officer on the oncoming watch would then discover that the lift was not working and would take some action. A minute or two later they started to move gently upwards and the crisis was resolved. No doubt some visitor — perhaps a child — had tampered with the controlling press buttons and cut off electric power from the lift unwittingly. After a drink or two in the gunroom all spirits rose, calm was restored, and when they went over the side an hour later, all three mayors each pressed half a crown into Hugh's hand. He tried to protest, but they thanked him profusely "for saving their lives", patted his shoulder in the friendliest way and scurried off down the ship's side ladder, no doubt with a dramatic story to recount to their wives at home. Hugh was not among those who made the Peace March through London because his stomach was now giving him frequent violent pains and he didn't think that he could keep on his feet for six hours. Thus it fell out that the mayors of Chatham, Rochester and Gillingham provided him with his most vivid memories of this historic celebration. They seemed to be a seal of guarantee that the war was really and truly over and done with.

In September, the 1st Battle Squadron and some destroyers visited seaports all around the country, and *Royal Oak* went to Scarborough, a popular seaside resort on the Yorkshire coast, and here Hugh experienced his first taste of the quite wonderful welcome and enthusiastic hospitality which ports all over the world were to offer to the Royal Navy represented by many ships in which he was to serve. An official programme of this visit survives. In addition to two ship's dances, cinemas, concerts, theatres, night accommodation at eight institutions and a long programme of sporting events including a sailing race, were offered to the crew. Officers were provided with golf, tennis, bowls, cricket and honorary membership of five clubs, and a civic ball at the largest hotel; in addition to which no member of *Royal Oak*'s gunroom was without at least one invitation to some private house on each of the seven days of the visit and there was a private or club dance every night to which officers were invited.

The only difficulty that arose was the business of landing at the jetty which was exposed to the effect of sea swell. Nobody was actually drowned, nor even fell into the sea, nor was any boat wrecked, though few escaped an anxious moment, and more than once boat traffic with the shore had to be suspended for a few hours.

They all had a glorious time, and perhaps deserved it at the end of a five-year war, and this was Yorkshire's gracious way of saying "Thank you".

The destroyers went to smaller ports because of their shallower draught. Two of these visited Yarmouth on the east coast, one of the historic fishing harbours of England where they received a truly royal welcome, which included on one evening a small private party in one of the trawler owners' homes. It was a family affair, and the two sub-lieutenants who were their naval guests enjoyed a splendid dinner and various games afterwards, one of which ended up with the two attractive daughters of the house sitting on the young men's knees to the uproarious laughter of the other guests — and that was apparently the signal that the party had come to its end. The two young men were offered substantial nightcaps by their host while mother and daughters were packed off to bed with kisses all round. Then Father settled back into his armchair and discoursed upon his daughters' charms, which:

"I'm telling you boys, are all yours. I don't mind telling you that kiss you got just now isn't the last one they plan to offer you tonight. Now you lads know what I mean. Be off with you to your beds and you'll find they are warm ones!"

They were. When they went into their respective bedrooms and switched on the light, bright eyes smiled at each of them from their respective pillows.

This was of course a great surprise to them, but it came in direct line from a centuries-old custom of welcoming an honoured guest and survived certainly in rural Finland and much of Lapland as late as the 1920s. One can imagine that many men will hope that it still does.

Royal Oak returned to the Firth of Forth in due course and Hugh and his term mates took the examinations for the rank of acting sub-lieutenant. This consisted of oral examinations conducted by the departmental heads: gunnery, torpedo, navigation, engineering and seamanship, and several written papers, such as the working out of star, moon and sunsights which they had taken with their own sextants, for each young officer had to provide himself with his own navigational sextant and had been continuously practised in its use at sea where the ordinary rolling and pitching of a ship creates difficulties that have to be mastered. They all passed reasonably well and were promoted to the rank of acting sub-lieutenant in October, a probationary rank to be held for six months before final Admiralty confirmation in the rank. So now they were "real officers", if only on a probationary basis, and they instantly tore off the white patches on their monkey-jacket lapels and then stitched on the first half-inch wide gold lace band round each coat cuff. It felt as if it stuck out like a signal flag and from time to time you would see them glance quickly down at the "curl" in the gold lace as if to reassure themselves that it really was there at long last.

They now began to take harbour watches on their own and other responsibilities were gradually increased, such as second officer of the watch on the bridge at sea, and more important action station positions.

During the autumn months dockyard workmen had come on board to erect a narrow platform suspended between the two 13.5-inch guns of the upper gun turret on the fo'c'sle deck. A great day came in November when a dockyard drifter arrived alongside with a very small single-engined aircraft (much like the later "Moth"), which was hoisted onto the platform; its crew, a probationary flight officer and a leading aircraftsman, accompanied their frail charge, and the officer was accommodated in the gunroom mess.

The business in hand was to discover how to fly an aircraft from an ordinary warship at sea, something which heretofore had never been done. The Firth of Forth was not the ideal locale for such an experiment, for the weather changed almost hourly and a thoroughly nasty sea could arise with a change of tide or wind at the shortest notice, and moreover, landing conditions at any nearby airstrip bore little or no relationship to the weather being experienced on the water only five miles away. It was almost a week before weather conditions became propitious and nearly the whole ship's company were on deck when the leading aircraftsman swung the little propellor to start the aircraft engine for its first trial take-off. The ship was lying at anchor head on to a brisk breeze, and the water was no more than ruffled as a lifeboat moved forward to be close at hand in case of a ditching.

The engine went "put-put" a few times and then died. They tried again. Two men took up positions to withdraw the wooden chocks which held the landing wheels. For several breathless minutes the engine warmed itself to the proper temperature and then the pilot held up his hand, the chocks were whipped away and, with a little roar like a rabbit might make, the tiny plane took to the air and did a steady steep glide down towards the water. The motor lifeboat shot ahead, and then, at the last possible moment, the little machine began to climb and it was safe away. The spectators let out a ragged cheer. The face of sea warfare thus began to be transformed. It was as great a change as the introduction of steam-driven propellors had wrought a century earlier, but nobody realised on this day how great that change was destined to be.

The trials went on for about a month because only occasionally were conditions suitable. In due course the captain appeared on deck in a flying helmet and climbed into the cockpit as passenger, and his, and all the dozen or so other take-offs were successful, though later on in other ships several ditchings did take place, one of them fatal. After his flight, Captain Whitehead was looked upon in a new light by his ship's company, for it took guts to face up to the very apparent hazards involved. Hugh and some other midshipmen were asked to tea at his house at South Queensferry one Sunday afternoon and he entertained them — all of course wearing their number one uniforms — with the task of cleaning out the small shed which did duty as his chicken house. Their protests had to remain unspoken for the moment, but must have been visible in the expression of horror upon their faces. However, the subsequent tea was superb, and they more or less forgot their indignation.

They finally left the ship just before Christmas and without regret said goodbye to *Royal Oak*. Hugh's father arrived from Canada on Christmas Eve and Hugh met him in London and they travelled together to Hythe in Kent on a train so hopelessly overcrowded that they were allowed to perch uncomfortably on trunks in the luggage car. It was the first time they had met since 1915. Christmas was enlivened and rather overshadowed by the birth of a granddaughter in the house on Christmas Eve.

Chapter 5

Off to China

A fortnight later, an appointment to HMS *Cricket* appeared in the mail on the breakfast table, and Hugh hurried off to London to find out from the Admiralty what on earth this ship was. He had never before even heard of the name. He learned that she was a China river gunboat lately returned from North Russia and that she was now refitting in Chatham Dockyard.

When his taxi from the railway station delivered him alongside on 6th January 1920, what he saw was a ship quite unexpected and looking down into the dry dock he discerned the unusual plan of this class of ship at a glance. It was about 230 feet long by 40 feet beam with a flat square stern; the freeboard forward was about four and a half feet, tapering aft to two feet six inches; there was no keel, but simply a flat plated bottom, the propellor shafts and propellors revolving in a tunnel open to the water below. A small superstructure arose amidships around the single funnel and short mast, the bridge being a simple little wooden box with glass sash windows all round. There were several small round hatches on the upper deck leading below to the officers' cabin flat and wardroom forward, and one to the cable locker right in the eyes of the ship, others down the sides provided access to coal bunkers, and those aft to the messdeck and store-rooms. Immediately below the bridge structure on the fore deck was mounted a six-inch gun which looked quite disproportionate to the size of this little ship. A four-inch gun was mounted aft, and on the wings of the bridge a pair of ten-pounder saluting guns on either side. A 24-inch searchlight was positioned on the after superstructure. Just looking at her, he wondered how on earth she could stand up to the shock of her six-inch gun when it fired, and wondered still more how such a ship could steam to Shanghai, which was her destination, because she was to serve in the gunboat flotilla on the lower Yangtze River. The captain, Lieutenant Commander

Morell, an elderly officer, and half a dozen engine-room ratings with their chief engine-room artificer, had already joined, and Hugh found that he was to be the navigator sub-lieutenant, Maurice Vernon being the first lieutenant. The ship was not yet habitable, so that everybody lived in the Royal Naval Barracks for the next ten days, while the refit was pushed ahead as fast as possible because the Admiralty had set a sailing date for mid-January in order that the later stages of the 15,000 mile passage should be made in favourable weather. The first leg down to Gibraltar might prove to be the most difficult of all since the Bay of Biscay is notoriously rough in early spring.

The *Cricket*, and her mate *Cockchafer*, which was refitting in another dock nearby, had returned from Murmansk a few months earlier, where they had been bombarding shore targets in support of General Wrangel's White Russians, fighting hopelessly against the Bolsheviks. When Hugh and Vernon started an exhaustive tour into every compartment, they discovered that almost everywhere sea water was leaking in. In some places rivets had fallen out of the hull plating and the holes had been plugged with wooden pegs hammered in, and some of these had become rotten. Two officially watertight compartments, when they were opened up, were flooded and found to contain ammunition stocks, obviously forgotten left-overs from the North Russian campaign; in one there were over a hundred Mills bombs, and in the other a few high explosive shells for army light guns, as well as a quantity of army machine-gun ammunition. After that first survey there was a concentrated hunt set up for plugged rivet holes, but it proved impossible in the short time still available to check all of the thousands of rivets that sew a ship's plating together; however about fifteen hundred had to be immediately renewed. When Hugh's father came down to say "goodbye" a day or two before the ship sailed, Hugh met him at the railway station.

As they were approaching the dockside Hugh said:

"Well Dad, there she is!"

"Where? I don't see any ship."

When they got to the actual wall of the dock and looked down, his father stopped and stared hard for a silent minute.

Then he said: "I've never seen anything like it! Do you mean to tell me you are going fifteen thousand miles to China in that?" Then he paused for a space. "Well, I can only hope they know what they are doing. Good luck to her — she'll need it!"

He was a seasoned traveller, having crossed the North Atlantic over forty times, and well knew what the sea can do to a ship.

The officers and ship's company were not fully confident; they were just hopeful, and everyone knew that the Bay of Biscay would be the first and crucial test.

All the 'tween decks cabin and messdeck accommodation was closed and battened down at sea. The wardroom mess was a wooden box-like ten foot cube-shaped structure which had been erected immediately behind the bridge. Down the centre was a table which could be folded up against one wall and around it were three cushioned settee seats, with stowage beneath for clothing. These could be converted into sleeping bunks for the three officers. There were some shelves and a couple of small cupboards and two small round scuttles. They fed, slept, and worked there at sea. The crew accommodation was a similar, but larger, temporary wooden structure further aft and fixed to the top of the boiler and engine-room casing which, as the coxswain remarked:

"Keeps us nice and cosy up here, it does; but when we get into the tropics I reckon we'll get done to a turn;" and in due course he proved to be a sound judge. You couldn't put a bare foot on the iron deck. Wooden decking, later fitted in Shanghai, didn't improve matters very much. Still, at this mid-winter moment in Chatham, it was nice and cosy for the time being.

They sailed from Chatham on 17th January: *Cricket*, *Cockchafer*, *Moth*, *Mantis*, and *Scarab*, with the sloop *Magnolia* in charge. It was foggy all the way down the narrow part of the Channel, and then, as they approached the Isle of Wight, the wind got up and they had their first experience of belting into short steep waves each one of which resulted in a resounding crash which broke crockery, glasses and other fragile articles. *Magnolia* quickly led them into Portsmouth harbour, having taken *Moth* in tow because she had suffered a machinery breakdown and she had to be put into dry dock. On 20th January the four survivors sailed again and made an eighteen-hour smooth passage to Devonport where Hugh's mother had hurried to see the last of him for a couple of years. A series of storms kept them in harbour for the next fifteen days.

Everybody went ashore almost daily to do last moment shopping and so on, and the flotilla sub-lieutenants organised a party in a box to see Marie Lloyd, the celebrated music-hall artiste in what must have been one of her very last stage performances.

She threw them kisses and they threw her oranges so that everyone enjoyed the evening's entertainment. Her broad jokes had been famous for several past decades.

The gunboats were to steam 500 miles on each leg of the voyage which was all that their oil fuel would permit, and after that the cruiser *Colombo* and four sloops would tow them onwards to their next port of call. The larger ships were already awaiting them.

At Devonport dockyard all of the gunboats required hull repairs, *Cockchafer* needing 1500 new rivets. She hadn't discovered the wooden plugs (probably overcoated with many layers of paint) before she left Chatham. The flotilla spent two weeks awaiting a favourable weather report, by which time the essential repairs were completed. Everyone in the dockyard viewed them with a question mark in their minds, if not on their tongues.

They sailed on the bright morning of 5th February with a light breeze astern and made an excellent passage across the Bay of Biscay through calm water, but with an enormous Atlantic swell on the beam. *Cockchafer* developed an engine-room breakdown, and she and her towing sloop were delayed while the remainder hurried on into Vigo, having received a report of an imminent westerly gale. The two laggards caught the beginning of it and *Cockchafer* was spitting rivets like a machine-gun before she got into harbour. As soon as she arrived all ships sent their shipwrights on board to cold-rivet about eight hundred leaks in her hull.

Vigo is a lovely place in spring, a fine long and narrow inlet sheltered beneath tree-covered hills, with a small dockyard and many jetties alongside where sardine boats were unloading heavy cargoes at that season of the year; later it would be tunny fish. The jetties were backed by fish canneries, and beyond these were great stacks of cased tinned sardines awaiting shipment. A tin cost only a few pennies and the newly-canned little fish were delicious — far better than those sold in English groceries, which no doubt were several years old. A walk through the surrounding hills away from the town took one immediately onto soft earthen roads bordered by primroses and other spring flowers, and over the doorway to many small untidy wooden cottages a green bough of some sort was hung. The sailors quickly discovered that the local wine was on sale here, and of course they drank too much of that — it was served in large earthenware pots and cost next to nothing, and none of them had ever drunk wine before in their lives. It was altogether a lovely four days they spent in Vigo harbour.

The next three-day leg was about 400 miles to Gibraltar and they were favoured by calm sunny weather as they passed down the Portuguese coast which was in sight most of the way. Cape Trafalgar was hidden in a haze, a promontory they all wanted to sight, for it bears a name to conjure with in the Navy. This was the most comfortable passage they made during the whole voyage, and the dramatic approach to the Mediterranean with Gibraltar like a crouching lion on the north side of the straits, and Ceuta gleaming a coppery gold on the African shore, was a sight that brought every man on deck.

They spent twelve days at Gibraltar refitting all the gunboats, for all their hulls were leaking. They were not designed to meet waves, but for the smooth shallow water of rivers. Gibraltar was Hugh's first contact with the "mysterious East". Here one sees Arab traders and Lebanese merchants with their characteristic type of Moroccan merchandise in almost every store. The polyglot population is more than half Spanish, and some thousands of Spanish dockyard workmen come in daily from La Linea and Algeciras. The frontier, a barbed wire line across the narrow mile-wide isthmus which joins the Rock to Spain, is strictly guarded on the Spanish side, and a good deal of formal fuss is made at the customs station, but it is noticeable that the natives treat it as a negligible sort of farce, and scarcely interrupt their newspaper reading or private conversation to observe the formalities. The foreigner — tourist, traveller, British resident — has to pay strict attention, or perhaps more important, deference to the control authorities. In fact one goes through very easily indeed and the only serious part is that face must be given, and if it is not, then delay and trouble quickly overtake the traveller. In those days the fortress was treated as such, and an unclimbable iron and barbed wire fence cut off the higher slopes of the Peak, which is the 1800-foot high summit of the Rock. No sooner had the sub-lieutenants of the flotilla discovered this bar to traffic than they made a concerted effort to find a way to climb over the fence. A couple of them succeeded by folding up two or three raincoats and laying them across the barbed wire, but the problem then arose of how to get up to the top of the very exposed rocky crest without being challenged and producing a pass. Hugh and a friend walked straight ahead up a little rough pathway, passing an antique 9.2-inch gun which looked fierce enough as they approached it, but was found behind its massive shield to be wrapped in old painted canvas which seemed to indicate that it had not been fired for a long time. No sentry was encountered, and peace seemed to reign undisturbed inside the fortified area, for they reached the highest point unchallenged, and only on their return when they walked down the main motor roadway and reached the guardhouse at the unclimbable fence entrance did they encounter a sentry. Before he challenged them they gave the name of their ship and that seemed to satisfy the regulations and no awkward questions were asked. The sentry obviously assumed that one couldn't get in without the proper pass. Not far below the unclimbable fence, a considerable park, the Alameda Gardens, has been laid out — a lovely steep-sloping place, the pathways lined with shade trees and a few ragged palms, and many beds of geraniums, arum lilies and cream-coloured freesias, which latter scented the air throughout the gardens in those early spring days.

At the opposite and northern end of the town is an area of narrow little one-way streets lined with tall seedy dark-looking houses, with washing flapping everywhere and a general air of dilapidation and poverty, some streets being the notorious red light district well known to all seafaring folk who have travelled to the East. At dusk small boys and a few sinister ragged men wait at the entrance to every bar, and patrol the busiest streets exercising their trade of pimp and guiding whoever will follow them "up the lines".

Following an expansive dinner shortly after their arrival, the sub-lieutenants of the flotilla decided to "go up the lines"; and they set off thither, not all of them too steady on their feet, one of them claiming to know exactly where to find the best girls; however, when the little group knocked on an obscure little door after quite a steep climb up the hill, it was opened by an enormously fat woman who burst into a staccato flood of Spanish, not one word of which could they understand, though she succeeded in making it perfectly clear that her house was an impeccably respectable one and not at all the sort of establishment they were looking for. Their guide subsided, lost, and they were obliged to turn downhill, coming out at the most distant end of the dockyard wall, and then had another mile or more to stumble along a rough unlit roadway before they could find the main gate (which is open all night) and get back to their ships.

When they sailed out of Gibraltar on 25th February all the younger personnel in the flotilla supposed that a Mediterranean passage (of some 1800 miles) would be a glorious yachting trip with blue skies and a warm sea — picture books always show it that way. But the first night dispelled the dream. A steadily increasing westerly wind threw up a choppy stern sea, certainly no more than five feet high, but absolutely devastating to gunboats. They yawed about uncontrollably and one of them parted her towing hawser. *Cricket* signalled to her towing mate *Bluebell* to slip her tow — which she did — and the pair of them turned north-east to put the sea on the port quarter, which made it possible to steer, although the course was forty-five degrees away from the desired easterly direction. They chugged along with Spanish mountains dark against the night sky to the west and soon lost the flotilla. The sea got steadily worse and they crept at minimum speed to keep Almeria light in sight for ten hours, and discussed by signal the possibility of putting into Valencia to await more favourable weather, but *Cricket*, crashing and shivering as each wave passed, seemed unlikely to get there, and so they anchored a hundred yards off shore beneath the lighthouse and then dragged their anchor and had to weigh again four times during the sixteen hours they sheltered there. At last the wind moderated and Morell decided to go off on the opposite tack and make for North Africa.

Bluebell replied to that proposal:

"I'll try everything but hope you won't lose your ship."

They weighed anchor and, if anything, the south-easterly course was a slight improvement though two forward compartments became flooded. It was really rather like a sailing-ship tacking to and fro. Two days later they made the Algerian port of Oran, being the second ship to reach it. The remainder arrived during the day, *Moth* rather badly knocked about and in need of dockyard repairs.

Oran is — or was — of course, a French naval base and a dockyard of considerable importance, though at that time there were only one or two small ships present, unmanned and lying in reserve. The French officials were most welcoming and really laid themselves out to entertain and assist the flotilla in every possible way, and the impromptu visit turned out to be one of the most enjoyable of the whole trip. An excellent British Consul organised an almost non-stop programme of social entertainments and sightseeing expeditions. Hugh fell on his feet straight away through his ability to struggle through a conversation in his schoolboy French. The town lies at the top of a wooded cliff about a mile above the docks, the business and shopping section, then "le quartier Arabe", and finally the French residential area, each fairly clearly divided from the other. The wooded cliff road was infested with brigands who had from time to time murdered and robbed a number of travellers, the most recent being a French businessman a few days before who had stopped his car because of a puncture. Cars were organised to transport officers and men up to the town at stated times, and after dark the cars travelled in pairs and the drivers were armed. "Le quartier Arabe" was out of bounds officially because of the risk of bubonic plague, and only certain bars, hotels and restaurants were allowed to be used elsewhere. The reputation of some Arabs was not beyond reproach — drugs and robbery being side lines they practised.

It all sounded rather dramatic, but the restrictions were proved to be essential. Hugh became acquainted with the chief of police, whose family entertained him almost every day, and he escorted the daughter of the house to a municipal ball that was given for the officers of the flotilla. Later the chief, wearing his uniform, took him on a short tour into "Le quartier Arabe", which, his host assured him, was not at the moment known to be plague infected, though it often was;

"And," he added, "we use this as an excuse to frighten you away. Presently you will see why!"

They drove in a police car through increasingly narrow tortuous streets, lined with one-story dilapidated hovels, many being open to the street and displaying goods of unimaginable kinds for sale. The stench of putrefaction and sewage was like a wall, it was difficult not to vomit. They came to a point beyond which the car could not penetrate, and got out and walked along the narrow street for a couple of hundred yards, jostling the crowds of Arabs on the narrow strip of trodden earth that lined the front of the buildings on either side. In the centre of what should have been the roadway was a continuous six-foot high bank of garbage, dead cats, rotting vegetables, excrement, flies, mangy snarling dogs, and little barefooted boys racing to and fro in all directions in their games; all of them had sore eyes. Flies were so thick that one was reminded of the ten plagues of Egypt. They dived into one of the shops where liquor was sold, and Hugh was pressed to drink an aperitif by the fat Levantine proprietor who was a friend of the police chief.

A couple of days before they sailed away the officers gave a lunch party on board for half a dozen of their hosts, and amongst those who came were the wife and daughter of the chief of police. After lunch the guests were shown over the ship. Mademoiselle la police wanted to see where the officers slept, and the deck hatch giving access to that compartment containing the three cabins was a small circular one. The young lady slipped down easily enough, and then, when her mama learned where she had got to, she insisted on following her, no doubt to see that all was fair and above board. But she was a large lady and only with the utmost difficulty did her hips, after an immense struggle, disappear below decks. Everyone had failed to realise that the upperworks were even more substantial, and of still greater circumference. The daughter hauled on the legs from below, assisted by the chief engineer — who was a married man, Hugh assured her hopefully — and those on deck tried to be helpful — but, as they say in North America, there was "no way".

"Ma fille! Ma fille! What will become of her, alone down there with a man?"

Her daughter's voice tried to reassure the distracted maman, but she was not to be consoled. Those on deck at last persuaded her that she could not get down and therefore must reverse course and come up. They hove and struggled; the daughter and the engineer officer below pushed and encouraged, but nothing budged the lady by even one inch, and she burst into tears. Hugh suggested that everyone should leave the fore deck and that maman should divest herself of as many garments as she could reach, and that her daughter should perform a similar office down below. Maman stoutly refused, but the daugher told the engineer to look the other way while she set to work. And then, with an audible "pop", like a cork bursting out of a bottle, maman started to rise, carefully pushing her skirts downwards to mask whatever deficiencies there might be below deck. The daughter followed up on deck immediately the hatch was finally cleared, clutching a bundle of clothing under one arm, and the two of them were hastily ushered into the captain's cabin on the upper deck to effect repairs. A bottle of wine had been thoughtfully left uncorked by the steward on the captain's dressing-table together with a couple of glasses. The ladies were effusive in their gratitude for this delicate attention, but they hurried ashore as quickly as courtesy permitted.

Here, too, Hugh met a hospitable owner of large orchards in the interior who drove him about fifty miles into the country to visit his estates. When the man called with his car at the dockside to pick up Hugh, the latter found two armed soldiers seated beside the chauffeur in front, and his host assured him that there was nothing to worry about as he had fitted armoured glass in all the windows, and the soldiers' rifles were loaded. He was well known on that road and bandits had never yet attacked him, though other people had been waylaid and robbed, and someone had recently been killed while riding out alone. They visited a vast area of lemon and orange groves and inspected a fruit-packing house, ate a sandwich lunch on the verandah of the manager's house, and sampled some wine made from the vineyards on the property. It was a brilliantly sunny day, almost the only one they experienced at Oran, which they found to be much as England is in early March.

They all remembered Oran as one of the most enjoyable experiences of the notable voyage upon which they were embarked. At the end of four days all ships were sufficiently watertight to put to sea again and they coasted along ten miles off shore to Bizerta. As they passed Algiers they could see the ships of the British Atlantic Fleet in harbour and a sloop was sent in to collect their mail, which had been brought from Malta in the Fleet flagship. Bizerta is a small edition of Oran, and they berthed alongside the canal, which is right in town with a picturesque white mosque close by, from which at sunset and sunrise they watched the muezzin loudly calling faithful Muslims to prayer from his high minaret. They stayed only overnight and left at midday on 7th March after taking on food and fresh water.

Through a 244-mile passage to Malta they experienced some of the roughest weather of the journey so far, and water leaked into every gunboat. Gozo came in sight first, and then shortly after, Malta itself. Both islands were seen to be very stony with little vegetation visible, and closely packed with cream-coloured stone buildings giving the immediate impression of overcrowding and intense heat. They had steamed 2,584 miles when they reached Valetta, and had established a confidence that their little ships could reach Shanghai — "with good joss", as the Chinese always carefully add.

Malta had been, for a hundred years past, a main naval base, and for these young sailors who for the first time entered the Grand Harbour on a glorious spring morning under a cloudless blue sky, it looked like a fairy story with its tremendous walls, castle towers and sculptured palaces of golden sandstone, some wreathed in purple bougainvillea. There are two large harbours, each with offshoot creeks. The flotilla berthed alongside the dockyard wall in Grand Harbour beneath the battlements of Fort Sant Anton, and they quickly learned the transport system of djhsias — a small double-ended brightly painted boat propelled by a single oarsman with his foot, the paddle sticking out over the stern into the water. All ships needed repairs, and this was the last Royal Naval dockyard they would see until Singapore 6,000 miles ahead of them.

They spent ten days there, tightening their belts, as it were, for the long passage across the Indian Ocean which lay ahead, and made some sightseeing trips about the island, and tried to swim in the cold sea. Dancing was the rage in those days — tea-dances in the afternoon at some hotel, and in the evenings more formal affairs in private houses or large hired ballrooms. There was hardly a night without one. It was an added experience to dine in the hundred-foot long hall at the Union Club, which once was the assembly place of the Knights Templar and still had its painted fresco decorations intact. Games facilities abounded, polo and tennis at the Marsa Club, football and hockey at the iron-hard Corradino grounds, and shore leave was given as liberally as possible to all hands.

Once again the sub-lieutenants set off one night, after an excellent dinner and dance at a café, to sample the joys of "going up the lines". This time they took three horse drawn cabs and the drivers made no mistake about the destination. A large beetling dame tightly upholstered in black satin introduced them very formally to the half-dozen girls who were sitting about disconsolately listening to gramophone music while awaiting customers in a dreary little stone-floored room with a minute dance floor around which were small tables. There they were to get acquainted over a bottle of the cheapest wine, as they propositioned whichever girl took their eye. Some of the young men passed up both the wine and the dancing, and were instantly led off into dark back premises. Others, slower off the mark, made an effort to dance and select more carefully, and when this group had been led off into the darkness at the back of the room it soon became obvious that the two or three remaining, amongst whom Hugh found himself, had found the few girls still on the floor singularly unattractive. When these damsels realised this they set to work with a vigour and purpose that practically amounted to indecent assault — which had the very opposite effect from that which they wished to achieve. The young men simply walked out of the brothel, got into a waiting cab and returned to their ships. Hugh found the whole thing sordid and pitiable that girls would be treated almost like cattle. When notes were compared later on, nobody appeared to have enjoyed the evening's entertainment very much.

The days at Malta seemed to pass in a flash and their next lap to Port Said was about as rough as the gunboats could stand. There were indeed some anxious hours during the last night when a very choppy sea developed, and the flotilla split up on a variety of courses in attempts to reduce damage.

Port Said in those days was a sink of iniquity unrivalled even by Marseilles, if the old hands could be believed. Its polyglot population seemed able to purvey every vice known to man and one or two new ones as well. As soon as a sailor stepped off the gangway one scout after another sidled up to offer him — well, just about everything that human perversity has invented, and several people had their wallets most expertly stolen while still in sight of the ship. It was said that the Greek section of the population preferred to take their sea bathing without the customary costume, and pretty well everybody made their way to the bathing beaches to check up on the rumour. Like the Norwegians, they did indeed dispense with a costume, and family parties were seen running cheerfully down into the waves laughing and holding hands.

Here the younger men for the first time saw the oriental system of coaling ship. Gangs of coolie women trotted up the gangway each with a small bucket perched on her head which she tipped down the coal shute into the ship's bunker, and then, without pausing, trotted off down another brow into the coal lighter where a gang of men filled the baskets, so that the coal came in an endless chain, and very high tonnages per hour were recorded. They were not sorry to leave at the end of two days, for the place stank, the streets were filthy, entertainment was mostly vicious and very limited, and flies swarmed everywhere. The valuable acquisition they made there was a local brown pottery jar for holding about a gallon of water. It was somewhat porous, and as the water sweated out through the porous walls it evaporated, and the temperature of the remaining water fell considerably. They could not make nearly enough ice, nor could they keep it for long in the primitive wooden ice boxes with which they were supplied — indeed the sick-bay consumed the whole production of the inadequate little machine with which *Cricket* was fitted. Refrigerators, as we now have them, had not yet gone to sea in HM ships.

The Suez Canal pilot took over the navigation on the bridge which presented no difficulties to the gunboats — they were so small that they were never required to tie up alongside to allow other larger ships to pass them safely, and they anchored for the night at Ismalia in the Bitter Lakes, changing pilots there. The hazy sunrise over the undulating golden desert stretching in every direction was breath-takingly beautiful, and on this morning a string of camels ambled across the empty landscape to complete an already perfect picture, and also served to emphasise that they were now indeed far from home. The temperature had risen sharply on leaving Port Said, and newcomers to the oppressive heat felt strangely out of sorts and exhausted. They got out their solar pith topees shaped like a London fireman's brass helmet, and were at least protected from sunstroke. The men's service jumper was thickly padded down the spine. It took forty-eight hours of sweltering before a signal came ordering white uniform to be worn, with its white jacket fully buttoned up to its high stiff collar; and prickly heat of course began to appear, for there was nothing like enough fresh water to allow bathing every day, and lukewarm salt water baths were only a partially effective substitute. The proper remedy is to wash all over several times a day, though they had not learned that yet.

They reached Suez at the end of the second day and stayed out in the anchorage for one night, so that the little white town was scarcely seen, though *Cricket*'s pilot invited the officers to supper at his bungalow. They walked through the empty dusty streets for the few minutes it took to reach the house. His wife, who was an Englishwoman and had been in the canal zone for many years, was delighted to make contact with her own countrymen and was able to give them some idea of the conditions in which the few Europeans in that area lived. It seemed to be a singularly dull and tedious existence.

Shortly after sailing (on 28th March) out of Suez the Admiralty chart informs you of the sight of King Solomon's emerald mines on the starboard hand, and if you look carefully you will also discover the "reputed site of Mount Sinai" well out of sight to port, but what concerned Hugh in his capacity as unskilled navigator was the paragraph in the Admiralty sailing directions which stated that at this season of the year strong to gale force winds from the north blew continuously down the northern half of the Red Sea, while, with only a narrow gap of calm water in the middle, mariners must expect equally strong southerly winds to prevail in the southern half. That meant that if they survived being pooped and flooded to begin with, they were sure to get a battering from head seas during the last half of the 1,400-mile voyage to Aden. Nor were there many sheltering headlands under which a lee could be found because coral reefs lay close to shore.

The Red Sea was going to be tough and unforgiving and so they found it. By steering a zigzag course for the first few days they managed to evade damage from the stern seas, and the wind fell light quite soon, so that they made good progress, though fuel consumption was much higher than expected owing to the irregular course and endless speed variations that were found necessary. Sleeping between decks soon became impossible due to the heat and lack of sufficient ventilation, and hammocks were slung all over the bridge structure. They found they needed to drink quantities of water and lime juice which upset some stomachs. Hugh discovered that red wine mixed with water was much better for him, and everybody began to appreciate the cool water that could be obtained from the Port Said porous earthenware jars.

Then the weather fell light and they slipped into Port Sudan to top up with fresh water and fuel. There were just three white men in the tiny place: the harbour-master, the engineer in charge of the railway terminal workshops, and the young assistant district commissioner who had been sent down to deal with the needs of the visiting flotilla. The harbour-master took some of them out fishing by night. A strong incandescent light was kept shining over the boat's side to attract the fish, and hooks were baited with the small fish that were immediately caught. Then lines tautened after a very short interval, but when hauled in again and again only the head of the bait remained on the hook and no fish was landed. Sharks were in the area and as soon as a larger fish was hooked they grabbed it. However, on the way back the light was rigged so that it shone across the boat directly abeam, and several flying-fish and one or two others of similar small size leaped into the boat, and were later welcomed at table as a pleasing variation to the menu.

Their visit lasted only two days and when they sailed the flotilla ran into the expected head winds which blew steadily at force 5, throwing up exactly the short breaking seas which the gunboats found the most difficult to endure. As each wave passed, the flat bottom crashed down with a shattering bump onto the next. During the second night out when just off Jebeltier the wind strengthened somewhat, and *Cricket* was making very heavy weather of it when a most almighty crash occurred, the engines stopped and everybody woke. The chief engine-room articifier ran up to the bridge to report that the ship's back had broken. The after deck, about forty feet from the stern, had a "wave" eighteen inches high from one side to the other across it, and the ship's side plating was split on both sides down from the deck about one foot, so that the crest of each passing wave squirted a stream of water into the engine-room. The danger was that the after part would break off and fall on the propellor shafts, causing them to rip through the bottom. Whether she could float under that condition was uncertain. However, in the event no further damage occurred. The light cruiser *Colombo* took the little ship in tow at daylight and began to creep at minimum steerage way speed of five knots back towards Port Sudan.

During the forenoon everyone packed a bag preparatory to abandoning ship if that should be necessary, and at about eleven o'clock it was found that the ship's side plating was splitting still further. Wood planks had been bolted along the upper deck to try to strengthen it, but they were rather light, and one or two of them began to break up. When these further defects were reported to *Colombo*, her captain immediately ordered *Cricket* to abandon ship, and a cutter (a substantial sea-boat thirty-two feet long) was dropped astern on a floating grass line to take off half the crew and their baggage at a time. The captain and Hugh were in the second boat, and while she was being loaded up, Hugh went a final round of the ship, and found the ship's cat, which had given birth to a litter during the night, installed in a straw-lined box with a large dish of condensed milk and some meat close at hand. As soon as she saw him she gave a wild shriek, rushed out on deck and jumped over the side — she had obviously gone mad. The sailors had thought it too risky to take her and the litter with them in the violently tossing small lifeboat, particularly since there was a good deal of difficulty in climbing up the jumping ladder over the stern of *Colombo* which was pitching quite violently. Anyhow they firmly believed that their little ship would somehow get into port, and that was only another day ahead of her if all went well.

As this second lifeboat came close under *Colombo*'s stern, the occupants became aware that there was nobody in sight on her quarterdeck. They shouted to no avail and bounced about in the rough water for quite twenty minutes so that some men became seasick. At long last an officer appeared and gazed down upon them, then hands appeared to help with the difficult disembarkation. When at last they did get on deck they saw practically the whole of *Colombo*'s ship's company packed into the waist of the ship admiring an enormous sixteen-foot shark which had been caught and which they had just finished hauling up to the davit head. As it was swung inboard they saw half a dozen shark fins swirling about in the sea. These had smelt the blood. This joyous event quite obliterated all thought for the unhappy shipwrecked mariners for the time being. There would be enough sharkskin for scrubbing the ship's woodwork for the rest of the commission. Later in the day they caught another and smaller one, only about six feet long, and that skin they presented to the *Cricket*.

They did everything on earth to make the *Cricket*'s company welcome and comfortable. The only thing Hugh had forgotten to pack was handkerchiefs — but of course some were immediately lent to him. It was before the days of Kleenex. *Colombo* skilfully towed her broken child into Port Sudan, and left *Bluebell* there to watch over her while she herself hurried off to rejoin the flotilla who were moving at a snail's pace against the contrary wind. They had to close the shore and anchor for a while under some convenient lee on occasions when the wind grew too strong for the gunboats.

Meanwhile the railway chief engineer placed his entire resources at *Cricket*'s disposal. There was no dry dock and so she was placed in a small wet dock, in reality a shallow depression close to the shore, where divers could work with the greatest of ease, though they did not have much underwater work to do. Stout iron plates were riveted over the two splits down the ship's side, and two very heavy railway lines were riveted by hand along the after deck where the buckled plating was removed and replaced with stronger plates. The whole work was completed in ten days. The midday shade temperature at Port Sudan was over 100°F, and it did not fall below 85°F at night, and, shut out from the sea breeze as they were, the whole ship's company felt the heat very badly. Neither ice, fresh fruit nor vegetables were to be had. Because the water was at its coolest the officers swam before sunrise in the wet dock for several mornings until a shark was sighted, lying under the ship. After that nobody was willing to bathe any more. A desert partridge shoot was organised by the assistant commissioner, and they had some good shooting between dawn and sunrise, after which it became too hot. When some stray dog died during the night a few yards from the gangway, a flock of about fifty large vultures descended at daylight and by ten o'clock only white bones were to be seen. These birds with powerful beaks and long scraggy bare necks are particularly hideous — one of the very few wild creatures that is truly revolting to look at. Nobody was sorry to leave Port Sudan, though the ship had been so well looked after by the minute community who were living there.

On the way south, *Bluebell* and *Cricket* met the sloop *Cornflower* employed on the Red Sea slave patrol. Her job, maintained by Britain alone for some sixty years, was to intercept dhows carrying slaves from Abyssinia to the Arab sheikhdoms on the east coast of the Red Sea. This trade had been a profitable Abyssinian speciality for centuries. Chieftains in the interior would raid neighbouring African tribes and capture men, women, and especially young boys. These latter had their genitals sliced off with a sword and about one in a hundred survived to reach an Arab sheik's court, where they were the most highly prized of his possessions and fetched very large sums of money, for they were destined to be the special companions of the ruler. Of the other slaves, male and female, about one-third survived the terrible journey to Arabia. They were chained together in lines, marched incredible distances and then battened down in the dhow's hold to avoid detection. This particular sloop had recently caught such a dhow, and when they broke open the hold dead bodies were putrefying and the few slaves still living had not been given water for several days as the dhow had run short of water. This trade, though now much reduced in volume, is believed to be still clandestinely functioning down to our own modern times.

The flotilla reassembled at Aden and prepared for the long voyage to Colombo. It was now touch and go whether the south-west monsoon, due in average years about 20th May, would break before they could reach Ceylon; and if they could not, then Bombay was designated as the alternative destination. The gunboats would be towed the whole way, but for the first 500 miles would also steam at their nine-knot economical speed, in order to reduce strain on the towing hawser, and the actual speed made good would be eleven knots. The towing sloops had just sufficient fuel to make this possible. It was a close calculation, and any breakdown or other delay at sea was likely to imperil both the sloops and the gunboats. At this season the Indian Ocean would be an oily calm, with a big swell developing as the monsoon drew closer.

The two days at Aden were busy ones with engine-room maintenance, ship's stores coming in, and fuelling. The Eastern Telegraph Company's station personnel of about twenty, including wives, did their utmost to entertain the flotilla. They formed very nearly the total European population at that time. Aden was blisteringly hot, and when Hugh took a broken-down old cab to the crater one day to look at it, he very nearly passed out with the heat. It was reputed to be the hottest spot in the hottest possession in the British Empire. Tennis in the late afternoon was just possible, and below the Eastern Telegraph Co. seaside bungalows, was a netted enclosure where everyone bathed. Sharks' fins could be seen patrolling just outside the net every time anybody went in to swim and some had got inside once or twice, but had been captured before any harm was done.

Sailing on 21st April, the flotilla steamed close along the north shore of Sokotra Island just south of the Gulf of Aden, and anchored for a few hours off the so-called port about two miles out because the water was so shallow. Quite close by huge numbers of pink flamingoes were standing on their enormously long legs on submerged sandbanks, and made a wonderful sight as small groups flew to and fro in search of better fishing grounds. The island is notable for the curiously named "Dragon's Blood Tree", which apparently grows nowhere else in the world, but the soil generally is too dry to be productive. Nevertheless it was thought that fresh fruit, vegetables and perhaps chickens and fish might be purchased there for the long sea passage ahead, and *Colombo* sent in a boat to see what was available. A contractor came out later in the afternoon in his little motor boat with a small load of fresh vegetables and fruit, which was all that the place could supply. As soon as this had been distributed amongst the eight sloops and gunboats they sailed onward for the East.

It was a twelve-day 2,140-mile passage made in intense heat and high humidity, and as the gunboats were in three watches, eight hours of each day must be spent on the bridge or in the engine-room, and there was little to break the monotony. Once they passed a small school of whales lying on the surface, apparently asleep, for they made no move as the ships approached and course had to be altered slightly to avoid colliding with them as they were lying very close together. *Bluebell* developed a defect which reduced her speed and the remainder of the flotilla drew ahead and finally disappeared over the horizon when only half the passage had been completed. From this time onwards the ocean swell steadily mounted and became shorter and steeper so that it seemed increasingly unlikely that *Cricket* and her escort would make Colombo. They seriously feared that the monsoon, now overdue, would break at any moment, and looked up the charts of the Andaman Islands and considered running there for shelter, but pressed on until the light on the small atoll of Minikoi was sighted. This was really the last hope, for it was still four days' steaming to Colombo and the skies were now low and heavy with grey scudding clouds; but they plodded on. When close to Ceylon *Bluebell* decided to slip the tow during the night as her fuel had run dangerously low and she steamed off independently.

At daylight the hazy palm-lined shores of Ceylon were dimly sighted with not one single feature to indicate the ship's position. A stream of traffic, both northbound and southbound, was visible but, since they had not had any sun or star sights for four days, they had no idea in which direction Colombo lay — and fuel was running very low indeed. Finally they asked a passing merchantman for their position and learned that Colombo was forty miles to the northward, a distance that might be too great for their remaining fuel. They turned north and presently sighted *Bluebell*, who offered to take them in tow again, an offer which was gratefully accepted as the weather appeared to be rapidly deteriorating.

About a mile off Colombo breakwater, and rather too close inshore, *Bluebell* suddenly slipped the tow, believing that it had caught on the bottom — which might, if it were so, hamper her manoeuverability and cause her to be cast ashore. In *Cricket*, the chief engineer reported that he was on the point of running out of the last drop of fuel, so the captain hoisted the international signal indicating "Emergency, keep out of my way", and made a bee-line for the entrance. About three hundred yards before they got there "Chiefey" ran up onto the bridge and reported:

"We've lost steam, Sir! There is no more oil!"

Cricket still had steerage weigh on her and gently slid through the entrance, dropped an anchor and signalled for a tug to come and berth her, for by now she had finally lost all weigh and was helpless. It was a close thing at the end of a two-thousand-mile passage. At Colombo they learned that the menacing weather they had experienced during the last few days was locally known as "the little monsoon", which indeed looked like the real thing, but failed to produce the expected gale force winds and heavy rains. It seems to occur most often in years when the real monsoon is late in breaking.

This was *Colombo*'s first visit to her titular city, and the place was *"en fête"* for the occasion, and she received a truly royal welcome which spread around the little flotilla. There was a civic reception, dinners at Government House, cricket and football matches, dances for the officers and others for the ships' companies, car trips out into the countryside and down to the ancient Dutch city of Galle, sailing races with the yacht club, picnics at Mount Lavinea, and a special train trip for a day up to Kandy, the ancient capital, where Buddha's tooth is enshrined in a splendid temple on the edge of a very beautiful emerald-green lake crowded with tortoises. Ceylon, one of the really memorable beauty spots on earth, did its utmost to make the visitors' short stay a success, and they never forgot the week they spent there; especially the *Colombo*'s chief cook, whose false teeth fell out of the train window and, in spite of half an hour's stop and intensive search by almost everybody on board, were never found.

But the monsoon was imminent and they had a thousand miles of ocean to cross before reaching the protected waters of the Straits of Malacca which separate the Malayan peninsula from Sumatra. Once more the sea was oily calm on a long ocean swell, and by now they had become acclimatised to the intense heat, and also had learnt about the sort of fresh food that would endure the longest. They made an excellent uneventful passage to Penang, passing many "floating islands" which are in reality large agglomerations of jungle vines, trees and shrubs bound together and swept down from the mountains by rivers flowing into the straits. Waterspouts were common as the sun began to set, and almost every afternoon a small violent tropical storm swept over them with torrential rain and forked lightning which came and went in half an hour. All night long there was a theatrical display of sheet lightning flickering over the Malayan mountains, so bright that one could read by it.

Penang proved to be another place of great beauty. The island upon which the port stands is quite small, and most of the European residences are on top of the hill that overlooks the harbour. A large hotel provides the background for every sort of party, and its bedrooms are separated by partitions that do not extend fully down to the floor nor up to the ceiling so that the draught created by the large overhead fans may produce the greatest possible effect, and it is felt even under the mosquito net over the bed, without which malaria would almost certainly be contracted. Everyone had been put on a low dosage of quinine a few days before entering harbour. Though never guaranteeing full protection, it did mitigate the severity of the disease in most cases, and only one or two occurred in the whole flotilla.

Here again the European population did their utmost to entertain both officers and ships' companies, the programme being much like that at Colombo — with rugby football added in a temperature of 97°F, which the visitors afterwards decided was about the maximum they could have endured. Hugh, visiting a home up on the hill, was introduced to his first gin and coconut juice. When this was offered to him at sundown he gladly accepted, and a "boy" (a Malayan servant) was sent out with a large heavy knife to climb up a nearby palm tree and cut down one or two coconuts hanging beneath the crown. The knife was then used to cut a hole in the thick shell of the nut and the white cloudy juice was poured into a jug. To his horror the coconut was thrown away on the ground, so he asked if he might retrieve it and take it back to the ship to eat the "white meat" lining. The shell proved to be extremely tough to cut.

In the streets they saw for the first time the colourful and quite amazing Chinese shops stuffed with European goods side by side with Chinese foodstuffs and curiosities. There was even a red-lacquered Chinese pagoda-roofed temple inside which they found a huge gilded Buddha, smiling serenely as he sat cross-legged on his gilded lotus flower. These temples — when well kept, as this one was by its wealthy trading community — can be very lovely examples of characteristic Chinese art. The calm and always graceful Buddhist priests were also something new to the visitor who learned that the acolytes in their deep yellow toga dress were local boys doing their adolescent four or five years of temple service as part of their education.

Every evening there was dancing at the hotel and the sub-lieutenants did not miss that. From the garden terrace where you sat out under the stars in comparitively cool air it was fascinating to watch the phosphorescent tracks of fish swimming and chasing one another. White mess dress, which included thick dark blue pile cloth trousers, and stiff white collars and starched shirt fronts and cuffs — and no doubt looked very smart and pleasing — made dancing a hot business, and before long the starched shirt front was likely to be sadly buckled, and the cuffs even more so; but they belonged to a more rigid and perhaps more hardy generation that observed social conventions and upheld accepted customs.

Penang, lovely and enervating as it is, came to a speedy end and they moved on down the calm waters of the Straits of Malacca towards the great island port of Singapore. The approach leads past a cluster of islands between this great port and the Sumatran coast, one given up to a huge oil storage depot; one an ammunition depot; another to aluminium production, and yet another to a convict settlement, brilliantly green with palms leaning out over the water. Singapore city fronts the wide and open roadstead and in those days laden merchantmen lay as far as two miles off shore and transferred their cargoes by lighter, towed by small motor boats, or sometimes propelled by enormous long sweeps manned by two or three sweating brown-skinned coolies in loincloths. The climate is humid, and the temperature hardly varies from around 89°F throughout the year. The sun blazes down with ferocity and drains the brilliant colours of flowering trees and myriad-patterned sarong cloths which are wound around the waists of men and women alike, the women wearing a distinctive bodice around the breast, leaving a gap of brown skin below it. All colour is annihilated in the noonday, and one only appreciates the brilliance of the street scene during the first and last hours of daylight.

They anchored half a mile offshore and saw virtually nothing beyond the town. As in every other port, the officers were made honorary members of the several social and sports clubs, and in addition the venerable Raffles Hotel was a principal meeting-place. The Tanglin Country Club provided tennis and a swimming-pool as well as tea-dances and evening dances several days a week. A sailing race arranged by the yacht club had to be abandoned at sundown as not even the slightest breeze arose.

Two or three of the sub-lieutenants found their way to a Chinese opium den — they wanted to discover what opium smoking was like. They travelled in rickshas drawn along by barefooted Chinese coolies wearing an open blue cotton shirt and shorts and a very wide-brimmed hand-woven straw hat as a shelter from the sun. At a slow trot it took about half an hour into the depths of the Chinese quarter of the city to reach a plain little wood-fronted street. A porter waited at the door, and a rotund smiling "host" welcomed them with cups of Chinese tea while they sat on hard wooden benches round the wall and he told them what exactly happens and collected his payment in advance. Then they went into an inner, airless chamber with a curious odour unfamiliar to them. This was divided into little booths by lattice-work wooden screens inside which were low wooden platforms along the wall, arranged very much like ships' cabin sleeping bunks, only there was no mattress, only bare polished wood and a little shaped block of wood to be used as a pillow for the head. You could either sit or recline, disrobe or not, and an attendant soon brought in opium pipes, a little wick lamp and a small pipe with a tiny bowl of brown opium and the couple of metal spoon-like tools used for heating the dry opium over the lamp and putting it into the bowl of the pipe. The bowl is very small indeed so that only a minimum quantity of opium is "cooked up" at one time. The attendant showed them exactly how to manage it all, and they lay down on the bunks and inhaled the delicate smoke, hoping for they knew not quite what exotic experience. Then the man hurried out, no doubt to attend to other clients. They felt drowsy; one fellow fell asleep and neglected to refill his pipe, there was the sound of a consumptive sort of cough nearby and one young man got up and peered into the gloom of the next cubicle where a pale livid face could be discerned, but no response came when he tried to talk to the man, who appeared to be dead — but no, not quite, for a gentle little sigh parted his lips for a moment, and so the officer returned to his own bed and another pipe. Time passed, four hours in fact, and no dreams, no beautiful houri in beads, just nothing. At last they got up, put on their coats and made their way to the door, where the patron, or whatever you call him, still sat fatly smiling, and they spoke to him of their disappointment.

"But Sir, you go home too soon. No dreams come for mebbe tree four day; you see! You come back, yes?"

And the answer to that, had they given one, would have been: "Not on your life. It's a busted flush! Twenty dollars down the drain." They were behaving rather like a litter of puppies; trying any and everything as it came along to see if it was fun.

That night Hugh had gone instead to Raffles Hotel to dine with friends who neglected to stop him when he called for a glass of water; they had all had several drinks at the bar beforehand and probably nobody noticed what he did. While they were still at table a snake charmer with his flute and little round straw-covered basket came and squatted down on the terrace a yard or so away beyond the opened glass door.

"Gilly, Gilly, you like to see snake dance? I show you! One dollar pleez."

Hugh threw him the coin and he started a quiet little tune on his pipe; the basket stirred and he addressed it with a stream of endearments and then continued his tune raised a pitch higher, bent over and very carefully removed the lid of the basket out of which a broad silver head with the black marking like a pair of spectacles emerged. It rose higher and higher until the four-foot-long cobra was fully out and practically standing on its tail on the stone terrace paving. The tune changed and the cobra spread its hood, opened its mouth, extended its two poison fangs and flickered its thin long red tongue, all the time waving its head to and fro from side to side in time with the music. At that point the head waiter dashed up, pouring out a stream of Malayan invective, and slammed the glass door shut.

"That man no good Sir! Him cobra come in here other day and one lady faint!"

The East seemed to be even more immemorial that day, and Hugh had unknowingly swallowed the germ of amoebic dysentery with his glass of water during dinner.

After a week's stay there they turned northwards with the Malayan coast in sight on the port hand and Hong Kong as their destination.

The sky was clear and the sun shone brilliantly hot, but once more a roughish sea got up and they had to make a zigzag course to keep the gunboats from breaking up. At one point it became bad enough for them to turn for shelter towards the uninhabited

Commander H. C. Guernsey, 1948

Gunroom (junior officers) Mess on *Colossus* — coaling ship —
on Christmas Day 1917, at Scapa Flow

HMS *Sandwich* on the China Station, 1929—31

Some of the crew of HMS *Sandwich* at a Buddist Monastery
at Fouchow, China, 1931

HMS *Sandwich* frozen in at Tientsin (North China), 1929

Box Gorge, going downstream on Yangtze River, 1921

Upper Yangtze River Gorges — towing upstream

Upper Yangtze River Gorges, 1921

Me and my kwadza leaving Chungking for home
on Upper Yangtze River, 1921

Going down the Yangtze River, 1921

Hugh Guernsey, Sub-Lieutenant,
at King George V's levee at St. James Palace, 1921

HMS *Sandwich*
firing a depth-charge, 1931

Mussolini and Vice-Admiral Imthurn
in *London* at Venice, 1934

Grand Harbour at Malta

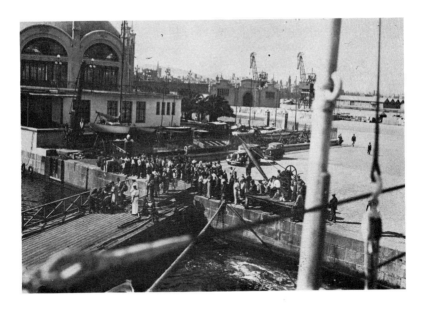

British refugees from Spain arriving on board *London* at Barcelona, 1936

Spanish refugees boarding HMS *Southampton*
near Santander, Northern Spain, 1937

HMS *Teal* at Chungking, 1921 — About 150 feet long

HMS *Colombo* on East Indies Station, 1928 — Steamed 220,000 miles on this commission

Sailing Dhow from Zanzibar to Malaya via Arabia,
West Coast of India and Ceylon. (Lasting two or three years)

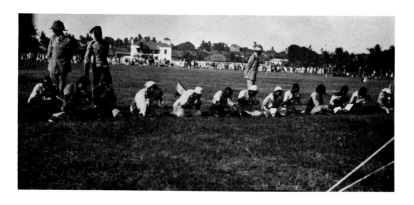

Coconut opening competition at Police Sports, Zanzibar, May 1923

Deck hockey with the German Pocket Battleship *Graf Spae*
at Barcelona during the Spanish Franco Revolution

Marconi's yacht *Elettra* and Mussolini's yacht *Aurore*
with two destroyers alongside at Venice, 1932

1st Cruiser Squadron at Alexandria
during Mussolini's attack on North Africa, 1935

Cruisers in rough weather in the Mediterranean, 1935

Sinking the *Bismarck*

The only shot (from *Bismarck*'s secondary armament)
that came close to Fleet Flagship *King George V*

King Boris of Bulgaria coming on board *London* at Varna, Bulgaria

Paracel Islands where Chinese fishermen land for water or repairs from time to time. However, the wind moderated and suddenly quite a large uncharted island appeared with some trees standing up at its centre. Hugh was dumbfounded and checked and rechecked his navigation and his charts and finally consulted the *'Admiralty China Sea Pilot, Vol. 3'*, and learned from it that in this area quite large floating islands are occasionally seen, having come down from rivers in Siam or Annam, and when they passed within a mile of this one, the binoculars revealed that such indeed was this curious apparition.

A day or two later a terrible stench of putrefaction swept into the ship — really sickening. A dark floating object came in sight several miles to windward and from it drifted a long shiny oil slick. Nearer approach showed the object to be a long-dead whale which they were glad to leave behind them.

Owing to delay caused by head winds the flotilla began to get short of fuel and they were ordered into Saigon, lying about forty miles up the slow-flowing Mekong River; this was their first experience of the river conditions for which the gunboats were designed. There were several miles of jetties and dockyard walls as one approaches close to the city centre and they berthed in a narrow reach just above the French fleet, and alongside a river-side tree-lined avenue of large and well-constructed houses — very much at the centre of the big city.

The French squadron seemed to consist of three rather old cruisers and several smaller craft — sloops, gunboats and auxiliaries. The cruisers had their quarterdecks decorated with flags and masses of potted palm trees and flowering shrubs and looked as if they had been in harbour for a long time. All ships had to turn and berth with bows downstream on arrival. When *Colombo* came up, her nose was pushed into the soft muddy river bank and a large part of a tree fell on the fo'c'sle deck as a tug hauled her stern upstream. The gunboats easily manoeuvred in the current, having no keels, and their officers appreciated for the first time how suitable they were going to be for their future duties.

The French fleet really laid itself out to entertain the flotilla, and tended to regard the British gunboat personnel as heroes for having successfully made the long passage from England. The visit happened to coincide with a great ball given at the Mairie in aid of some charity; the Governor-General and the official world all attended in full dress. Hugh dined out beforehand at the splendid residence of some important banker and went with the family to the ball as escort for the daughter of the house. He was introduced all round and his programme was filled for him by his hosts in no time at all. Quite early in the evening he found he was to partner a very fat dusky lady who spoke in French as halting as his own — the wife of some provincial official. She could talk of nothing but her daughter, a very pretty brunette maiden who was obviously having a success with the French officers. The waltz was encored and just as Hugh was turning to lead off his heavyweight partner once more, she threw up her hands in the air and gave a piercing shriek which brought everyone in the great room to a halt.

"Ah, mon Dieu! Ma fille, elle est morte, elle est morte!"

And Hugh had seen the girl and her young officer partner running towards an open window out of which they jumped hand in hand and disappeared. Maman could not move herself, but continued screaming. Hugh ran to the window and looked out — to see the young couple leaning over a balustrade laughing and talking. They were on a small balcony, down a few steps below the ballroom level. He turned back to explain to his partner what had really happened, only to find the Governor-General glittering in medals patting her on the back and offering her his handkerchief as he tried to console her. Hugh's rudimentary French was not really geared to do justice to the situation and he dragged maman by the hand to see for herself. The ball revitalised itself and they arrived back on board at daybreak.

After five days in Saigon they sailed for Hong Kong and arrived a few days later without further adventures.

In those days there was a teeming town clustered along the waterfront of Hong Kong island with perhaps a hundred thousand inhabitants and across the mile-wide harbour Kowloon lay in a leased territory about ten thousand strong, packing itself close to a range of commercial wharves. The place was growing yearly, but the extreme shortage of water appeared to be likely to limit much further growth. The port was the key to the valuable Chinese foreign trade, said to be valued at four hundred million pounds sterling a day, a sanctuary from which foreign, and especially British, business operated. There the money in a bank was felt to be safe — and the same claim could not be made for any other place in the whole of China, for Yuan-Shih-Kai, the first president, was not long dead, and the Provinces were falling apart each under its Tujun, the local military commander, and also at the same time its political head. A vague lip service was paid to Peking central government officialdom, but decrees coming from there were being increasingly evaded or disregarded, and already several Tujuns were at war with their neighbours. The country was in the process of disintegrating into general turmoil, and officials had little or no interest other than to feather their own nests.

Chapter 6

On the Yangtze River

It was very apparent that the gunboats were going to have plenty of work to do. *Cricket* and *Cockchafer* with their towing sloops sailed for Shanghai after a few days, leaving *Moth* and *Mantis* to serve on the Canton River. It was a long, slow, very hot, and often rough journey up the coast of China, but they could frequently take advantage of inshore waters in order to avoid heavy seas, and so they arrived after a ten-day passage at the season of greatest heat and humidity. *Cricket* went straight into dry dock to undergo long refit, the officers being housed in a mess in a nearby rented house, or at the Shanghai Club, and the ship's company in a nearby barracks accommodation. It all felt luxurious and comfortable after their six month travels in very cramped conditions.

Everyone was carefully warned of the danger of sunstroke at that particular season, and a spinal padded shirt and shorts was the rig of the day, with — most important of all — a solar topee, the back of which extended outwards several inches like a fireman's helmet. Nobody under any circumstances was allowed to be out in the sunshine unless he was wearing a topee. These heavy cork-lined hats were uncomfortable and hot, and for the first few days there was trouble in making the men obey the order. Then, after only a week in Shanghai, a rather fat stoker, who was carrying the cooked dinner from the kitchen across a courtyard only about thirty yards to the living quarters, neglected to wear his topee, perhaps not for the first time, and he died a day and a half later. After that the crew remembered their topees.

Shanghai, a vast city on both banks of the muddy Wampoa River, with a population guessed at over three million, was all things to all men. It was the business centre of China and nine foreign consulates lined the Bund on the river front, where the foreign concessions, ceded after the looting of Peking in 1904, joined one another in a mile-long block. Each had its own police force and law court, and worked as a self-contained national administration. Probably only the Chinese, of all the peoples on earth, could have coped successfully with such a complication. Money smoothed all paths, for the foreign presence did bring a very great trade to the port. In later days, when the Communists came to power, they attacked and overpowered the indefensible area and abolished all foreign concessions throughout China, but that was a generation ahead.

Hugh sank — they all did — into the wide arms of Shanghai with no trouble at all from the moment they got there. The several clubs made all officers honorary members, and wherever the visitors appeared they were instantly recognised — probably by their pale skins — and the foreign community as one man stepped forward to welcome them, give them a drink, take them home to meet their families, arrange tennis, swimming, a Saturday afternoon at the races — the magic carpet seemed to unroll itself before them. The thing that the young men enjoyed the most was the perversity of going out after dinner to one of the small dance-halls where an excellent Philippino band would play till tomorrow for a dozen couples, the girls being hired as partners for so much a dance. Their real business was not, as was anticipated, to become sleeping partners, but to persuade the young men to buy them drinks. A long night of really good dancing under almost perfect conditions cost about five dollars, a sum which a sub-lieutenant could afford. A hard-faced woman was present and in hawkeyed control, and saw to it that none of her girls left the room, and also supervised the endless whiskies or granadines which they drank. Overhead fans provided a cooling draught on the hottest night; the music was very good; there was plenty of comfortable seating; and the floor was perfectly polished. The girls were, of course, accomplished entertainers, some of them White Russian refugees who had escaped from the Bolsheviks across Siberia into China, and quite often were daughters of well-born parents.

Nanking Road led off the Bund into the hinterland of the city, and Hugh out shopping one day, walked quite a long distance up the busy street, interested in all the new sights and sounds around him. A vacant gap in the wall of buildings came in sight where evidently a whole block had burned out. A crowd of two or three hundred was packed into the space at the back of which he could see a small raised slope upon which a man was gesticulating and shouting while two girls stood immobile beside him. He thought it was perhaps a political meeting and stopped to watch the goings-on. Presently the two girls were bustled off the stage and a dejected youth was pushed up on to it from the side, while the shouting man bent down and collected a handful of dollar bills from someone in the crowd. Hugh was puzzled, and asked a Chinese standing beside him what was going on. The man could talk halting English and explained that this was an auction of slaves. Some had come in voluntarily because they were starving and unable to get work; parents had sent unwanted surplus daughters; brigands might have sent some of their captives, and so on. It was all perfectly legal and above board. A strong and comely girl might fetch three hundred dollars, and a sturdy youth of about twenty only a little less. An elderly man or woman could be picked up often enough for ten dollars, sometimes even less. Then the Chinese pointed out a youngish fat man in a rich silk robe wearing one or two jade ornaments.

"Watch him!" he said, "he has surely come to buy another concubine. There must be something special coming up today. I know who he is — the son of a very rich merchant!"

And sure enough a buxom girl, with paint on her face, all smiles, presently minced up onto the platform. A few minutes later Hugh saw the fat man leading off the maiden by the hand. It was being said that unwelcomed competition had forced him to pay five hundred dollars for her.

Chinese families have owned slaves from time immemorial, and the lot of such a servant in a wealthy man's household is a good one. The slave is treated with care, well fed, clothed and housed, and usually married off to a suitable mate in due course. It pays to treat them well, for then they give willing service and last in good condition into old age. They cannot be cast off; the owner accepts legal responsibility for them for the remainder of their lives. A dissatisfied slave might run away, but in most cases he won't get very far before he is recognised, and then traced to his owner.

This was the only slave market Hugh ever attended — or indeed, actually heard of, though they must have been in existence in other Chinese cities at that time.

The converted river paddle-wheel steamer *Kinsha*, flagship of the Commodore commanding the Yangtze Flotilla, lay at her mooring buoy off the Bund for the greater part of her naval life, though she had been built for Christian missionaries for their transport on the river many years earlier. Her sub-lieutenant had lately been invalided home. As *Cricket* was to be under refit for at least three months to come, it was not long before a signal arrived ordering Hugh to be loaned to *Kinsha* until *Cricket* should come back into service again. And so he packed his bags and went on board the little flagship. She carried a commander in command, a surgeon-lieutenant commander, a paymaster-lieutenant secretary to the commodore, and his flag-lieutenant, and they all seemed pleased to see him, especially as the ship was due to set off on her annual inspection cruise up the river almost at once, and another watchkeeper was badly needed. At the last moment the cruise was cancelled. War had broken out between two provinces up river, and the commodore must remain at the centre of communications ready to deal with whatever emergency situations were sure to arise.

Hugh was very disappointed, but in one way somewhat relieved. He had been feeling increasingly unwell ever since arriving at Shanghai, and put it down to the high temperature and humidity, but in the past few days an internal bleeding had become evident, and so he went to see the doctor who, of course, diagnosed dysentery and dosed him with emmertine — the only remedy then known. It seemed to control the condition but not to cure it, and he became increasingly weaker and was sent to a large nursing home, a lovely airy building staffed with, he thought, the most beautiful nurses. He was to be given a three-week course, involving chiefly diet and complete rest in bed. He had quite a romantic time there, especially with a handsome Estonian nurse, the daughter of a general who had escaped from the Bolsheviks with his family through Siberia. The parents were now dead, and the nurse's only brother worked in Peking. But from this time forward for the rest of his life Hugh was almost never without some sort of pain or discomfort, for these particular bugs destroy part of the intestinal fabric and nothing can replace it.

At the end of his treatment he came out as thin as a rail and wobbly about the knees and was ordered off to recuperate at Kuling, a curious mountain four thousand feet high, rising up in the middle of the flat Yangtze plain, originally a missionary sanatorium, and now a summer escape resort from the heat of the plains for the wives and children of foreigners working between Shanghai and Ichang, a thousand miles upriver. On the mountain there were many private bungalows dotted about, a golf-course, tennis-courts, a swimming-pool and a sprawling bungalow hotel.

There were a very few recuperating men up there, wives and children far outnumbering them, so that Hugh's arrival at the hotel was a popular event, and he became very friendly with a young English wife from Hankow accompanied by her little five-year-old daughter. They soon seemed to be doing things together every day.

At first there was puzzlement over the missionary contingent who mostly lived in their own bungalows about half a mile from the hotel. The ladies wore the huge straw hats and the long sweeping skirts and pinched-in waists of 1910, and the men seemed to favour striped college blazers and straw boaters. It emerged that they hadn't been "home on leave" since before the war, and in the summer of 1920 the backlog had not yet been worked off, the ill and elderly being dealt with first, so that those one saw at Kuling were dressed in the garments they had brought perhaps in 1913 or even earlier.

The journey of five days up river from Shanghai to Kukiang was an adventure in itself, though passed in bed or reclining on a deck-chair. Hugh's river steamer had three decks, the lower stuffed with mixed cargo, the visible upper layer of sacks containing brown sugar, upon which camped a mixed teeming multitude of coolie-class Chinese of every sort, shape and size. It was wiser not to contemplate what might be happening to the sugar. There was a latrine somewhere, but the cooking, washing and feeding went on just where the family squatted. On the deck above a more opulent class of Chinese, some in cabins, were tightly packed, but they at least had chairs or benches and a sort of self-service cookhouse. The top deck had proper cabins, a shower, and meals in the saloon, and a deck outside where there was room to walk. This catered for the twenty-odd foreign passengers and one or two obviously wealthy Chinese families, with whom Hugh tried to talk a little, though no other white person could be seen to do so.

The ship would be of perhaps 2,000 tons burden, and steamed at about twelve knots. They carried four white officers and a Chinese crew, and the officers were scarcely seen, for they were hard at work all day. She stopped at the three or four treaty ports — Nanking with its immense castellated stone wall being the most important — and also at many smaller places out in the stream where there was no berthing alongside; sometimes, too, a passing junk would hail her and unlaod a few Chinese or sacks of cargo. There is a curious and indefinable smell about China; it may come from the cooking oil; it is concentrated in the lacquered coating applied to preserved dried duck and chicken, and it clings to any room where they are stored. In Shanghai it had been detected everywhere, but normally at a distance; here, on board this packed ship, it became overpowering until acclimatisation overtook it. The Chinese, for their part, say that the European smells like a sheep, and can make him feel sick in an enclosed space. A Chinese once remarked to Hugh:

"I suppose you Europeans have not yet learned the benefits of frequent bathing!" There are two sides to all coins, the young man was beginning to observe.

At Kukiang, which was a small treaty port, and therefore had a British Consul, Hugh was met by some clerk from the Consulate who produced a coolie to carry his suitcase ashore and put him into a sort of palanquin chair which, manned by six coolies, would carry him up to the top of the mountain. These chairs were similar to the sedan-chairs of olden times. A comfortable reclining seat with a cushion was slung between two stout bamboo poles about fourteen feet long, the ends of the poles resting on the shoulders of four coolies, while two relief men trotted ahead, ready to take over from the bearers, each in his turn. They ran quite fast through the mile of rice paddy-fields before the ascent began, but from then onwards for about four hours it was a steep climb up stone steps with only one or two very short level spaces. Much of the pathway was hewn out of solid rock face and occasionally a deep chasm yawned alarmingly below. Orange tiger-lilies and a few flowering shrubs and many ferns made the whole way very beautiful, and the view out across the flat Yangtze plain from the higher levels was a stupendous one, stretching for a hundred miles until lost in the heat haze. At corners, if one met with a down-coming chair, there would be a brief but heated battle of words between the two coolie crews as to who should give way, for both wanted the safer inside track. At one such corner, edged by a precipice, Hugh's chair was elbowed into the outside berth, and as he looked down he realised that a drop of a couple of hundred feet lay beneath his seat. He fainted right off for a brief moment in his weakness, but didn't fall out of the chair, which had good solid rails to it. The jerking motion as the coolies leaped from step to step was at first agonising, but one grew accustomed to it and nausea died away.

When they put him down on the ground at the hotel he was so exhausted that he had to be lifted out and carried to his room. However, a few nights' good sleep in the cool air, and the invigorating altitude did wonders for him, and in less than a week he was able to get out for short walks and to enjoy meeting the other hotel guests. The month allowed him passed very quickly, and he returned to Shanghai, if not in full vigour, at least able to do the peaceful duties required on board the *Kinsha* lying at her buoy. The only disagreeable thing about that was the daily passage of the fou-fou fleet of junks carrying the city's sewage down river to the farms in the lower reaches. The stench began about two o'clock in the morning and awoke Hugh in his early days as he slept on a camp-bed on deck. At six o'clock he was up with the hands as they turned-to for scrubbing decks and cleaning ship, and by then the sun had been operating on the fou-fou fleet for more than an hour, and there were times when he leant over the guard-rail and vomited into the river. This traffic eased off to a mere trickle by ten o'clock, and after a few weeks, one became hardened to it and the reaction was much less violent.

However, *Cricket*'s refit came at last to its end and Hugh rejoined her and she went slowly up the Yangtze, stopping at each treaty port for a day or two, and then turning into the Po-Yang Lake.

By now half the *Cricket*'s crew were Chinese. Each officer had his own "boy" and the wardroom had a Chinese messman, chosen as much as anything for his ability to speak the various dialects, which changed about every two hundred miles. There was a sort of river "lingua franca" which all the watermen understood, but once the messmen went ashore to buy fresh food he would find that the people in the towns could not understand the "river talk", and with this situation he must be able to cope. Especially in the treaty ports a pidgin English was widely spoken, but beyond their narrow boundaries nobody would understand this. The local consul was always able to furnish an interpreter where possibly complicated official business had to be conducted by a gunboat. The fact of the matter was that, in spite of these difficulties, the gunboats did manage to carry out their role with marked success. After all, they had now been on patrol since 1906 and the Chinese whom they encountered were familiar enough with them and their habits.

The capital of the province, Nanchang-fu, a city of half a

million inhabitants, lay at the far end of the lake about thirty miles to the south, and, as the river level slowly fell during summer, so did the lake drain away into it, making the passage increasingly shallow and difficult, and it took some days before a pilot could be found who was willing to navigate a ship the size of *Cricket* through the shallow waters. He insisted on testing her in the Yangtze for a few hours to satisfy himself as to her draught and handling capabilities, and was amazed to find how very well she performed in river conditions. No ship of comparable size had ever before made this passage.

But a visit was imperative because the small European population had been cut off from the outside world for a month past during which the Communist Army from Canton in the south had overwhelmed the city and massacred thousands of people, according to public report.

Cricket made a successful passage through the lake, which had by now almost vanished, leaving only a few shallow lagoons connected by short lengths of narrow sluggish streams. They were often so close to the banks that it would have been possible for anybody good at the long jump to have leaped ashore. At one such point they kept pace for a while with a gaily-dressed Chinese lady being wheeled in a painted wheelbarrow by a coolie along the low banks enclosing rice paddy-fields. Evidently she was on her way to a gala social function, for she had flowers in her glistening black hair, and her minute bound feet hanging out of the end of the barrow glittered in the sunshine with some bejewelled decoration, and for a moment she seemed to be waving her little fan at the admiring sailors — which would have been very unorthodox behaviour indeed for a Chinese lady of high degree.

News of *Cricket*'s progress had flashed ahead of the gunboat, and a knot of officials and one solitary European could be seen waiting at a dilapidated jetty alongside which they berthed. The dark grey mud bricks of which Chinese cities are constructed gave a gloomy impression of doom and devastation. There were handshakings and a formal speech of welcome from a well-dressed official, for the surviving merchants had already formed an *ad hoc* city council, and then the solitary European came on board, very glad and relieved to see them. He was an Australian merchant, the only foreigner in the city, and had been living here for thirty years past, and had not been away from it for the past eleven. He had married a Chinese wife, and his only child, a very precocious son of fourteen, accompanied him. The Australian spent several hours acquainting the gunboat officers with the local situation, and was really excited that he found he could still speak his own native language.

About three weeks before this an invasion from the south had threatened, but nobody had been unduly troubled because the city was held by a strong well-equipped garrison commanded by a renowned general. Then suddenly, during the dark hours one night, the garrison had vanished together with its general; though nobody was sure of what had happened. They were probably purchased outright and changed sides. However that may have been, in swarmed hundreds of Communist troops the next morning. They made directly for the mayor, but the city yamen people had already shot him, dealing likewise with the whole body of officials. Next, strong detachments moved out along the main streets and into every building, shooting on sight all the well-dressed and elderly people, and herding all the teenagers into groups under guard. Sometimes younger children were killed, others were passed by and ignored. This went on for most of the week, by which time they had visited almost every street in the city, and had collected many thousands of the youth, whom they penned into the large open area of the racecourse.

When "peace", as they put it, had been "restored", the youth were divided into small bands over each of which was placed a Communist officer. He told his group that it was now free from past generations of oppression and must make its choice of either joining the Communist Army or being shot, and at the same time pointed out that all, or at any rate, nearly all their friends and relations were already dead, so that they had nobody to turn to, and moreover that all houses had been cleared of "stolen goods" which had been distributed amongst the glorious Communist Army, and that they would find no place to shelter since all private dwellings were that day in the process of being burnt down, because the glorious Communist Army would no longer tolerate the evils of private ownership. They must understand that they had no friends, no possessions, and nowhere to shelter; thus, if they "liked" to choose the Communist Army, all these things would be provided for them, and China would soon be freed with their help.

It is no surprise that they all marched off to the quartermaster's store and got fitted out — boys and girls — with the grey cotton Communist uniform. This is the way, though not the absolutely universal way, that Communism took control of China in the initial stages.

A few days later the soldiers marched away with their new recruits in the middle of them — surrounded. Now the local survivors were licking their wounds, and of course there were many who had hidden or run away into the countryside, or were just left in the few streets that had escaped visitation. They were too stunned to make any sort of a move, and obeyed without question the decrees of the handful of Communist officials who had been left in charge of the city.

There was nothing that the *Cricket* could do. The Australian and his wife and son had hidden, their house had never been visited by the Army, nor had the new officials taken note of them, realising of course that they were completely powerless to harm the new regime in any way, whatever they may have thought about it.

For the four days of their visit the Australian was constantly in their company, overjoyed to make this contact with his own kind. They visited him in his large Chinese house — for lunch, tea, or dinner, where his wife, after the Chinese fashion, stood and directed the servants or perhaps served some particular delicacy herself, but never sat down at table with the menfolk. Hugh was interested in the Communist philosophy which did have some good points and was progressive, and yet, in those days, employed such harsh and apparently unnecessary methods. There were long discussions with the Australian on this question, and one day he said:

"I don't understand the Chinese, though I talk their language like my own. I've lived as a Chinese amongst them here for thirty years, and I took my Chinese wife twenty-seven years ago; yet even today, I just don't know what she is thinking about. No woman could be a better wife. I owe everything to her, and yet when I turn over in bed and look at her sometimes, I just wonder what sort of person this stranger really is."

Officialdom, apart from the initial reception at the dockside, took no further notice of them, and when the time for departure came, the jetty was empty, and they had to cast off their own mooring hawsers, although they had informed the port office in advance of their impending departure. The Chinese pilot firmly refused to put a foot on shore — he said he could not trust the new regime, and the ship felt very much the same way about the situation, having kept ammunition on deck and a gun's crew inconspicuously ready to man the armament at a moment's notice; also steam was kept continuously ready for the duration of their visit in case trouble should arise. The further they steamed down the Po-Yang Lake away from Nanchang-fu the happier they all felt. It was the first time a gunboat had been up there for a dozen years.

Cricket moved on to Hankow, which is really three cities separated by the confluence of the Yangtze and a large tributary, the Han River. There was difficulty in obtaining fresh water because the city system had become accidentally contaminated. The medical health department assured them that if they would move out into the main stream a few hundred yards from shore, the water there would be perfectly safe for drinking, though the mud in it should be allowed to settle for twenty-four hours before use. *Cricket* struggled along on her own distilling plant, but some foreign gunboats there took in the river water as advised and suffered no evil consequences, though they did find that it tasted of mud.

There was rain, or rather frequent showers throughout the week of their visit, and so shore-going in the intense heat was not very agreeable. Everybody bought an oiled paper bamboo-ribbed Chinese umbrella which looked very odd sheltering a white uniform, but proved remarkably efficient. When Hugh went to the club one afternoon to meet some Kuling friends at tea, he had the unusual experience of seeing an exact double of himself seated at another table. He had heard already of this young man's existence, but when he suddenly saw him he was indeed startled. He went over and spoke to the man, who looked as surprised and uncomfortable as he was feeling himself. It was an uncanny, alarming, experience. They never again encountered one another.

A few days later the ship was ordered to relieve *Aphis* on guard duty near the entrance to the Po-Yang Lake, where the Communists had been fighting. The heat and the humidity were intense, and the wardroom mess moved itself up onto the fore deck to get whatever breeze might arise. Hugh awoke next morning to an appalling stench and got up to find the quartermaster in the eyes of the ship with a long boat-hook in his hands trying to disentangle a cluster of three or four putrefying Chinese soldiers' corpses which had been swept by the river current onto the anchor chain cable. Others were drifting past in the water all day long. In the evening, as soon as lights were switched on, clouds of cream-coloured flying ants flew inboard, and when dinner began these creatures smothered the table-cloth, dishes and food, so that they could not eat their meal there, and were obliged to move down to the sweltering heat of the wardroom mess again. Next day they set up spare mosquito nets and enclosed a small dining space on deck to use as their dining-room. The flying ants swarmed onto the outside of the netting at dusk and shut out most of the air, so that once again they were compelled to go below before the meal was half done. These insects descended like a heavy snowstorm every night as soon as lighting was switched on.

A European who came on board told them of the Buddhist Monastery of Fung-Tu which was built on the vertical side of a tall pillar outcrop of rock about two miles distant in a series of galleries nine stories high in all, a most extraordinary construction originally designed for defence against brigands. The abbot had received authority — nobody knew from whence — to issue "tickets to Heaven", an engraved certificate on thin yellow paper, which, if presented to the proper Buddhist authority at the pearly gates, would ensure the admission of the holder. Everyone wanted one of these insurance policies on the next world, but alas! brigands now resided inside the monastery and it would be dangerous to go there in person, so, in the usual accommodating way of China, a messenger was sent with the necessary funds at two dollars a head, to obtain certificates for those who were prepared to pay.

Later *Cricket* moved on to Ichang, a thousand miles from the sea, and at the upper end of the Lower River, and here the hills they had been passing for the last two days had grown into mountains, and the placid Yangtze alters its character to become a swirling torrent cutting its way down steep canyons from Szechuan Province, a mountainous region leading on to the eastern borders of Tibet.

On this upper stretch of the great river were two elderly gunboats, *Widgeon* and *Teal*, about a hundred and fifty feet long, with a crew of twenty-five. *Widgeon*, commanded by Commander Jukes-Hughes, had a warrant-officer gunner, and *Teal*, the junior one, commanded by Lieutenant Commander Henderson, an elderly officer, had a surgeon-lieutenant on board. The young doctor had become ill and had to be invalided home, and so Hugh once again, was ordered to catch the next steamer to join *Teal*. He just managed to hurry on board the new fast twenty-two knot ship *Soong Mow* on her last passage of that season up the rapidly falling Upper River, and found *Teal* at Wanhsien, a large town half-way up to Chunking. It was now October, and the weather was cool and sunny, a perfect autumn scene with trees beginning to turn colour.

The Upper Yangtze — about six hundred miles of it — was then perhaps the most dramatic water in the world regularly navigated by steamers. For ages past traffic up and down was carried on by junks, and in both directions the journey was a saga in itself. Seldom was there sufficient wind to enable a junk to progress against the current, and accordingly they were equipped with towing lines of twisted bamboo up to two miles in length depending on the tonnage of the junk, the inboard end being fastened to the base of the mast. Small sampans would carry the towing end to the shore where a waiting gang of towing collies, anything between 300 and 400 strong, hooked on their individual short ropes which they looped diagonally across their chests. Round their foreheads they bound a coloured sweat cloth, and their winter clothing was a pair of blue cotton shorts and perhaps a ragged shirt. In summer they worked naked. The gang-master was accompanied by a man carrying a drum slung round his neck upon which he beat out the time while the coolies stamped their short pace forward, muscles bulging and bent almost horizontal to the ground. In the case of the longer tows, one or two assistant drum-beaters would be stationed along the distant sections of the line, and these joined with the master in chanting ancient towing songs which the coolies took up, and this helped them to pace in unison, and also to cheer them on. The tune would mount to a high-pitched shriek that echoed to and fro between the rocky cliffs on either bank and curiously resembled the high-pitched sea songs that can still be heard amongst the Gaelic-speaking people along the west coast of Scotland, where the cry of the seagull weaves in and out of the music, which is both barbaric and inspiring. Where the cliffs rise steeply out of the water long sections of pathway have been carved out of the rock, and in some places at two or three different levels in order to cope with the rise and fall of the water. This section which we particularly describe here is known as "The Gorges". The Windbox Gorge, where at one point the cliff is nearly four thousand feet high, is the most spectacular, and a little higher up there is a two hundred and twenty-foot difference between summer and winter levels in the river. In early summer, when mountain snows farther inland in Tibet are rapidly melting, sudden freshets often occur and make the river so fast flowing and violently turbulent that all navigation must be suspended for a few days until the flood water crest has passed. The current at such a time exceeds twenty knots. Above the top of high water, galleries could be seen at many places where wood coffins were laid, safely beyond the depredations of dogs, the river, or wild animals, and yet still close to the benign river gods — the last resting-place presumably of towing coolies who had failed to "make it". Nobody was quite sure about this.

During the journey to Wanhsien, Hugh made the acquaintance of the Methodist Bishop in Western China, a widely travelled man who had served his missionary church in China for nearly twenty years, and consequently was able to tell Hugh a great deal about the Chinese and their habits, and also about the political and military situation with which he was now involved, for Szechuan Province was seething with disorder as the Communists sought to penetrate and the Tujun and other generals attempted to enhance their various positions. The gist of the information seemed to be that the only people who would not sell out their own side were the Communists, and even then an occasional commander amongst them did fall for a bribe and change sides. It was nearly impossible for a foreigner to keep pace with events, for military commands, cities, even whole provinces switched their allegiances overnight at the rustle of a wad of dollar bills.

The *Teal*'s motor sampan — the envy and admiration of the waterside population who had nothing but oars — collected Hugh from the passenger ship on the fourth day, and his new captain welcomed him kindly and set about teaching him the peculiar lore of the upper river, where an ever-changing stream was the controlling factor in what the ship could or could not do.

The next day the postmaster, Greenfield, a senior official in his branch, came on board for lunch to meet the new first lieutenant. A part of the treaty with China signed after the inter-allied sacking of Peking in 1906, was that the Customs, the Post Office, and the salt trade were all placed under foreign administration in order to secure payment of war indemnity. A further provision was that at about twenty ports, "foreign concessions", involving nine powers, were established where a small strip of land, usually a few acres, was placed under the administration of each foreign consul and was treated as foreign territory where a trading post could be safely established. Chunking was the farthest inland of these ports.

Greenfield, a delightful person, was in close touch with many Chinese officials and heads of business, and often had better information about what was going on than even the Chinese themselves. He used his wide network of sub-post offices with their telegraph hook-ups to supply him with a continuous stream of instant local intelligence. For the time being Wanhsien was at peace, so that Henderson and Hugh were able to come and go to the Post Office Yamen with ease.

Greenfield, a widower, told them that one day he and his wife in their two sedan-chairs were going through the city, when a traffic jam held them up for a few minutes. A rather drunken coolie on the roadside began shouting abuse of a very damaging sort at Mrs Greenfield. The husband, who spoke fluent Chinese, was furious, jumped out of his chair and punched the coolie, knocking him down. For a moment the situation was explosive, and the Greenfields were in danger of being attacked by the crowd, but a Chinese of high class stepped forward and in a loud voice commended Greenfield for having taught "good manners" to the coolie who, he said, "has shamed our people in the eyes of these foreigners". The coolie had never imagined that the two Greenfields understood Chinese, and would probably not have opened his mouth at all if he had known who they were; for in normal circumstances, even the very lowest classes were polite in public places, though the whole population in reality detested the foreigners because of their privileged position in China.

Presently an invitation from the city governor came to the two officers of the *Teal* to attend an official dinner in honour of some visiting "bigwig". It was arranged that Greenfield would meet them at the jetty and guide them to the governor's house, a prominent building high up on the city wall which at that point was a hundred feet above a small stream bed. They were on deck in full dress uniform wearing their swords, ready to step into the motor sampan just coming alongside, when a yellow painted Post Office sampan was seen rowing furiously out to the ship at her anchorage in the stream — so they awaited its arrival. In it sat Greenfield's personal "boy" whom they knew well, and when he jumped on board he blurted out:

"Master says tell captain he no come ashore. Something wrong at governor's yamen!" And so they remained on board. Obviously the message was a last-minute warning sent with the utmost speed, or the personal servant would not have been despatched to deliver it by word of mouth.

That evening a report came in that there had been "trouble" in the city, but nothing could be learned of its nature, and they were anxious about Greenfield's safety, since no further word had come from him. A day or so later he came on board and told his tale.

He had received a warning through a chain of servants that the governor had been acting in an unusual way about preparations for the dinner, and had given unexpected instructions to the servants, and they suspected that "something was up", though they couldn't put a name to it. However, since he himself was not implicated nor threatened in any way, he decided he would attend, and in particular because he knew the governor well and their relationship had always been cordial, but he felt that the British officers might be used as a cover-up for whatever mischief was afoot, and that, of course, ought to be avoided.

It was a dinner on a grand scale with about twenty guests and the twenty-four course meal, beginning at noon, wound on and on till almost four o'clock. There were musicians and singing, and each guest had a singsong girl beautifully dressed at his elbow to supply hot towels to wipe his fingers, fill up his cup with hot rice wine, make gay conversation, attend to his water pipe, and prop him up in his chair as round after round of toasts slowly eroded his abilities. Indeed, several guests had subsided under the table where their snores could be heard punctuating the tinkling laughter of the girls long before the twenty-fourth course was reached. At last the governor arose and led his principal Chinese guest, together with one or two other men, out onto a little balcony from which a fine view of the city could be seen. Suddenly there was a crash, and then some shouts and bustle as those on the balcony ran back into the room — but not the principal guest, for he, they assured the company, had drunkenly staggered and topppled over the balustrade to his death on the rocks in the stream bed a hundred feet below. The still suspicious Greenfield, who had his eye firmly fixed on the balcony, saw at least two arms push the honoured guest from behind and tip him over the coping of the balustrade. Needless to say he held his tongue, as did all the other guests. They condoled effusively with the governor over this tragic accident — his hospitality had just been too generous! Being inside the governor's house they would never have got out alive if they had shown the slightest sign of being aware of the murder that had been committed. What the distinguished guest had done to deserve his untimely fate was never divulged.

Hugh one day was out for a walk with Greenfield on the outskirts of the city when they passed a small group of police hustling along an old and decrepit man who appeared to be almost insensible, and Hugh asked his friend what was going on. They were at an empty open space beside the city wall, and the old man was pushed up against it and then the police stepped back a few paces and shot him. Two or three lookers-on who had been following the posse ran forward weeping and loudly wailing and picked up the corpse and carried it away — they would have been relations.

It was an established custom that when a member of a well-to-do family committed some serious crime and was sentenced to death for it, relatives would, if they could pay for it, bribe the police to turn a blind eye and produce a substitute for the malefactor who would be put to death instead. The police only wanted a body to show in support of the death certificate should any enquiries be made afterwards. This was obviously such a case, for there was little difficulty in finding some destitute family who would sell an old, infirm, or diseased member to stand in place of the criminal. They argued that the substitute was no longer of value to himself or to them, so they stuffed him with narcotics beforehand, and after execution buried him with all the honours they could afford.

On another occasion Greenfield took Hugh to see a spacious temple out in the country beyond the city walls. It was well maintained; the red and gilded paintwork bright, and jade green glazed roof tiles, with a guardian Kalin at every terminal, fairly glittered in the pale winter sunshine. But the glory of this temple was its bell, hung in a separate building. The diameter at its base must have been close to thirty feet (Hugh paced it off), and its height was lost in the gloom of the wooden roofing far above. The rim of the bell was only about four feet from the ground, and the clapper was a huge bronze-shod wooden beam operated from outside by several priests at the end of an exotic train of wheels and ropes. Somebody in the little party struck the bell with a stick and a thunderous deep note bewildered those inside. The Buddhist priest who was showing them round was appalled and threw himself against the rim in an attempt to stop the vibration — and the party was hustled away out of the temple gate as quickly as possible. The bell, it emerged, was reserved for special occasions and ceremonies, and its misuse would draw vengeance from the gods. They heard it being used on one or two occasions later — there was no mistaking the deep resonant note that must have been heard many miles away. How such a gigantic casting had been successfully managed in the first place was not known.

On one lovely spring day, Greenfield arranged an expedition on foot out into the hills from behind the city, for half a dozen ratings and officers from the *Teal* to visit a particularly interesting temple, supposedly originally dedicated to Confucius. In the course of centuries the various doctrines propagated by the most distinguished sages became eroded, or modified, or perhaps half forgotten, and to the foreigner they all appeared like variants of Buddhism, which was probably the principal religious cult of the country. When, after several miles' walk, they reached the temple, they found it more or less embedded in a series of hollowed-out shallow caves linked by a single path along the steep face of the mountain side. They met the chief priest, and a couple of monks with yellow Buddhist robes and shaven heads who were sent to guide them through the several detached buildings, all of them filled to overflowing with carved gilded and brightly painted deities who presided over different activities. Presently they came to a small shallow cave where the mountain stream had been harnessed to turn a water-wheel. This, through an astonishing web of wooden shafts and wheels, turned five small brightly-decorated prayer-wheels, where one could insert into a small sort of pocket one's prayer written on a sheet of thin paper where it would turn round and round until the paper disintegrated and blew away perhaps a week later — depending on the weather.

Hugh, because of his very rudimentary ability to speak any Chinese at all, never did find out from temple inhabitants how exactly they rationalised in their own minds the activities of the multitude of gods and goddesses, some of whose functions seemed to be contradictory. The Chinese have an extremely logical mind, and they never gloss over difficult issues, and normally they pursue a line of thought to its ultimate conclusion. How then, come prayer-wheels, which are apparently of Tibetan origin?

After about a month at Wanhsien, *Teal* was ordered down river to Yung Yang, a small walled city about a day's journey away, where there was some trouble brewing and a missionary station might be in need of protection, or perhaps evacuation. They anchored at dusk and the leader of the mission, a pleasant Eastern Canadian, came on board at once and told them that so far no trouble had arisen, although the military guard on the walls and at the city gates had been strengthened and was very much on the alert. He knew some of the local officers and it was only because of this contact that he had been able to get out, and he had to go back immediately because the gate was about to close for the night. It was a huge mediaeval wooden structure twenty feet high studded with enormous iron bosses and suspended between two massive stone circular towers facing the river.

Next morning, shortly after the hands had turned to scrubbing decks, Hugh was in his cabin having a cup of tea, when the quartermaster came to report that a large fleet of junks coming down river was turning in towards the city. Most of them grounded on sandbanks and then lowered ladders over the side down which grey-clad soldiers swarmed into the water, which was only waist high. Several horses also landed and a bucking stallion got out of control and threatened to hold up operations for a while until he was eventually tamed. It could be seen that they were also unloading very long bamboo ladders, and this army moved down towards the stone city walls, which were about thirty feet high. Another body of troops could be seen going up the hill behind the city dragging two or three heavy carts of peculiar construction.

Then there seemed to be a pause, perhaps for breakfast, so the ship's company went to their breakfast, keeping, however, the twelve-pounder gun manned with its ammunition at hand. Presently flags could be seen to wave on poles and a general advance towards the walls began. One could see defending soldiery looking out between the crenellations on top of the wall, and also the smoke of several fires, and apparently steam. Something seemed to be cooking.

The invaders ran the last few yards shouting as they hoisted their ladders up against the stonework of the wall and began to climb up. Only one or two soldiers got to the top, and these were thrown back onto the ground. A rattle of rifle fire could be heard all round the walls, and evidently attacks were beginning on other parts out of sight. This must have gone on for half an hour, when suddenly from the hill a loud explosion was heard and a cloud of white smoke arose. The attackers cheered and rushed once more at the walls, and the defenders threw stones down on them and tipped up large cauldrons of boiling oil, which caused loud shrieks when they found their mark. The battle swayed to and fro until another cannon shot from the hill, this time with a very loud bang indeed, and an even larger cloud of smoke, produced a sudden dead silence. Later it was learned that the ancient piece had exploded and killed its crew. A small party could be seen emerging from the rear of the city waving a flag and they disappeared amongst the attacking troops, who now seemed to be getting out their lunch. No city could be expected to stand up to that sort of violence. The silence lasted for an hour or so, and then desultory rifle fire could be heard from inside the city. As there seemed to be a truce, the captain of *Teal* decided to go in and find out how the mission was faring. He and Hugh, dressed for tennis, carrying Very's coloured signal lights and the pistol which fired them and covered by the twelve-pounder gun, landed right opposite the city main gate and walked straight up to it and knocked loudly upon it. A little postern opened and a sentry pointed his rifle at them, but a Chinese boy whom they had brought as interpreter talked hard and fast and they were let in. The officer in charge provided a guard of two armed soldiers who conducted them through a quarter of a mile of deserted streets to the missionary compound, about a third of an acre surrounded by a twelve-foot-high stone wall. The missionaries, who had been playing tennis, welcomed them warmly, and those on the court continued their game. Tea was served on the overlooking verandah, and then Hugh was invited to join the next set to play. Meanwhile spasmodic rifle fire and marching troops could be heard close at hand, and several spent bullets hit the walls surrounding the court, but all appeared to be above the heads of the players so that their game was not interrupted. The missionaries behaved as if the afternoon was the most ordinary tennis tea-party in the world, and showed little concern about the fighting which was going on all around them.

"Oh, I don't think they will try to come in here. The word will have got about that gunboat officers are with us today, and we have told the gatekeeper not to open to anybody on any account. We shall just have to wait till they quieten down" — so said the senior missionary lady in answer to Hugh's questioning.

Darkness closed in, and then the head of the mission was called to the gate. A messenger from the incoming conquering general had appeared to inform him that the general would be coming to call upon him shortly, and indeed he did appear a couple of minutes later, and was brought into the drawing-room where everyone was gathered, talking.

General Fu was a small slender man with a long, grey, very thin beard, dressed in a stiff black gown to his feet, with a couple of carved jade buttons at the high collar. He was extremely polite and smooth, with hooded eyes that flashed and darted about once in a while. He had come, he said, to see for himself that the mission had not suffered any sort of damage, and then waited for confirmation that that was so. Then he smiled and talked about the shortage of food in the town, and did the mission need anything? No, they had their own stores which they always kept replenished, thank you. Then: Was the gunboat paying an extended visit? He hoped he might have the pleasure of entertaining the officers a little later on when he had got settled into his own quarters. The fighting was over and there would be no more trouble. He would send a guard to escort the officers back to their ship because just for tonight things were still a little unsettled in certain quarters of the city. And so he bowed himself out. It was a beautiful performance. He was a successful brigand who had lately purchased a small army, and surely looked like becoming a successful general.

The name of this game was "Face". To a Chinese "face" is even more important than money, so much so that they will sometimes commit suicide if they lose it irretrievably. Things had to go well for the new general, especially at the start of his career, otherwise people would not forget that he had once been a brigand, execrated by all. He must create a good relationship with the potentially powerful foreigners in his city since they had behind them the overwhelming legendary power of the gunboats. He had selected this relatively prosperous little town as a first upward step in order to squeeze money out of its merchants wherewith to pay his troops, and the merchants would be much more easy to handle if they realised from the outset that he was not a mere brigand, but a successful and powerful military leader with whom foreigners were willing to deal, and he had quickly cornered them so that they had really no choice at all in this matter, but were in fact compelled to give him face by the act of receiving him.

There was nothing more to be done that night, so the captain and Hugh left almost at once. Outside the mission gate, the guard, consisting of two rough-looking sulky customers — perhaps until lately brigands — didn't at all want to go down to the water gate, but the missionary persuaded them firmly, and decided that as they were unreliable he would therefore accompany the officers. They carried lanterns both before and behind the little group of three foreigners. When the roadway came close to the wall, a sentry challenged, loaded his rifle and pointed it at them, and some very high-pitched excited exchanges ensued, and the missionary suddenly said:

"I don't like it at all. They won't accept our credentials. They have orders to shoot on sight."

At which point Hugh stepped behind one of the two guards, so placing him between himself and the challenging voice coming from the wall. Voluble exchanges continued for several minutes, and then at last they were allowed to proceed unmolested. Another excited exchange took place at the city gate, but the missionary talked fast, and they were allowed out and flashed a signal for the ship's motor sampan to be sent inshore to collect them. Without the help of the missionary that night it is very doubtful if they would have got back to their ship alive. The situation was electric and the discipline almost non-existent; foreigners were not loved anywhere in China.

The next morning clean-up operations were obviously in progress. Along the shore opposite *Teal* and immediately outside the city gate about fifty ordinary trading junks were moored close together with their long bows inshore, making it easy for the soldiers to jump on board, which they now began to do. The soldiers herded all the occupants of each junk together at rifle point and then tore open the tunics of both men and women; several persons were seen by the grey uniform underneath to be soldiers in disguise — obviously from the defeated garrison. These were quickly bound with hands behind their backs, and then led to the high stern of the junk and thrown overboard into the swirling deep water. Some were swept away at once, others bobbed about in the eddies, and the few who were washed back in among the junks were pushed out again into the current with long bamboo poles. Ammunition is expensive and this was cheaper than shooting them.

Later on, when things had settled down, Henderson, who was a keen shot, took Hugh off on a number of occasions to look for pheasant reputed to be numerous in the hills a few miles outside the town. It turned out that there were very few of them, and they only bagged one brown one. They saw, however, quite a lot of the magnificently feathered Chinese golden pheasants with their enormously long sweeping tails glistening in the winter sunshine, sitting up in the trees. The coolies urged them to fire, but they would not shoot such a magnificent and rare species. However, Hugh found a cook in the galley at that time plucking a golden pheasant for the table, which he had bought in the town market, and he said that they were very often to be found there. On other occasions they went off in the motor sampan shooting waterfowl, of which large flocks were beginning to arrive from the north for the winter, appearing in reedy lagoons and backwaters. The sampan would stop its engine a mile up river and let the current carry them down amongst the waterfowl, but so often at the last moment the current would sweep the boat away out of range so that much time would be lost, and in fact they bagged very few birds, mostly teal and widgeon, who proved to be easier to approach than the duck, and anyhow provided excellent fare at the table.

During this autumn period junks were often seen going down river with high stacked cargoes of persimmon, a brilliant gold-coloured fruit somewhat like an outsized plum, which would be sold at the large river ports. It has a curious but not unpleasing flavour. Early in December *Teal* was ordered further down river to guard the Standard Oil Company's oil-carrying *Mei-tan* which had got stranded and suffered a hole in the side. They found her spa-moored in a very rocky, steeply banked section of the river. This particular mooring device, necessary in the peculiar conditions of the Upper Yangtze, is managed by laying two heavy timbers, one forward and the other aft, straight outboard from the deck until they touch the shore and then putting out mooring lines which hold the ship's side pressed to the inboard ends of the timbers. The usual mooring wires fore and aft prevent her moving lengthwise, and when springs are set up she is as tightly berthed as though she were lying alongside a dockyard wall. It is thought that this ingenious Chinese device is possibly not used in any other part of the world. *Teal* spa-moored immediately above *Mei-tan*, whose captain, Micklow, was very glad to see them, as he was almost out of drinking-water. He was an old and widely experienced American seaman, a cheerful and interesting companion, and they spent the days together until the hull plating had been repaired and *Mei-tan* was able to move up to Wan-hsian under her own steam for the rest of the winter to await the reopening of the Gorge

Passage the following April when she would go down to Shanghai to dry dock.

Christmas was approaching, and *Teal* was ordered up to Chungking to relieve *Widgeon* as guardship there. On the way they passed a series of sandbanks exposed in the middle of the river at this low-water season. On each of them was a little cluster of huts with fires smoking up into the still cold air. Small quantities of gold were panned from the sand, and it was said that the industry was centuries old, though it yielded only a minute profit.

When Chungking comes into sight at low-water level one sees a dun-coloured muddy shore where rows of huts have been temporarily erected during the low-water season to trap the gangs of towing coolies and the crews of the junks they have brought up-river. Within are food booths, opium dens, bars selling heady alcoholic concoctions, lodging houses, and above and before all, brothels, at the doors of which lounged highly-painted and brightly-garbed young prostitutes with permanent smiles fixed on their faces. The coolies have just been paid off, and for the first time in several months they have coin in their pockets. It is a matter of chance into which of the several establishments they first enter, but it is likely to be a bar, and then straight from there into a brothel. Many of them don't get out for a week, by which time they are almost penniless and likely to have contracted venereal disease. The captain of *Teal* fell in the ship's company and told them all about it, but not everyone listened, and more than once sailors could be seen exploring.

Then, up a steep two-hundred foot cliff with many staircases cut in it, the strong city walls mount another thirty feet high, and in behind them over an irregular acreage, with many small hills and some streams, spreads the grey city with its narrow stone or unpaved muddy streets, along both sides of which small low buildings, mostly of grey mud brick, are huddled in unbelievable confusion. A few large municipal buildings and five Christian Church missions, whitewashed and visibly foreign, stand aloof in spacious walled compounds with uniformed servants guarding their impressive gateways. It would, in those days, have taken more than an hour for a chair to thread its way through the tangle before emerging at the wall on the far side of the city, where grey-coated soldiery would have demanded an exit tax, pocketing part of that quite openly for themselves. It was said that three million people lived there in 1920, but there was no sewage system and the stench that arose in the hot summer weather was like a formidable wall. Nor was there any street cleaning; if a dog killed a cat it lay putrefying — or it might be seized upon and eaten by a destitute beggar, of whom there were swarms, mostly diseased. The infinite variety of smells, sights, sounds, buildings, people from as far away as Tibet, shops, antique dealers, goldsmiths and silversmiths working in the open-fronted booths was overwhelming — only think of something and Chungking had it.

The postal commissioner for Szechuan Province, of which Chungking is the capital, became an almost instant friend and occasionally took Hugh into the city to shop. His sedan-chair led the procession with four armed guards going ahead to thrust a way through the dense crowds, and Hugh in his chair followed behind. The bearer coolies and guards wore coats with the description of the occupant sewn upon them in large Chinese characters. Hugh's read:

"Exhalted Hugh, the Great British Gunboat Teal." The postal commissioner's was much more florid, but perhaps only one in five hundred could read, so that the impressive advertisement drew stares but little comprehension. Nevertheless it would be wise to keep out of the way of important people because the guards going ahead would not hesitate to use their wooden truncheons to clear the way for the great man.

They stopped to watch the goldsmiths at their intricate and beautiful work, making mostly jewellery. At the silversmith's next door a small solid silver ashtray with a somewhat debased silver dollar as its base could be bought for two dollars and fifty cents. But the antique dealer's street was a serious objective. It proved to be about three hundred yards long and five yards wide, and was surprisingly clean and not very populous. However, when they got out of their chairs, the *lao-pan* (head of the guards) organised the whole sixteen coolies into two forces and from the middle of the road they marched arm in arm in opposite directions and cleared the whole street. It seemed to Hugh to be a somewhat dictatorial way of ensuring that the two foreigners would not be molested while they inspected the antiques, but this is how a high official like the commissioner must maintain his "face", and the Chinese would have been shocked indeed if less had been done to ensure his comfort. An important official had to be treated with visible, tangible deference. It was, after all, only sixteen years since the deposition of the emperor, and old customs take longer than that to die in China.

The antique dealers' street was a fascinating gold-mine which

Hugh was far too ignorant to exploit. He turned away from a jade inlaid opium pipe and bought a little plain wooden one — what he wanted was to examine it closely in his cabin and learn the detail of smoking it. The little implements required accompanied the purchase. He knew nothing about porcelain, but purchased a pair of small decorative plaques mounted in free-standing beautifully-carved frames, and backed with ancient fragile glass, and they decorated his cabins, and later on his various homes, until 1974. No one ever identified the porcelain. Right at the end, as they were preparing to leave, an old Chinese led him into a back room where a very large volume about thirty inches square lay on a table. The outer binding was of parchment, and inside were perhaps fifty or more pages, with most beautifully written Chinese characters on one side, and on the opposite page hand-painted scenes of every known means of making love — a pornographic prize of obvious value. He wondered what he would do with it when he got home and his mother unpacked for him, and so he left it where it was, though with lasting regret, for that kind of treasure does not come to anybody twice in a lifetime. It was a real work of art, and the price seventy dollars in Chungking currency. This was probably a "pillow book" and worth quite a lot of money.

The next time he visited the antique dealers' street he found a miniature painting on glass, about four inches square, of a young court lady exquisitely painted in brilliant robes. This is a museum piece, for portraits of women had never been permitted — apart from the funeral painting of a mother, dutifully hung in the family shrine by her son. The exception to the rule had come about two hundred years ago, during the fifty-year reign of one of the emperors. He commissioned portraits of his favourite wives and concubines, one or two examples of which are known in European museums, though very few people have ever heard of them. The glass of Hugh's miniature was cracked from one side to the other by a supposed expert employed to tighten up the antique original frame fifty-three years later. When foreigners came to China at the end of the nineteenth century a very few important personages allowed their wives to be photographed, and some taken of the Empress Dowager were published. The Chinese were deeply shocked.

This was the first time Hugh realised that unusable bric-a-brac is best left wherever it is found, and in his many travels there were very few useless articles that he brought home with him.

Christmas drew on, and *Teal* issued a general invitation to the foreign community to drinks on board after the morning church services. The Chinese stewards loved a party, and the cook prepared plates of beautifully cut little red chili sandwiches, amongst other goodies. Some of the missionaries came and one of their ladies had apparently never before had a cocktail. She asked how it was made before accepting one, put it down after a couple of gulps and had a refill before feeling the usual effects, and then slumped into a chair and demanded another. Hugh was at his wit's end, and pressed sandwiches upon her — which she also found delicious — and yet again met a new experience in those chili sandwiches, which have a distinctly delayed action, but are considered good blotting paper in a case of alcoholic excess. By now the lady had ceased to be responsible for anything, and a meek little husband lost in the background had to be pulled out of his chair to escort her to the gangway, and the man seemed amazed to find her hiccoughing, with tears streaming down from her eyes as she kissed the delighted quartermaster goodbye, thanking him as "the captain" profusely, if a little thickly, for a wonderful Christmas day. She must have felt awful on Boxing day, but that, of course, is one of the hazards attendant upon Christmas hospitality.

They finally got rid of the last of the guests at two o'clock in the afternoon, the ruined lunch was abandoned, and they went to sleep in their cabins, for more partying still lay ahead of them.

On the opposite side of the river to the city rose a steep-to range of hills up which wound many paths, most of their way being stone steps, leading to the residential bungalows of the foreign community, and the several bachelor messes maintained by the larger trading companies. A remarkable breed of small sure-footed ponies carried most of the men up and down on their way to their city offices each day, the ladies usually preferring a chair, for the ponies liked to gallop down the stairs at a frightening pace. There was even a polo ground and a mud-surfaced tennis-court up in these hills.

On Christmas night the Standard Oil Company's mess gave a dinner party for twenty-four to which Henderson and Hugh were bidden, and they decided to walk the mile or so up the hill, feeling exercise would help them through the last hours of the day. They were met at the door by one of the younger men who warned them that their president, an older man in his fifties, had woken up that afternoon from his siesta to see the pictures on his bedroom wall sway to and fro a couple of times, and was convinced that he was on the threshold of delirium tremens, and was terribly upset and anxious about it. Hugh suddenly remembered that he had been awoken in the afternoon by a quite violent lurching of the ship and had gone out on deck to see if some ship had passed at speed, but found nothing, and now realised that there must have been a minor earthquake; such were quite common in Chungking. The mess president was a shattered wreck when they met him, and his colleagues finally told him there had been an earthquake, which several of the guests confirmed, and so he went joyfully back to his tippling. At dinner a whole roasted suckling pig was put upon the table — a dish Hugh had never before seen — and to his chagrin, its curly tail was put on his plate, and no more. There was much mirth at the expression of dismay on his face. The rest of the evening was given over to games, and when the time came to go home they found that it had begun to snow, so their hosts lent the two officers ponies, which, nothing daunted, galloped all the way down the hill so they had a hard time to avoid falling off. This sort of light-hearted jollification went on wherever there was a foreign community in China, and was of great value in combatting the feeling of isolation and of fear about the many real dangers of their situation; there never was a failure of morale amongst these isolated foreigners.

About this time reports came in that two middle-aged women from a mission station some days journey inland had been seized by bandits who were demanding a ransom of about a quarter of a million pounds. The Foreign Office in London took over the case and negotiations had dragged on for some weeks when a messenger arrived at the consul general's office in Chungking with a human ear which he said had belonged to one of the ladies, and moreover, unless the ransom was paid by a certain date, other organs would be chopped off and sent in to hasten negotiations. Almost the whole foreign population living in China joined in the controversy, some holding that surrender would inevitably lead to future repetitions of the incident, others that government was not elected to consent to the mutilation of any British subject. Then a second ear arrived at Chungking, and finally a finger, and with it a note from one of the hostages to say that the ladies were both well and decently treated — a confession which of course could have been extorted under duress. Somehow after about three months money was said to have been sent to the bandits and the two ladies were released, not really very seriously harmed by their experience, though minus two ears and one finger. What precise sum of money was handed over was never officially revealed, but the story went round that the British had cunningly seized some person related to the bandits and a simple exchange of prisoners had taken place.

In the middle of all that a hostile army began to move in on Chungking, hoping to seize the city and extort money, which had become almost a recognised custom, the city fathers preferring to pay up rather than to be burned down and killed, or more expensively they must raise an army and fight.

The consul general had made the strongest repesentations to both sides that British property must not on any account be violated — but the invaders were daily coming closer in to the area in which the consulate general's large compound was situated.

At this time Hugh was invited to lunch there, which involved a journey of over an hour in his coolie-borne sedan-chair right through the centre of the city and out beyond the walls on the far side. He borrowed his captain's crew of six chairmen and had them dressed in his own men's white uniforms emblazoned with his Chinese title and rank, and the long poles which rested on the four coolies' shoulders as well as the small awning poles above the chair were all shod with large polished brass balls, rather like our door handles — just to give it an air of grandeur and importance. Four coolies ran ahead with sticks in their hands to clear a way through the crowded streets, four more carried the chair on their shoulders, and four more followed immediately behind the chair, and "Exalted Hugh" climbed into his seat wearing full dress white uniform and his sword. It ought to have made quite a dignified picture, but nobody was on hand with a camera.

There was a small crowd when the cavalcade landed on shore, and after the slow climb up the steep stone staircase, as soon as they passed through the gate in the city wall, the coolie crew, well aware that this was "an occasion", burst into a sort of loping gallop which was not stopped even to change bearers, a drill carried out every ten minutes with skill and precision. At the running speed of this cavalcade some of the milling crowds could not or would not get out of the way fast enough in spite of the coolie leader's shouts, and when a brass knob hit someone in the chest he was simply spun aside out of the way. Hugh, when he saw a woman hit squarely in the chest fall to the ground under the

K

coolies' feet, exploded in a fury of protest which had no effect whatever, he realised that he could neither get out of the chair nor ease its speed, so he just sat more or less grinding his teeth. The Chinese had characteristically taken over the whole thing and were doing the duty they considered the important occasion required.

As they passed outside the city walls on the far side into an open country dotted with trees, the crowds vanished and the coolies slowed their pace; and almost at once the sound of rifle fire could be heard. When they reached the brow of a little hill they found themselves almost surrounded by grey-uniformed soldiers, who stood back off the narrow pathway as they passed, staring in obvious astonishment. Firing died away and soldiers climbed out of the shallow trenches to get a better view. Hugh was considerably relieved to see a large white English-style country house with many outbuildings and large gardens, the whole surrounded by a massive stone wall, down at the bottom of the little hill, and as the chair charged through the tall open gateway, he sighed with considerable relief, and the gate clanged shut behind him.

The consular family welcomed him warmly and the children and one or two secretaries joined them at lunch. Later he asked the consul general many questions about the two missionary women still in captivity and also about his surprising gallop through the city. The official view was that in such a vast country, and in the presence of widespread disorder, the only possible protection government could give to its widely scattered people was through prestige, something which generated respect in a population long experienced in corruption and violence. The gunboats were there to enforce respect, but they could take physical action in only a very limited geographical area beyond which an attitude of mind had to be created among the populace, and it had to be strictly maintained. Hugh's journey through a nervous city could serve as a boost to British prestige, and must be conducted in the kind of manner that would impress a Chinese mind. What a Britisher thought about it was, quite frankly, of no importance at all.

In retrospect he realised that he had learned some important political lessons that day, and they were to stand him in good stead, for he would spend some four years of his life in China.

Henderson and Hugh would often go up to the tennis club at Chungking and play on the mud courts, which in the frosty air only needed the snow to be swept away, for they maintained perfect condition unless rain fell and turned to ice. Even that disappeared if there was a very rare gleam of sunshine, but Chungking has a winter of heavy low cloud. A little later, in the very early spring, Hugh noticed from the tennis-courts many long strips of what looked like gold being stretched on the far shore of the river between wooden frames, and was told that this was the silk from local silkworm farms. He went over there to take a closer look as soon as he could. The silk had already been spun into fine thread, and this thread was wound on wooden stretchers about thirty yards apart to dry out, or perhaps "ripen" would be a better word, in the sunshine. This raw silk thread was a brilliant shining buttercup yellow. Weavers' hand-operated looms were to be seen in nearby sheds, but here only locally grown cotton was being woven into lengths of material. The shed seemed to have little or no ventilation, and the soggy hot air was thick with cotton dust which evidently affected the weavers, all of whom were coughing and appeared to be ill and emaciated.

Teal was ordered to go on up the two hundred and forty miles to Chengtu, the ancient Western Capital, as soon as the river should rise sufficiently in the spring, and they were all looking forward to a journey that was very seldom undertaken, but the water did not rise sufficiently in the early weeks, and they remained at Chungking a long time. The Baptist Mission in the city issued invitations to about three hundred people, including all the principal Chinese officials, to witness the first talking cinema film ever shown in Szechuan, and the *Teal*'s officers attended. Tea was served after the film, and Hugh found himself chatting to a very tall and richly dressed elderly Chinese who spoke perfect English, a very unusual accomplishment so far from the coast. Missionaries came into the discussion, and the Chinese gentleman said:

"There is something which I do not understand — perhaps you can explain to me? There are five foreign missions in this city, and all of them say they are Christians; but as you can see if you will look around this large hall, each of them has separated itself into a little group of people isolated from all the others, whereas the rest of the foreigners are all mixing and talking to one another, and here are you and I, very different sorts of people, but finding it easy and agreeable to join in this conversation. I understand quite well what they all teach about the brotherhood of man, but why is it that these people don't talk with one another when they meet?"

That question haunted Hugh for years to come. At the time he found he could not — perhaps dared not — answer it.

Presently they went off on a cruise down river for a short period, visiting half a dozen disturbed areas. At one such place a sampan came off to the ship loaded with fresh meat, some game birds, and a lot of fruit and vegetables, "as a present from the colonel", the messenger said. They were surprised but were just starting to unload it when the messenger plucked Hugh's sleeve and hauled him to one side and took a letter out of his bosom.

"You Captain, Sir, eh? This letter very private for you!" Hugh took it to the captain's cabin, and when the ship's interpreter had translated it, it turned out to be a request for a secret passage down to the next port of call, and a second envelope contained four thousand dollars as a "present". The dollars and the messenger and the fresh food were quickly bundled into the sampan, and it was pushed off into the current. Later they heard that the "colonel" had been shot, and it became obvious that he had wanted to make a quick getaway from some danger. This sort of thing, and also bribery to transport opium, was attempted on many other occasions, as other gunboats reported.

There was a young seaman only twenty years old on board who had begun to make a habit of breaking his leave — a naval offence of course, but also potentially dangerous, for he might be seized and held to ransom, or even killed. Probably women were at the root of his trouble, but his offences were so numerous that on the Home Station he would have incurred a prison sentence. Here there were no prisons, and the loss of even one member of such a small crew would have been a blow to efficiency. At last, after so many repeated offences, the Admiralty Regulations compelled the captain to discharge the man from the Service forthwith. He was sent to pack up his gear, and the sampan was at the gangway ready to put him on shore right there, in Western China, when suddenly a fusillade of rifle fire, apparently directed at *Teal* from the shore, burst out and the alarm for action stations was immediately sounded. The young seaman leapt up the ladder, ran to his twelve-pounder gun and fired it, hitting the building on shore from which some shots were coming. It was a smart bit of work, and when Hugh asked the captain later if he would delay the discharge of the young man, he smiled and said:

"I've got to. We must get under way at once and go down river!"

Hugh had the man into his cabin and tried for half an hour to change his habits for him, without apparent success, and he was transferred to another ship to be taken to Hong Kong to serve a gaol punishment. About twenty years later, when Hugh was visiting a ship with friends during Navy Week at Portsmouth, a small curly-headed petty officer stepped up to him smiling and said:

"Do you remember me, Sir? Charman, in the *Teal*, Sir!"

He had hardly changed at all. He was now gunlayer in a fifteen-inch gun turret, married, obviously reformed, and making a success of his career. It was a very pleasing moment.

At about this time they came to the junction of the Si-kiang tributary river with the Yangtze. This junction is a right-angled corner hemmed in by cliffs on either side, where the river is only fifty yards wide and the current very fast and turbulent. The only way of getting round the corner is to steam at full speed directly into the cliff, where, about ten yards before the stem hits it, the Si-kiang stream catches the bows and hurls them round ninety degrees to port, thus negotiating the turn. The swing when it came was so violent that everyone on the bridge was thrown into a corner off their feet. The Si-kiang river junks have their sterns built several feet outwards on the port quarter so that their steering sweep can be operated there with maximum effect in order to get round this hazardous bend. No other exactly similar navigational conditions are known in the world.

Hugh's time on the China station was rapidly drawing to its close; he was due to be in England by May to commence his sub-lieutenant's courses. Moreover, his general health was not good; amoebic dysentery had taken a severe toll of his strength and tended to erupt frequently, and he would almost certainly have been invalided home before another summer because the heat of the Yangtze could have been disastrous.

The order from the Admiralty to leave *Teal* and get to Shanghai as quickly as possible for passage home reached him when the ship was back again at Wan-hsien. Greenfield made all the arrangements for hiring a passenger junk (a kwadza) with a *laopan* qualified as a pilot and known by the Post Office to be reliable, and he drew his necessary bedding and other equipment from the ship's stores, and took his "boy" with him to see to the cooking, for the journey to Ichang could take ten days. He had a cabin aft which was reasonably comfortable and took a deck-chair. Two Chinese passengers also embarked, but spoke no English and were accommodated elsewhere. His only means of communication was through his "boy" who spoke very little English, though he seemed to understand a good deal. And so in mid-March they set off, hoisting the great mainsail as a sort of act of faith, since there was no wind on that frosty, raw morning. The river was at dead low water which would make some rapids easy, while others would be at their most dangerous.

The first obstacle was the Hu-tan, just above the city, and this consisted of a very narrow vertical-sided gorge which, when the river was in spate, acted like a hose through which the water squirted and boiled at over twenty knots. No pilot would think of entering it; the turbulence at that time was unpredictable, and no craft could be steered through it. On this day it was a smooth swift stream without problems.

Presently they met the Hsin-tan rapid, at that time a vertical fall of about ten feet stretching from one bank to the other, and broken with outcrops of jagged rock, which was reputed to cause the loss of every third junk that attempted to go down. The true performance was more like one junk in twenty for total loss, and one in ten for a grounding. All junks pulled inshore a mile or so above Hsin-tan to check their gear, land objects of special value, offer incense to the river gods, and permit passengers to walk past the rapid and rejoin their junks below.

Hugh decided to land and walk; he could see no merit in challenging whatever river gods were in control; and he was suffering severely from yet one more outbreak of dysentery which left him very weak. The cold water would have killed him even if he had been washed ashore or hauled out by one of the several rescue junks that patrolled the water with a long line to the shore immediately below the rapid. As he walked along the shore he saw two junks in quick succession shoot over the fall and disappear head first into the boiling froth below, and hoped that neither was his, carrying all his worldly possessions. He decided not to look again.

There was another compelling consideration. Overlooking the rapid and only about four hundred yards from the water's edge, Captain Plant had built his bungalow many years ago and now lived in retirement, well past seventy. Word had spread up and down the river in recent months that the old man was ill, and that now his life was in danger. The Chinese on the river regarded him as the most distinguished Britisher who had ever come to China, for he had developed and perfected the pilotage technique of the Upper River so that some thousands of junks and their crews were now saved from destruction each year. Because of his work increasingly larger steamships now travelled these waters for seven months out of every twelve. Trade increased to an enormous extent, which opened up the isolated province of Szechuan with its sixty-seven million inhabitants to the civilisation of the twentieth century. More than all that, he had created a morale and an expertise amongst the hundreds of local pilots he had trained that would carry into the future the benefits that in his own lifetime had already begun to accrue from the courage and good judgement which had enabled him to master the mighty Yangtze. This river is no mere waterway, it is a cunning, infinitely powerful and dangerous tiger, as the Chinese who live by it have always said.

So Hugh tottered unsteadily up the little slope to the house, wondering if he could reach it, determined not to turn back. Mrs Plant, who had evidently seen him coming, opened the door, a sad-looking elderly lady, and when he had introduced himself and explained the purpose of his visit, she shook her head:

"No. I'm afraid I must say no. He is asleep just now and he gets so little sleep these days. I just can't wake him. I'm not sure he could even understand who you are. His mind wanders a good deal and he is so very frail now."

She wept a little and then said that they dared not take him down to Ichang by junk with its total lack of facilities, and she feared the first steamer coming through when the river rose might be too late.

It took Hugh almost a month to reach Hong Kong, and when he got there he learned that Captain Plant had arrived a few days earlier, and died the next day.

Life on board the junk was reduced to its simplest dimensions. In the well of the ship forward a small charcoal fire was kept burning with a huge wide flat iron cauldron endlessly cooking rice. Every now and again the cook would dip a long wooden handled gourd over the side to scoop up water which he poured tenderly over the steaming rice, keeping it moist — not wet — and stirred almost without intermission. Another smaller deeper cauldron boiled up green Chinese beans and a lettuce-like vegetable. The crew, expert with chopsticks of course, ate morning and evening, and the two Chinese passengers cooked up their own food when there was a lull around the charcoal fire. Calls of nature were obeyed as in the days of the old sailing ships when the men climbed over the gunwale right forward, clutched onto the rope netting and hoped that no passing wave would sweep them away. At daylight and after mooring up for the night everyone took his turn with one of the three wooden buckets on board, tossed it over the side at the end of a short line and, removing his shirt, sluiced his head and torso liberally with the cold, somewhat muddy water. They slept in heaps about the deck, on top of the cargo hatches, or under the small roof projection forward of the cabin. When it rained they got wet unless they could curl up under an umbrella, which is difficult to manage.

Hugh's food was cooked over a wood-burning stove made out of an old gasoline can, and he had a basin for washing. There was a hole cut in the poop deck aft, well above water-level, with a canvas screen around it, to be used as the toilet.

Once or twice he landed in the evening to take a short walk if the place was considered quiet and free of brigands, but on one occasion he was misinformed and as he approached a small village, armed men suddenly appeared out of the bushes on all sides. He greeted them with bows and smiles and effusive shaking of his clasped hands in the Chinese manner, calling out "Ding-how! Ding-how!" which, if he had got his tones right, would be translated as "How do you do!" On the other hand, if he had got the tones wrong it could mean something quite unmentionably vulgar, and he experienced a moment of panic when the nearest of the brigands — for such they were — burst out laughing. At that instant a rather handsome, well-dressed English-speaking Chinese appeared from nowhere and he hoped he was saved. He told the man who he was and where he was going and they carried on a cheerful spirited conversation about the singsong girls of Shanghai, but when Hugh invited his new-found friend on board to have a drink — he had a bottle of whisky — the man looked about him nervously and said no, he couldn't, it would be misunderstood by his companions, who knew nothing of foreign ways. And with that he and the gang vanished like smoke and Hugh turned about and went back to the junk, which immediately took in its mooring ropes and moved on down river a few miles. The *laopan* had no mind to be raided in the dark. Hugh himself thought that there was little risk, for he felt sure in his mind that it was the aura of "Da Bin-Shuan Inguea" — the Royal Navy of which he had been careful to speak — that had protected him in an impossibly weak position only an hour ago.

Nobody would expect the fierce Yangtze to abandon a last effort to conquer a mere seaman stripling, and it was not many hours later that the *laopan* was warning them to make ready for the Yeh-tan rapid. The water began a preliminary swirl that embraced both banks and then slowly concentrated in the centre surrounded by tall forbidding rock faces. The swirl became a circle and the centre of the circle rapidly lowered itself about fifteen feet as the junk commenced to swirl round and round at rapidly increasing speed. The whole crew of about fifty manned the huge sweep which was half as long again as the junk, but their efforts did nothing to pull the junk out of the rapidly increasing swirl. At that moment two Post Office sampans shot out from the bank making to throw a line to the junk and haul it out of the swirl. Each of these missed his throw in turn and things began to look desperate. The junk was going to be sucked down into the centre of the maelstrom. The *laopan* was wringing his hands and Hugh was quietly stripping off spare sweaters. Then Yeh-tan flipped itself suddenly to one side, brushed the junk against the rock wall and flung the whole thing with a splash out at one little corner of the swirling river and on beyond into a small sort of lagoon, and they were safe. That was one of the rare occasions when Hugh drank whisky, almost all the small store he had brought with him, because the *laopan* would not have known what to make of such liquor.

When they reached Ichang he returned all his service equipment — bedding, mess utensils, etc. — on board the *Aphis* which happened to be guard ship there at the time, and got a paymaster's receipt for it. But storekeeping accounts probably took a long time to travel from the Upper Yangtze to the Admiralty, and almost two years later when he was doing his courses, a very starchy official letter came to him demanding an immediate explanation as to what had happened to his stores issued to him on leaving *Teal*, and rather hinting that embezzlement, theft, or whatever it was, was something upon which their Lordships looked with grave displeasure. He sent the letter on to *Aphis*, which in the meanwhile had been paid off and laid up in Shanghai; so there this matter rested for evermore.

Chapter 7

Home Again

After a few days at Shanghai, Hugh got a passage to London in a Blue Funnel Line cargo ship of fifteen thousand tons named *Tiresias*, and was given a fine airy cabin next to the captain's quarters just below the bridge. She carried thirty-four passengers, mostly missionary families going home on leave, a couple from Sarawak who whetted his interest in that beautiful and primitive state governed by an English rajah, and the remainder were unremarkable people from the foreign business community in China. It seemed to be rather a dull passenger list, but by now he was too weak and ill to do much more than walk to the saloon for meals and then lie out on a deck-chair, or else in his bunk when the weather was wet or rough.

Singapore was their first stop, but he was not fit enough to go ashore and visit friends, and so lay sweltering on deck. After lunch he had fallen asleep and was dreaming when he awoke confusedly to see a dark face leaning over him. The man was an Arab fortune-teller and Hugh told him to go away and leave him alone.

"But Sir! I have just been reading a part of your hand while you were still asleep, and it is so interesting that I had to wake you. Only one dollar, Sir, and I tell you all!"

Finally he succumbed. The man was glib, and tried several devices to get Hugh to tell him who he was, but finally he had to rely on palmistry alone. He was very accurate about things that had already happened. Then came the future:

"I cannot see any wife! Are you already married, Sir?"

"No."

"But this is remarkable! It is not marriage though. Past middle life you will suddenly change your whole work, the way you live, everything! You will go off to an entirely different kind of life. I have never seen this before! You will live to be very old!" He got his dollar and, as we shall see, proved to be accurate.

Next they called at Penang for a few hours and later on at Malacca where the temperature on deck was 105°F. Hugh didn't stir from his deck-chair, and watched a group of monkeys playing on the shore while the ship was mooring alongside the jetty. A surge of native salesmen swarmed up the gangway as soon as it was out, and the duty officer turned back all those who had not got a trader's licence which did at least something to weed out the crooks, though of course a trader could without detection easily rent out his licence document to someone else, no doubt for an adequate fee. They sold fruit, embroideries, handmade lace under which was hidden a bundle of "Filthee postcards, only ten cents, Sir!" as well as jewellery and loose precious stones. There were "diamonds" from Burma manufactured by some secret process, rather dim stones that could never be mistaken for a real diamond; zircons which change colour, and after a few months' exposure to light might lose all their lustre; gold (reputedly); silver (perhaps); and last of all out came a little paper package of rubies. This last caught Hugh's attention.

The salesman told him all about the reconstructed rubies — of which he had several — made out of the dust and chippings of real stones under great heat — and at last brought out from his bosom a little bit of twisted paper from which fell into Hugh's hand quite a large ruby, somewhat different in appearance to the reconstructed ones he had already been shown.

"This, Sir, real Burma ruby! You see the difference? Very good stone this one Sir! You like to look-see?" Hugh continued to say no to all blandishments, and the salesmen were now being chased ashore as the ship was about to sail. He walked over to the gangway head to watch the last scene of the Far East. Suddenly a brown hand was thrust into his own and the little package of rubies fell into his palm.

"You choose any one, Sir! Only five dollars." And there amongst them was the larger, "different" stone which was really beautiful to look at. He picked it out and pushed a five dollar bill into the man's disappearing hand. It was just a sudden impulse which he regretted at once, but it was too late to grab his money back and return the stone; the brow was being hoisted and the man had to jump off the end of it onto the jetty.

He kept looking at the stone all the way to Colombo. Had the salesman inadvertently dropped the stone amongst the others in the last hurried moment and unawares? It unquestionably was different from the others he had seen. At Colombo he went ashore as soon as they arrived to take his ruby to Louis Siedel, the world authority on Ceylon gems, with whom he had made friends on the outward journey eighteen months before, but the old man was at home unwell, and only an assistant was in charge, so he told his ricksha to go on to a well-known Ceylonese jeweller a few yards further up the street. He explained exactly how he had got possession of this stone, and as soon as they saw it a little cluster of dark heads bent over it, all talking excitedly. Finally the largest and fattest of them turned to him and said that if he would leave it with them for a few days they would set up a special apparatus for examining stones, and then would be able to value it for him — but this was impossible as *Tiresias* was sailing early the next morning.

"Then, Sir, I am very sorry; we cannot do what you want in so short a time. But Sir, we think you may have a very good Burma ruby indeed. You should keep it in a safe place!"

He spent the remaining five weeks of the journey in a state of suppressed excitement, not daring to hope. Bombay was next, then Aden, where that day the temperature fell forty degrees as they passed up the Red Sea into the zone of northerly winds. He found the cold on deck unendurable, put on two sweaters and his warmest coat and trousers, and remained blue with the cold. Port Sudan brought back memories indeed of *Cricket*'s broken back. Then Suez, the Canal, and Port Said where they only stayed a few hours. On then to Malta and Gibraltar, by which time he was wondering how on earth he would survive the cold of England in April, though he felt that he was getting just a little bit more used to it, but still hating it as much as ever. And at last the port of London, shrouded in mist with a hazy sun giving hardly enough heat to be felt on one's face, but that didn't matter; there were four weeks of glorious leave ahead!

When that was over he, together with about fifty of his contemporaries, "joined" Cambridge University as undergraduates for eighteen months' studies in nine subjects, half of which could be chosen from a short list. As undergraduates they wore cap and gown, and were subject to the university rules and procedures. Each college offered a small number of vacancies, and Hugh was allocated to Selwyn, in those days a "new" college which did not inspire him.

He liked the master, who was very kind to him and quite often invited him to his lodgings. But the bathing arrangements were primitive indeed. One had to walk about thirty yards across a courtyard to a brick-walled enclosure only partly roofed with corrugated iron, upon the plain concrete floor of which were several shallow round tin baths, such as he had used in *Colossus'* gunroom bathroom. A cold and a hot water tap stuck out from one wall and the bath-tub had to be pushed underneath — unfortunately only lukewarm water ever emerged from the hot tap so that it was necessary to carry small kettles of boiling water from the undergraduates' rooms if one did not care to be frozen to death. Protest to the authorities produced no more than the obvious retort that a cold bath was very healthy and thirty yards ought to be within the distance an undergraduate could be expected to walk. But in cold or stormy weather undergraduates did not bath at all and Hugh's marine servant looked and sounded very shocked when he told Hugh about this.

Hall, in which one was obliged to dine several days in the week, produced one nightmare moment. A uniformed butler thrust a large and dirty card into Hugh's hands as he was about to sit down and commanded him to "read the grace", which was announced by ringing a handbell. When Hugh looked at it he saw that there were half a dozen lines in Latin, and the last Latin he had read was in 1911. Hardly a word was familiar to him, and he was dripping with perspiration when he sat down, and so never dined in hall again. Evidently no proper check was kept, for no rebuke came his way.

He shared the marine servant with another officer, and lived in two small rooms in college where no water was laid on, and was allocated a tutor whom he saw very briefly once a fortnight when he presented the essay he had been told to write — always on some academic subject about which he knew nothing whatever, and doubtless designed to make the young men read and learn. He invariably left the tutor in a rage. The tutor showed little concern — after all, these young officers would never take a degree.

The object of the whole business was, of course, to educate them up to the standard they should have achieved if they had not been sent to sea a year and a half early. But Cambridge during the "Long Vac" in summer is both lovely and beguiling, and sufficiently uncrowded to make life very easy and many lectures were cut on a sunny day. Hugh spent too much time in a punt on the Cam poling his way up to Granchester for tea and swimming in the rather muddy river on the way back in the evening.

Such great men as David Hannay, the naval historian, who unhappily was a poor lecturer and consequently disgracefully abused by the young men, and Sir Arthur Shipley, master of Christ's College, who called his fascinating talks "Aspects of Life", were among their lecturers. Sir Arthur was particularly kind to Hugh and occasionally asked him to lunch where he always met interesting people from many walks of life, and probably received more education than from the whole of his formal courses. Shipley was an inexhaustible story-teller and recounted one day how the Crown Prince of Japan had come to lunch which was, since the prince spoke no English, a difficult meal. Afterwards Sir Arthur brought out two desiccated rats which had lost their lives five hundred years ago during the "Black Death" plague for which they were responsible as germ carriers. This electrified the Japanese party, who burst into a tremendous spate of conversation and smiles all round. He never knew why they were so interested. The rats had been found when some panelling in the Master's Lodge had to be repaired. Another discovery in the same house was a whole room papered with copies of a proclamation Henry VIII had made when he came to the throne. Apparently the young king was very proud of his proclamation and had given spare copies to his mother who lodged in the master's house at that time. On another occasion his guests were led up to the master's own bedroom which was once occupied by Lady Margaret Tudor who had a window cut through the wall which enabled her to hear mass being said in the chapel below without getting out of bed.

Sir Arthur had put on too much weight in his later years:

"My dear boy, I haven't seen my feet for ten years, but my valet tells me they are in very good order. He, poor man, has to lace up my shoes in the morning and then unlace them again at night, no matter how late I am in getting to bed!"

Sadly the Geddes Axe (a government commission appointed to cut down unnecessary expenditure) fell on the course at Cambridge, and the sub-lieutenants were whisked away after completing only the "Long Vac" and the Michaelmas Term which followed. Hugh felt that the whole experience was of the greatest value to him, and although his examination results at the end were merely average, every one of his special essays he wrote on subjects ordered by the naval instructors was commended and sent to the

Admiralty, who indicated that they were pleased, in a language invented and understood only in Whitehall.

In January 1922 he joined Portsmouth Barracks for the sub-lieutenants' courses which were designed to qualify the young officers for the rank of lieutenant. These were Navigation, at the School of Navigation in the dockyard with practices at sea in a sloop; Torpedo at the *Vernon* just outside the dockyard; a very brief look at Signals; and then the one he found most difficult, Gunnery at Whale Island up the harbour. He never did master parade ground drill and perpetrated the classic boobs of marching two platoons into each other, and on another day of sending a small army over a steep bank down which they would have tumbled onto the football field, but for a purple gunner's mate who roared "Halt!" at the last possible moment. He had always hated cadet corps drill at his "prep" school and continued to do so in his later life.

At the end they were all sent on leave to await appointment. When Hugh opened the Admiralty envelope he learned that he was promoted to acting-lieutenant and was to go to the battleship *Malaya* preparing at Portsmouth to carry the Prince of Wales on a long tour round most of the world. He went on board the ship lying in Portsmouth dockyard and found that he would be the junior watchkeeper, and also that he would need to equip himself with full dress uniform and generally smarten up his wardrobe. A week before he was due to join, the appointment was cancelled, and he felt very downcast because the *Malaya* was obviously a number one assignment.

Then on 17th January 1922, came another appointment to the cruiser *Colombo* on the East Indies Station, and he would join her at Bombay, taking passage out in a Bibby Line ship. That took some little time for the authorities to arrange, but it was a quick journey with nothing new nor particularly interesting about the sea voyage which he had already experienced on two previous occasions.

When he went on board *Colombo* she was still in the Royal Indian Marine dockyard in the last and dirtiest few days of a periodical refit.

Chapter 8

East Indies Station

Hugh's appointment as acting-lieutenant to this smart little six-inch gun cruiser was very much to his satisfaction after the disappointment of missing a Royal Cruise in the *Malaya*. *Colombo* would do a two and half year commission on the East Indies Station, which extended from Aden and East Africa as far east as Burma and the Andaman Archipelago and as far south as the Antarctic, which frigid territory was never visited by warships, since no particular British interests lay in that area at that time. It was now March 1922, and *Colombo* was to be the first British warship to visit most of the ports since 1914. This unquestionably enhanced the warmth of her reception everywhere she went. The isolated — often numerically very small — British communities scattered over this vast area all regarded the ship as a breath from "home", which some had not seen for eight years; she was a visible link with their country and families. In these latter days the whole position of what used to be very loosely called "the Colonies" has by a later generation been not only misunderstood, but sometimes jeered at. The men who left home to earn their living in distant lands, and the wives who followed them, did so out of economic necessity, and with the commendable spur of adventure. None of them was highly paid, and few saved more than enough to buy a house on retirement. Their very circumscribed lives were frequently rather dull and isolated, though usually comfortable enough, in the sense that abundant servants were available, at any rate on this station, to deal with the domestic chores which difficult climates, business, or a profession prevented the white man, and often enough his wife, from tackling with his own hands. For example: the oriental market is a noisy, dirty, and often diseased area into which a white woman sometimes could not safely go. The "boy" did the shopping much better than she could, for he was born into the almost universal bargaining system that prevails, and he knew about the quality of produce and where it came from in a detailed way which a white woman would take years to learn. The language difficulties almost compelled the employment of some sort of "middleman", even where the white people had learned the local dialect. In India, for example, there are over six hundred dialects in use, though Urdu was likely to be understood by somebody, even out in a distant village. Europeans who worked abroad were moved fairly often for climatic reasons, amongst other considerations. Nearly everywhere children had to be sent "home" at an early age partly for their health and partly because education was not available in the outposts of Empire.

Colombo, the main naval base on this station, is a busy international crossroads of the sea and had, at that time, quite a large British population. The Governor of Ceylon — then Brigadier General Sir William Manning — headed the civil administration, and also formed a focus of social activity. The ship was often at Colombo and Hugh always joined in the Saturday sailing race at the Yacht Club, where two boats were reserved for naval use. There were two tennis clubs, the Garden Club being his favourite, partly because of easy access from the ship, and partly on account of gin slings, a delicious and perfect sequel to a game of tennis close to the equator. A more distant, but idyllic setting for any sort of a party was Mount Lavinia Hotel, on a small promontory seven miles south of Colombo. On the way one crosses a river where elephants would be seen working with logs or having their evening bath, depending on the time of day. Below the hotel on the sandy beach on many Sunday evenings a dozen young people would gather for surfing and then a fried chicken supper on the beach presided over by Bill Veach, the American Consul, whose sister was the prettiest girl in the place. There is something magic in a sunset at Mount Lavinia seen through the spray of the breaking rollers with palms along the shoreline rustling in the breeze.

Hugh occasionally accompanied a keen fishing friend on sea trips in a Mount Lavinia catamaran. These primitive boats built out of a hollowed log with two wooden beams holding the small wooden outrigger, have only a foot-wide slit opening running the length of the eighteen-foot hull into which the legs are thrust as far up as the knees. Your tail is balanced in mid-air over the side and gets wet — not that it matters in a temperature of over 80°F. A thin rough twelve-foot long pole does duty for a mast upon which a square cotton sail is hoisted and this gives the little craft a surprising turn of speed. They left shore at daylight and sailed straight out seven to ten miles where schools of swordfish were usually seen porpoising at great speed through the water, and their long serrated swords sometimes six feet in length looked really dangerous. Hugh never caught one, and perhaps it was just as well. The largest ones were twice the size of a catamaran. Many other varieties of fish abounded, so one was always certain of getting something for the pot.

Another fishing expedition, which was apparently a new adventure amongst Colombo residents, was often made to the lagoons which run parallel to the shore and immediately behind The Galle Face, a mile-long grassy promenade lined with palm-trees where the Indians, especially, like to parade up and down with their lovely sari-clad women to catch the sea breeze at sunset. These lagoons were found to contain a small salmon-like fish of about five pounds weight, which fought with tremendous gusto and were excellent eating. At that time nobody knew their name, and only a few small Ceylonese boys would be found trying to catch them with a bent pin for a hook, and a rough bough pulled off some tree serving as a rod.

The manager of the Colombo city waterworks, a friendly Scot, had a bungalow perched on a steep hillside above one of the large reservoirs in the foothills, twenty miles out from the city. It was a particularly delightful expedition to go there to dinner, as most of the road wound through coconut palm plantations, and after dark the car lights would make them look like tall columns in a cathedral. The pathway up the final hundred yards to the house had to be climbed on foot, and the host always sent a boy down with a light to chase away whatever snakes might be lying on the warm stone steps. Dinner was sometimes served on board a large raft floating on the lake, a lovely experience on a moonlit night. However, on one occasion a young python swimming in the water decided to come aboard to investigate, and when one of the guests saw it slowly emerging from the water beside him he let out a yell and jumped over the other side and swam ashore, followed by most of the rest of the party, except the host who was familiar with their habits and knew that they were relatively harmless, except when hungry. Their habit there is to go swimming in the lake after waking up from a substantial meal, not before one. But the place was also infested with various poisonous snakes, all of which like to swim, and nothing could be done to clear them out. Hugh fortunately never saw one on any of his visits.

The first Christmas they spent at Colombo was one that they would all remember. Hugh found himself much involved with friends, and on Christmas eve dined in the city with a Scots family who put on a large and heavy traditional dinner that lasted far into the night. Next morning everyone on board went to the cathedral at nine o'clock; over three hundred from the ship attending the Holy Communion Service. This great influx fairly swamped the small cathedral staff and the last sailors did not get back to the ship until nearly midday.

The captain's rounds of the messdecks started off almost at once. This is a customarily convivial affair for which the sailors save up their rum ration in order to entertain the officers in each separate mess — and *Colombo* had more than twenty. This happy naval tradition provides a moment when hard feelings — and there are bound to be some when six hundred men are enclosed in a small iron box for two and a half years — are relaxed, even forgotten — and a sailor might without offence say to his captain:

"You did treat me awful hard that time, Sir!" and the captain could answer with a smile:

"But you could have gone to detention, you know, and would have too, if you hadn't stroked the seaman's cutter to win your race in the regatta last summer. Make sure you do that again next summer, and the best of luck!"

This was the sort of thing that was getting mixed up with the grog all through that morning — to the very great benefit of the Service.

Hugh had become involved in a variety of ships' entertainments, shore-going expeditions, and so on, and had become familiar with far more of the men than just those of his own division; indeed there was hardly a mess in which he did not have one or two special "buddies", the result on Christmas day being that at every stop on the rounds somebody insisted on his having a drink with them. He had no objection to that of course, but his capacity did have limits. He never was quite clear how he got back to the wardroom, but when he did he found that a forenoon cocktail party for visitors from on shore was in progress and it was only at two o'clock in the afternoon that the surviving officers sat down to their Christmas dinner of turkey and plum pudding, the pride of the wardroom messman's heart.

In the late afternoon two or three of the younger officers went to swim in a little sandy cove just where the breakwater joins on to the shoreline, and they found that the ocean swell was sending in very large breakers which were exciting to ride upon, but could be disastrous if misjudged. There was always a cohort of small naked Ceylonese boys there either fishing or swimming, and one was sure to see some spectacular upsets, though these youngsters never seemed to get damaged by the big waves. Hugh felt clearer in his head after his dip, and returned to the ship to dress for his third Christmas dinner at the beautiful home of the leading industrialist of the town and his Scots family, where entertainment was provided in lavish style. The large maroon Daimler was awaiting him at the pierhead, and on the way he pondered whether it was actually possible to eat three Christmas dinners in twenty-four hours — it was a vain meditation, for he knew that he must. They were the kindest and most generous family in the world and did a great deal to make his visits to Colombo a joy which he liked to remember in later years. He would have liked to marry the daughter of the house, but could see no way of supporting a wife on a lieutenant's slender pay, and he had no other income.

This was an era sometimes described as "the dancing years", and appropriately so. At Colombo there were always one or two private dances whenever a cruise ship came in or some other special event deserved a celebration, and that of course included Saturday nights. The best dance band of five pieces was undoubtedly the one run by a bachelor mess, and whenever there was a momentary lull in the social programme they put on a dance in their own large house. Nobody willingly missed this.

The official base on the station was Trincomalee, a good harbour on the east coast of Ceylon, and it was from there that they did their gunnery and torpedo exercises. It was a hot airless little town, the dockyard consisting of a few storehouses from sailing days, and having only a shallow water wharf from which sharks could almost always be seen hunting for small fish which were plentiful. Almost every evening Hugh and the young ship's doctor hired a dug-out canoe manned by a very ancient fisherman. They paddled out to the fishing grounds and caught some most exotic varieties, and others highly poisonous, about which the ancient mariner warned them. One night, after dark, Hugh was fishing from a rocky place on shore and hooked a five-foot shark which put up a great fight but was eventually hauled up on a flat sloping rock, and he began to wonder what he would do next. It made a leap towards him, which dislodged the hook, and the creature slid back tail first into the water, which was probably just as well, though a disappointment at the time.

A small island, Sober Island, near the anchorage, had been given to the officers of the Fleet many years before as a club. There was a little mat-shed building, with an ancient retainer, Paramu, in charge, and a cook and a bar. The place was popular at weekends and a superb meal was served — especially gulu Malacca, Paramu's masterpiece, made of sago, coconut milk, fresh lime and other delicious ingredients.

The little town lay half a mile across a narrow flat palm-covered isthmus, and consisted of a couple of rows of palm leaf huts, half of which seemed to be arrack bars. Because of malaria the last boat left shore at sundown. One evening when Hugh was officer of the watch there were five absentees who early next morning were brought back by a local boatman in a dazed condition. When the men got to their messes they drank water or tea, which is the fuse that detonates the local brew of arrack, a really dangerous type of spirit. In a few minutes all hell broke loose, nobody realising what was the matter. Four of the drunks were successfully locked up to sleep it off, but the fifth, a burly Royal Marine private, needed five stalwart men to hold him down. Irons were clamped on him and he broke two sets in quick succession, and then suddenly passed out peacefully. They all eventually sobered up twelve hours later.

On one occasion one of the ship's company developed smallpox, and an immediate general vaccination followed. Fortunately the man suffered only a very mild attack, and nobody else caught the infection. Hugh landed one day to visit the sick man in the hospital, a small comfortable and airy bungalow at the dockyard. As he was about to enter the gate he looked up into the trees overhead and saw long green snakes swaying from the branches above, so he jumped back and climbed over the wall at another place. Later he counted no less than five of these snakes, which seemed to be about six feet long and very slim. They were supposed not to be poisonous, but the information on this point was conflicting, so he continued to climb over the wall when visiting the sick. There were cobras in the district, especially in the ancient stone fortifications which surrounded the harbour, but nobody wanted to go and investigate.

There was a wealth of shooting available at Trincomalee, and Hugh went quite often to a "tank" about four miles walk into the jungle. A tank might be anything from two to four hundred paces in extent. These ancient, sometimes stone-lined cisterns were dotted about all over the country for water storage, but had long been out of use and now harboured fish and crocodiles. One day, on the way out, a shooting party passed a railroad gang renewing sleepers with ebony and satinwood from the jungle treees alongside. It seemed a curious usage for such valuable timber, but the Ceylonese foreman when questioned said:

"But Sir, we cannot get trees out here to market, and we have found that both these woods make very good sleepers. They last much longer than anything else we have tried!"

Nearing the tank they ran into some peacock, reported to be very good eating, but in spite of their size they disappeared into the jungle in a flash and could not be followed, for it was an area where snakes, leeches and scorpions were known to be plentiful, and one had therefore to keep to open ground. Jungle cock — closely resembling the gamecocks used a hundred years ago for cock-fighting — were numerous, and two or three of these could usually be bagged on the way. There wasn't much to eat on them, but what there was tasted very good.

When the party got to the tank they spread out along one side to try and get crocodiles. Hugh was looking out over the water where it was always possible to see the raised pair of ridges above the eyes and the rather bulbous tip of the nose projecting an inch or two above the water. He heard a sudden rustling noise, and a grey log he had already glanced at was sliding into the water a couple of yards away. He had disturbed a sleeping crocodile, but was so surprised that he never fired at it. It was the only one he ever saw that offered a real target. Firing at those in the water was almost useless, for the visible parts were not vital, except for the actual eyeball, which was a difficult target. Even if a crocodile was killed, it did not float to the surface for four or five days, and boatmen did not willingly venture out to collect the corpse when so many of its relations were cruising around waiting for it to ripen before eating it.

Monkeys usually gathered in trees nearby, apparently to inspect their two-legged relatives, and it was worth the walk to watch them playing among the branches, and quite often a family, the children being led by the hand, would walk down to the tank to drink.

The great day came when a rogue elephant was reported in the district. Hugh and the navigator went out after it in the afternoon, but saw only a couple of huts it had pulled down and some vegetable gardens decimated. Next morning at daylight the sub-lieutenant went out alone, found it, and killed it with a single shot and was back on board for breakfast. Rogues go savage — perhaps insane — which is not the same thing as the periodical "must" — and they are then boycotted by the herd, and, apparently in resentment, destroy practically any living thing, or even a stationary object, which comes into their view. There is no plan, no objective, and no known reason for this, and nobody is safe until such a beast is destroyed.

In order to give some relief from the very hot weather experienced all over the station, each ship in turn sent its crew once a year up the mountains to Dietawala Camp, which had been built for prisoners during the South African Boer War. A month in the cool air at five thousand feet did wonders to restore vitality, and also gave the opportunity to carry out musketry courses and field exercises. This was a tea-growing area, with the campsite in a large, grassy, open basin several miles across. The governor's bodyguard horses were stabled at the camp and the aide-de-camp in charge of the guard was always glad to lend a mount to any officer who cared to ride. Hugh often went riding and so was able to get easily over the area. One day, while out exercising his horse, with a groom up on a second mount, they were going down a wide path through a little wood when his horse suddenly leaped sideways into the brush, and out of the corner of his eye he just caught a glimpse of a tick palonga, a broad twenty-inch long viper, slowly wriggling off the path. These are the most deadly snakes in Ceylon, and account for some hundreds of deaths on the island every year. They look exactly like any small stick of wood lying about and they move very slowly. They were believed to be deaf. Whenever Hugh's duty involved going night rounds he held a long stick out ahead of him along his pathway and had a man with a lantern accompanying him.

A couple of miles from the camp a small river wound its way across the plain to which a few energetic people used to walk for a swim in the shallow pools. One Sunday afternoon two young seamen went there and on the way back one of them was bitten on the ankle by a tick palonga. His mate sucked the wound for about twenty minutes, and as the victim did not collapse, they walked slowly back to camp where a doctor inspected the wound. There was a slight trace of poisoning, but it cleared in a few hours and no evil consequences of any sort followed. It was a remarkable case of cool-headedness, and one of the rare occasions when a person survived a proven bite from this particular type of snake. The young fellow who sucked the wound was officially commended and well deserved this recognition.

Hugh and one or two others were invited up to the Haputale Tea Factory to inspect the operations there. An open linesman's "flat" was hooked onto the tail of the morning train for the seven miles up a fairly steep grade, and in the evening the flat was simply lifted onto the line and rolled down again to Dietawala. They were taken for a walk through the nearest part of the tea-gardens and saw the small waist-high bushes planted close together on the steep stony mountain side cleared of all other growth, through which gangs of Tamils, originally imported as a labour force from Travancore State in South India, and mostly consisting of women and children directed by a male overseer, were picking the top and freshest leaves, which they dropped into a sack hung across their chests. They worked on the piece-work system at amazing speed, and the small fingers of the pickers were perfectly suited to the little green leaves. This estate is situated on a weather divide in the mountains, much prone to wet mist and light showers which improve the tenderness of the tea leaves so that the product of the factory was judged to provide the highest quality of tea that Ceylon could then supply. The factory beside the railway is a large open-sided building on two levels, and when the pickers' bags are emptied there, each day's picking is weighed, stacked on the wooden floor, and spread out to dry. The leaves go through a series of drying and heating processes over a period of several days, depending on the moisture prevailing in the air, and then the finished product is packed in lead-lined wooden cases ready for shipping. A tea-garden may last thirty years, much depending on the rainfall, but eventually the fertility of the hillside becomes exhausted and that particular land is abandoned and allowed to revert to jungle once more. Large areas have run out in recent years, and it is not yet known how long it will take before the land recovers. Ceylon is all mountainous country in the interior and there are large reserves of hill jungle available for future clearing and planting, but the quality of the crop varies with the height, the rainfall and the aspect, as well as the soil.

Royal Naval Reserve officers, and also Royal Indian Marine officers, were drafted to the two cruisers on the station to carry out the periodical training and instruction that their services required, and *Colombo* always had at least one of these on board.

Lieutenant Paliser, an RNR officer, came to Colombo for his six-month re-training period and became a close friend. He had made his home near Haputale Station, and his wife was in permanent residence there. She was a great lover of animals and kept horses, a pedigree bulldog, and also a mongoose which ruled the whole establishment and killed the snakes which had originally been numerous in that region. She had been a noted horsewoman in Australia in her younger days and seldom missed a day's riding, Hugh often being invited to accompany her.

One day when shopping in Colombo she chanced to pass by the place where the horse-drawn cabs waited to be hired, and at once noticed that the animals were uneasily lifting one foot after the other because of the intense heat of the stone pavement where there was no shade whatever. She hailed a policeman to complain about this but, getting no satisfaction, went off to the headquarters where the chief of police told her that no law was being broken and that he could do nothing. From there she walked to Government House, which was not far away, and chanced to meet the governor just as he was getting out of his car. She buttonholed him on the spot and prevailed upon him to walk outside the gates and a short distance down the road to inspect the cab-horses for himself. He too was a horseman and was horrified by what he saw, and in due course the hire cabs were moved to shady places and their horses were fitted with heavy leather shoes. Hugh checked up on their welfare twenty-two years later when he visited Colombo again and found the horses still wearing their leather shoes.

Later on the ship went north to Madras where the "little monsoon" was just breaking with its light winds and heavy ocean swell outside the harbour. The Yacht Club arranged a sailing race of six a side in their sixteen-foot dinghies, and supplied a yacht club "boy" as crew for the visitors. The swell had risen overnight and looked formidable for such very small boats, but the sailing committee did not want to cancel the race since improved conditions could not be expected, and off went the starting gun. The boat was unfamiliar and the crewman practically froze as soon as Hugh's boat passed outside the breakwater. He saw very little of the other eleven competitors during the four-hour race because their mast-heads were well below the crest of the rollers when they went into the trough. He quickly found that all wind was lost in the trough so that the brief period on the crest must provide enough speed to negotiate the following crest which was sometimes breaking, and could have swamped the boat if not taken at the right angle. It was more like mathematics than sailing. However, he got the hang of the thing almost at once and practically forgot the race in his concentration on keeping afloat. He did see one upturned boat and two broken masts, but there was a large motor boat patrolling the course and she was well able to take care of whatever accidents might be happening. Quite by chance he briefly spotted the sea mark at a critical moment, but never actually saw it when he thought he ought to be rounding it; however, as time was getting on he decided to turn back for the harbour entrance, and eventually came in alongside the Yacht Club jetty in twilight. Three boats had finished the course, two from the club and himself, and the patrol boat said he rounded the mark — so mathematics had paid off in the end. Several had capsized, some masts were broken, and the balance gave up and abandoned the race. Hugh was to remember this event as the most difficult and unpleasant sailing experience he ever had, but felt that he had learned a lot on that day about handling a small boat.

Lord Willingdon, perhaps the most successful of all the proconsuls who held office in India, was Governor of Madras Province at that time, and both he and his immensely energetic wife did their utmost to make the ship's visit to Madras a happy one. Government House had a beach hut at a sea bathing place outside the city and Hugh and some others were taken out there by one of the ADCs or Lady Willingdon on several occasions. However, the place was reputed to be infested with snakes and one was constantly being warned not to do this or that because a snake was likely to be hidden there. Nobody saw one, but the ADCs said they usually did, and they didn't at all like going out there. Lady Willingdon enjoyed swimming and was never for a moment deterred. She was a remarkable woman, no longer young, but nevertheless, as soon as lunch was over, guests were carried off to play table tennis for an hour while the rest of India enjoyed its daily siesta. When the Willingdons went off to their summer residence at Ootacamund in the hills they took two of the officers with them to play polo for a few days.

One very interesting visit was that paid to the government clinic where anti-snake venom serum was produced. It was the only source of supply in the East in those days, and the whole technique had been developed at Madras from scratch. The staff said that there were forty thousand deaths annually from snake bite in Madras Province alone. India is not crawling with dangerous snakes by any means, but there are locations and conditions where they proliferate, and equally there are large areas where they are a rarity and one needs to be informed of the varying situation when travelling.

Their next port of call that spring was Trivandrum, the capital of Travancore State on the south-west coast of the Indian peninsula. As the ship rounded the southern tip of the country, a white painted mission station was passed quite close-to, which claimed to have been founded by St. Thomas the Apostle, who, tradition says, went off to evangelise India after the ascension of Jesus Christ. Certainly the Ma-Thomist Church has been established in Southern India for many hundreds of years.

At Travancore they lay out in the roadstead almost two miles from the shore on account of the shallow water. The commissioner, the British official overseeing the general administration of the state, was a splendid person and invited everyone to tennis at his pleasant house, and organised expeditions out into the countryside where tarred roads ended at the edge of town and mud and potholes made the driving of an ordinary car nearly impossible.

The maharajah, whom they never actually saw, gave an enormous dinner for the officers, sixty persons sitting down at a U-shaped table in a very large pillared white room open at both sides to surrounding gardens. His orchestra played in an overhanging gallery and his prime minister acted as host in his place. In this state was a matriarchal system of rule, the mother of the maharajah taking precedence over him in all things. In fact his only explicit function seemed to be the siring of a sizeable number of heirs in order to ensure that neither plague nor murder would be likely to sweep away the dynasty.

The meal lasted for two hours with a dozen courses served from silver dishes on a table profusely decorated with Indian silverwork candelabra, cups, trophies and huge bowls of tropical flowers, which gave off an overpowering scent of honey. The temperature was in the nineties, and everyone was glad when the time came to go home, for starched collars, cuffs and shirt fronts had wilted into a soggy mess almost before they had sat down.

The ship was thrown open to visitors, and arrangements were made with the local police to control the safe landing of the small native boats at the town jetty. Unfortunately the police were not seafaring men, for every boat arrived at the ship loaded to the gunwale, and one or two sank before they came alongside, which meant that the ship's motor boat was kept busy fishing out submerging passengers. As the boats neared the ship the boatmen, challenging one another to get there first, put on a final burst of speed and excitedly rammed whoever got in the way regardless of possible consequences, so that boats dashed alongside, some colliding, some flooding, one or two overturning, and the passengers apparently enjoying the fun, quickly leaped into the next boat already overloaded, which then slowly submerged so that many of them were wet up to the waistline when they finally reached the upper deck, cheerfully laughing and calling out encouragement to the ever-increasing flood of humanity still afloat on the water below. Nobody was actually drowned alongside the ship, but the side party attempting to control the boats spent a breath-taking afternoon. When once three hundred people had got on board an urgent message was sent to the police to stop all further traffic, but they had apparently given up all hope of controlling anything anywhere, for the boatmen had made up their minds that this was to be the day on which they were going to make their fortunes. A patrol was finally sent ashore to put a stop to any further embarkation of visitors.

Arrangements had been made on board to entertain the children with games, swings, slides, and so on, but the crowd became so dense on deck that it was impossible to keep an open space for any such activities. The people had evidently never before been on board a warship, and they were removing and pocketing small fitiings to take home as souvenirs, and also relieving themselves wherever they happened to be standing at the moment. A movement was begun to get them back into the boats waiting to take them ashore, but the boatmen started to raise the price, and the high-pitched haggling at the gangway drowned out every other sound and delayed the exodus interminably. It was dark before the last boats left. Later it was learned that five visitors had been drowned during the day, which sadly marred the occasion for the ship. Nobody on board had ever before seen an Indian crowd, nor had they dealt with the native police. Thereafter the ship always took over control at the embarkation point, which seemed to be the only sure way of protecting ships' visitors from themselves.

Colombo moved on to Bombay and on the way northwards, and quite close to the coastline, the ship passed through a vast shoal of cream-coloured jellyfish. The sea water inlets to the condensers became clogged with these creatures, thus causing a failure of steam to the turbines, so that the ship was only able to move at about three knots speed for several hours until they had passed beyond the twenty-mile wide jellyfish concentration. A little further north they ran into masses of sea snakes, a highly poisonous cream-coloured serpent about six feet long with dark bars across its back — a particularly loathsome-looking creature. One night on watch on the bridge Hugh sighted light-coloured water ahead, and as the ship drew closer it sounded like surf breaking on a reef. He quickly altered course away and called the captain and the navigator because he thought some navigational error must have been made, or else that the gyro compass had failed. Everything was carefully checked and as no error could be found the captain resumed course and they entered what appeared to be white breaking water, but it was in fact a large area of phosphorescent plankton which is occasionally seen in those waters. Those who had come up onto the bridge also thought they heard the sound of breaking water as the stem of the ship entered the white water, but this must have been some freak of auto-suggestion, for there were no wavelets other than the breaking of the bow wave, and plankton does not make audible sounds.

Bombay is seen from the harbour entrance to be a very large city indeed, spreading far inland, and as densely packed with people as the harbour is with local boats in addition to steamship traffic. They anchored for a few days off the Gates of India (a memorial archway at the landing place) before entering the Royal Indian Marine Dockyard for a two-month refit during which the ship's company was accommodated in an army barracks, and the officers found whatever accommodation suited them as near to the dockyard as possible. They were made — as everywhere — honorary members of the local clubs, and Hugh lived at the Byculla Club some way out for a couple of weeks in an atmosphere of old-time grandeur, though the buildings reeked of mould and damp. It was, however, too expensive in taxi transport, and he was offered a share in the large and pleasant flat which Engineer

Commander Deans and his wife had secured overlooking a park with cricket fields and tennis-courts. The damp heat of the monsoon was upon them, and overhead electric fans did little more than stir up the steamy atmosphere. Within a week they found that they had acquired nine servants to look after the three of them, and planned to cut down this ridiculous establishment. But it couldn't be done! The man who cleaned the shoes was not permitted by caste to sweep the floors. The amah who looked after the lady would not wash the men's clothes — and so on and on, until they gave up the attempt. The cost was minute; what all these people really wanted was food, and shelter from the rains.

One afternoon while Hugh was waiting to bat in a ships' cricket game there was a thunderstorm which flooded the ground within a few minutes, making any further play impossible for that day.

As soon as the downpour stopped he set off for the nearby flat on foot and chanced to pass a theatre where Pavlova with her ballet company was billed. The matinee performance had only just begun and he decided to go in, as he had always wanted to see the famous dancer. He was completely captivated, and at the intermission hurried to the box office and booked a seat for each of the remaining five days of the programme. Pavlova was then forty-seven years old, but showed no sign of diminished powers. She was the greatest dancer alive, and from then onwards he became a ballet fan.

On Saturdays the three flat-dwellers, who were all keen racegoers, usually went out to the weekly meeting at Bombay Racecourse and on to the Willingdon Club for a drink afterwards. This Saturday, Pavlova was to be seen in the Government House box, rather a gaunt woman with colourless skin and tired eyes, her hands and arms showing the marks of age. Hugh hung about and followed her closely when she went off to place her bets. There was something electric, he felt, about her every movement, and it was not the effect of stage costume or lighting that gave her the magnetic attraction she seemed to exude; so thought the new fan at the age of twenty-four.

Racing was good at Bombay and some well-known jockeys were riding there during the off-season in England. Hugh always took just the amount of money he could afford to lose, and, with the exception of a couple of days, he always lost it. Mrs Deans, on the contrary, always made money, and on one occasion had a seven hundred rupee win and treated the two men to dinner at the Yacht

Club. The Willingdon Club always seemed to produce people they knew after racing was over. It had been founded by Lord Willingdon when he was Governor of Bombay Province some years earlier in order to provide a social meeting-place for both Indians and foreigners, and was, at this time, the only club in India which had such dual membership. It was for this reason that Hugh particularly liked to go there; it gave him at least a chance of meeting Indian people in whom he was always interested; nevertheless inter-racial relationships did not always work out happily. The Parsee community in particular greatly valued their pale — almost white — skin, and sought to maintain or increase that quality. In the waterside bars used by the sailors they sometimes met an ex-sergeant of the British Army, a handsome fair-haired youngish man who, some years earlier, had struck up a friendship with a well-to-do Parsee family who often entertained him in their home, and finally one night when he was drunk contrived to bed him down with a daughter of the house. When the girl became pregnant the family persuaded him to marry her, and they bought him out of the Army and set him up in his own home, but, as always in India, in their compound. The sailors said that he invariably appeared in a chauffeur-driven car — so that he would not be able to escape if he ever wanted to — and that he had every luxury that money could buy; but he was the most sad and unhappy man they had ever met, even though he loved his wife. He could not grow accustomed to the Indian way of living, nor to the isolation from his own people.

Hugh met a similar case at the Willingdon Club where he would often see a vivacious blonde girl with a group of expensively dressed Indians. It transpired that she was married to a good-looking young Indian who was obviously very much in love with her. Hugh eventually made their acquaintance and found out that the girl had been a member of a theatrical touring company which had gone broke in Bombay a few years earlier and left her stranded. She married the wealthy young man, but could not always conceal her utter misery, for although she enjoyed every luxury, she, too, could not accept the Indian way of life, and felt desperately lonely, for she had no real contact with the European community. She said one day to Hugh:

"I only come here so that I can just look at the people from home. But I hardly ever meet any of them. They don't go to Indian houses and they won't invite me to theirs!"

There was another case of a different sort which much exercised the minds of the British residents at that time. A young girl from a touring English theatrical company had got herself involved with a rich landowner living out in the country, and he claimed that he had married her according to Indian rites, which was probably quite true, even if the girl had not understood what the ceremonies really meant. She fled from her husband to Bombay, and he pursued her, forced her into his car and compelled her to go back to his home. But was she bound by Indian law? Nobody believed that she could be held against her will under British law. It was a tragic position for the girl who, of course, had no real understanding of the situation into which she had entered, and it seemed that she would be unlikely to escape from her marriage, if such it really was, and this incident ended with her suicide.

About six miles across the harbour the renowned Ajanta Caves are situated — really an ancient temple inside extensive caves, the walls of which are elaborately carved with giant figures of the innumerable deities of Indian mythology. Exaggerated admiration for the artistic merit of the statuary has been widely expressed by foreigners, and the caves have become one of the principal sights in India for travellers; but Hugh found the endless sensual posturing of the figures cloying and ultimately disgusting, although the execution is often exquisite. There was, for him, something heavy, overpowering and fundamentally unpleasant about the whole erotic concept.

There was good weekend sailing to be had from the Yacht Club where Hugh was lucky enough to become crew to the owner of one of the large class of forty-five footers which raced far out to sea where the air was fresher and less damp than in Bombay harbour, and he got leave whenever he could to go off sailing.

They all very quickly met people amongst the large and hospitable British community, the more wealthy of whom lived out at Malabar Hill, which was much less steamy than the city centre. The Deans became interested in a group of table-turning fans and Hugh joined in this curious activity on several occasions. The planchette — a small wooden table standing on legs about a foot high — was placed in the middle of the polished dining-room table and people sat round with both hands resting on the planchette and touching the fingers of the adjacent person. Silence must be kept, and one is asked to concentrate the whole thought on one particular thing. After a few minutes the planchette begins

M

to move about at random, and a pencil attachment records these movements on a piece of blank paper already in place on the table beneath. Someone asks the planchette to answer a question, and, if all goes well, the pencil quite often scrawls out a word or two which may reasonably be judged to give a reply. It is a queer business, and creates an eerie feeling of supernatural forces in operation. No rational explanation of these results seems to come to hand and it is difficult to see how a person "in the know" could control the movement of the planchette so that its pencil spells out a word — yet this seems to be the only available explanation for the results which are quite often achieved. Hugh decided in the end that it was not a bad entertainment for a wet afternoon, but if the day was fine he would much prefer to be out of doors playing some game.

The theatre at Bombay had some good shows while they were there, and one of the better ones was the appearance of a renowned conjurer who did numerous wonderful tricks during the first half of the programme. The second half turned out to be a "thought reading" session. Ushers handed out papers upon which the audience was asked to write out their questions. Mrs Deans asked when she and her husband would be returning to England. A jockey and his wife whom the Deans had met at Colombo happened to be seated in the row immediately in front and they asked if the offer of a move elsewhere would be advantageous. The conjurer, pointing at Mrs Deans, read out her question and said:

"Your husband will be appointed to a shore job at home and you will be leaving in June." This happened.

Later the man pointed to the jockey and his wife, and said:

"You really want to know whether or not to accept an offer to go to Australia which you have just received. It is a good one and I advise you to accept." Again this was exactly their question, though they hadn't mentioned Australia on their bit of paper.

After that they hurried back to the Deans' flat in a high state of excitement and enjoyed several drinks. It would not have been difficult to identify the questioner if the ushers marked each paper slip, but the correct answers given cannot be so easily explained. The papers were drawn at random out of a hat. Everyone who attended this particular show left in a state of wonderment.

About once a month the governor, Sir George Lloyd, gave an evening reception to which about three hundred people were invited. The night Hugh went was particularly hot, and after shaking hands with 'their excellencies' in the ballroom, the company moved out to the illuminated gardens where a buffet supper was served from several long tables. There were about equal proportions of Indian and foreign guests. Hugh, while admiring one of the enormously tall Sikh bodyguards in his bemedalled scarlet uniform, with his long bushy beard in a sort of hair net, got into conversation with an Indian gentleman who spoke perfect English, having been at Oxford. Gradually he began to take in the jewellery worn with the stiff brocade tunic and draped white cotton trousers. There was a long necklace of large pearls alternating with rather larger carved cabochon emeralds, and three or four other less dazzling necklaces, and in the turban a six-inch long aigrette made of graduated diamonds sprouting out of a very large aquamarine. Both arms from wrist to elbow were encased in many jewelled bracelets, among which were the largest sapphires he ever saw. The man was the son of a maharajah and must have worn quite half a million pounds' worth of precious stones that night.

Another very old and distinguished-looking Indian with a long white beard was seen to be wearing a choker necklace of pearls approaching the size of a thrush's egg, the largest pearls Hugh ever saw in his long life, and reminiscent of the magnificent necklace given to Mary Queen of Scots by King Henry of France on the occasion of her marriage to the Dauphin. These are pictured in two of her very early portraits, and mysteriously vanished at the time of the queen's execution by Elizabeth I who refused to buy the necklace when it was later offered to her.

This calls to mind the largest collection of precious stones in the world belonging to the Nizam of Hyderabad. Captain de Winton was in command of the nizam's bodyguard at this time and came on board the *Colombo* for a cruise to East Africa as a guest of his brother, one of the ship's officers. One of the captain's special duties was to see to the security of the nizam's jewel house and to supervise the periodical checking of the inventory. The value was at that time well beyond a hundred million pounds. There was a twenty-foot long carpet made of pearls which hung on a wall. Other loose pearls were stowed in large bins on the floor, rather like root vegetables in a cellar. There were boxes of uncut diamonds, and of course an endless variety of jewelled articles. Nevertheless, whenever an important gem came on the market, no matter in what country, the nizam was immediately informed, and more often than not he bought it. It was a form of obsession with him, and since his large state was the wealthiest in India and he personally owned all its revenue, he could always afford to buy whatever took his fancy — and that meant any gem of top quality. In later years when the republican government dispossessed the ruling princes, he managed to hold on to this collection of precious stones after he lost his principality. It was said that it would take half a century to dispose of the collection because it was so large that the market could be swamped, and the only way would be to sell off small parcels of jewels at wide intervals of time.

He had the reputation being parsimonious, but de Winton did not agree with that. The nizam supported the three hundred immediate members of his family, placing as many as possible in government jobs, but insisting on absolute obedience to his orders and also upon personal efficiency. Those who rebelled, or were incompetent, were dismissed from whatever appointment they might hold, cast out of the family, and sent into exile. There weren't many rebels, not that that mattered to the nizam, for he always had a large roster from which to fill up gaps in the hierarchy. His personal life was extremely frugal; comforts and necessities were provided, but never a useless luxury. The same rule was followed in public administration, and the state was considered to be the most undeveloped territory in India; but the nizam saw no reason to alter ancient practices that worked satisfactorily, and thought that modernisation for the mere sake of being "up-to-date" was simple stupidity. What his people thought was unknown, but they were at peace and adequately fed and clothed.

One of Hugh's hostesses in Bombay had arranged a dinner party, and the day before had gone with her boy and the amah and a coolie to the market to shop for supplies. This left her house deserted for two or three hours. When she came home she found that the dining-room — where silver and glass were laid out in readiness for the party — had been almost stripped, and that many small articles in other rooms were missing. She informed the police immediately of course, but they offered little hope of recovery. Several other houses in the district had been similarly robbed, and they thought a gang was at work, and advised her always to leave a servant on duty when she went out. All of that was of no help to her in trying to find a means of coping with her dinner the next day. Presently the boy came in with his list of the losses to be sent to the insurance people, and then he said:

"Maybe you can buy back your things. I go to thieves' market tomorrow and see if they are there." He did so, and found nearly the whole list of missing articles for sale and was able to buy them back in time for the dinner party.

Mrs Deans was busily shopping for her forthcoming return to England and they made a number of expeditions into the various specialised markets. The street of carpets was a wonderful experience where every sort of carpet from all over the world was displayed for sale. Hugh even recognised some made in Szechuan and others probably from the American Indians in Arizona. There was a rug from an Indian source made of gold silk interspersed with gold wire threads which had a raised pattern in coloured wools. Hugh had seen one of these lent by Queen Mary for an exhibition in London. The silk market, too, was a riot of colour — and temptation. The dealers sat crying their wares on a raised platform in their open-fronted booths, as they did in China, and the shelves behind them were stacked to the ceiling with rolls of every imaginable colour and pattern. Those were the days before real silk was degraded with fibre threads as it almost always is now. Fifty-five years later Hugh was still wearing a cream-coloured silk suit made in Bombay at that time for use in the tropics and still in excellent condition.

Everybody was glad when the refit came to an end and they were able to sail for Karachi, for the summer climate had been extremely enervating, and although Bombay was wonderfully hospitable, it was wholly alien. While they were anchored out in the roadstead preparing to leave, and Hugh was officer of the watch on deck, a dishevelled and unshaven man came over the side from a bum-boat. There was something vaguely familiar about him, and as Hugh was questioning him he realised that he was wearing very dirty white trousers that looked like a uniform article. The man said he was Stoker Jones, which did ring a bell. The man had been absent without leave many times and was now a deserter and also of poor ability and worse character, and it had already been decided that he would be discharged from the Service.

The captain was informed immediately, and the master-at-arms, as is usual in any case of serious default, brought him up before the captain.

"What is the charge, Master-at-Arms? This man does not appear to be a Naval rating; he is not in uniform."

"He came on board in a bum-boat half an hour ago, Sir, and says his name is Stoker Jones. But that Stoker has been reported as a deserter to you, Sir, already, and the shore patrol have not been able to trace him."

"Do you recognise him as Stoker Jones, Master-at-Arms?" and the master-at-arms looked him up and down:

"No Sir, I can't say as I do. He don't look very clean. I never let one of our men pass me looking like that!"

"Officer of the Watch, do you recognise this man as Jones?"

"No Sir, I don't know what the Stoker Jones looks like."

"Well my man, we don't know who you are, and you will leave my ship at once. Master-at-Arms, see that he gets back into his bum-boat!"

"Yes, Sir."

And that ended the Naval career of Stoker Jones. Hugh was worried about this, fearing that he had been stranded, and later spoke to the master-at-arms on the matter.

"Lor bless yer Sir, not a bit of it! There are a dozen British ships in port, and he can get a berth on any one of them if he wants work and a faster passage home than we shall!"

As soon as they were at sea everybody felt better; the air was fresh and quickly blew the fuzziness out of the ship with every scuttle and ventilator open in the calm weather. It is only a two-day passage due north, but by the time they had come alongside at Karachi they were all shivering and the order was piped — "Hands shift into half-whites!" And everyone scurried below to put on his blue serge coat or jumper. Nevertheless it was delightful to feel cool air about one again.

Half a dozen officers, including Hugh, were due to go to the Army Staff College at Quetta to work on a Combined Operations Scheme, and they boarded the train that night for the two-day journey into the Himalaya Mountains. The first hours were spent crossing a dun-coloured arid plain dotted with scrub and furrowed by dry watercourses, but next morning they were in the lower foothills, still very dry, but with some scattered trees. As they climbed higher the train moved more slowly, and it got colder and colder. They piled on every garment they had brought with them, and hadn't nearly enough blankets for the night. The second morning they were in the Khyber Pass at daylight, a rocky, steep, and narrow gorge, and the one or two men they did see at wayside stations were six-footers, ragged, with large beaky noses and tall spiral turbans and a long rifle slung on the back and a pistol in every belt. They looked as if they were ready to shoot at the shortest notice, and the train guard said that on the downward journey a few days earlier the train had been peppered with rifle fire twice and everybody on board had been told to lie flat on the floor, which was very dusty and not over clean. He didn't know if it was a new tribal war breaking out, or just the usual brigands hoping to stop and loot the train.

The station at Quetta was crowded and a transport officer led them into a waiting-room where they were introduced to their hosts for the visit. The staff college quarters were full to overflowing with representatives from regiments all over India, and it had been arranged that the officers of the college would put up the small Naval contingent in their own bungalows. They were whirled away in horse-drawn gharries and given a few minutes to wash and change and then went on to a large reception given by the general in command at Quetta for all the visitors who had come for the course. Then back again to the bungalow to change for dinner at the staff college mess which was attended by about sixty officers in a wonderful variety of uniforms. The Naval contingent were very conspicuous in their white mess dress — and also cold, for it was freezing hard out of doors. Then on to a big dance given in a large hall at the other end of the town, and mercifully that ended at midnight. The last thing Hugh's host said as he was seeing him up to his bedroom was:

"Now which would you prefer, to go riding at six or to practise polo down at the club?"

He was called at half-past five and went off riding with his host and hostess at six. They got home an hour later, then bath and breakfast, and up to the Staff College to begin work on the Combined Operations Scheme at nine. They were free after lunch until half-past four, and worked again for three more hours. They went out to a dinner party at eight and got to bed about midnight. The week, crowded like this, passed in a flash. One afternoon a Royal Air Force pilot offered to take Hugh up in his Bristol fighter. Hugh had never flown before and was delighted. When he got into the machine he found that it was open to the four winds of heaven, and the pilot strapped him into his seat with a single belt round the waist — and up they went. They climbed in wide circles until they could see over the surrounding mountains, and — in the form of a very distant smudge of smoke — Kabul, the capital of Afghanistan, could be dimly identified. Then the pilot began half an hour of aerobatics. After two minutes, when he had caught his breath for a moment, Hugh said several prayers and closed his eyes, but it was no use, the blood rushed to his head and when he looked out the ground was above him. It was exciting and alarming and the wind roared and he scarcely heard anything the pilot was saying; but presently he found he really could, after all, still breathe, and that clutching onto the seat was useless; he scarcely touched it at all, but felt the strap taking all his weight. When they landed he was speechless for a few minutes, and saw the flight lieutenant looking rather searchingly at him, and he blurted out:

"It's all right, George. I think I'm still alive." He never could make up his mind whether fright or excitement dominated his feelings.

Towards the end of the week the Quetta Hounds held a Meet, and almost everybody on the scheme was excused work for that day. The country was endlessly strewn with outcrops of rock of all sizes, and was much divided by jumpable stone walls; but the real hazard was a "choraze", a stone pit of varying diameter up to thirty feet, and the worst ones apparently of about the same depth. They were unfenced and almost always masked by bushes and brambles so that the rider never did know what was in front of him. Some of them looked as if only a crane would be able to rescue a horse and its rider should they inadvertently jump in. Hugh, who was not at all a skilled rider, looked carefully at the iron hard ground and frozen ponds in all directions and told his host he would not go hunting.

"I am so glad! I felt I ought to offer to mount you, but I don't believe any of my horses can stand up to the ground today. They would come home lame, I'm sure."

However, his wife, looking reproachful, announced that she was going anyhow. She was thrown and broke a leg and retired to hospital. Hugh, instead of hunting, went off for a long ride alone, and was warned not to go up the valley beyond a certain point because the Afghan border was close at hand, and once it was crossed all the bandits felt free to ride you down and strip you. He went up the road some distance, and was about to turn back when a very large dishevelled beaky-nosed man on a scruffy little pony rode up to him all smiles, and said:

"I show you the way, Sir! You follow me up this way."

The path seemed to vanish into a narrow side valley, and Hugh quickly turned his horse and cantered off back the way he had come. That evening his host told him he was sure he had met a decoy and must have been very close to the frontier line.

Another day one of the officer's wives took him off to look at carpets. A Russian couple ran a small store and had some good ones, and at that moment a consignment of Baluchistan rugs had just come in. They were magnificent, very thick and close woven with the elephant foot pattern in dark red with a purplish sheen on them. He went back twice, undecided, but in the end did not buy anything because he had no home where they could be used — and regretted the decision for the rest of his life. He had long ago realised that his small pay left little margin for luxuries, and that he must buy nothing for which he had no immediate use, and he seldom broke this rule.

Each year when the summer monsoon made the climate of the Indian Peninsula unpleasant, the East Indies squadron cruised to the East African coast, their southern boundary being the frontier of Portuguese East Africa, and the northern limit, Aden. This involved crossing the equator at least twice and of course King Neptune came on board and a large part of the officers and ship's company were required to pay their respects at court after the traditional fashion. The canvas swimming-pool was rigged and the king, his queen and the court appeared on the fo'c'sle head suitably attired; the success of their appearance was Aphrodite in an enormous golden wig manufactured out of teased-out new rope and carefully dressed in dozens of curls. Hugh with the rest got his mouthful of soap and a ducking, but they were gentle with him while some others (who had probably offended the ship's company in some way) had a really severe initiation. The fun occupied almost the whole day, and in due course decorative certificates were handed out signed by King Neptune.

On their first cruise they were in company with the cruiser *Southampton*, flagship of the Commander-in-Chief of the Station, Vice Admiral Sir Lewis Bailey, who had his wife on board. They rigged up a canvas awning and a screened enclosure for Lady Bailey on the quarterdeck, and there she spent a good part of her time, for it was about the only place on board where a breeze could be felt.

The usual custom at sea when the men muster at 4 p.m. at evening quarters, is to execute some special drill or perhaps a manoeuvre. Divisions are fallen in on the upper deck and mustered, and the signal bridge has observed the admiral walking forward and climbing up onto his bridge. So has everybody else for that matter, for *Southampton* is only 2 cables (500 yards) away on the beam. Her signal deck, immediately abaft the bridge, is astir. A good telescope will discover flags being pulled out of their locker and bent onto the signal halyard. A moment later they flutter up to the fore yardarm and "tow aft" is the order. Divisions break ranks to race on to the quarterdeck with a grass floating hawser to the end of which is bent a lifebuoy or a barrel that can be picked up by the ship to be towed. Then a heavy hemp hawser follows, and a wire one which is wound round the stern capstan, or mooring bollards. When all is complete, a signal pennant indicating "evolution completed" is hoisted. The competition to be first is intense.

But have pity for poor Lady Bailey sitting at a little tea-table with perhaps a book in her hand! The canvas screens have vanished and she is almost buried in coils of rope and wire and someone can be seen helping her to climb out of the entanglement. The tea-table had, alas! capsized.

When someone spoke about this to the admiral his answer was:

"Well of course I chose that evolution because both ships would have expected that the one thing I was certain to do would be to leave my wife in peace. Anyhow she's got to learn that she is on board a warship and not in a P & O liner."

On this station the commander-in-chief held a unique position in the Service. His rank was "Excellency". He came next in precedence after the viceroy and the army commander-in-chief came after him. There was in Bombay a large and mouldering Admiralty House provided for his official residence, but its whole maintenance had to come out of his own pocket and in fact he never spent as long as two weeks in a year at Bombay, so that over the years the place had become more and more dilapidated. Hugh went there one day to call on Lady Bailey and she was wringing her hands over the sad condition of the old building. The gardens were an overgrown jungle and they were actually sleeping in a little outhouse in the garden because the main building was reeking with damp. At a later date the Admiralty sold the property, since successive admirals flatly refused to live there.

On the way westward, a first stop was the Chagos Archipelago. The main island, Diego Garcia, is a rim of coral (varying in width from a mile to a few hundred yards) surrounding an almost circular sheet of water in which is a good but shallow anchorage. The land is only a few feet above sea-level and is closely covered with coconut palms and jungle. A copra company leased the island and a Goanese manager lived in the only conventional dwelling, a small decayed wooden bungalow, at the head of a short rickety pier where sailing schooners from Colombo loaded the nuts. The population of about four hundred mixed Arabs and Indians living in palm leaf huts, worked the copra and grew just sufficient rice and vegetables to feed themselves; a flock of goats supplied their meat and milk, and a few ragged hens their eggs; and the lagoon teemed with fish.

This place, only a few degrees south of the equator, is the dream tropical island of any romantic traveller. *Colombo* arranged to make her approach at daylight, and there sure enough, in the early horizontal rays of the copper sun lay in the distant haze a smudge of grey, soon turning into a central darker patch with several outlying small islands, and within minutes the graceful form of palm trees could be distinguished leaning outwards over the sea at the edges. As the sun rose a little higher the pale colours solidified into green land encircled by a white line of breakers on the outer coral reef. A gap in the breakers showed up the entrance with a golden sandy shore extending away on either hand. As they passed through the gap the crash of the breakers died away to a murmur and they found themselves in calm blue water bordered by palms that seemed to droop with the intense humid heat. A little group of dark-skinned people in white loincloths stood watching near the pierhead where two men were launching a small rowing-boat into the water. No sound came from the shore; nothing moved; only the two boatmen seemed to be alive. When they came alongside the ship's gangway, the frail-looking little Goanese estate manager shuffled up the ladder and looked about him in a dazed sort of manner. He had never before seen a warship, though he had been on the atoll for fourteen years. No; they had no fresh provisions for sale; in fact they were always on short rations themselves, for neither their goats nor their chickens throve on the unsuitable food which was all that was available for them. Their water was brackish and it took some little while before one grew accustomed to it. Most of the children born on the islands died in infancy, probably from malnutrition, so they had to depend upon recruited labour from Ceylon, which the schooners brought in as it was needed. The breath-taking calm beauty of their surroundings was about the only redeeming feature of life on these islands, and no one lived very long in that hot humidity and with the unsatisfactory rations.

The ship's people landed close to the ship on a small beach and walked the short distance through the jungle to the outer shore, a superb coral sand steeply sloping beach extending right around this main island. The manager had warned that the outer shore was unsafe for swimming because of strong currents, and that the inner harbour was infested with sharks, so that walking was the only exercise the island provided. One would see tree crabs climbing up and down the palms in all directions, but they only ate the insects and never attacked the coconuts. On the sandy shore flocks of hermit-crabs engaged in a never-ending race with the incoming wavelets to catch the small hoppers and other minute critters upon which they fed, and there were quantities of their ornamental shells strewn above the high-water mark. At certain times of the year turtles came in to lay their eggs which the natives dug up and ate. No place Hugh ever visited produced a greater atmosphere of decay; it was beautiful in a gentle drowsy way, but somehow deadly. During World War II the archipelago was developed as an air staging port, and still later leased to the USA as an air force base, the inhabitants being removed to Mauritius which had a shadowy sort of claim to "own" the archipelago.

Then *Colombo* went on to Addu Atoll further to the west, the latest survey of which had been made seventy years earlier, and the small scale chart showed soundings inside the lagoon, but provided a little note that a strong cross-tide might make the entrance difficult. A boat was lowered to investigate and signalled back to the ship that a cross-current of seven knots was running. Soundings inside indicated a sufficient depth to accommodate the ship and there was a clean sandy bottom, and no coral heads were found. So *Colombo* pointed towards the harbour, and picking up a speed of sixteen knots, fairly shot through the two hundred yard wide entrance. She was not alone; as soon as the anchor was down a number of copper-coloured six-foot sharks closed in and began a continuous patrol around the ship. They could best be seen jockeying for position near the chute over the ship's side where garbage food was dumped after each meal. Several people tried their hand at shooting, but only once was a small shark hit. As soon as blood was seen streaming into the water, all the other sharks rushed in and the water fairly boiled as they quickly tore their wounded companion to shreds. Obviously there would be no chance of getting the coveted shark's skin, nor of landing a fish, for the bait on every hook that was cast into the water was quickly snapped up with the loss of the hook as well.

A boat went inshore and ascertained that all was well with the minute population who worked the copra. A schooner called most years to collect their harvest and nobody could remember any other steamship of any description having called at the atoll during their lifetime. The only animal native to the atoll was a small chameleon lizard, and one wondered how it got there in the first place. Addu must surely then have been among the most isolated of inhabited places on the earth. Its population at that time was about twenty souls. The ship's boats were kept busy surveying the anchorage during the three days of their visit. Today Addu is an active airline staging port.

Further west they came to Réunion and Mauritius, both originally colonised by the French, and still speaking that language, and too, still retaining a French style of education and society. Indian and African labourers had been brought in to work the sugar cane plantations, and intermarriage had united the two races to the apparent detriment of both, for physically they had become poor specimens indeed, and there had been no intellectual advancement. Réunion in particular seemed to be the home of a sickly, emaciated population, probably hopelessly inbred and inadequately nourished during the past two hundred years. The only person they found there not bound down by tropical lethargy was the young Irish Roman Catholic priest who was heroically trying to improve the condition of the people but, as he said:

"I don't think I'm making much impression on their way of life. Perhaps the prior necessity would be a different climate and a different diet, and after that an infusion of new blood."

It is interesting to compare the case of Réunion with that of Tristan da Cunha, a rather smaller island even more isolated out in the South Atlantic with probably only one twentieth of the population, but of British, not mixed Afro-Asian stock; and a temperate, not a subtropical climate. A young doctor whom Hugh met later on had spent three years on Tristan da Cunha and found that, although the original stock had numbered only about one hundred and twenty persons, the three or four hundred he had found there were in excellent physical condition and showed no sign of degeneration due to inbreeding. Their minds and intellectual standard were unimpaired. In later years the eruption of the volcano on the island compelled evacuation, and the islanders were brought to Britain where the young people nearly all decided to remain while the older generation almost all elected to return after the danger subsided. Inbreeding does not, apparently, lead to physical or mental deterioration in the case of Nordic people, and this speculation is supported in some measure by the experience of the Aran Islands off the Irish Atlantic coast where the garrison of about seventy soldiers placed there in the time of King Charles I was forgotten by London during the revolutionary period, and too, for long after. Then, when almost two hundred years later the islands were, in a manner of speaking, rediscovered, the population was found to be among the most robust in the world. There had, of course, been some occasional dilution of blood through intermarriage with people from the Irish coastal areas, though this has always been an infrequent occurrence right down until very recent times. Now tourists flock to Innishmore in summer.

On her second cruise to East Africa, *Colombo* was alone and the long lovely days on a glassy sea became tedious. The glare off the water actually caused some cases of sunstroke, and those on the bridge quickly learned to wear dark glasses.

One night at dinner in the wardroom, with the ship's side scuttles open for ventilation during the meal, a small flying fish about a foot long flew in and landed right on the table and became somebody's breakfast next morning. It had no doubt been attracted by the bright lights. Almost every morning, when hands turned to at six o'clock to scrub decks, half a dozen flying fish would be found on the upper deck. They also saw large fleets of Portuguese-men-of-war, a curious sort of mollusc that raises a white membrane a couple of inches above the surface of the sea to catch the breeze and sail away — presumably in search of new pastures. They are said to be a rarity, but in those waters they were numerous.

Presently a signal came indicating that a medium size cargo ship named *Trevassa* was sinking five hundred miles away to the south. Her cargo of iron ore had shifted in heavy weather and burst open some side plating in the hold. Then they learned that boats were being lowered — and after that, silence.

On the reasonable chance that one or more boats had indeed successfully got away from the plunging ship, the captain worked out that they would make for Réunion or Mauritius, which were the nearest landfalls, and so went off to take up a suitable line of search which was maintained for five days until fuel became so short that *Colombo* put in to the small port of Réunion to conserve what remained, so that she would be able to take whatever action might be needed should any further report be received. None came in, for it was a singularly empty ocean that any surviving lifeboat would have to traverse.

At a later stage survivor's reports became available, and this, roughly, is what Captain Foster of *Trevassa* told Hugh:

As the ship slowly sank, her lifeboats were provisioned and one after the other lowered into the raging sea. Some were smashed to pieces alongside the ship, but two of them, one under the chief officer and the other under Captain Foster, each carrying about eighteen men, managed to get safely away. Instructions had been given to make for Réunion or Mauritius and to keep within sight of each other. After only a few days they lost sight of one another during the dark hours. Captain Foster had his sextant so that he was able to calculate his latitude, but no chronometer, and was thus unable to measure his longitude. He did have a small chart so that he planned to sail north and, as far as the wind allowed, westward until he reached the latitude of the two islands and then make due west which the boat's little compass would help him to do. As empty days passed and provisions ran low some lascars attempted to seize the food box, but Foster managed to get hold of it and thereafter sat on it in the stern sheets. Water presently ran out, and some men drank their urine; several lascars drank sea water which killed them, so that their bodies were thrown overboard. A few more became insane and jumped overboard, but now of course the dwindling rations would hold out for just a little longer. Some providential rain showers occurred and they spread an awning to collect water and partly refilled the water cask. At last, after about three weeks, Réunion was sighted one evening. At daylight next day they were very close to the island and made for the harbour entrance which is somewhat blocked by an off-lying coral reef. Some fishermen putting out to sea at dawn spotted a strange-looking boat, and as it was steering straight for the reef where it was certain to be swamped, they rowed towards it, took it in tow and delivered it safely to the Eastern Telegraph Company's jetty, where several men had gathered in the expectation that it might be a boat from *Trevassa*. As soon as they had identified the boat they sent off a message to *Colombo* and to Mauritius to inform all shipping in the area. Mauritius sent out immediately whatever patrol craft they could muster, hoping to find the second boat. Meanwhile Captain Foster and the half dozen other survivors were brought on board *Colombo*, who immediately put to sea to search for the second lifeboat. Her fuel would only last for two more days, and then she was obliged to put into Port Louis on the north coast of Mauritius. The surviving *Trevassa* men on board were sent directly to the hospital. The very day they arrived, some fishermen on the lookout along the southern coast sighted an unfamiliar boat near the reef in a position they knew to be dangerous. They rowed out at full speed and guided the boat — which indeed was the one in the charge of *Trevassa*'s chief officer — safely through the reef. A little group of natives helped the very weak handful of survivors ashore and took them to their cottages, where they gave them brandy or other sorts of spirits in a effort to revive them, until ambulances, which had been called for, could arrive. Tragically that killed every one of them, the chief officer lasting the longest, and fortunately being able to give some account of his boat's experiences, which were much the same as his captain's.

This story received world-wide publication, and it stands as one of the most dramatic sea stories of all time. It is sad to recall that Captain Foster, who was well looked after by his company, lived on only for five or six years.

Mauritius from early days had a considerable French population — government officials, a military garrison, and a significant number of owners of sugar cane plantations. Most of the white children were sent to France or to Britain for the main part of their education, and were certainly the intellectual equal of their contemporaries in either of their mother lands.

Port Louis, the capital, and only harbour of Mauritius, has a polyglot population drawn from both Africa and India as well as Europe, and in the nineteen-twenties was out-of-bounds to visiting warships on account of endemic bubonic plague. The isolation hospital almost always had one or two cases, and the overcrowded steaming hot little town with its ancient dilapidated slums had never been seriously cleaned up. Probably it could only have been effectively treated by being burned to the ground and rebuilt on a new site — a project so expensive that no government could be found to contemplate it.

The ship was received with open arms and nowhere did Hugh ever experience greater friendliness and hospitality. Every day of their stay was filled with entertainment. The centre of the island — some forty miles long — is the elevated crater of an extinct volcano and Port Louis is isolated by the towering cliffs and black peaks of the surviving few miles of the crater rim. The volcanic soil is immensely rich and mostly given over to sugar cane, though there is other cultivation of food crops, and a good deal of virgin forest land still remains. Outlying coral reefs almost surround the island, and on the southern shore in particular, there are many very lovely palm or casuarina fringed coral sand beaches.

One expedition was to the reefs at low tide, where, safely shod with heavy soled boots and armed with a spear, one could catch a great variety of fish, crabs and even sea slugs, which were appreciated as a delicacy by the French. There were also some poisonous marine creatures to be found, so that local guidance was needful. Other fishing could be had in two or three small rivers yielding small trout and a freshwater miniature crayfish known as *camprement*, most delicious to eat. The botanic gardens keep a herd of giant tortoises over 200 years old, and some of the sailors were allowed to go for a short ride on their hard and slippery backs. One of the happiest aspects of these years of service abroad was the invariable effort made by British communities to provide entertainment for the ship's company, usually in the form of games, or perhaps races, of visits to places of local interest, and of course dances. Many invitations to private homes were always received by the crewmen.

On this island the great event of the season was, however, a deer hunt. There was a large number of deer in the wooded interior, needing to be culled each year in order to keep them healthy and within reasonable bounds, and the sportsmen of the island had formed a St. Hubert Club which controlled the herds. The clubhouse was a small well-equipped building out in the middle of the largest forest area, with a little wooden chapel built near at hand where mass was said before dawn by the chaplain of the club. About twenty huntsmen would arrive by car before four o'clock in the morning and, after mass, and coffee and sandwiches served at the clubhouse or from the assembled cars, the club official in charge of the hunt would allocate their stands to the guns, who were spaced out along thirty-foot wide *allées* cleared right through the forest in straight lines, each gun being about a hundred yards from the next one on either side of him. They were spaced so as to form an "L", the deer, when located, being driven by beaters into the point of intersection of the two arms of the "L". Pellet shot, not ball, was used. Some forty beaters, spread over a wide arc of the forest, set off at the call of a bugle which most of the guns would be able to hear, but in any case, as the beaters slowly approached, their shouting grew louder and louder as they moved forward beating the tree trunks with long staves.

Tension steadily rose as the shouting came still closer, and presently the breaking of some falling branch would be heard close at hand, but the bush was so thick that nothing could be seen.

Hugh was stationed one place from the end of one of the arms of the "L", and presently heard a rumbling sound as of many feet. Then the gun at his left — the end of the line — fired, but nothing could be seen, though there was a rustling sound in the bush. Very suddenly, in an open glade covered with low bushes which was exactly opposite where Hugh stood, a solid mass of antlers and heads suddenly appeared and a close-packed group of about thirty deer of all sizes charged out directly towards him from not more than twenty yards distance. He sprang towards the trunk of a small tree, and as he reached it the leaders rushed past him, their flanks or tails touching him as they ran. He would have been trodden to death had he jumped more slowly. They crossed the *allée* so quickly that he had not fully turned round before the last one vanished, and then the dust slowly settled on the trampled branches of the bushes. He was glad he had not had time to fire, for the stags were in the middle of the mob and he would never have succeeded in picking out an antlered head in such a confusion.

A whistle blew the signal for lunch and everyone unloaded and moved towards the clubhouse where a monumental buffet was spread out — hot soup, casseroles, cold meats, desserts, and a tall pillar of brandy-flavoured ice-cream studded with nuts and crystallised fruits. Aperitifs were handed to each guest as he arrived and several wines accompanied the feast, which was topped off with coffee and liqueurs. They learned that one of the ship's officers had shot a stag with a fine head, which was later taken down to the dockside strapped over the bonnet of a car, and then hoisted on board, much to the glee of the ship's butcher. As soon as the lunch was over they set off for new lines in the forest and a second drive was set on foot. Within a few minutes a very large stag with what turned out to be a record head stepped out directly between Hugh and his next neighbour, who fired and instantly killed the animal, Hugh reflecting that a miss would almost certainly have hit him. The day's bag was four deer only, which seemed minimal when so many had been put up, but the forest was thick and open spaces very small, so that only a fleeting chance was likely to be offered to the guns. They got back to their ship after dark, very weary but triumphant.

Tennis parties were arranged almost every day, and someone conjured up the idea of a hockey match between the ladies of Mauritius and the ship's officers who were to play left-handed. Two of the men were quite soon knocked senseless — but not seriously injured — and at half time, when the ladies had scored six goals to nil, it was decided that the men should play right-handed. They proceeded to score two goals and the ladies again surpassed them by adding a further three goals to their score. The tea-dance which had been arranged to follow the match was abandoned because both teams declared they had had more than sufficient exercise for that day. A concert, with turns by both local people and the sailors, and daily football matches were arranged for the ship's company, and they enjoyed their visit as much as their officers did.

On the occasion of a later visit the time had come round for the main race meeting of the season, which was always regarded as a gala benefit affair for the jockeys, and on this occasion it was to mark the final retirement of one of them who had spent almost all of his career on the island. The whole population seemed to have turned out, including the governor, and the leading families each occupied their boxes in the front row of the grandstand where a champagne lunch was served. The ladies strove to outdo one another in their toilettes. The course was not quite a mile in length and looked a bit rough in some places, but the rocky ground had prevented much improvement. Hugh was the guest of the Anderson family and was so often called away to visit other boxes that he had little time to look closely at the horses. In a programme of seven races none had more than an entry of six, and one or two started with but three runners. The retiring jockey was soon pointed out to him and he noticed that the man was quite old, and also that he was riding in every race — which looked as if that might prove to be a very severe test for an elderly person. However, he won six of the races and scratched the seventh, and it seemed as if all the riders held back their mounts to let the hero of the day through. Hugh, who thought that the age of this jockey was against him, of course lost all his bets, while those who were locally experienced won all of theirs. It was one of the more dubious race meetings among the many he attended all over the world, but he treasured its memory as one of the most entertaining.

Hugh became close friends with the Franco-Scottish Anderson family, bankers of Paris, who spent part of the year at their villa at Curepipe in the Highlands, and he was entertained both there and also at their lovely sugar cane estate, Bel Air, on the southern coast, where a summer cottage stood among feathery casuarinas at the very edge of a sandy beach from which it was safe to swim. This was one of the most beautiful places Hugh ever visited; the crystal clear water was a brilliant turquoise blue and the breakers thundering on the reef off shore glittered emerald green in the sunshine. Nature had been left untouched and the cottage was nearly invisible amongst the trees and shrubbery growth.

As in all the larger ports on the station the ship gave a dance before they left. Here at Port Louis, it was a large affair and very crowded and Hugh was in charge of the organisation. The captain gave a dinner party in his cabin beforehand to which the governor, Sir Hesketh Bell, was invited. During dinner his excellency suddenly noticed that the Star of his Order was missing from the breast of his tailcoat. The dinner party became a search party, but the Star was not found on board, and so the ADC was hastily sent back to Government House to search there. The governor's car had already gone home, and as soon as someone opened the door the Star tumbled out onto the ground and was rushed back to the *Colombo*. By that time guests had begun to arrive, and the captain was standing at the gangway to receive them. Hugh hurried in to the governor and helped him pin on his Order, and calm was restored, and he was able to step out onto the quarterdeck to be officially received with everyone standing at attention while the National Anthem was played, and only then could dancing be properly allowed to begin.

A small island, a thousand miles from anywhere out in the Indian Ocean was not only reminded but also reassured that it was a living part of the British sovereign's dominions, a concern of the homeland and entitled to its support; this was the inner meaning of such visits with their ceremonial, and it gave a deep satisfaction to the small and isolated European community, particularly to the French part of it.

The Director of Public Works, de Segrais, had been responsible as chief engineer for the conservation of water and had constructed five dams to hold water in different parts of the island. Hugh, who became a friend of the family, was conducted round the dams and saw the foundation of a new one in its very early stages when the clay core was being poured into the cutting that had been opened to hold it. He also visited a sugar mill that same day and watched the raw cane being brought in on a miniature railway line to be crushed, the sticky juice running into a holding tank to await the several refining processes, and finally the bagged sugar being loaded onto trucks to be conveyed to the Port Louis dockyard and loaded onto a freighter. Sugar during World War I had risen to astronomical prices and estate owners had become wealthy men. Cane is one of those satisfactory crops from which nothing is lost; the cane residue is ploughed back into the land as green manure, and the coarse final residue of the juice becomes molasses which is added to silage to provide cattle food.

Another group of islands they visited was the Seychelles, which was also previously a French possession. This colony, consisting of over sixty islands scattered across many miles of the Indian Ocean, may perhaps claim to be the most lovely of all the island groups in the world. Port Victoria, the only town, and in reality not more than a scattered village in those days, stands at the head of a deep bay on the largest of the islands. Here, once again, the little community extended a warm welcome to *Colombo*. It was extremely hot and humid and between noon and dusk scarcely anything stirred — except the flies. Everyone retired to their beds under a mosquito net from lunch onwards until four o'clock.

Hugh and another young officer were invited to stay at Government House where almost every day a lunch or dinner party was arranged to meet a few local official people. The governor, at that time Sir Joseph Byrne, who had been head of the Royal Irish Constabulary, and whose life would not have been safe for an hour in Ulster, was a warm friend of the Royal Navy, and had no doubt been sent to this distant outpost in order to ensure his safekeeping until Irish tempers should have time to cool.

The two teenage daughters of the family were full of energy and took their guests out riding at six o'clock each morning across the hills to the other side of the island, which seemed to be uninhabited, and they all went in to swim in a shallow bay where sharks were not found. The rocky terrain and lush tropical growth combined to make the cross-island pathway they followed a memorable experience of jungle exuberance and beauty.

This island group was very sparsely populated by a mixed Afro-Asian people, wizened, emaciated and diseased — amongst the poorest human specimens the ship ever encountered. Their livelihood was derived from fishing, and the waters abounded in sea creatures of every description, especially sharks. Only in a very few places was it safe to bathe. The most profitable harvest was tortoise-shell obtained from the huge tortoises that come ashore to lay their eggs. The government took all shell that was brought into the depot at Port Victoria and marketed it abroad on behalf of the fishermen, and its quality is nowhere surpassed. A few of these creatures are kept in Government House gardens, and as in Mauritius, some have lived in captivity for over two centuries. Hugh took a short ride on the back of one of the largest specimens.

As one drives up the avenue to Government House the roadway is bordered on either side by fifty-foot high coco-de-mer palm-trees, a variety found on this island and on one other in the group, and nowhere else in the world. The reproductive organs of this extraordinary tree appear somewhat embarrassingly to be almost identical with those of human beings, but on a gigantic scale, though the actual mating looks as if it would be difficult to achieve and is in fact, in natural circumstance, infrequent. Some sea legends derive from the curiously divided female nuts which have from time to time been washed up on distant shores.

The day *Colombo* left Port Victoria the fleet oiler came alongside to replenish her fuel. The Government House family came on board to lunch with the captain, after which 'his excellency' and his daughters were taken on a tour round the ship by their host. Lady Byrne, somewhat overcome by the heat of the steel-walled cabin, decided that she would prefer not to clamber about the ship, and Hugh, who was also a guest, was left behind to look after her. He took her out to sit on the quarterdeck right aft where whatever stir in the heavy atmosphere there might be would most surely be felt. Presently the oiler began to prepare to leave, having completed the refuelling of the cruiser. Hugh took Lady Byrne a few yards forward to watch the unscrewing of the oil hoses and their careful withdrawal back onto the oiler's deck, immediately after which the mooring wire hawsers were cast off. The after one got caught up and seemed to be jammed around a guard-rail stanchion and a lascar seaman gave it a couple of sharp jerks, and then suddenly it broke loose, snaked across the oiler's deck, caught the lascar across the back of his knees and flicked him over the side and into the sea immediately below where Lady Byrne and Hugh were standing. As the man hit the water, the black shiny head of a shark was seen as it seized him and carried him down out of sight. The whole thing lasted only two or three seconds, and the two horrified watchers looked at each other aghast and helpless.

"Did I really see that man taken?" exclaimed Lady Byrne. "Can nothing be done?"

"I'm afraid not. One bite of the shark must have finished him. In any case no diver who went after him would survive. By now other sharks will have closed in. There are always several patrolling round the ship," said Hugh. It was the only time he saw a man actually swallowed alive.

The onward passage to Mombasa, the chief port of Kenya, took the ship close round the northern end of the large island of Madagascar, where cross tides cause a considerable swell to run. On the East Indies station almost all who were able to do so chose to sleep on the upper deck both at sea and in harbour in order to get whatever cooling breeze there might be, for it was always very hot in the steamy damp atmosphere between decks, in spite of the ventilation fans kept running at full speed. Air conditioning had not yet been invented. Hugh found his cabin almost unendurable at night and always carried his mattress up on to the quarterdeck and laid it down well aft in order to get the full benefit of the stirring air there.

On this particular night, half an hour before the ship was to enter the rough waters off the northern point of Madagascar, the officer of the watch sent a messenger down from the bridge to waken all who were sleeping on the upper deck and warn them to move their beds. Hugh, with all the others, was called but fell back again almost immediately into deep sleep, and the next thing he knew was that his bed was whirling on top of a wave towards the wire guard-rails. A green sea had swept inboard, but by a miracle the mattress became entangled for a moment in the wire and gave him time to seize that with one hand while his legs and half his body were hanging over the side. The salt-soaked mattress could not properly be dried out, and a new one had to be obtained, but apart from this no other harm was suffered. This was the second time he was almost lost at sea, but the warning had struck home and he never again took such a risk, though he continued to sleep on deck as long as he was on the station.

East Africa provided, in those days, a wonderful experience. During their commission *Colombo* visited Zanzibar, Malindi, Lindi, Dar-es-Salaam, and Tanga, as well as Mombasa, and the officers were able to get away on big game shooting trips in both Kenya and Tanganyika, so that they managed to see a great deal of these enormous territories.

Mombasa is a large flourishing commercial port at the terminus of the railway which runs inland as far as Victoria Nyanza Lake, and it had a considerable European population at that time. As was the case with most of the ports they visited, *Colombo* was the first British warship the people had seen since the termination of World War I, and their welcome and their hospitality was all the warmer on that account. Football, hockey, cricket, squash, tennis, bathing, and dances were organised, and it was difficult to muster a respectable number of officers to appear at every event to which all were invited. One of the best evenings was a concert at which local people and the ship combined to put on a programme led by a lady who had been on the London revue stage at one time, and of course she inspired the amateurs to give of their best. She was a very spirited woman and at once the sailors took her to their hearts, and the evening was a riotous one. The enthusiasm was so marked that the company put on a matinee performance for local charities, and everybody hoped that the many children who attended would have missed a large part of the sailors' somewhat broad sense of humour. A pair of pink drawers was entangled in a part of the script, and when the ship sailed away a couple of weeks later, this brightly coloured garment was to be seen wildly waving from an upper storey window overlooking the harbour as they steamed out. A roar of cheering went up from the ship.

Hugh had been invited by the Boyce-Agetts, friends of his parents, to go on a big game hunting trip from their farm at Kijabe in the interior highlands of Kenya, and he duly took off in the train out of Mombasa one evening. The next morning sunrise woke him, but as his eyes opened they were filled with the fine red dust which was stirred up by the train and had seeped in and covered everything, as they sped across the vast arid Serengeti Plain. The water in the little sleeping car wash-basin looked as if cocoa dregs had been poured into it. When he did succeed in getting his eyes more or less washed out, the sight from the train window was wonderful indeed. To the south, away high above the clouds the volcanic cone of Mount Kilimanjaro floated glittering white nineteen thousand feet above the earth. Nearer at hand flat-topped green tamarisk thorn trees thickly dotted the sandy dry landscape and big herds, some numbering over a hundred, of striped zebra, then wildebeeste resembling the North American bison, and the bright fawn-coloured antelope kongoni galloped away in every direction as the train passed close to them. Smaller "buck", such as Thompson's gazelle and Grant's gazelle, bounded off into the lower bushes. An occasional spotted cheetah leaped across some open space as it fled at an incredible pace away from the noise of the train.

Hugh sat in his bunk transfixed by it all, and then presently saw something like a red-brown pole moving along the flat tree-tops. Finally a giraffe poked a head up to look at the passing disturbance and then Hugh was able to distinguish the fawn-coloured rectangular markings on its incredibly long neck. Once or twice the whole animal appeared in an open glade, and he appreciated what a very big beast it is. When it ran it took up a swaying motion exactly like a ship pitching in an ocean swell. Right up until the train approached the outskirts of Nairobi, the capital of the colony, big game of many varieties was almost continuously in view — but he never saw a lion in the wild in East Africa.

When they got out of the train his host, a retired naval officer, took him off to stay in the "chummery" in which he lodged. It was the custom throughout the East Indies station towns for several young batchelor business men to form a group of perhaps half a dozen, rent a large house and hire an English lady to run their "mess". Everybody gained; they lived in comfort in a fine house in a healthy situation, properly managed and which they could all afford, because they combined. In these hot tropical climates it is not at all easy to maintain good health. A lot of rules have to be followed carefully in order to maintain a sound physical condition, and the newcomers are always ignorant of the local limitations, especially with regard to food.

This Nairobi chummery was occupied by five members and their housekeeper, a widow, and the big house in which they lived was on the outskirts of the city, with a large garden and a wonderful view across the plain. It seemed to be a social centre, for endless friends dropped in and Hugh found himself quite unable to cope with the many invitations that poured in upon him. Lunch at the Nairobi Club, and a long session in the bar beforehand, had already been preceded by a visit to the wine shop of the locally famous Emile Jourdain where they were entertained with champagne. After lunch they arrived rather late for a tennis party and tea. Then a rush home to change and hurry off to Government House where tradition demanded that a visiting officer should "write his name in the governor's book" as soon as he arrived in town, and that was usually followed by an invitation to lunch or dinner. However, on this occasion His Excellency was away.

Hugh had been dropped off on the street from a friend's car and walked up the quite long avenue to the big house set in a small park. As he walked along he spotted a pair of cheetahs playing at some distance, and then, just as he was approaching the house, a lioness stalked past him thirty yards away. Then a small lion with a beautiful mane appeared and stood and stood gazing at him. That stopped him; he had no gun and could only stand still and look the lion straight in the eye — which is the heroic way one is told that alone masters the king of beasts. The lion didn't seem to care much about heroics, and started to move very slowly in the direction of Hugh, who reached the end of his fortitude at that moment and bolted faster than he had ever run before for the Government House front door, where the policeman on duty eyed him with cold suspicion and surprise. It was a minute or two before he got back enough breath to explain his unceremonious arrival. The man said nothing, merely pointing contemptuously to the large visitors' book lying open on a table in the porch.

But how on earth was he going to get away from the place again? He asked to see the ADC, for he suspected the native African policeman might not have understood a word of his story about the lions. After some delay the young army officer appeared, and when Hugh explained the hazards of approaching Government House, the young man roared with laughter:

"Oh, the lions! Of course you didn't know about them! We keep five in the gardens. They are very well fed and never attack anybody. They don't jump into cars, you know.''

"I didn't come in a car. I walked."

"Well, they've never attacked us, and some of us are always walking about in the grounds."

So he left and scurried down the drive, breaking into a run as soon as a curve in the road carried him out of sight of the front door. He didn't look about him for any more wildlife but just kept running till he reached the gate, where the military sentry stared at him in evident surprise.

That evening there was a dance at Muthaiga Country Club. They got there early and all went swimming in the large pool and then changed into mess dress before dinner, for the ball was an official entertainment given by the governor for the ship's officers. During dinner Hugh had fallen in with Lord Delamere, one of the leading men of the country. He proceeded to gather half a dozen people together and carried them off to another dance in a private house. This nearly led to a fight, for the elderly peer had been attracted by quite the prettiest woman in the room, who turned out to be the new dentist's wife at her first party. The husband came up and said that he must go with his wife, otherwise she could not go.

"Old D", as he was universally known, hadn't been thwarted, evidently, for many years past, and a heated dispute raged round the doorway. Finally when Lord Delamere's car drew up he seized the lady round the waist, swept her into his car and drove off at a great pace. The rest of the party piled into other cars, and the last they saw of the furious dentist was his clenched fist shaking in the air. They got home at three o'clock in the morning, and Hugh's host told him that a polo practice had been arranged at Muthaiga Club at six and a pony was placed at his disposal, but he was tired and had to face another packed day of social activities prior to taking an evening train onwards to Kijabe, and preferred to get some few hours of sleep. He joined the party for breakfast at Muthaiga, after which they played tennis until he had to go to a lunch party at the Nairobi club. After that several people piled into cars armed with cameras, and they drove out from the city to the plains to try to get photographs of lions which were likely to be found in certain locations. Though no lion appeared, Hugh saw a lot of different varieties of game, including a distant rhinoceros which was too far off to photograph.

The following day his next host met the train at the little wayside halt of Kijabe, which turned out to be a cluster of half a dozen grass huts and an open-fronted little store where a few canned goods and some locally grown fruits and vegetables were usually available. There he found the large and long green local bananas which were the best he ever ate, and they grew, it seemed, nowhere else. The Boyce-Agetts had a large farm, several thousand acres in extent, and their house, built of wood cut on the property, was perched on stilts high up on the mountainside with a tremendous sweep of country spread out below, bounded by the distant crater walls of the extinct volcano Sisera, and they could also see a part of the Great Rift Valley stretching away to the south.

The house had been built high above the ground in order to defend itself against the attack of termite ants, and was an open-plan airy structure surrounded by a broad shaded verandah, so that there was always some cool place to sit, even in midsummer. Much of the furniture was made on the property — the dining-room chairs seated with tanned antelope hide, tanned skins of several animals on the floor were used as rugs, and a large sofa was a splendid sight upholstered in striped zebra skin. The mounted heads of several varieties of antelope, a huge buffalo, and cheetahs and leopards decorated the walls, and a most realistically mounted lion head glared from one dark corner. The prize amongst these game trophies was a bongo head, the rarest antelope in Kenya, which had been shot on the property directly behind the house, where, oddly enough, a large herd of the very rare black and white colobus monkeys also lived. They went out in the evening to try to see these creatures, and a couple of colobus were spotted in the high trees, but no bongo appeared that day.

The next day was spent looking around the shamba and preparing for a shooting expedition. Camp cooking equipment, water cans, bedding, a shot-gun, a couple of rifles and appropriate ammunition, and suitable food were all loaded on to a high four-wheeled wagon by sunset. Breakfast was at six o'clock next morning, when Hugh learned to his dismay that his host was unable to accompany him because of some suddenly urgent business on the farm, and so he climbed up onto the seat of the wagon accompanied only by the driver and a trained "shikari" (hunting guide), neither of them speaking English. Four fairly frisky mules were impatiently stamping to be off and could scarcely be restrained by a man at their head. The driver handed him the reins, but when he tried to explain that he had never driven a four-in-hand in his life and needed instruction, it immediately became plain that the man didn't understand a word he said, and most certainly was not willing to take charge.

Boyce-Agett shouted at him: "You'll have to drive them yourself, that man will never be able to get them down this hillside!" The groom at the mules' head let them go and they sprang away at a smart gallop, and Hugh willy-nilly found himself trying to learn to drive. He hadn't held driving reins in his hands since he was a boy of ten. Ahead a gully, a dry watercourse, sloped steeply downhill roughly strewn with small stones and an occasional large boulder, and the mules seemed to think that this was the way. Hugh tried to get information from the driver, who was clutching at the iron side rail of the seat, obviously terrified, and prepared to jump for his life the moment impending destruction should overtake the wagon. The team couldn't be held while going downhill and to turn them at their present pace would certainly capsize the wagon — so on they galloped at breakneck speed. If there was a road somewhere, Hugh never saw it, and apart from a general description of the journey ahead, and the identification of several guiding landmarks in sight from the verandah where drinks were being served at sunset the previous evening, Hugh had no more than a sketchy idea of where he ought to be heading. He didn't worry about that just yet; there was little reason to expect that the lurching wagon could hold together for longer than the next few minutes.

However, natural forces turned out to favour survival. The mules presently began to get blown and reduced their speed, and at the same time the slope moderated and then gradually levelled off into a vast plain. On the right was thick forest with occasional outlying clumps of scrub and trees; everywhere else the plain dissolved into a soft sandy waste dotted with patches of trees and scrub at ever-widening intervals, and presently the wind-blown tracks of wheels began to emerge from time to time so that Hugh judged he was moving in the right direction. About this time the shikari, crawling out from amongst the stores in the back of the wagon, burst into a stream of Swahili, pointing excitedly towards the ground. He had spotted the fresh tracks of a lion, and kept repeating: "Simba, Simba!" which was one of the half dozen words Hugh recognised, and so he pulled up, handed his reins to the driver and got down and extracted his .405 Winchester repeater rifle from the back of the wagon, and led by the shikari, followed along the pad marks until they led off into the jungle, by which time he was wondering how he would deal with a lion at a couple of yards' distance; on balance it seemed that it would be the lion who would deal with him. The Boyce-Agetts had told him of a young daughter of the Williams family of the neighbouring shamba who, out for a walk alone one evening and carrying a single-barreled shot-gun loaded with only a No.9 cartridge with which she hoped to bag a pigeon or two, suddenly saw a lion a few yards ahead on the path. It reared at her and charged, and she fired at a couple of yards range. Its brains spattered on her feet as it fell almost touching them. They assured him that this was really the safest way to deal with any charging animal. You didn't even need to be a good shot; a cool head was all that was required. It was good advice, of course, but he wondered if in his total inexperience he would take it with the necessary speed should the situation arise.

The shikari suddenly released a voluble flood of words and plucked at Hugh's shirt tails, but he didn't want to turn round in case there should be something close ahead. At that moment the crash of some large animal and the sound of heavy galloping feet enveloped them and they saw bushes moving about twenty yards away — evidently a buffalo had been watching them, and he is the most dangerous beast of all in a thick jungle situation. So they turned round and went back to the wagon. It began to seem as if there was never a dull moment to be expected in Kenya.

The day passed, dry and very hot at noon, with game of many varieties appearing and then galloping away at least a couple of times in every hour. About sunset they sighted a large log barn close to a cluster of half a dozen mud and wattle beehive huts which was to be their camping place.

The driver and the shikari unhitched the mule team, watered them and then took them in under the barn where there was a pile of hay, and carefully closed the barred door. Then they carried Hugh's chop box, water cans and bedding up some steps into the barn which he found to be dusty, empty and stinking with putrescence, and very dimly-lit. No cooking was going to be necessary this first night, and so Hugh lit the kerosene lantern he had brought with him, and when he had hung it on a nail, turned to look about him and saw in a far corner the long white horns of an African ox. It was the whole head, from which came the stench, so he dragged it outside, where it fell down the steps and lay in the dust.

After he had swept out a corner, made a bed, and later supper, he lay down to sleep, but the stench was more penetrating than ever, so he went out and dragged the ox-head a few yards downwind from the corner of the barn, and now hoped to get some sleep. It was only a short while before he heard a puffing and snuffling sound outside, seemingly very close to his head — a leopard, he wondered? He got up and, for camouflage, put on a brilliant patterned purple silk dressing-gown he had purchased in the bazaar at Bombay, loaded his rifle and went out and sat down on the barn steps facing the ox-head. As soon as he was quietly settled the snuffling noise — now much louder — recommenced, and in the moonless darkness he thought he saw a movement where the ox-head lay as a vague shadow on the yellow sand. He fired; there were yells of alarm from the beehive huts, and then a scuffling noise from the direction of the ox-head. He had been blinded temporarily by the gun flash but fired a second shot in the same direction — and then went back to bed, for if the predator was dead it would be there in the morning, and if not, then you must never follow a wounded leopard in the dark. He slept like a log until sun-up.

Next morning, as soon as breakfast was over, he went out and followed the marks of the ox-head in the sand for half a mile and, when he found it, saw that it was stripped absolutely bare of meat and fur, and noted that there was dried blood on the ground, but whether from the head or from the animal that had dragged it there, was uncertain. It was a stony place and footmarks could not be clearly distinguished. He cast around for a while hoping to find a dead leopard or cheetah, but saw nothing at all.

The rest of the day was sheer frustration. The shikari led him off to an open area where there were patches of grass and detached clumps of bushes and trees surrounding several glittering black lava cones about three hundred feet high. Cheetahs were repeatedly seen racing across the plain apparently hunting antelopes. Several small families of gazelle of different species were surprised feeding in grassy patches. He shot a Thompson's gazelle buck for the pot since his little party must rely upon the gun for their supply of meat. Late in the afternoon, walking through an open wooded glade, a herd of giraffe suddenly appeared only fifty yards ahead; there were fourteen ranging from two enormous bulls which seemed to stretch their necks twenty feet high, right down to a gentle-eyed little calf obviously born within the last few hours. This one walked unsteadily directly towards Hugh — who had not yet been detected by the herd. When the mother saw him she swiftly interposed herself between Hugh and her baby and gently nudged it away in the opposite direction, while the two bulls turned and slowly walked towards him shaking their heads with a menacing gesture from their fantastically long necks. He quietly backed out of sight, not knowing how such an animal might behave in this unusual encounter. It was the picture of a lifetime, but he had no camera of any description.

That evening he decided to scale the steep cliffside of Sisera which towered above the camp on one side, and by means of gesture, sketching in the sand and his six words of Swahili, ordered the shikari to be ready to set out at 3 a.m., by which time the moon would be well up, and, as it was almost full, should give them sufficient light to cross the plain. The first light of dawn would appear as they began to scale the mountainside, which looked as if it would be very tough going indeed. All went according to plan, though Hugh had not realised how bitterly cold the air would be during the first hour; still, they warmed up as soon as they began their climb among the broken rocks on the hillside. The crest, or rather the crater rim of the extinct volcano, seemed to be almost three thousand feet above the level of the camp, and they reached it at about seven o'clock, almost an hour after sunrise. The top of this rim was a fifty-yard wide platform, never level at any part of it, and they lay panting and exhausted in the early sunshine as they ate their iron ration breakfast. There was a noticeable "height effect" in their breathing, for they were now at an elevation of probably 9,000 feet. The green floor of the crater lay far below them, patched by dark forest growth, and emitting clouds of steam in several places, and also from the silver thread of a hot water stream. Very large herds of game moved across open grassy spaces where they were grazing, but they were too far away to be certainly distinguished, even through binoculars. Hugh quickly made up his mind that it would be beyond his strength to go down to the floor of the volcano and then climb up again, and then finally descend to the camp all in one day, and because of the cold after sundown, a night out at that elevation would be out of the question. He wore only a pair of shorts and a khaki cotton shirt.

They spent more than an hour watching the distant game and examining the rather misty interior of the crater through binoculars. Then the shikari proposed walking along the narrow rim, which after about half an hour suddenly fell away in a one-hundred-foot vertical drop. Below this was an open sand-pit perhaps two hundred yards wide in which were some two hundred antelope of all the common species, some standing, some rolling in the sand to try and scrape off the ticks, and many young ones galloping round in little groups just playing games. They silently watched this enchanting sight till noon, by which time the sun had become so hot that they were forced to take shelter among the trees. They had spotted three varieties of gazelle, the kongoni antelope, zebra, wildebeeste, oryx, all in or around the sand-pit, then well beyond it a huge impala with its long corkscrew horns, the only one he ever saw.

After a little sandwich lunch it was time to start back for camp and so, with the greatest reluctance, they turned away downhill. Later they spotted a family of water-buck about half a mile below them, and, as Hugh had never before seen this variety, they climbed steadily towards the group and an hour later, coming round a bluff, spotted them on the far side of a water gully only a couple of hundred yards away. The shikari urged Hugh to get the large buck which he evidently thought to be a prize well worth having, but to get a closer shot was going to involve a long and hard climb that might take an hour, by which time the group could easily have moved elsewhere. At that moment they stood perfectly still, a big buck and a smaller one, two does and a calf, surveying the plain below and unaware of their enemies' presence. Hugh decided that his Winchester could do the job, though at that range the occasional quite violent and unpredictable blasts of wind might deflect even the best-aimed bullet during its flight. He waited some time until it seemed as if the air was still and no leaves stirred, and then fired, hitting the big buck in the shoulder, too low to be fatal. The water-buck family bounded downhill out of sight. A long and difficult climb amongst the heaped rocks eventually brought them again within range, this time only about eighty yards away, so that a second shot was effective and the large buck lay dead. The delighted shikari was beside himself. He quickly skinned the carcase, cut out the horns and divided the most edible parts so that they carried home as much meat as they were able to bear, reaching camp after sundown. It had been a tremendous day, and Hugh could scarcely keep awake to eat his supper.

The following morning he awoke very stiff and tired and made the idle driver boil water for a bath which had to be managed out of a bucket. Later the mules were hitched up and they drove on

o

and upwards to the southern end of Lake Nivasha, a very large sheet of water, their end of it being quite shallow far out so that thousands of pink-legged flamingo stood there feeding; and there were also waterfowl, white crested egrets, heron, and two giant species of crane standing six feet in height, together with a host of smaller birds, among them parrots. Probably no greater bird sanctuary existed in the world at that time. After an hour or two of bird-watching the shikari indicated that more meat for the camp would be welcome, and so they moved away out on to the wide open plain, where herds of hundreds of kongoni and zebra seemed to dominate. One kongoni took five shots from the heavy Winchester rifle to despatch, and while the shikari was cutting up the carcase and stowing meat in the wagon, Hugh decided to try for a zebra skin. He hit a suitable fine-looking specimen, but had to make a considerable detour to reach the animal, and when he did he found marks on the ground but no zebra anywhere to be seen. The shikari told him that a lion had surely taken it.

The next day they returned to Kijabe where they found that the game warden was staying overnight with the Boyce-Agetts. He examined Hugh's water-buck head and pronounced that it was a quarter of an inch below the world record, which was, of course, a very pleasing tail-piece to the finest hunting trip he would ever take.

Back on board *Colombo* at Mombasa a heavy monsoon had broken, but it was decided to go ahead with a big farewell party for the children, and more than fifty of these, accompanied by mothers and many black nannies, came off in cabin launches hired in the port to protect them from the rain. All sorts of ship's games were organised, including the ever-popular merry-go-round on the capstan. There was also a good smooth chute rigged from the boat deck down on to the quarterdeck, and of course an enormous tea in the wardroom and a smaller one in the captain's cabin. All went very well until after tea — and then the heavens really opened; they never saw such rain again. It slowed up the disembarkation of the hundred and more guests, and those mothers who were the last to leave entertained themselves while waiting, regardless of the weather, by sliding down the increasingly wet chute, and really were completely soaked through by the time they got into the boats. With a temperature of over eighty degrees no harm was likely to result, and the guests really enjoyed themselves. During the next twenty-four hours, twenty-three inches of rain fell. It seemed like the second flood. There was great anxiety about the ship's boats, which are drained only by one small hole, and they filled up to the gunwale until a carpenter went round and drilled several additional holes so that the water could escape more quickly and reduce the danger of bursting the planking apart. In the end none was seriously damaged.

Another port visited more than once was Tanga, the terminus of the railway into the interior of the colony of Tanganyika. It was a small place and an important communications link with the African interior. The town organised a *n'goma* in honour of the ship's visit, and every officer and man who was not on duty landed for the event, which was held on the large football field at the club. Various African groups — tribal, social, religious — had a trained team of dancers to represent them at celebrations of every kind. In most villages the whole population takes part from white-haired grandmothers down to little four-year-olds. They wander into the dancing group, join in for a while, and when tired, wander out again, and it is common for the dance to go on from evening until sunrise, and sometimes it does not cease for a couple of days because the dancers become self-mesmerised. The *n'goma* is a form of racial or tribal self-expression, sometimes an historical recitation, and all the figures and motions are the physical representation of a continuing story which could quite well be written down if the African had ever developed a literary art.

The costumes are endlessly varied. Very few tribes go completely naked, and a minimum primitive breech-clout of some sort, in the interior probably woven from palm fronds, is almost universal. To this is added decoration of every imaginable sort, including coloured feathers and dyed bands, with necklaces of animal teeth and inlays of bone and shells; and the body, or parts of it, are roughly daubed with colour. Flowers are not often seen; they would soon perish in the violent movements of the dance.

Some two hundred assorted dancers emerged from the surrounding forest with strident yells and a furious beating of drums, and then drummers and singers settled in a group on the ground close beneath a sloping bank where a few seats were provided for the principal white people, while the remainder of the spectators stood or sat on the bank. The performers drifted into circles, or groups or lines, their feet stamping out a complicated rhythm set by the drums. Occasionally the figures could be understood — clearly a hunt was afoot and a lion was killed, or scouts searched for a hidden enemy, or there would be a battle, a stirring charge, a triumphant victory procession, and so on. The climax of this particular *n'goma* came after dark with the whole body of dancers organising themselves in battle formation and making a charge directly towards the spectators, at whom they hurled their spears, which struck the ground at the very feet of the front row of the white men's chairs. It was extremely dramatic, and Hugh noticed that the several policemen on duty round the seats drew their revolvers, evidently to be prepared in case the excitement got out of hand — but it didn't, and the provincial commissioner provided a great supper later on for the dancers on another part of the grounds. The spectators had been almost overwhelmed by the fierce drama of the performance and drifted away in thoughtful and almost silent little groups. Once the drummers and dancers really get dug into their rhythmical trance out in some jungle clearing they will not stop until physical exhaustion, at the end of perhaps a day and a night, will at last bring them to a halt as they fall panting to the ground.

Lindi, a much smaller port, and a place of great tropical beauty, came later on their cruise. In earlier days when the little port was no more than a tribal village where half a dozen foreign bungalows had been built on the outskirts to house the government officials and representatives of trading companies, a pride of lions had moved into the area. These discovered that it was easy to seize a child or someone alone and unarmed, and they settled in the neighbourhood, killing not only some humans but also stray goats, dogs and cattle, so that a veritable reign of terror developed. The local administrative officer armed his police and established protective patrols, but the lions were quick to discover these enemies and seemed to watch for them and avoid them. One morning a message came in that an outlying farm had been attacked and a child and some animals taken, and the officer and some of his men set off immediately to investigate. Almost as soon as they had gone, three or four lions appeared at one end of the village street, and with a roar, rushed upon an African woman drawing water. Her screams reached nearby neighbours and they began beating an alarm drum which alerted all the village. Doors and windows were closed and shutters put up as the lions moved up and down and around every house in the place. Almost every gun had been taken out by the patrol earlier, and the two or three white men, who had been in conference out in the street, had to bolt for their lives into the nearest house, so that they could not get at their weapons. The morning slowly wore away in a state of intense anxiety, husbands, wives, children in many cases, being separated and unable to communicate. At last gun-fire burst out; the patrol had returned and caught the whole pride of four lions right out in the open and shot them all.

Malindi, further north, was visited for a couple of days, and a little mound of stones on a promontory still shows the mark set up in the seventeenth century by Portuguese navigators who penetrated this far north on the East African coast on their pioneer voyage to discover a route to China. Half a dozen bungalows had been built to catch the breeze on a little ridge close to a pleasant sandy bathing beach, and these were used as a sort of convalescent and holiday resort for government people living in unhealthy places in the interior. Later the area was considerably developed and a hotel was opened. One or two hunting expeditions were organised into the hinterland, but proved unproductive in the thick jungle where only a few narrow paths wound their serpentine way towards native villages.

While the ship was at Tanga, Hugh and another officer were invited to go shooting on a large company sisal estate, a twenty-four hour railway journey up-country. They boarded the train in the late afternoon and next morning were invited to get on the engine. The train stopped while they walked up the line carrying their guns, for the driver proved to be a keen shooting man. His train had at one time or another been charged by an elephant and also a large rhinoceros, which lost one of its horns in the encounter. Fortunately the cars were heavily loaded and were not derailed. On another occasion an elephant had run alongside the train trumpeting angrily, but they were able to put on more steam and got away from it without harm of any sort. Presently the two officers pulled out a seat cushion and sat out in front between the engine buffers with guns across their knees, for the engine driver told them they were entering an area where big game had often been sighted, and he was quite ready to stop the train if something worth shooting should appear. They perched there until evening, protected from burning their tails and legs by the cushion, for it was very hot in the bright sunshine and any metal object would burn a hand or leg severely. However, no wild animal showed itself on that day.

At two o'clock next morning they pulled into their destination which turned out to be a long concrete platform in the centre of which was a block of station offices and the station-master's house, all windows being fitted with heavy closed shutters. No light was to be seen, and apart from the hissing engine, dead silence reigned. The train guard went to the little house and banged on the door while the two travellers disembarked with their bags. Eventually a dishevelled little Greek came out into the bright moonlight, and immediately insisted on dragging the protesting passengers inside his door. He explained that there was "trouble, very bad trouble", and his Greek assistant had been killed the previous day by local tribesmen who were "on the warpath". He was shaking with terror and clung desperately to a rifle, his only defence.

At this point the distant noise of an approaching car made itself heard, and the English estate manager drew up in his truck. They piled in their luggage and climbed aboard. Yes, there was indeed trouble. The East Indians and the Greeks who provided the bulk of the sketchy services — mail, railway, shops — that existed in the interior had infuriated the native population over many past years of alleged financial extortion and oppression, and the situation had recently deteriorated into violent indiscriminate attacks upon all foreigners. This particular area around the railway station and its nearby village was one of the worst hotbeds of violence, and several murders had been perpetrated. However, the sisal estate compound was about a dozen miles distant, and so far had not experienced any trouble. All employees suspected of dissension had been quietly weeded out during recent months, and the company had increased the food ration so that it was hoped that the storm would presently pass by. Hugh was told to load his shot-gun and keep it on his knees with the safety-catch on, but not to fire unless told to do so by the manager. The drive out to the shamba was a bumpy but happily uneventful one.

As they drew up at the manager's house the first streak of dawn was appearing in the east. An enormous and really coal-black African servant in a long white cotton garment enveloping him down to his bare feet and wearing a red fez perched on the back of his close-cropped curly head, slowly opened the door after a coded knocking signal twice repeated, and then he again locked and barred the door behind them. All the windows had heavy wooden shutters upon them, which closed out the cool night air, and indoors it was stifling. Cups of cocoa served in tin mugs were passed around, and they were told that the servant, coming from a distant primitive village, could not understand the frailties of crockery, and in his first month had broken or damaged every single piece of either glass or china in the house, so that now they had nothing left but tinned kitchen articles and one or two native wooden calabashes.

The first day they accompanied the manager on his normal round of duties, which spread in wide variety over the 25,000 acre property, all of which was in cultivation. They drove out to a distant cotton plantation bordering on the edge of the forest and saw the considerable devastation wrought by a herd of elephants, who ate some of the tender leafage and apparently became very irritated by the cotton bolls and then rooted up the plants. Their shooting trip here was going to centre on an elephant hunt, to try to drive the herd away. Close to the African huts they saw the twelve-foot high "mealies garden" being harvested. The heads containing the seed were cut off and pounded by hand in a wooden or stone bowl and then cooked, forming the main staple food of the sixty estate employees. The green stalks and leaves — resembling maize — were fed to cattle, pigs and chickens; almost the whole of the process was performed by the women and children, while the menfolk worked among the sisal plants. These are huge bulky eight-foot high cactus-like plants, silver grey in colour, and the long spiky leaves are cut off with heavy sharp iron "machetes", and then placed in water, which softens the fabric so that their fibrous threads can be stripped off and eventually spun into rope in the neighbouring factory. Some cattle for both meat and milk, and a few riding horses, were also kept near the compound.

That evening they drove off to the headquarters of the manager of the nearest estate about thirty miles away, again a predominantly sisal operation. The man was a Swiss and had his wife and two small children living with him there. He also was anxious about the prevailing agitation amongst the native population, and his house was prepared at every point for any possible attack. They watched him while he collected the machetes from the sisal workers as they came in to the compound from the fields, and then he stowed them in a locked cellar under the house, turning to his guests and saying:

"They'll have to get me before they can get at the machetes! Once they run amok with those only a machine-gun would be of any use." Fortunately government attended to the various grievances so that no serious outbreak occurred at that time, though of course twenty-five years later the Mau Mau rebellion devastated much of East Africa.

The Swiss wife was a superb cook and the whole house was organised on modern European lines. It was a joy to be a guest there, and in striking contrast to the spartan rough domestic arrangements at the English company's house where no woman presided. This Swiss lady showed the visitors with great pride an enormous bed covering which she had made from twenty-two leopard skins her husband had shot during the several years of his service in East Africa. One of the leopards which he had only wounded with his first shot very nearly killed him. It was twilight when he fired, so that he could not pursue the wounded animal till next morning, when, for some reason, he did not take his dog with him. There was no difficulty about following the blood marks, and he fully expected to find a dead animal. Suddenly, without any warning whatever, the leopard sprang upon him from the side of a little jungle pathway. He saw that one hind leg was paralysed, but nevertheless the animal landed on his chest and tore him badly before he managed to seize it by the neck and choke it with his bleeding hands. The wounds, of course, were infected, but a doctor happened to be passing through the district and was able to save his life. He was fortunate, for doctors were very few and far between in those days.

The next day, accompanied by their host, the two officers set out on the projected elephant hunt, now urgently necessary they realised when they passed through several acres of newly-uprooted cotton plants and saw a considerable length of heavy wire fencing torn to pieces. They found an elephant path directly into the jungle, occasionally seeing the large round mark of a pad where the ground was soft. Two guns led the procession, another was placed in the centre, and a fourth at the tail, Hugh and the shikari being in front. In an open glade Hugh stopped to count the party, straggling out over two hundred yards behind him. They numbered fifty-two; he could hardly believe it. There were tents, cooks, a couple of personal servants, men with machetes to cut a pathway through the jungle, water carriers, boxes and baskets of food, and finally several young sons of the shikari out to learn the art of hunting elephant. All was peace and jungle beauty until sunset when a sudden rushing and snorting warned that a buffalo was about to charge. The shikari fired two or three wild shots in the direction of the noise, and several of the more timid domestic staff at the rear burst out with shouts of alarm and wailings, and, as they found later, some porters dropped their loads and fled for home and safety. About a dozen in all disappeared, and the hunters felt that they were well rid of them.

The night was anything but peaceful. No sooner were they bedded down under mosquito nets in their tents, than lions, at least three of them, probably scenting the meat they had brought, began an intermittent roaring from different directions. The native contingent, lying out on the ground around the camp-fire, let out piercing yells and the cooks stoked up the fire to a crackling blaze. The disturbance never really settled down until dawn broke, and nobody had much sleep. It seemed likely that any elephant in the area would have moved elsewhere.

However, by five o'clock they were off again on the trail and by noon seemed to be closing in upon the herd, for fresh droppings were seen and, as they stopped beside a little stream to examine these, Hugh suddenly let out a wild yell. Red ants had climbed up inside the jodhpurs he was wearing, and were biting fiercely. It was some minutes before he could tear off the tightly fitting trousers and sit down in the stream in order to dislodge the ants, and there was such merriment amongst those who had not been bitten. They all gathered together on a sandy island in the middle of the stream to eat their luncheon sandwiches in safety and refilled the water-bottles that each one carried slung over his shoulder. A council of war was held; it was obvious that the elephant herd was moving as fast as they were, feeding as is their habit on greenery as they marched. But a flat marshy area could be seen lying ahead and the herd might stop there to browse for the rest of the day.

And so they hurried on full of hope, but the speed did not last for long. As soon as they entered the marsh elephant grass up to eighteen feet in height blocked out all view and only when they fell into the four-foot-deep holes made by the elephant pads in the soft ground did they know for sure that they were still on the trail. On several occasions people got jammed down in some of the deepest holes, and had to be pulled up again to level ground. The advance was reduced to a snail's pace and in mid-afternoon the manager called a halt. He estimated that the elephants had already left the swampy area, which did not appear to contain any large pond in which they would have stopped to bathe. The chance of catching up with them was now a remote one, and the herd would probably be moving off at a fair speed to some other area where water was more plentiful. He decided that he ought to return to the plantation, and it was arranged that the two officers and the shikari with only three porters would move up on to higher ground and circle back to the farm along a low range of hills for about two days, hoping to find other game there before their small food stocks ran out.

And so they parted company and moved off in different directions. Half an hour later Hugh stumbled upon a steaming elephant dropping, but the ground was now hard stony uphill going and pad marks could not be distinguished. They made for a high point, still hoping to sight the herd from there before dusk, but when they reached it nothing was in sight, and so they camped in the open for the night, getting very cold once the sun had gone down. During the night the three porters ran away, and now they were alone with the shikari, so that they had to carry their rations as well as guns and ammunition and were glad that they had brought no other equipment. They toiled on along the hillside for two days, sighting a distant buck once or twice, and Hugh managed to shoot a dik-dik, the very smallest of all the antelope family, and they were indeed glad of the meat, for food was almost exhausted. It was interesting to note that two inexperienced Europeans wholly unaccustomed either to the heat or to the hard physical exercise were able to outwalk and outlast the many Africans who started on this five-day trek, but they were dead tired when they did finally get back to the shamba. Even the shikari himself had to be helped along the last two miles of the journey.

This did not exhaust East Africa, for they visited the coast again the next year and took in Dar-es-Salaam. From this port and rail terminus two or three different hunting expeditions set out. Hugh and two other officers went by train, a night's journey into the interior — about 160 kilometers — and were met at a wayside halt by a planter in the district, and set off at once to establish a camp about twenty miles "out in the blue" where a wide variety of game could be found. The ground was rolling sand with occasional woods, a distant lake, one or two streams, and scattered shrubs and groups of trees in all directions. Each day a shikari was appointed to guide a single officer to a particular area well clear of all the others.

Next day they all set off in different directions as soon as the sun was up, and of course all had different stories to tell when they got back to camp at dusk. The first thing Hugh saw was a family of wart-hogs trotting along in Indian file a couple of hundred yards distant and too far away for a shot, so he moved off in a direction that would intercept them, for the large boar had a magnificent pair of ivory tusks curved like a scimitar. Just as he started to move, the shikari behind him plucked at his shirt tail, hissing in a loud whisper:

"Simba, simba, Bwana! Simba, simba!" That meant lion, but Hugh's mind was on the wart-hogs, just passing out of sight, and he impatiently turned on the man and jabbed a pointing finger in their direction, indicating that he intended going after that great pair of tusks. The shikari hopped up and down agitatedly repeating "Simba, simba!" several times, but Hugh was already running as fast as he could from one bit of cover to the next in order to keep out of sight of the wart-hog family. Five minutes later he saw their erect tails waving through thick undergrowth so that no shot was possible, and as it was noon and now very hot, he dropped to the ground and ate his luncheon sandwiches under the reproachful gaze of the shikari.

When they got into camp in the evening the planter questioned each shikari carefully as to what his charge had done during the day. The best story that evening was that of the officer who sighted a rhinoceros which trotted towards him evidently to investigate, and as at that moment he had only a shot-gun in his hand expecting to shoot a guinea-fowl that had just flown up into the tree, he darted behind a tall anthill and called to the shikari to let him have his rifle, but then the rhinoceros chased him round and round the anthill and only moved off when another one, probably his wife, suddenly appeared out of the bushes and snorted. By the time the officer had at last got his rifle the two rhinoceroses had disappeared into the jungle and were not seen again.

When the turn came for Hugh's shikari to make his report Hugh watched him talking volubly, and then the planter swung round towards him:

"Why on earth didn't you take that lion? You'll never get a better shot than that was!"

Hugh said that there hadn't been any lion. The shikari made further explanation and it finally transpired that at the very moment Hugh had sighted the wart-hogs, the shikari had spotted a sleepy lion lying in the shelter of some bushes five yards away from the game track they had been following. He had done his best to alert Hugh — but the language difficulty could not be overcome in the heat of the moment, and Hugh never saw this lion of his life.

It was superb hunting district in which they were camping. On a subsequent day Hugh came across a large lake about a mile long with reeds extending far out from its edges. There was a tremendous variety of bird life to be seen, white egrets, enormous cranes standing six foot high, flamingo, parrots, guinea-fowl and hundreds of duck. After watching for some while Hugh fired a shot to put up the duck. They circled round and round the lake but always out of range of the spit of sand which extended far out into the lake and upon which he stood. He appreciated that he was far too conspicuous and so walked along the lake shore for some distance and then waded out to the edge of the reed growth and from there began to fire away at the duck as they passed overhead, bringing down about a dozen in all. That would be enough to feed the whole camp, so he stopped and looked about him to pick up the fallen birds. As he did so he could only count three, and was wading up to the armpits towards the nearest one when he saw it suddenly vanish in the midst of a swirl of water; then another one disappeared in exactly the same way, and it dawned upon him that there were crocodiles about, and he was two hundred yards from the shore. He turned and waded as fast as he could towards the nearest dry land — but he was not alone, for a lump of floating wood nearby, which he vaguely noticed, suddenly became the head of a hippopotamus, and the enormous bulk of the animal slowly emerged as it made its hurried retreat to the shore and the jungle beyond. All that he really saw was a large black blob and a stumpy little tail furiously wagging in the middle of it. On the way back to camp he shot a small buck from a little group of Grant's gazelle, for it was his turn today to supply meat for the camp.

At this port the commissioner asked the captain to transport the dangerously ill wife of one of the officials to the hospital at Zanzibar, but regulations forbid a woman sleeping on board. However, the lady was brought to the ship only an hour before she sailed, and the signal requesting the commander-in-chief's permission was not transmitted until she was under way. It had to be referred to the Admiralty, and when at last a sort of qualified permission was received, she was half-way to Zanzibar anyhow.

On their last cruise to East Africa they visited Zanzibar, chiefly to be present for the celebration of the end of the Mohammedan feast of Ramadan. In spring the faithful fast for a month and at the appointed end, as the moon rises above the horizon, a cannon is fired and the whole town bursts out in shouts of joy and fireworks explode in every direction. Drinking, singing and dancing go on all night long, and night leave to the ship's company was stopped on this day because of the risk of some sort of a drunken brawl — though Moslems are not supposed to take intoxicating liquor, nevertheless a lot of drunks were staggering about the poorer streets of the town. On the morrow the ship fired a salute in honour of the feast and the sultan held a reception at his palace on the waterfront in the middle of the town. All available officers attended, wearing full dress uniform, and there were two hundred guests gathered in a large salon on the first floor facing out over the roadstead. High tight collars added to the discomfort of the midday heat and one or two white uniforms showed signs of stress as drinks and trays of little sweet cakes were handed round by a regiment of white uniformed servants wearing turbans, for the sultan is an Arabian prince and wears the flowing robes of an Arab sheik. Presently he appeared on a dais at one end of the room, a small neat man who, when one got close up, showed evident signs in his face of a heavy night out. He made a short speech of welcome, which the British High Commissioner translated, and then the company lined up and passed before 'his highness', making a slight bow as they reached him. It was a relief to get back on board and take off the full dress uniform.

That afternoon a garden party was held at the club and the sultan attended for a short while. Hugh was swept off into a croquet game, partnering a beautiful young lady, and when they tossed for colours he and his partner got the red ball. As the game progressed they drew ahead of their opponents, and Hugh noticed that people were crowding round the croquet lawn where, at the end of the game, which they won, almost every person present in the club, including the servants, were craning their necks to catch a glimpse of the final shots. At the final stroke an enormous cheer went up, but when Hugh turned to congratulate his partner he found her dissolved in tears burying her face in a handkerchief. He couldn't imagine what had gone wrong. The High Commissioner came out and presented the prizes, and as they left the field Hugh asked the commissioner quietly why on earth his partner was weeping. He roared with laughter and explained:

"We have an old tradition here that whoever first wins with the red ball after Ramadan will be certain to produce a baby nine months later! You'd be surprised at how often this has actually happened, so you'd better be careful!"

He never heard whether or not the tradition was fulfilled that year.

While they were there a clove planter — Zanzibar produced almost the whole crop of cloves for the world at that time — with whom Hugh was spending the day, received a telegram announcing that he had won the Calcutta Sweep on the Derby worth about sixty thousand pounds, and so yet another celebration was in order. After lunch they walked through the scraggy-looking clove tree plantation — they were untidy, gawky fifteen-foot high shrubs — and then drove off to the south end of the island where a cliff bordering on the sea-shore has been eroded, and there one could pick up Persian coloured glass beads six thousand years old that kept falling from the remains of an ancient city long buried beneath the tropical growth. Little glass flasks and other statuettes and other interesting objects were constantly being discovered, but these were claimed by the museum. The island had for long ages been an Arab trading settlement, and even still, in the early 1920s, an Arab prince, the Liwali bin Salim, who lived in Mombasa, was a powerful personage along the coastline for five hundred miles, and controlled the dhow traffic with the Persian Gulf, and in fact had more power than the Sultan of Zanzibar possessed. Since the abolition of slavery — and Zanzibar was the principal port for the export of captured African slaves to Arabia — the wealth. of the Arab traders had steadily declined and was no longer of great importance.

While at Zanzibar, Hugh used the excellent weather conditions to take out classes of young ordinary seamen for sailing instruction in the ship's 27-foot whalers. This boat carries a crew of five and a leading seaman as coxswain, and the warm sunny weather and pleasant light winds made this a very enjoyable morning for all concerned. Several sharks were sighted, and one morning when a flat calm had suddenly overtaken the boat and it was stationary, Hugh went forward to deal with some small matter and leaned over the side for a moment and saw lying on the clear sandy bottom an immense shark with an apparently square nose, from which projected a large fin on either side. Its tail stuck out a little beyond the boat's stern, for it was indeed a real monster of its species. The sight created a distinctly queasy feeling, and Hugh ordered "out oars" and they returned to the ship, for it was approaching the dinner hour anyway.

Later they took a senior commissioner northward to Jubaland, which Britain was to cede to Italy — one of the later adjustments made to the provisions of the Treaty of Versailles at the end of World War I. This same desert territory on the equator had a predominantly Somali population and there was strong native opposition to the intended transfer of sovereignty, and the mission of the cruiser was to overawe the local representatives, and if that did not work, then to protect the life of the commissioner. The local council was assembled in the port, and the commissioner was landed with some ceremony and a small escort of armed seamen. The preliminary conference which ensued was a stormy one, and when he got back on board in the evening the commissioner felt that rebellion was likely to break out. The two or three local British officials were brought off to live in the ship for the time being while negotiations proceeded and a stream of telegrams passed to and fro between Nairobi and London and the commissioner in the *Colombo*. The debating stage lasted through about ten days during which it was, of course, not safe to land the crew on shore leave; nor indeed was there anything for them to do beyond one football game with the local police, the effect of which was to improve relations between the negotiating parties to a marked degree. Each afternoon a large party rowed away in ship's boats to cast a seine net and drag the catch onto a distant isolated sandy beach. At every cast sting-rays formed the larger part of the catch, and these dangerously poisonous flat-fish were a serious menace, so that those handling the net in the shallow verge of the water wore sea-boots for protection. Nobody actually got stung, probably because the young ship's doctor always accompanied the party and the men regarded him very highly and listened to what he told them.

A fancy dress dance was organised on board one night, chiefly in honour of the two wives who were temporarily accommodated on board, and one of the male guests proved to be a real inspiration. Bluebeard and his "wives" appeared in one group and a dramatic beheading occurred just — but only just — off-stage; and there were other similar groups, the South Seas hula dancers being very popular, though certainly their performances would not have been licensed on the London stage. But the prize went to Adam and Eve, a muscular stoker and a young and handsome seaman, both of them appropriately dressed in fig leaves, who between them swept the two ladies quite off their feet for much of the evening. Their husbands looked really anxious. It was all an enormous success, and served to break the monotony of waiting about in idleness. Some of the costumes were wonderful to behold, especially when one considers the inadequate resources of a warship lying off a desert coast.

Meanwhile the local authorities presently considered it safe for a small hunting expedition to go out into the hinterland, and so Hugh and another officer set off with two local shikaris towards the Juba River. The whole land was loose dry sand into which the feet sank at every step so that movement was slow and the first day they followed a vague track for twenty miles that led to the river where they were to camp because the water would attract whatever game existed in the area. Nothing beyond an occasional bird was seen that day, though while they were in the process of setting up camp on the river bank a small covey of desert partridge flew in and they shot a couple of brace which were a welcome addition to the menu, as they had been able to carry only a small load of food on their long and very hot march.

Each of the three days they were there Hugh and his friend took a shikari and went off in opposite directions so that game would not be unduly disturbed. Hugh found himself in a large open plain with hardly any cover beyond a few knee-high shrubs and the occasional undulations in the ground. A group of oryx was sighted about two miles away walking along as they browsed upon the shrubbery. A very long stalk — over two hours — brought him at least within a possible range of two hundred yards, and the oryx must have seen the gun flash, for they turned and fled at great speed probably before a bullet reached them. At all events there was no sign of a hit. A still longer stalk in the afternoon brought him no nearer the herd, for they moved continuously as they grazed. He had been walking since before dawn and was now tiring, and so returned to camp. That evening the nearby village was holding an *n'goma* to celebrate some tribal anniversary. The shikari told the two officers that they were invited to the entertainment as honoured guests, and so of course they had to attend. It was dusk when they arrived and the whole company had already been dancing for many hours. When someone tired, he (or she) stepped out of the gyrating stamping circle of perspiring bodies, tore off a piece a meat, or perhaps a bone from the roasting carcase of some unidentified animal spitted above the wood fire, and swigged long draughts out of a calabash dipped into a dark pot. As soon as they arrived the headman greeted them and offered both meat and drink to them, and then sank with a sigh down on the ground and passed into a peaceful sleep. The meat was very good, but the drink was fire-water and they spilt most of it on the ground unnoticed. One after another the villagers sank exhausted to the ground; small children strapped to their mothers' backs or chests were already dead asleep. But the circle of dancers was replenished from time to time by people who had awakened, and it never seemed to grow any smaller. After a couple of hours the officers slipped away, for they, too, were very tired. Next day Hugh's friend found himself very footsore and decided to return by the shortest route to the ship at once. Hugh, after consultation with the shikari, decided to return by a longer route through a shallow valley where game might by found. In the event he walked almost up to the ankles in soft hot sand for thirteen hours and saw no living thing beyond a few squawking crows.

They left Jubaland to the Italians without regret, for in it they had seen nothing beyond an empty torrid desert, and were glad to sail back to Ceylon.

Towards the end of this two and a half year commission on the station, Hugh found himself occasionally invited to dine and dance at Government House in Colombo, and a particular pleasure was the approach in a ricksha after dark when one passed beneath an avenue of trees producing a strongly scented white blossom shaped like a ball the size of a large orange. It seemed to be entirely composed of fine hair-like stamens and opened only after dark, and fell to the ground at dawn. He never saw it elsewhere. Many of the residential roads were planted with the heliotrope flowered Judas tree, others with the flame-coloured "orchid-blossom" tree, all of which came into flower early in the new year and continued spasmodically and with diminishing florescence for several months.

As a final effort — and to offer thanks for endless hospitality in Ceylon — the *Colombo* gave a ball for fifteen hundred guests at the largest hotel in town. The governor, the Kandyian chiefs (the remains of the ancient Ceylonese royal families), the foreign

P

consular body, the principal business people, the small army group and the chief government officials, and of course all the personal friends the officers had made, were invited — and yet some had to be left out of the list that night. Hugh had a large part in the organisation, including the decoration of the very big galleried ballroom which was done with red and white flags and lights, and green potted plants. The effect was brilliant. Other side rooms were embellished with flowers and plants, but a long and mouldering corridor leading to the usual cloakrooms seemed to present an intractable problem. It was such a let-down from the brilliance of the rest of the setting. At the last moment Hugh decided to line the whole thing with foreign ensigns which were large enough to hide all its ugliness, and the very last flag to be hung was a green one draped over the ladies' toilet doorway.

Shortly after dancing commenced Hugh was buttonholed by a very large perspiring portly olive-coloured young man who was spluttering with rage. It appeared that every country was honoured that evening:

"Except my country, dear Lebanon, Sir! I wish to make my formal protest, and indeed complaint, for I am the Temporary Acting Vice-Consul of my country, and I expect an official apology to be made for this insulting omission!"

Hugh, who had been dining at Government House beforehand and was due to partner Lady Manning for the next dance, had to think quickly.

"Do I rightly remember that your flag is green with, let me see, yellow, yes, a yellow device?"

"Indeed it is Sir!"

"Well then, would you please come with me. I believe we have not forgotten Lebanon," and he hustled the young man down the long flag-lined corridor.

"There, Sir, is your flag, accorded the special honour of guarding the privacy of the ladies!"

The first bars of the next dance could be heard in the distance as a seraphic smile spread over the moist countenance of the Temporary Acting Vice-Consul of Lebanon, but Hugh waited for no more and fled to the red-carpeted dais where the governor and the principal Kandyian chief were chatting, and her excellency, sitting in a gilt chair, was tapping her foot. As soon as they got onto the floor he told Lady Manning why he had been unpunctual and the little story quite made her evening.

He felt that nothing in England would compare with life on the East Indies station, and he had no home to go to. Only his mother and a young schoolgirl sister were in England, and they were moving from pillar to post as school holidays came round. During the last six weeks spent in Colombo harbour, Hugh's diary reveals that he attended forty-six dances, on some occasions two in one night, and once even three. He managed this by exchanging watches with other watchkeeping officers who were less keen than he was, sometimes coming back on board from a dance at midnight and then keeping the middle watch, going ashore again at four o'clock in the morning to continue the party. They did get tired, of course, but a swim in the sea usually put that to rights.

At last the old coal-burning cruiser *Weymouth*, on her way trooping home from Hong Kong, picked up *Colombo*'s party of about three hundred and delivered them at Portsmouth late in October 1924. It was an uneventful trip, but the gritty coal soot from the three funnels quickly piled up aft to a depth of a couple of inches, and the upper deck had to be swept several times a day. Even so, the grit was tramped down to the decks below, and nobody could continue to keep clean.

On passage through the Mediterranean, it being the season of the year when the quail fly across from Southern Europe to North Africa, all the ship's seine nets were rigged between the masts and the funnels, and arc lights placed to shine on them, so that flocks might be attracted and dazzled and trapped in the netting and fall to the deck. Sometimes huge quantities of these little game birds had been harvested — sufficient to give a whole ship's company a meal of fresh meat. But this time they were out of luck, for only four birds were caught, and these were cooked for the captain's table, where Hugh happened to be a guest that night, and tasted this delicacy for the first time in his life. It was a modest tailpiece to a wonderful commission.

Chapter 9

In the Doldrums at Home

Hugh, up till now, had held a succession of exceptionally interesting appointments, but the Admiralty policy had for long been to give officers alternative periods of service at home, and then abroad, and he was overdue for home service, where, on the whole, he found that life moved at a pedestrian pace.

He had applied some time ago to train as an interpreter in French, hoping that this might lead to activities of more than ordinary interest. So it was that, after a period of foreign service leave to which he was entitled, he found himself on board the cross-channel ferry from Dover to Calais which was making its passage in storm force winds. He went down to the saloon with the intention of getting a meal, but what actually happened was that he was flung off the staircase through the air and grabbed hold of a pillar stanchion to which Mr Neville Chamberlain, the future prime minister, was clinging. They disentangled themselves with mutual apologies, but neither food nor drinks could be served, and the battered passengers on board were thankful to reach the calm shelter of Calais harbour only a few minutes behind the programme schedule.

The train journey to Paris across the frost-bitten flat countryside provided views of occasional fortified farmsteads with defensive towers at the corners of their yard walls; some houses having strong stone walls and castellated embattlements. There were also occasional later pink brick villas beautifully sited among tree plantations and ornamental lakes — altogether an interesting scene in spite of the dead flatness of the land.

Arriving in Paris, he was interviewed by the Naval Attaché, Captain Holland, in his office at the British Embassy in Rue St. Honoré and spent a couple of nights at a small nearby hotel while making arrangements to live at Tours with the family of a young

213

French professor. The "Institut Français pour les Etrangers" where he enrolled for instruction was a sort of extra-mural university college which gave it a certain status in the eyes of foreigners. Half the students were American and the remainder drawn from a dozen different countries, but only three from England. The professor's wife and two young children did their very utmost to help him talk French, and the professor administered grammar in the evenings. The formal class work was, however, less helpful, for a large part of that consisted of erudite lectures on French literature — of which Hugh was almost entirely ignorant, and then, too, on philosophy, chiefly that of Descartes who, even at his best, is but second-rate. The instructors, young professors, were evidently enthusiastic about their subjects, but spoke in a manner far too rapid and too technical for the completely ignorant students, amongst whom Hugh was probably the least competent. He learned very little at Tours perhaps because his out-of-school hours were spent usually in the company of English or Americans.

One Sunday the professor walked him the four miles down the banks of the Loire to Vouvray where they spent the afternoon sampling the lovely, but somewhat heavy, local gold-coloured wine sold under the village name. They were able to walk soberly enough home again in the evening; but they passed occasional sleeping casualties of Vouvray tippling along the pathway.

Hugh attended high mass at the cathedral in Tours, in order to exercise his ears to French speech, and on one occasion there was a liturgical reception of the Cardinal-Archbishop of the Province where the full ceremonial magnificence of the Roman Catholic Church was displayed. The several processions of dignitaries took nearly twenty minutes to reach their seats while a magnificent choir chanted. This basilica, dedicated to St. Mark, shows traces of Roman brickwork in the lower parts of some of its walls and exhibits a wide variety of architectural styles prevailing during the long centuries through which construction and alterations proceeded, and it is indeed one of the most architecturally interesting buildings in Europe.

After a couple of months, Hugh decided that progress was too slow and that what he needed was a concentrated "crash course" if he was to pass his examination, and so moved to Paris to live with a French family living close to the famous Madame Calléde, teacher of British Service interpreters over the past forty years. She was well into her sixties when Hugh arrived and immediately assumed the position of a sergeant-major, brooking no interference from outside interests, no slackness in personal effort, and least of all accepting any condition other than perfection. She firmly drove the French language into the heads, and probably usually into the hearts, of her pupils. She had no hesitation whatever in casting out whoever failed to make the full effort of which she considered a pupil was capable. She made it quite clear at the first encounter that her pupils were expected to get a first-class pass in their examinations, and from that objective she never relented. They almost all succeeded, even Hugh, though obviously he had little talent for languages, and no asset beyond a kind of apprehensive goodwill and a disposition to plod on, come what may.

On Sundays he walked many miles all over the more interesting streets of Paris, visited the Louvre galleries and the Cluny and Rodin museums, inspected the Sacré Coeur Basilica, and fell in love with the Sainte Chapelle on the Isle St. Louis. He often visited the Andersons in their beautiful home in Neuilly, and called occasionally upon the de Segrais family, now retired from Mauritius, looked at the Eiffel Tower but never went up to the top because the lift was under repair, and for weeks longed for English afternoon tea which he finally tracked down at a little students' restaurant beside the Sorbonne. For a short while he was threatened with being caught up into the aristocratic society of which Edmond de Chazal, a friend of Mauritius days, was a member, and through that family began to receive invitations to receptions from some of the old princely families who still live behind closed shutters in the gilt and carved "grandes maisons" where a powdered footman may well open the door to a visitor. One evening at such a house he fell in with a young Russian refugee prince whose escape from the Bolsheviks made an interesting story. By now the young man, unable to get work because he had no qualifications nor experience whatever, said he was determined to commit suicide when he awoke next morning. Hugh in part believed him, and so stuck beside him until he reached the door of his lodgings in some back street and extorted a promise that he would telephone Hugh next day before he fired the fatal shot. No message came, and Hugh was unable to find the lodging-house again in the broad light of day — and he heard nothing more of the young man. The fate of some of these people was indeed pitiable because their education and upbringing deprived them of ordinary human resources which most of us take for granted.

Quite often Hugh would take the train to Versailles with a packet of sandwiches and an exercise book in his pocket and he became thoroughly familiar with that vast and truly magnificent palace, and also the more homely but no less beautiful little palace of Trianon. Between them these two structures had played a fundamental role in the eventual first appearance of modern democracy which erupted through the French Revolution.

Just after Christmas 1924, which Hugh had spent very happily with the Anderson family at Neuilly, his mother and youngest sister came over from England to spend a fortnight's educational visit. A young Irish schoolgirl friend of the sister was living with a French family and arranged for Hugh and his sister to accompany her and several of her friends to a state ball at the opera in aid of some charity. The president, most of the government and also Generals Joffre and Weygand attended. There was a presidential guard of honour outside at the entrance and the very grand staircase was lined on both sides by cavalrymen in full dress. "Tout Paris" was present, together with all the theatrical stars, including Mistinguette and Josephine Baker, a dusky lady of talent who had discovered a way of obeying the law clad in a stage costume consisting of three rose-buds. Happily on this occasion, though, she had added some sort of diaphanous material, but not very much of it. Madame Mistinguette, who had shortened somewhat her customary display of ostrich feathers above her head from six feet to only two feet, was very much "in evidence", and her famous smile really was six inches wide when you got close up to her. Altogether it was an evening to be long remembered.

Another of Hugh's theatrical experiences at this time was one of the (several) "final appearances" of Sarah Bernhardt, who was playing "L'Aiglon" at the Comédie Française for a week — at the age, it was believed, of eighty-three. This most moving play is a representation of the death from tuberculosis of the Roi de Rome, Napoleon's sixteen-year-old son.

Madame Bernhardt had suffered the loss of one leg, and was not able to stand unsupported, much less to walk, and she played the whole thing clad in a scarlet military uniform reclining on an army camp bed in a subdued light in a tent. Hugh, who had only been able to get hold of a single returned ticket the day before, quickly bought a copy of the play and read it right through the night, in order to ensure as far as possible that he would be able to understand what he feared might turn out to be the indistinct speech of this very old lady. But he was mistaken. The old, very old, sometimes cracked guttural voice, frequently punctuated with racking coughs, came across the air of the large auditorium syllable by syllable in a very low key but missing not one single note of the tragedy which this play presents. The performance was staggering. He regarded it as the finest theatrical presentation he ever saw, and the "Divine Sarah", as she had long been known, had no peer.

At the end the audience stood and cheered again and again; Sarah struggled to stand up to acknowledge the applause, but could not, and an usher came on stage to lift her to her feet and hold her up so that she didn't collapse, and then one saw the deep wrinkles on face and hands as they really were. She appeared genuinely moved by the tremendous reception and the applause continued for twenty-five minutes until finally she held up her hand: "Ladies and Gentlemen, I can do no more. I must get to bed. Thank you, thank you, and God bless you," and she sank into a wheelchair which was pushed off the stage. A lot of people were mopping their eyes as they went out onto the street.

After six months in France he passed his examination as first-class French interpreter and for twenty-eight years thereafter was daily paid a supplement of two shillings and fourpence, although he was only on one occasion officially required to function as an interpreter. But he always claimed in later years that it was only through the Chinese and the French that he had ever been able to grow into a civilised citizen of the world — something that very few insular Englishmen had the least inclination or desire to do in those days.

Now began a series of moves from pillar to post which provided experience but little satisfaction. At the end of April 1925 Hugh was appointed to *Dido*, a very antique cruiser moored four miles up a narrow creek from Portsmouth which acted as depot ship for a variety of experimental and trial operations. He joined an old destroyer, the *Rapid*, which had only a skeleton day crew and sailed out into the channel five days a week to carry out gyro compass trials which were directed by the Admiralty's very distinguished chief scientific adviser. These compasses were still in their early days and were proving far from reliable in ships at sea.

The two months now spent working on them finally resulted in a cure for their various teething troubles.

That much was satisfactory, but Hugh wanted to be in what he called "a proper ship", which really meant one with a permanent complement and a settled objective to pursue. In his cabin in *Dido* he began to detect a queer smell and told his Royal Marine servant to investigate. The man called him down there a few minutes later to show him the brown imprint of his body on the mattress cover which, when it had been removed, revealed the ticking of the mattress partly rotted away and the cotton stuffing fermenting with dampness. It must have been there for years in a cabin where the scuttle was probably never opened. Fortunately he suffered no harm as he had only slept there on occasional nights.

At the end of July he was appointed to serve in the reserve Eighth Destroyer Flotilla berthed close to the bridge across the Firth of Forth at Port Edgar. He found that he was to be a spare first lieutenant to be moved from one destroyer to another as each boat took its turn to go to sea with instructional classes of boy seamen. He started off in the *Bruce* under the command of Captain J. C. Tovey who was "Captain D 8", and in due course moved to four other destroyers of this flotilla. They did short one-week cruises up the east coast of Scotland all through the foul winter weather, anchoring each night because there was only one third of a crew, and that was insufficient for night steaming.

When at Port Edgar he met Captain A. B. Cunningham in command of the base and went occasionally to meals at his official residence. These two captains became during World War II respectively the Commander in Chief of the Home Fleet and Commander in Chief of the Mediterranean Fleet, the two principal operational commands of the Royal Navy.

That winter Hugh had his first experience of skiing with a party of friends at Montana in Switzerland, and, as most other beginners do, he suffered from more falls than successful runs, but he enjoyed the sport enormously and went to the Alps for winter leave whenever possible in the following years, finally, at the age of fifty-two, qualifying for the Ski Club of Great Britain Silver Badge awarded to second class skiers. Then an injured knee cartilage compelled him to abandon the sport, to his great sorrow.

In March 1928, Hugh was appointed as first lieutenant to the coal-burning minesweeper *Badminton* at Portland, where the only minesweeper flotilla in full commission did training and experimental work, some of which was of great interest. But *Badminton*, which was a survivor of World War I, was almost worn out, and he moved to *Sutton*, which was about to be converted to oil burning. They did at least one extended cruise a year and spent a few weeks on fishery control duty in the North Sea which entailed visiting the fishing fleets at work at sea, and also the ports from which they worked. A few days at Aberdeen would long be remembered. The captain and his first lieutenant called officially on the provost at the Town House, an ancient and stately building, where several of the bailies in their robes of office were also in attendance. The officers were conducted first to the council chamber where official greetings were exchanged, and then the whole company of about a dozen men moved into the adjoining dining-hall and sat round a large table making polite conversation while a scarlet-coated butler poured out whisky in two-pint cut glass tumblers and distributed cigars and cigarettes. Hugh, who had still a long day's duty on board ahead of him, tried to stop the butler pouring when there was an inch in his huge tumbler, but the man pushed his hand aside:

"Whist, mon, ye dinna ken the sort o' stuff ye are drinkin'," and poured out another couple of inches. This was unquestionably the finest whisky Hugh ever drank in his life. The bailie next to him spent a long time explaining the lengthy processes involved in its production. Meanwhile cigarettes were being passed round and Hugh, who did not smoke, refused these. Finally, and by now the whisky had ensured a lively buzz of conversation on all sides, the butler offered two large boxes of cigars on a silver tray. Again Hugh refused, but the bailie couldn't bear this and stretched over his hand to seize three or four cigars which he stuffed into the breast pocket of Hugh's uniform jacket.

"Tak them, mon; tak them; an' if ye won't smoke 'em yersel gie 'em tae yer friends. They're the finest that Cuba produces!"

The two officers went on, with some doubts about the wisdom of it at this stage, to call upon the president of the university, an aged professor of great distinction, but when they arrived he was unwell and had deputed a small delegation of his council to receive them. They were conducted on a sightseeing tour of some of the buildings and were very thankful that no further refreshments were offered.

Next morning the ship was coaling alongside when three bailies arrived in an antique Rolls-Royce with a scarlet-uniformed chauffeur to pay a return call. The provost was sitting on the magistrate's bench that day and could not come; so the bailies were shepherded through the coal dust down below to the wardroom where the steward had prepared an extra special cocktail such as they had never before experienced, and nothing would stop them for the next two hours from asking for refills for their "wee small glasses", by which time they were well dusted with coal and verging on speechlessness, but gloriously happy. In the end they had to be almost carried out to the Rolls-Royce and only at the very last moment could the chauffeur be retrieved, for he had been entertained with service rum in the chief petty officers' mess and at long last came lurching towards the gangway through the coal dust. Hugh hastily consulted with a policeman on duty on shore who agreed that it would be wise to desert his post of duty and get into the provost's car to sit beside the chauffeur and assist him to find the way home.

Everybody concerned considered that Aberdeen had been a great success and Christmas cards were exchanged with the provost for several years to come.

That summer *Sutton* went on to Norway visiting ports in the south and then putting in at Bergen to show the flag at an International Cheese Festival where, amongst other surprises, a whole meal consisting of nothing but cheeses of many sorts, and a few suitable biscuits or breads, was advertised and indeed eaten. Too much of a good thing was the verdict. The ship was royally entertained, but they made a hurried departure when a typhoid epidemic broke out and they discovered that a town drain discharged from the wharf where they were berthed and were, very wisely, requested to distil their own water.

During the cruise they were practising for the flotilla annual regatta, and the boat's crews went away in succession after the hands turned to "scrub and wash decks" at six a.m. daily. After a couple of days Hugh noticed that every boat immediately disappeared behind a headland, and when he went off with the crew he was training and started away in another direction, the coxswain protested:

"No, Sir. That's the wrong way. We go round that other point over there!"

Hugh complained that made a dog-leg and the regatta would be pulled over a straight course.

"Well Sir, yes, of course. But you first try this way, we all like it much better!"

"Oh, well, have it your way if you must."

When the boat rounded the point, behold the ladies' swimming-club was not far beyond it, and there costumes were not worn.

Norway was a great success, and they threaded the narrow inshore passage through the Indreled and got almost as far north as Trondhjeim, but Marsten Island with its white lighthouse at the entrance to Bergen Fiord was the thing that most interested Hugh when seen on a fine sunny day. He was going to value immensely this firsthand experience of this part of the Norwegian coast later on in 1939 and indeed in the years following.

Then at long last appointment to a "proper ship" came in the first days of 1929. It was to the new sloop-minesweeper *Sandwich* building at Hawthorne Leslie's yard at Hepburn-on-Tyne, where a most interesting few weeks passed before commissioning. The captain and the engineer officer and a dozen senior engine-room ratings had already joined and the whole period was filled with tests and trials of every kind, finishing up with the complicated business of a first storing of the ship. They went down river for steaming trials, and, when power failed, had to call a tug alongside to get them back to their berth at the yard. For nearly the whole period Hugh lived at an hotel out in the suburbs where his mother joined him for a week's visit. One of the coldest winters ever experienced in England developed, and the water supply for the whole city froze up for five days. The problems that arose were endless; no sewage disposal; no domestic water supply for drinking or cooking, and the closure of a variety of public services, including electricity, where water was a part of the operation. It even came to the point that one had to go to a pub and drink beer, and that of course quickly ran short. The thaw, when it came was providential.

Finally they got away early in March, and after a week or so of sea trials, *Sandwich* sailed for China in company with *Bridgewater*, who had been building in the same yard.

Chapter 10

The Sandwich *in China*

The passage to Hong Kong in company with their twin, *Bridgewater*, was uneventful, but on arrival they went into dockyard to fit out extra refrigerators, awnings and so on, which were locally known to be desirable for the service required in the several widely varying climates on this station, and they took the opportunity to land a lot of useless stores and some fittings that had proved unsuitable.

With a draft of fourteen feet, as opposed to *Cricket*'s four feet, their operations would be to seaward and in fact they seldom went up the rivers for any great distance, so that Hugh was now going to see a new aspect of China.

When winter came they went to Wei-hai-wei, an island treaty port used largely as a summer recreation facility for the Fleet. Here they acted as guardship for three months. A captain of the Royal Marines was in charge of the island where sports fields, a canteen and a small hospital had been constructed, but the little ship was really too small to make much use of these facilities, the ground was frozen hard and a game of football with a beer after it was the limit of possibility. The British resident lived in the small town on the mainland. Sir Reginald Johnston had been tutor to the last Emperor, Pu-yi, who, while he was still a boy and under the regency of the Dowager Empress, was evicted from his ancient office and now lived in a modest house behind a high wall close to the river bank and docks at Tientsin, in North China, a permanent military guard being maintained at the only entrance gate.

Sir Reginald, now getting on in years, was probably the most knowledgeable foreigner in China, and a visit to his Chinese house was an education in itself. He was most helpful in organising shooting parties for waterfowl among the chain of lakes and swamps that lay a few miles inland. Usually four or five guns would set out at daylight in two cars with a steward and food for

223

the day, and beaters were already waiting at the particular ground to be shot over. They were experienced at their job and were controlled by an old head man who had been employed by the Fleet for many past years. Duck, geese, widgeon or teal, and wild white swans and snipe in season were plentiful. The waterfowl could be seen far out on the lagoon and boats would put out to drive them towards the line of guns, or sometimes the guns would go out in boats strung out in a long line. One could have imagined that the ducks, too, had long experience of what was expected of them, for Hugh never once got a likely shot; either the birds were too high, or they sped away over the far end of the beaters' line to come down again on another lake. At dusk or dawn one sometimes heard spent pellets on their wings, but they always flew too high.

One day when the guns were lined up along a high embankment and the lake in front was teeming with birds, a snow shower came down. Birds could be heard whistling low overhead in all directions and a few shots were fired, but Hugh saw nothing, and so began walking along towards the next gun, when suddenly in the snow something looking like a great white sheet seemed to be waving ahead of him. He called out and stopped, but hearing no answering shout he began to move cautiously forward again in the blinding snow and all but collided with a large swan standing with uplifted wings ready to strike with its heavy yellow beak. Both Hugh and the swan called out loudly in alarm and the bird flapped away, a mere shadow in the snowstorm. Later he asked if he would have been allowed to shoot the bird, and the answer was "most certainly yes". The beaters regarded the meat as a rare delicacy.

On other occasions they went out after geese which were feeding in their thousands in the rice paddy-fields. Here again all the birds seemed to know at what point they would come within range and were wont to take off loudly honking at that critical moment. They were never once seen to disturb themselves when a Chinese farmer trudged across his fields. One European told Hugh that his method was to dress in Chinese coolie clothing and then lead out a water-buffalo drawing a farm wagon, and always he came back with a comfortable bag. "It was all very successful, especially as the cart hauled the heavy birds and I never had to carry them home!"

Once a year the seafaring coastal inhabitants of Wei-hai-wei held a festival in memory of members of their families who had been lost at sea. A special family feast was prepared and eaten in the late afternoon, after which the relatives would go down to the seashore and fix small candles to wooden planks or to a small roughly-fashioned boat. As the sun was setting the candles were lit and the floats pushed off where the evening breeze would carry them out to sea, while the people lining the shore chanted prayers to the water gods that their lost ones would see the lights and be guided back to shore once more.

The commissioner hired a large seagoing junk and invited about fifty guests on board (of whom Hugh was one) for the ceremonial feast and to launch their own candles out to sea. The guests stood, some praying, transfixed as the daylight swiftly died out, and all remained gazing silently to seaward until the very last candle light disappeared. This simple ceremony was somehow intensely moving, and the handful of foreign spectators felt themselves as deeply involved as any one of the weeping women scattered along the shore line.

Wei-hai-wei was being returned to China, and on the commissioner's last night he gave a dinner to about a dozen of the leading men of the territory, Hugh also being invited. It was a formal Chinese 16-course dinner with all the traditional ceremonial foods being served. At one point a small charcoal brazier was placed before each guest so that he might grill little pieces of pork, dipping them into a bowl of sauce. Hugh's Chinese neighbours on either side — who had been chosen because each of them spoke some English — were endlessly helpful in showing him how to manage chopsticks with the various different courses, and his end of the table was in an almost continuous uproar of laughter and jokes which did much to lighten what was for both Chinese locals and the two Englishmen a sad, mournful, sort of farewell. Johnston had built up a solid respect and admiration for British administration and the officials regarded him almost as a beloved father. He had through the years selected and trained and guided them, and oppression, famine and real poverty were no more than a distant memory. People kept coming to the door to say goodbye all through the evening.

Early next morning *Sandwich* put to sea flying the commissioner's flag for the last time and saluting it with the prescribed eleven blank charges. Hugh had already seen Jubaland in East Africa given up at the behest of the League of Nations and felt sad that Wei-hai-wei, such a successful and happy little

Q

kingdom, must fall back into obscure poverty and perhaps misery, for it must henceforth be just another little fishing village.

Later they moved on to Tientsin in the dead of winter. The treaty port lies about thirty miles up a river and is sixty miles from Peking, and the docks are well downstream from the town which is almost never seen. The weather was well below zero and a bitter wind never ceased to blow Mongolian sand which penetrated everywhere. Presently the river froze over and ice began to accumulate inside the piles that supported the jetty so that the ship was gradually pushed out. The steam in the officers' bathroom bulkheads froze to a depth of nine inches and on the crew's messdecks ice was five inches thick on the ship's side plating. Perpetual rivulets of water dribbled down and across the decks. Arctic clothing was worn by everybody, and the only comfortable place was in bed. When the ship arrived the Chinese officials paid the usual formal calls which were returned, but they asked that nobody should go out of sight of the ship because "there were bad men about, very bad men".

A week or two later they sent a message to say that "the bad men had gone away", and that it was now quite safe to go on shore without restriction. A day or two later the Chinese messman, who had been into the city to do some shopping, came back with the report that the whole brigand band had been surprised in their hide-out and captured, and then flayed alive, and this was later on reliably confirmed as true because a mutilated body was washed up on the river bank.

On another occasion when they were in the North they were diverted to Shanhaikwan, which was a summer seaside resort chiefly used by foreign embassy personnel to escape the torrid summer heat and dust of Peking. The ship had already met quite a few of the people who usually went there, including a young couple named Pawley. Mrs Pawley one day went out into the country for a walk with another woman, and when she failed to return home in the evening enquiries were started and a search set on foot. The two ladies had been captured by a brigand band and taken off into the gauliang fields, the crop being a sort of millet grain sown thickly and standing twelve feet high, and at that season covering many square miles of the countryside. The search produced nothing at all, but after a while a message came through from the abductors demanding a huge ransom. The diplomats took over the negotiations, and after some weeks the British

Government paid up and the ladies were released unharmed.

China always in those days had this kind of overhanging unspoken menace that made life uncertain, and from time to time the reality of the threat was proven.

Their next visit in the North was to bring the British Ambassador, Mr Miles Lampson, and his staff from Tientsin south to Nanking on the Yangtze which had lately been established by Chiang Kai-Shek as his capital. At this time Hugh was invited up to Peking to stay for a week in the embassy compound with one of the secretaries. He spent each day seeing or doing some special thing under expert guidance, and the vast Imperial Palace, covering several square miles and surrounded by an immense wall, occupied several of his days. The roofless Temple of Heaven, a series of circular white marble terraces of great beauty, is perhaps the jewel of it all. This palace almost beggars description, it is so large and so varied. On one guided tour he took, the party was shown the last emperor's personal quarters, and as they moved on from these rooms, built in low bungalow-style, they crossed a long wandering courtyard where a small dilapidated wooden gate idly swinging on rusty hinges chanced to catch Hugh's attention. He walked over to it and was looking to see what was beyond as the party moved off in some other direction. What he did see was a ragged overgrowth of bushes and weeds and a decorated wall with a little tiled gable end above it. He went through the gate, pushed his way through the bushes and came on a small marble-floored pavilion brilliantly decorated and painted in Chinese style, but now sadly faded and damaged by weathering. There was a long verandah behind which doors led into a range of several small rooms. The dust everywhere was inches deep. He pushed at one door which finally opened a little and went inside. There a carved table had fallen over on its side. Shelving lined part of the inner wall and, when some of the dust had been swept off, it was seen to hold a number of small carved objects — animals, groups of flowers or leaves — such as Chinese sculptors have always produced. Some of these articles were in different coloured jades. Then he realised that two small carved wooden chairs stood away as if suddenly pushed back from the upturned table. On one of these was a black silk mandarin skull cap with a green jade button on top and the remains of what might have been a peacock feather such as only a high official would have been entitled to wear. He wondered if two men might have been playing at some table game when the Allied Army burst into the Imperial City and sacked it in 1906. Perhaps they fled in panic and it appeared as if nobody had ever been in this little garden pavilion since.

Time had passed and Hugh hurried away to catch up with his "tour" and found difficulty in doing so in that labyrinth of buildings until he heard foreign voices in the distance.

Elsewhere a very lofty and brilliantly-decorated pavilion housed some three hundred clocks of every imaginable shape and size, gifts from foreign heads of state to an emperor who had reigned over two hundred years ago. They were very tightly arranged into the large space available and many of them appeared to be in working order. Their cases were lavishly decorated with gold, jewels and coloured enamel work. There can be no other comparable collection in the world, for these gifts had been designed with the single objective of flattering an emperor whose power was acknowledged and whose favour would be of advantage.

Yet none of these striking objects lingers in the mind as being typical of Chinese art and skill; but rather one remembers the roof-tops of this palace. Here all roofs are tiled in shining but soft shades of many different colours. Buildings are spaced widely apart and only very few are large. The eaves extend well out beyond the walls and at every roof corner and along the ridges there is a sort of frieze of ornamental tiling culminating in a dragon figure with his long sinuously curling tail. The Kwelin (guardian dog-like figure at the entrances to all temples) stands at every possible point of vantage as a defence against noxious spirits. All these decorative ceramic figures are in brilliantly glittering golds, greens, blues, even occasional reds. They are designed to be highly visible and they create an impression of alert power. Their colours are unforgettably brilliant, and beautiful, and do not seem to be known elsewhere. This is the unique glory of the "Forbidden City".

On another day he visited a very fine temple where Confucius' Tomb is housed and the keepers made for him a rubbing on a piece of paper of the brass plaque that marks the place of burial under the floor. Black-robed monks were quietly moving about and one of these gently took Hugh's hand and led him away through a number of passages and rooms and then vanished. A moment later two dishevelled-looking monks with their robes discarded and wearing only a loincloth, and with hair awry, appeared from nowhere and came to him offering him postcard size obscene photographs. One glance was enough to alarm him and, as he looked more closely at the two men, he appreciated that their eyes were glazed as though they didn't focus properly, and one of them, who was standing in the full light of a high window, was streaming with sweat. There was a curious unidentifiable odour about them and they were pressing him almost frantically to buy the postcards. In fact, as he learned later on, they were probably drug addicts and would go to any lengths in their frenzy to get money to buy whatever it was they were taking. Hugh turned and fled, and as he did so, one of the men burst into tears and the other was wringing his hands in misery, so Hugh threw a couple of dollars on the floor as he went. The whole thing was an eerie sort of experience that made him more cautious about moving about alone amongst the many fascinating old buildings in this country.

A few days later at Tientsin they embarked the ambassador, the Chinese secretary, Eric Teichman, and the other staff members together with some servants and many boxes of embassy archives. An ice-breaker came to make passage for the ship. Hugh at his station on the fo'c'sle head was clearing away the anchors so that they could be let go if required, but when he looked over the jetty, he saw that a solid block of ice was cleaving to the forepart of the ship on both sides. An anchor was lowered onto this, but it did not break, and so he hove up the anchor again and let it fall with a thud. That, too, failed to dislodge the ice. On both banks of the river the ice was piled thirty feet high with huge up-ended blocks and slabs, and, as the ice-breaker steamed ahead of them they saw that she was breaking a passage through a thickness of about four feet. They would not have been able to get out under their own small steam power and possibly the hull forward could have been damaged if such an attempt had been made.

The diplomatic party were all on the bridge to watch the proceedings, and as the sun set it became intensely cold. Mr Teichman quite unthinkingly put out his tongue which touched the bridge side railing and it froze solidly to the metal. As he stepped back the skin tore away and for the rest of the journey he was in great discomfort and hardly able to speak at all. Finally they were free of solid ice twenty miles out to sea.

When they entered the Yangtze a few days later the water was everywhere dotted with duck and other waterfowl and almost everybody tried to shoot some of the game. One evening after they had anchored in the river for the night the captain and the ambassador went off in the ship's motor sampan and managed to get a couple of birds in the dusk. The ship's machine-guns were also exercised at these moving targets, but no birds fell and they seemed always to keep just beyond range.

On a later visit to Nanking in the autumn the ship learned that there were pheasant beyond the city wall to the south. The wall is about forty feet high and of similar width and encircles a perimeter of forty-seven miles. At the time much of the inside area was empty countryside or scrub woods with some scattered small farms. An enormous and impressive memorial tomb had been built for Sun Yat Sen, the father of the republic, and there was a ceremonial approach staircase of white stone stairs about a hundred yards wide and, at the top, a large pavilion housed the actual remains; the elevation was over two hundred feet. Distinguished foreign visitors and all diplomats were invited (and expected to accept the invitation) to drive out to the memorial, walk up the tremendous steps and lay their wreaths of flowers in the pavilion. The whole ceremony was a sheer terror to the elderly and the obese, and it was said that several persons had died from the exertion.

Hugh went out to this place — not of course being an "official" sort of visitor, but a mere sightseer — and started up the steps, but gave up when scarcely a quarter of the way, for he had dysentery and almost blacked out. This pilgrimage was a favourite expedition for the Chinese people on holidays and special festival occasions, and one would often see little family groups sitting on the steps having a picnic meal.

The consul-general had arranged for the captain to pay his official visit to Generalissimo Chiang Kai-Shek on a certain day and drove with him into the city for this purpose. When they arrived they were received by Madame Chiang Kai-Shek, who, she explained, had been asked to deputise for her husband because he had been called elsewhere on urgent public business. This famous lady was as beautiful and as charming as public report indicated, and it happened that the subject of shooting game came up. When she found that the ship's officers were keen on this sport she said that it was the general's favourite relaxation and that she would arrange for him to go out to a specially favoured area with them one morning early, as soon as possible. All was in due course arranged and the motor sampan was repainted for the occasion.

But at the last minute a message came that a riot had just broken out in the city and the general could not get out to the river. Evidently his recently acquired control of the countryside was still in some state of dispute.

Much of China including Nanking City was at this time in a condition of intermittent ferment, and the ship's people could only go inside the walls of Nanking if and when the consul-general made special arrangements. One morning a little delegation of five youths came alongside in a sampan and explained that they were members of the university football club and would like to have a game with the ship's team. When approached about this the consul-general was nervous about the possibility of some sort of anti-foreign demonstration erupting, but in the end the ship's team did go ashore and the game was played on an open field only about three hundred yards from *Sandwich*'s anchored position. The captain accompanied the football team and Hugh watched from beside a four-inch gun with HE ammunition at the ready beside it. At half time, through his binoculars, he could see that the two teams had equal scores and during the interval the considerable crowd swarmed all over the ground, but no Very's light signal was fired, so he hoped all was well. When a student's patrol had at last cleared the field, the game was resumed and *Sandwich* got the deciding goal. From the ship's deck Hugh could see a small group of people rushing onto the field waving their arms, apparently bent on assaulting the sailors. In the nick of time the students' patrol headed them off and could be seen belabouring some of them as they dragged them off the field. When everyone was safely back on board the captain said that he had the Very's light pistol cocked at the ready and thought there would be trouble. After the game was over the student team gathered round him and were profuse in their apologies, so he invited them all to come aboard next day and look round the ship and they, when they came, seemed a fine healthy set of young men and certainly the sailors were delighted to show them round, including their messes between decks and the engine and boiler rooms.

Another day the captain and his first lieutenant were invited to lunch with Chiang Kai-Shek, and were on deck in their best white uniforms ready to leave, when a sampan shot out from the shore displaying the consular flag. A messenger delivered a note from the consul-general saying that Chiang Kai-Shek had been obliged to cancel his invitation because, for the moment, a riot was in progress and it would be unsafe for the officers to go into the city.

However, later arrangements were made to land a little party above the city where the consul-general met them and the whole party walked about two miles into a lightly wooded area, passing through what was evidently a city burial ground, for on all sides graves and tombstones were around them. Poor families could not always afford to have a grave dug and the corpse would be laid on the ground in a winding sheet, and stones, or logs of wood cut in the neighbourhood, would be laid to cover it, but not always effectively, because they saw that dogs had got at some of these makeshift graves with gruesome results. Fortunately the pheasants were still further afield, and they were delighted to see a few migrant woodcock which always offered a most challenging target. A member of this party was the captain of a small American warship then stationed at Nanking, and he used a remarkable new type of gun not before seen by the British sportsmen, and with this weapon actually brought down one bird at one hundred yards range, and secured others at seventy yards. It was the best pheasant shoot Hugh ever had.

Most of their visits were to 'treaty ports' where there would be small numbers of British people in addition to the consul; Chefoo was a memorable one. It was noted for the production of the best foreign-style needlework and embroidery obtainable in all of China at that time. Hugh was interested in getting some of this linen to take home as presents to his relatives, and he got the help of a local lady when he visited the workplace. This was a large European wooden house a little outside the town, where they were received by a middle-aged Chinese woman who spoke some broken English and conducted them through the entire building. In each room several work tables, each with a small stool, was attended by a young girl seamstress, the youngest starting at seven years of age, and none was older than nineteen, for by then they had become blind, and were returned to their homes. This horrible exploitation had gone on for many years past, and the workmanship was said to be unsurpassed anywhere in the world. Chinese gossamer-thin "ricecloth" was used and also linen from Northern Ireland and cotton from America to make embroidered cloths, while lace was also produced, and all at extremely low prices.

Later that year *Sandwich* moved to South China with orders to investigate several anchorages and harbours. In one uncharted inlet they entered at high tide cautiously with the motor sampan three or four hundred yards ahead sounding, and found anchorage off a fishing village where it looked as if the whole population had turned out to see a sight they had never seen before. The houses were all of light wood standing in rows upon wood piles about twenty feet above the high-water mark, and joined together by a narrow plank pathway to the shoreline almost two hundred yards away. Hugh landed with a Chinese steward and was received with smiles, and although the dialect was unknown to the steward he succeeded in getting the people to send off small quantities of eggs, vegetables and chicken, and then they were directed onwards up a small hill to a very primitive temple where it seemed the headman lived. He was old and evidently infirm, but the customary bowls of most beautiful tea and some little sweet rice cakes were offered and a sort of amiable conversation was conducted through smiles and pointing to different surrounding objects. On their way back to the shore they came upon a minute shop where decorated rice bowls of an unfamiliar pattern seemed to be on sale. Hugh tried to buy some but couldn't make his wish known and told the steward to get some if he could the next time he went ashore. However, he did not succeed because — as far as he could understand — whatever was in stock was the reserve for the whole population and the storekeeper could not hope to replace it in the near future. It had probably come from some obscure pottery in the interior and a journeyman would only come to such a small village very seldom. Certainly the attractive pattern was never seen elsewhere. After three days of sounding from the ship's boats, they established the limits of the anchorage which proved to be too small ever to be of much value. The gentle nature and ingenuous behaviour of the people seemed to indicate that they had but little contact with the outside world.

A visit to the port of Fukien, which is a provincial capital about thirty miles up a river estuary, was a very different matter. The city is the river terminal for seagoing junks. There are some antique fortifications on the river banks, and it is a prosperous trading centre, a few miles below which is the principal Chinese naval training depot, established many years earlier by British naval officers. *Sandwich* was immediately made to feel warmly welcome there and everything was put at their disposal. The city claimed to produce the finest lacquer ware in China, and Hugh was conducted over the extensive workshops and learned that the best quality gets seven coats, each of which takes a week to dry. The two or three pieces he bought there were still in perfect condition fifty years later.

On a Saturday — which curiously enough was universally set aside there as a work holiday, after the British tradition, and the only place in China that Hugh found where the Chinese observed this custom — a cricket match between a university team and the ship was arranged to take place on the large polo field. Hugh, who had been lunching at the consulate beforehand, arrived a little late, but saw that everything had been arranged as though it were taking place in an English country village. Even a tea tent was to be seen, and several European ladies carrying parasols, not the usual oiled paper and bamboo Chinese umbrella. He was walking round the perimeter with a Chinese businessman he had met, and had already noticed that the foreign community seemed to be gathered in three widely separated groups, sitting on their own chairs and keeping exclusively to themselves. The Chinese called his attention to this.

"Can you tell me," he said, "why the foreigners are all separated out as you can see? Down there are the Baptists and that tall man is their minister. And that next is the Methodists. And here, where your consul is sitting with the captain are all the Church of England people in Foochow. They all say they are Christians, but I cannot understand why they do not seem to be able to speak to each other."

This was the second time an educated Chinese had put that question to him. He felt confused and ashamed and could not give a straight answer.

The Chinese naval base commander arranged for the whole ship's company to walk several miles up into the hills to visit a large and celebrated monastery where people were accustomed to go for meditation retreats, or simply to visit and see the sights and have a free meal if they wished. So it was that at six o'clock in the morning almost the whole of the ship's personnel landed, leaving only one officer and about twenty essential ratings on board for that day. The walk was steep, rocky and often wooded, with streams and some splendid views, and it took them about six hours, including a couple of stops for a rest. Some of the older petty officers only just managed to reach the monastery, for it was a blistering hot day. At the entrance was a series of bridges over stream-fed pools where huge carp leapt out onto the rocks to gobble up bits of bread which a coolie was selling out of a basket for a few cents. Inside was a series of courtyards connecting to one another where all shapes and sizes of ancient stone buildings seemed to be scattered about haphazardly, and one of these was pointed out as the pavilion where Chiang Kai-Shek had spent some time on a pilgrimage only a few days earlier. The place had been famous throughout China for centuries past. The kitchen was an earth-floored roofed area about fifty feet square with several wood or charcoal fires surrounded by a few stones laid on the bare ground. On some of these fires was an enormous shallow metal basin, perhaps six feet in diameter, where rice was being cooked, and on others, large bubbling iron cauldrons contained soup, or vegetables and stews. Cooks offered Hugh a taste here and there from very long-handled ladles or spoons. The ship's party, however, had brought sandwiches and carried water-bottles and sat at a long table out in one of the courtyards where cooks brought them Chinese handleless cups and, of course, Chinese tea, neither of which had the sailors ever seen before. The messdeck habit is to boil up a strong brew of black tea and then add a large spoonful of sugar and a generous quantity of thick condensed milk, the result bearing no resemblance whatever to the almost colourless and delicate flavour of China tea. They could hardly believe that what they were being offered was real tea.

The ship went on from there to Hainan Island, a large area well away from the coastline and without a harbour, notorious in those days for brigandage and piracy. Ships must anchor a mile or more out from the port, and cargo is transported by small junks. The little town had a deadly dull sort of air about it. Everything looked faded and roads were unpaved.

Hugh had difficulty in hiring a ramshackle car to drive him along the only road that crossed the island to the far shore on a sightseeing expedition, which very few of the resident Europeans had ever done. The drive was a rough one through slightly undulating farm lands and wooded areas. In those days quite a number of foreigners collected silver dollar coins and had them made into ashtrays. Hugh had found five with considerable difficulty, but here he met an interesting long-time European resident who had fifteen and told him that the maximum possible was twenty-one. This man also had some pieces of the *sycee*, which was the medium of exchange up until about 1900, and consisted of various sizes and shapes of silver bullion which was valued according to its weight, so that almost everybody needed to keep a small scale, even when going to shop in the food market. By now almost all *sycee* had been gathered into the banks, and not only the Central Peking Government, but many of the several independent *Tujuns* (Provincial Governors) struck their own coinage, so that when one crossed a provincial border — and some of these were always in dispute — one's coinage had to be exchanged. Business men had to get used to this, and the abacus which the Chinese invented (and which is said to be the first step towards a computer), was a very rapid method of doing the necessary arithmetic. A good deal of faith also entered into such money transactions because almost nobody knew the true degree of purity of the silver, and some *Tujuns* were accused of debasing the content in the dollars they minted. Yet trade went on and almost nobody complained; and had they done so, nobody in authority would have paid the least attention.

China governed itself by custom rather than by law; indeed the first breakaway from that came in the Western World with Napoleon Bonaparte's "Code Napoleon" which defines legal obligations, and it is interesting to recall that still, today, Great Britain has no completely written constitution, but relies rather on precedent.

In the middle of *Sandwich*'s commission on the China station piracy erupted on the central coast. Numerous small vessels traded between the many small seaports, and brigandage began to take to salt water. The method adopted was for a gang to board the trader as "deck passengers", and when she was well out to sea they stormed the bridge, put armed guards on the engine-room hatches, and compelled the captain to alter course to some lonely pre-selected place where junks would come alongside and the pirated cargo would be discharged. The gang would then escape in the junks and the ship would be allowed to proceed on her way and of course report the piracy far too late to permit any effective action.

The procedure was simple, and about once a fortnight some such looting was occurring, so that an emergency wireless signal procedure was introduced, and a warship, stationed in what was hoped might be a suitable area, would hurry to the scene of the piracy. The pirates got to know about these signals and began to destroy the ship's wireless office as their first action. They had to take a chance on the warship's position because one method was to anchor at night and move off to a patrol area at daylight. On no occasion was a pirate gang actually caught, though once or twice they had to leave their captives in a hurry without their full quota of loot.

Sandwich worked mainly in the Bias Bay area about a hundred miles north of Hong Kong and was perhaps moderately successful as a deterrent, though she never managed to catch a gang. Chilang lighthouse, standing six miles out on a narrow promontory, was a good position to take up as that area was the scene of the most active pirate enterprises. The lighthouse, with its keepers' houses, stands on a very small rocky island, and at that time there were three European keepers, each with his own Chinese wife, a "boy" (who is a personal servant) and of course the indispensible messman. The tour of duty there was two years, with a voluntary extension for a third year, and after the tour a keeper was given four months' leave which was usually spent in Hong Kong.

One day when *Sandwich* was not going to sea, Hugh went into the island lighthouse in the ship's dinghy to invite the keepers to lunch on board. It was getting on for midday, and as he walked up the rocky pathway to the quarters he passed a little well-kept graveyard where headstones indicated the burial of a woman, two children and two men. They had all died from one single infection, but nobody knew what it was. The doors and windows were all open in the spotlessly white building, but when he knocked at the entrance and then called out, no answer came, so, supposing that the keepers were asleep, he walked in and called out again, but still no answer came. He passed on into a large airy room with shutters closed, and at a small table a man in white shirt and shorts was sitting eating his dinner with a Chinese woman in the customary black dress standing at one side; neither of them moved a muscle, so Hugh explained his errand, and the man, who never ceased munching, pointed with his knife to a door and said simply:

"In there!"

Hugh walked through the door into an identical room where two men sat at two tables with two black-clad Chinese women in attendance as far apart as the walls allowed. Neither of them stirred, so Hugh repeated his invitation speech. One of the men stopped munching, so he walked over to him and began a single-sided conversation. Presently an answer came:

"No. We can't come."

Hugh argued, and after almost half an hour walked back to his boat and semaphored to the ship that he was bringing two men off to lunch shortly. It was sheer optimism, but by now having got two of the keepers to speak and answer questions, though haltingly, as though speech was an uncommon experience for them, he expected to persuade them, and presently succeeded in doing so. Their tours of duty had extended beyond a full year, and their silent colleague had been on the lighthouse just short of three years and was due for relief quite soon. Later, on board, after a number of whiskies, the two men couldn't stop talking. They had all agreed among themselves long ago that they had said all they had to say to one another and that it was pointless to invent matter for conversation. Only the simple repetitive operation of the light itself remained as a subject of conversation, and as all of them had been tending that same light through several past years, it provided virtually nothing to talk about. There was no picture other than a faded photograph in a frame, not one spare chair, nothing but each man's white shirt and shorts, his bed and bedclothes and mosquito net inside that building — no calendar, no book, no magazine, no radio set — just nothing. They said that they used to fish, but after one man fell among the rocks and knocked himself senseless, they gave up that activity, and anyhow the fish were tasteless when cooked. They had not walked into the little town at the inshore end of the promontory for over a year because it was reported to be the headquarters of a band of brigands and would therefore be dangerous. The Chinese wives were part of the furniture. When you arrived for a tour of duty the comprador in the town sent out two or three girls and you took your choice — spare daughters in China were always an expense and always available for loan or purchase to any man who appeared to be in a position to feed, house and clothe them. A lighthouse ship came once a quarter with supplies for the station, and staple foodstuffs, and a contract had long ago been negotiated with the comprador in the local town to furnish whatever more the keepers needed, sending in his bill to the Hong Kong headquarters, where each man's private bills were deducted from his pay-roll, so that keepers had no money, which, in their complete isolation, might have tempted robbers. It seemed as if everything on earth had been catered for, except perhaps for illness, and, as the five graves outside testified, nothing could be done about that in a hurry. Anyhow, nobody except the five dead people had ever become ill at this lighthouse as far as was known. They just never thought of illness — it had not happened for a very long time.

There were other anchorages in Bias Bay and a favourite one was a mile offshore from a small, and apparently dry island where a beautiful sandy beach could be seen. Hugh got swimming competitions under way, being an enthusiastic bather himself, and eventually at the end of a summer's season a test was set to swim from the ship to this island, three ship's boats being stationed along the course to rescue anyone who might find that he couldn't manage the distance. Five men were forbidden by the doctor to take part, and every other man in the ship actually did complete the mile without physical help. At the outset of the commission there had been about fifty non-swimmers. A huge picnic and a bonfire on the beach after dark was organised as a celebration of this satisfying effort.

As time went on it was noticed that fishing junks started anchoring overnight about half a mile from the *Sandwich* and numbers steadily increased to about sixty. This led to the uncomfortable feeling that they might be planning to pirate the *Sandwich*, which they would know had enviable rifles and pistols and ammunition, and so the small arms were locked away at night in a secure place below decks, and through the night three sentries were placed on the upper deck. Hugh always slept on a mattress on the quarterdeck with a loaded revolver under his pillow and the quartermaster on watch and the sentries were similarly armed.

Hugh decided to go out on his aquaplane, towed by the ship's motor sampan and tour around and in amongst the anchored junks whose crews thronged on deck to gaze at a sight never before seen. So he went alongside one of them and bought several crayfish which gave the opportunity to have a careful look for any sign of arms on board. He noticed nothing suspicious. However, the season of fogs was coming on, and he doubled the sentries on deck at night and also illuminated the ship's side with arc lights during the night hours. One night he woke up suddenly to hear a peculiar swishing sort of sound, and there dimly through the fog he saw the fishing fleet drifting on the tide past both sides with sails set, but no wind, simply drifting out to sea with the tide. Some of them were only fifty feet away and for a moment he fortunately hesitated about ringing the action alarm bell — but no junk made the slightest sign of coming alongside and they were probably using *Sandwich*'s bright illumination as a leading mark out of harbour in the dark.

A few days later a much publicised piracy did occur while they were just entering Hong Kong harbour to refuel. But it was about two hundred miles north, and they couldn't reach the area in time. A young girl clad in green silk jacket and trousers led the gang and actually shot down one of the crew who tried to resist; this gang got away with the ship's cargo which no doubt furnished the lady with a comfortable dowry. *Sandwich* hurried off to the scene but when they reached the place many hours later and sent a boat ashore to investigate, they found nothing but half a dozen large junks all with empty holds.

A dockyard refit now became due and they were to spend about two months under repair with many of the usual domestic services out of action, and that implied a great deal of dockyard dirt and disorder in almost every compartment. In addition to all the turmoil, the humidity in Hong Kong was now very high, and much of the ventilation system would be out of action. Hugh went off to the garrison commander and succeeded in borrowing a part of the army barracks buildings which had been built on a small but beautiful island five miles down the harbour from the naval dockyard, and there the ship's company, except for four or five security men, were installed for the period of the refit. The excellent canteen, football and cricket grounds, and two tennis-courts made the place an ideal summer resort for the sailors who had more space around them than they knew how to use. The officers, except for the warrant gunner and Hugh, who elected to live on the island, housed themselves with friends or at the Hong Kong Club. Hugh sailed early each morning up to the dockyard in the ship's dinghy, and back to camp in the evening.

The captain of the ship was at this moment recalled to England and Hugh was appointed to take command pending the arrival of a new commanding officer, and held this position for three months, the ship finishing her refit only about a week before the new captain arrived.

Presently a typhoon was reported to be approaching. *Sandwich* was towed by tugs out to a mooring buoy about three hundred yards off the dockyard wall, and the engineering staff worked round the clock to raise steam in one boiler. Two bridles of chain cable and a four-and-a-half-inch wire hawser were shackled to the buoy, and by nightfall the typhoon was reported as almost certain to hit Hong Kong early the next day. Every movable object on the upper deck was lashed down, even the blacksmith's heavy iron anvil, and all breakable articles, such as awnings and wooden gratings, were stored below, and watertight doors and ship's side scuttles were carefully closed.

At daylight next morning the sky had an unhealthy yellow haze about it and the humidity became torrid. Junk traffic was intense with sails and oars propelling the thousands of small craft to whatever typhoon anchorages were not yet jammed full. When breakfast was piped at eight a.m., a blustery breeze had set in and before it was over sudden gale force winds would make the ship jerk at her cables in a way that could be felt from bow to stern. At ten a.m., the typhoon signal was hoisted at the observatory and the last telephone communication with the shore was that the centre of the typhoon was headed directly for Hong Kong and should reach it in an hour's time. By now steep confused seas were breaking in all directions and the driving spume steadily reduced visibility. On shore traffic could be seen darting for shelter in all directions and the tops of some palm trees were being torn off. To the east there was a hazy sand-coloured bar where sky met sea and a blue-black obscurity above it. A sedan car was seen driving along the bund when suddenly the top lifted up in the air and the four passengers could be seen sitting up. Then the iron and glass canopy sheltering the main entrance to the Hong Kong Club lifted bodily into the air and disintegrated. Trees could be seen bowling along the roadway nearby. On board *Sandwich* the propellor was going slow ahead to reduce the strain on the cables, and the ship was being violently tossed about in random directions and the cable kept crashing down on the fo'c'sle deck and jerking wildly in the hawse pipe. The wind force increased moment by moment, and really big seas were built up; then, just as the ship was rising up to the next oncoming wave, its whole top would be swept up and it would disintegrate into the air. The howling noise drowned out all speech. It was impossible to keep one's eyes open. Quite suddenly the wind died out; the sea fell back on itself boiling and confused; the dockyard wall emerged from the twilight gloom. About eight minutes later the wind broke out with a roar like a huge waterfall from the opposite direction and the ship lurched violently as it quickly swung round. The utter confusion of the scene was indescribable, but within a minute or two the ship was again jerking at its cables more violently than before, and Hugh decided to go forward to see if they were damaged. He put on a bathing-suit and over that an oilskin sou'wester, and crawled forward from the shelter of the bridge structure, holding onto a wire jackstay

R

that had been rigged from one deck fitting to another. He felt that he would be blown over the side unless he lay flat down on the deck, and so very slowly wriggled little by little forward, blinded by the driving water and only occasionally getting a momentary glimpse of his surroundings. He eventually reached the hawse pipe and was able to see that both cables looked normal and that the wire hawser was also in good condition, though brightly polished. The return journey to the shelter of the bridge was a similar experience, though easier because he knew what to expect. As he got hold of a hand railing and brushed the water from his eyes he saw that a little group of seamen clustered behind the bridge structure were roaring with laughter at him, and so he spoke up:

"It's all very well for you to laugh, but when you get out there it's no laughing matter!"

"Well, look at yourself, Sir!"

He did, and found that he had nothing on him whatever, and that several scratches were bleeding slightly — every stitch on him had disintegrated; someone put a coat about his shoulders as he went below.

Within a short time the violence of the storm had passed and the seas subsided in a light wind. Ashore the destruction was very great. A car on the tramway up to the Peak had been blown off the rails, but its hauling cable held it. Trees and greenery were piled everywhere twenty feet high. No glass remained in any window. Iron park railings were twisted and torn from their concrete bases. The tale of damage was endless. *Sandwich* suffered no more than a few dents from the heavy anvil which had broken away from its lashings and bounded across the deck into some solid fitting. The junks began to come out cautiously in ones and twos from wherever they had hidden themselves. Many must have been destroyed, for the harbour was littered with bits of broken wood and also some branches of trees.

A Blue Funnel Line ship of 15,000 tons had been moored to a buoy three hundred yards from *Sandwich* and had dragged the buoy and its anchor sixteen miles through the many adjacent islands. Tugs fetched her back again that same evening. The anemometer at the weather station on the Peak had blown away at 140 miles an hour, and the weather men estimated that the wind force reached 165 miles an hour, and also that the centre of the typhoon had passed six miles south of their position. The whole thing came and went in about an hour and a quarter. The frightening violence of it has to be experienced, for there is no weather condition that parallels a cyclonic storm.

The commander-in-chief's yacht, the sloop *Cornflower*, ran on a rock in a fog at about this time and of course had to be docked as soon as she managed to get back to Hong Kong. But the admiral had an engagement to pay an official visit to the provincial governor at Canton, and only a small ship could get through the shallow waters. Hugh was hurriedly sent for and interviewed by the flag captain and given the order to prepare to embark the admiral and his staff for the Canton visit. They would have to sail in five days' time. Cabins must be refurbished and the ship painted and spruced up everywhere and everyone worked at full speed to get things ready in the short time available. Then it was found that the ship could not hoist the admiral's barge because it was too heavy for the davits; nor did the admiral like the lack of air conditioning; so at the last moment *Sandwich* was informed that she would not be required, and everyone heaved a sigh of relief and relaxed.

The new captain arrived on 13th March 1931, and took over command, and Hugh's relief also joined a few days later, and so he was free to go on leave until his passage back to England could be arranged. He was invited to go as a guest up the Canton River on one of the gunboats, and the day before she was due to sail he had spent all of it at a bathing party at Repulse Bay beach. It was a day of low heavy clouds and very hot, and nobody had appreciated that the invisible sun would burn the skin all the more fiercely. By the time Hugh got back on board that night he could feel that he was badly burned, and next morning could not get out of his bunk because huge blisters — one about six inches long on his forearm — had developed during the night. The doctor did what little was possible, but Hugh was in acute pain. However, he decided to go to Canton anyhow, as the gunboat carried a doctor. By the time they moored up there at the island wharf he was no better, and as snipe shooting had been arranged, and he was unable to lift a gun, they took him to a large house on a canal where the student-consuls were trained in speaking Chinese. The five young men studying there welcomed a fresh face in their rather restricted sort of life, and did what was possible for him, but even sitting in a chair was agony. The second day he decided to go out with the shooting party but remained in the motor sampan to organise their lunch. It turned out that the migrating snipe had already mostly left for the north and only a very small bag was brought home.

By the time he had returned to Hong Kong his passage home had been organised and he sailed a few days later for Yokosuka in Japan. Just across the road from the jetty at this port there was the very high wall of the naval shipyard, and armed guards not only kept the gateway, but roughly moved anyone who might stop to look through if it happened to be opened for a moment. He was warned that, as an obvious foreigner, he would be arrested at once should he pause for even a moment while passing by, and he saw pedestrians who were actually being arrested.

The Japanese system was to provide all workmen and women with living accommodation inside the dockyard wall, and they were contracted for a period of years and never allowed outside during that time. Moreover, foreigners who spent over 48 hours in any one place in Japan were obliged to report to the police, a long and tedious process, and to explain why they wished to extend a visit beyond that time. Hugh had worked out a fortnight's itinerary that would avoid reporting to the police and carefully preserved all hotel bills in case any enquiry should be made.

On board the ship from Hong Kong he had made friends with a Belgian couple, the de Koechlins, who were doing an almost identical tour, and so they happily travelled together for almost all of his fortnight. Tokyo, the first stop, was disappointing, as the famed cherry trees were not yet in blossom. The centre of the city which had lately been almost wholly destroyed by an earthquake resembled a giant builder's yard. They hired a car, drove through the city and round the parks and the Imperial Palace precinct, part of which was open to the public at that time. While they were walking about with a guide, Mr de Koechlin chanced to get into conversation with some workmen who were engaged in repair work, and as he spoke Japanese fairly well one of the party, who seemed to be a foreman, invited the three visitors to come with him and he would show them what he was working at. They passed through one or two gates and courtyards until they came to a modest-looking sort of pavilion from which a lovely view spread out, and in they went. It was the palace of imperial installation, a series of spacious interconnecting rooms with extremely simple restrained decoration, but each of them more impressively splendid than the last. Then they entered the actual empty chamber which had a small low dais along one wall and upon which a single chair stood made apparently of superb lacquered wood, and this was the place in which the emperor was officially installed. There is no crown nor religious ceremony in Japan. As they looked about them they realised that at every point their surroundings were of a quality and workmanship never before seen. One wall which seemed to have gold leaf applied to wood, so that it glowed but did not shine or reflect light, had a widespread design of autumn-coloured maple leaves, as though a branch of a tree had been fixed to the wall. They learned that only about thirty persons would be present at the installation ceremony, and elsewhere they saw some of the special ceremonial robes that were worn, the sort of silk material that practically stands up on its own, it is so stiff. It is difficult to describe the subdued colours in their harmony and the sheen upon rich materials and the extreme simplicity of wall decoration which created an impression of a magnificence one had never before imagined, and the contrast with equivalent western exuberance of decoration was very striking. Probably very few foreign people have ever seen the interior of this building which must represent the very summit of Japanese art and decoration.

That night they took a train to the north hoping to see Fujiyama early next day, but it was pouring with rain and even the nearby countryside was shrouded in mist. However, they reached a lovely hotel on a lake in the hills and from there drove a hired car up into the mountains to a resort at a height of 7,000 feet, the narrow, often only one-way track zigzagging up what was in effect a steep cliff. At one point, the turn was so sharp and the road so narrow that the car had to reverse twice to get round it, and as he looked back Hugh saw that the corner in the road at that place was built on a heavy wood platform which was suspended by several wire cables to other parts of the cliff. It was an altogether unique piece of construction and a clever solution of a difficult problem. Up at the top, snow still persisted and skiers were weaving their way through tall clumps of green and white-leaved bamboo. On the lower side of the roadway one could see bushes of familiar red japonica just breaking into flower where the snow had melted. An extensive European-style resort lay scattered along the lakeshore below and was used chiefly by foreign diplomatic personnel to get out of the humid heat of Tokyo in summer. Altogether it was a drive to remember and some car passengers would not face the precipitous descent in the evening and got out of their shaky vehicles and walked down the more hair-raising parts.

On another day the Belgian couple, who were keen bow and arrow people, made contact with a Japanese who shared their enthusiasm, and the little party of three Europeans spent an afternoon out in a field behind the residence shooting at the targets. Hugh had never before had a bow in his hand, and after suitable instruction from his Japanese host, shot off his first ever arrow which hit the edge of the bullseye and of course drew loud applause. The next time his arrow hit the ground and wriggled its way through the rough grass exactly like a snake, and he never again got anywhere near the target centre. When they all retired to the house they found that the entrance was through a high-walled little courtyard about five yards square and this was laid out as a bonsai garden. Some of the plants had been in the family for three hundred years and the whole effect was exactly that of a Japanese painting — exquisite, complicated, and somehow unnatural.

During their extensive tour of Kyoto they went shopping at several stopping places and Hugh stocked up on what he hoped would be suitable presents for his family. On one shopping expedition the storekeeper beckoned him into a little windowless room at the back of the shop and carefully closed the door. Hugh became intensely alert, ready to cope with whatever oriental mystery was to be revealed. After unlocking a large chest and some rummaging amongst the paper packages it contained, out came a little wooden box about a foot high, sealed and tied up with tapes. When it finally did open a small squat black vase with a stylised chrysanthemum in cream was revealed. It was explained that this black Satsuma almost unique treasure had come to hand by accident. A courtier of ancient lineage in attendance at the Imperial Palace had gone bankrupt and his house and its contents had been sold by his creditors, and the shopkeeper had bought at the auction a box full of odd bits and pieces, some unseen and wrapped in paper.

This little vase was undoubtedly an Imperial treasure, perhaps had been a present, and, as its decorations showed it to be a personal treasure of the emperor, it could not be displayed to public gaze, and any Japanese who was discovered to have it in his possession would be judged as a criminal and be imprisoned.

So the storekeeper thought that a good way to get rid of the embarrassing possession would be to sell it to a travelling foreigner who would soon spirit it out of the country. Hugh bought it for a few yen and slipped it into his raincoat pocket.

When he went aboard ship next day at Yokohama, the numerous customs and emigration officials examined the passports and also the possessions of the passengers with the utmost care. Why, since his passport showed that he had been in Japan for the past fourteen days, was there no police report noted? His reason was that he had not spent forty-eight hours in any one place. The emigration officer didn't believe it, he was sure that Hugh had broken the law; the penalty was imprisonment. So Hugh, who had the black Satsuma vase in his overcoat pocket, was obliged to go and open a suitcase, extract his hotel bills, the railway timetable, the hire-car receipts and several shopping receipts, and went over hour by hour his fortnight's travels. It all took a long time, and the ship's captain was champing in the background because the tugs were already made fast, and it was now five minutes past sailing time. Finally the official stamp was applied to the passport and the officials hurried ashore. Fortunately the customs men never had a chance to examine his luggage nor to find the black Satsuma vase still in his coat pocket.

That night at dinner in the saloon Hugh happened to look out of a ship's side scuttle, and there saw the vision of Fujiyama-San, as though floating above the last pink mists of sunset, glittering in its amazing perfection of symmetry, immaculate and white, the most beautiful mountain on earth — a sight no man forgets once he has seen it.

The fourteen-day passage to Victoria in the province of British Columbia in this eight-thousand-ton Japanese cargo ship, endlessly rolling in the long Pacific swell, with only sixteen passengers on board, might have been dull, but once the ship's officers discovered that Hugh played mah-jong he was kept at it for many long hours each day, and they taught him many of the expert tricks of it so that, at the end of the voyage, the chief engineer owed him five yen, and this he always regarded as a real triumph.

He had so much looked forward to spending his ten weeks foreign service leave in Canada where his father, whom he had not seen for ten years, and also two married sisters and a flock of unknown nephews and nieces were living, all more or less concentrated in the British Columbia coastal area. A small sort of delegation of relatives was actually on the dock as the ship made fast in Victoria and he was soon driven away to a sister's home on the sea-shore facing Mount Baker through flower-lined streets, at that season at their very best. It was, of course, a most joyous occasion, but his health was not good and a long spell of Japanese food brought on a crisis. A duodenal ulcer was discovered and a severe major operation performed, so that his time in Canada was spent partly in hospital and then in the early stages of convalescence, and he was far from fit when the time came for him to report back to London. Fortunately an old friend met him with a car when he staggered unsteadily out of the Admiralty, and drove him down to the Naval Hospital at Chatham where he collapsed at the door and was of course put to bed. The damp cold, to him at all events, was paralysing, but the permitted season for fires — and that meant coal fires in each room — had passed, and regulations forbade them. He could not get warm and simply stayed in bed, and when the surgeon rear-admiral in charge came round on his weekly inspection and found him so, he was not pleased. Finally Hugh stretched out his two blue icy hands and said:

"I simply can't stand the cold, Sir, after so long abroad. Just look at my hands, even here in bed!"

Everybody looked shocked. The admiral couldn't avoid looking, and went somewhat red in the face.

"But we can't allow fires. It's against the regulations at this time of year! Dammit, Matron, get a fire lighted in this room at once and see that it is kept going. How I'm going to explain this away I don't know!"

"I don't think there is any coal left, Sir!"

"Then telephone for a load and light that fire as soon as you can. Tell the coal man it is urgent."

And out he went, followed by the usual tail of doctors and starched nursing sisters. Later they sent him off on six months' sick leave and very slowly he improved. He always claimed it took six years to get over that operation. The techniques of 1931 were not what one would find today.

Chapter 11

The Mediterranean Station

At the end of his six months' sick leave, a medical board recommended Hugh for Home Shore Service and he was appointed to Devonport Barracks in charge of the training of new entries, which comprised about two hundred and fifty youths of ages 16 to 18 entering the Service for the first time and allocated to all branches. The engineers, joiners, carpenters and shipwrights went to learn their trade in the dockyard; the tradesmen cooks were taught in the large kitchens of the barracks; and the remainder — about three-quarters of the total — were directly under Hugh to be trained for the seaman branch, some of them at a later stage being allocated to the signal and telegraphist branches, most of their instruction being given by specially selected petty officers and schoolmasters. Some parade ground drill, swimming, and gymnastics were in all these programmes, and outdoor games such as football, cricket, hockey, field sports, boxing, sailing and swimming were encouraged to the fullest extent of the facilities available at Devonport.

One of the interesting classes was the needlework one. A man at sea must be able to sew on a button, to make repairs to torn clothing, to darn his socks, and especially to wash his clothes. Hardly any boy had ever done any one of these necessary things before he joined the Service, and of course some initial efforts were very comical — but six months later their mothers would have found it difficult to match their workmanship in many cases. At the end of each cook's course the passing-out examination consisted of the production of a hot dinner made entirely of Service provisions and using Service utensils that a ship would normally carry. The warrant cook instructor loved above all else a symmetrical plum duff pudding which is made mostly of flour, lard and large raisins and is boiled in a cloth.

Hugh's stomach was now working again quite well but needed continuous care and attention to diet, and these heavy puddings were exactly what could knock him out for a week. When he went for the first time to inspect the cooks' passing-out dinners — and there were ten of them spread along a large table — the warrant cook asked him to judge the quality of the puddings in order of merit — and that of course meant that he had to eat a slice from each one. He munched up half his slice of the first one, and from within came unmistakable warning signs that something close to death was approaching. He had a lot of trouble talking himself out of this job, and solved the problem by altering the positions of the other nine puddings so that the boys wouldn't know which was which and then made each examinee taste them and produce what the boy thought was the correct order of excellence. But he had to be off duty for two or three days after that. He did much of the instruction in boatwork himself, including rowing and sailing, and enjoyed getting out of the dockyard smoke or merely sitting in an office.

The dockyard is, of course, a civil department, and is organised on civilian shipyard type rules. One of its functions was to attend to the upkeep of the barracks, and that included the painting. The commander-in-chief was due to inspect the barracks and would be certain to take an interest in the training department, so Hugh arranged to get the boys' living-rooms painted out and generally spruced up. They had all worked "after hours" to complete the work, and it was very nearly finished when Hugh was sent for and had to explain to the commodore in command why dockyard painting regulations had been "disobeyed". He answered that he had no idea that anyone could forbid the smartening-up of a naval establishment, and a purple-faced trade union official standing by said that bread had been taken out of the mouths of dockyard workmen, and demanded Hugh's head on a charger. The commodore said some fairly severe words, and then announced that he would give his considered decision later, and everyone filed out of the office. Hugh felt apprehensive, but heard no more about it, and suddenly a gang of dockyard painters moved into the boys' quarters and in a single day repainted the whole thing — which for months they claimed that they hadn't time to get around to. So at least bread had been restored to the hungry mouths, but at the cost to the Admiralty of two coats of paint where only one was necessary! The commodore became a real friend and Hugh was quite often invited to his house, but he never told Hugh what his "considered later decision" was. It was all very typical "Navy", and a good deal of fun is extracted on the way through these kinds of hassles with shoregoing departments, who are in fact expert in their chosen sphere.

When long summer leave time came round one of the boys spoke up and said that he didn't want to go home, nor could he find any other place where he could spend a month. After tactful investigation it emerged that his father was a commercial traveller hardly ever at home, and in his absence his son was compelled to sleep in his mother's bed. He hated it and had joined the Navy to get away from the situation. One of the instructor petty officers invited him to spend his leave in his home with his own family, so that the problem was solved. It was the first time Hugh had come face to face with such a situation, and in discussing it with the petty officer was astonished to learn that it is common, especially in the families of men whose work takes them away from home a great deal. Hugh was beginning to learn many new facts of life other than the one at sea which he had blindly chosen.

The wardroom mess at the barracks, where usually over a hundred officers are accommodated, was in the process of being redecorated and generally improved, and the famous marine painter, Wylie, had designed a frieze in carved wood which encircled the dining-room ceiling and was written up in the press and much admired at that time. Someone had observed that a "plate store", a small but very substantial stone building standing near the mess, seemed to be something of a secret. The keys could not be found on the normal keyboard and nobody knew where they were. It was therefore carefully broken open and inside was found a mass of silver plate brought in by ships when they paid off, apparently through almost a century past. Much of the contents could not be identified and no complete inventory existed. A committee investigated the whole matter and selected articles that should be preserved, such as cups that bore ships' names that were likely to be repeated in future construction, or that commemorated some historical event, and what remained over and appeared to be of no general interest was melted down and cast into a four-foot high statue of Drake playing bowls on Plymouth Hoe, a really impressive work of art in itself. Since then it has been the centre-piece of the naval barrack's dining-table.

Hugh was in no way involved in all that, but his time was very full with football matches, sailing and rowing races, and weekend picnics with a couple of boat loads of young sailors right up to the end of this appointment in the spring of 1934.

And in a way it all rebounded to his credit, for, after a month's leave, he was appointed as first lieutenant of the 8-inch cruiser squadron flagship *London* on the Mediterranean Station, and that would certainly be considered as a "promotion job" for a lieutenant commander. Out of his seniority batch perhaps twenty from over a hundred officers would be promoted to commander in the normal course of events, and he would be in the promotion zone for about four more years; once out of that zone an officer was never promoted. He felt that his spell of ill health had evidently not blackballed him entirely.

London was duly commissioned in April 1934 just as she was coming out of a long dockyard refit. The Lord Mayor of London telegraphed the city's good wishes and the commander-in-chief at Portsmouth inspected the ship which was still in a considerable mess as dockyard workmen were on board hurrying the completion of their work. The ship was the inheritor of a long line of predecessors of her name, and during the previous commission had won almost every cup and trophy that existed in the Mediterranean, and in a large glass case forty-seven pieces of silver were proudly displayed. They undoubtedly served to set up a standard for the new commission and in the early days one would usually see two or three of the ship's company gathered round reading the inscriptions. It was said at that time that no ship had ever held so many trophies.

By the time they had got to Gibraltar, where they spent a month doing working up practices and training drills, the ship was cleaned and repainted and officers and men had got to know one another and had settled down in their jobs. At weekends Hugh went by rail up to Ronda, a picturesque small Andalusian town on a mountainside divided in two by a deep chasm spanned by a bridge where there is a rambling nobleman's dwelling, housing antique furniture and pictures of beauty and interest to which the public are admitted. Indeed, the whole town is picturesque and has a large and excellent hotel. The officers also sailed across the bay for picnics on the Spanish Coast, and on one occasion had inadvertently landed within the prohibited area of Spanish coast defences, and then quickly found themselves surrounded by several angry Spanish soldiers with whom they were unable to talk, neither side understanding a word of the other's language. Suddenly a tall grey-haired man in bathing rig appeared and quickly settled the incident. Later on they discovered that he was General Harrington, Governor of Gibraltar, who had in fact put ashore in his boat a mile or so to the north. The governor invited the officers to join his party and meet his wife and everyone enjoyed their picnic all the more. Later they found that Lady Harrington loved gypsy music, and an officer who had Spanish friends managed to engage a tzigane band to play on board to entertain a large reception the ship gave to the people of the fortress.

It became showery, and the guests, who were mostly on the quarterdeck, left almost at once. But the band had been taken down to the wardroom and about twenty people had followed them below to listen to their haunting music — among them Lady Harrington, who was completely captivated by it and kept on and on asking for still one more last song, until it was past the hour for the staff to prepare the mess for a farewell dinner that was to be held that night. The captain told Hugh, who was responsible for the arrangements, to "get Lady Harrington out of the ship", which he didn't know how to do in view of her official position. At last came inspiration, and he managed to get the tziganas to announce that they would play no more and were going ashore; and so one of the most enjoyable parties they ever gave came to a perfectly harmonious end.

Malta was the Mediterranean Fleet base, and they were in and out of Grand Harbour many times during the next two years. In the spring the Home Fleet came out for about a month of combined fleet exercises usually held in the Atlantic west of Gibraltar. When that was over, Mediterranean ships dispersed for summer cruises. One year *London* visited Greece, stopping at Milos, a very hot sandy island famous through the discovery of the statue of the Venus de Milo, now in the Louvre in Paris. Then Skiathos, very small, with only a few farms mostly producing olives. The next place, of great beauty with perfect sandy bathing beaches and a Greek naval base, was Poros, where a whole fleet of boats from the Athens Yacht Club sailed in for a weekend during which parties were almost non-stop. Hugh long remembered a very beautiful young woman who spoke seven languages fluently, a total not achieved by any other person he ever met. *London* was now practising hard for the forthcoming fleet regatta, and Hugh, in charge of the training programme, was away in the boats many hours each day which made it impossible for him to accept the invitation of several of the yacht owners to sail up to Athens with them.

He had acquired an inflatable rubber mattress, known as a lilo, which, when out bathing one day, got caught in a strong current sweeping him along the coast out of sight of the ship and, unable to guide the float into the shore, he wondered what he could do to save himself. Presently the tide turned and carried him in towards the shore where he landed and then had to walk about four miles back to the bay where *London* was anchored. There was much fraternising with the crews of the Greek warships present so that days passed very quickly there.

Later they put in at Argostoli for a few days. It is a very large sheltered anchorage which the Mediterranean Fleet had often used in times past. The mayor, who spoke only a little French and no English, was invited to lunch with the admiral, who hauled in Hugh to do some interpreting, and that didn't go too well, for Hugh's French was rusty and the mayor had an accent that made too many words unintelligible. However, it was fortunately not a very long-drawn-out meal and they all went up on deck to watch the seaplane catapulted for a short flight and then land again, these operations being under Hugh's charge. After the signal had been given to the plane that the water was clear of obstruction and fit for landing, the flashing gold-coloured head of a powerful swimmer was sighted making to cross the path the plane would take. It was already too late to abort the landing and no amount of yelling and blasts on a bugle attracted the attention of the swimmer; they all thought the seaplane floats were sure to decapitate him. It was not so; the pilot saw the swimmer and thought the head had passed through the narrow space between the floats; the spectators held their breath; then the golden head reappeared in the wake of the seaplane. The mayor explained that the man was the local champion swimmer, but was stone deaf. Later it was learned that he had seen the shadow of the seaplane on the water and, not knowing what it might be, had dived at once. He never did see the seaplane and was unaware of his escape until much later in the day.

The ship also visited Corfu, one of the most developed and attractive of the islands, which still bears many evidences of its past status as a British possession. The town has a good hotel, a few shops and an impressive cathedral with a great square in front of it. At a short distance out of the town an attractive villa overlooking a most lovely bay belonged to Prince Andrew of Greece (a brother of the king) who no longer lived there but placed the bathing beach at the disposal of the Fleet. At the entrance gate to the estate was a little lodge where visitors identified themselves before admission, and Hugh made friends with the old couple who lived there. The husband had been a Foreign Office courier long ago and his wife a maid in the British ambassador's household and they delighted in talking of England where they had not visited for many past years. Tea and crumpets were produced and it was difficult to get on for a walk on the beach a mile away. But they were a delight to meet and their stories of life half a century ago were full of interest.

A short drive out into the country to the Villa Akelion, Kaiser Wilhelm's summer residence in past days, hidden behind an enormously thick hedge, was an interesting expedition. The modest house, though empty of all furniture, still reflected in its decoration the ugly and ostentatious bad taste of the emperor. There were in one room groups of plaster cupids in the ceiling, each one having an electric light bulb in its mouth. One went away from the place marvelling that a German emperor could have been capable of creating such an unremittingly hideous dwelling.

There is also on Corfu a village in the interior named Paleokastritza where a small and very ancient Greek Orthodox Monastery is perched on a hilltop from which a marvellous view can be seen in all directions. The interior of the buildings is generally dark, for there are no windows, and the pictures and other furnishings look as if they had not been cleaned for centuries. Outside, the terraces and courtyards are hung with bougainvillea and grape vines and the few monks seem to drift about noiselessly so that the whole effect is one of peace and quiet. There can be very few visitors there who have not been impressed with the general atmosphere of calm.

The first winter on the station, *London* went on a cruise to Istanbul and then Varna in Bulgaria on the Black Sea. They took the opportunity to steam close inshore past the beaches on the western coast of Gallipoli peninsula where British and Imperial troops had landed and fought so desperately and unsuccessfully during the First World War, and one realised how wide open they all were to the Turkish gun-fire. The almost wholly unsheltered beaches gave the impression that only a miracle could have saved the army from annihilation during the evacuation. Inside the straits, on the other side of the peninsula, the allied fleet had steamed up to bombard shore defences and several heavy ships had run into a minefield and been sunk. Had the combined forces pressed on for only one more day disregarding their heavy casualties, they would have captured the whole peninsula at once because the Turks who had run out of ammunition and fresh supplies, could not have reached them in time. But that intelligence came in only at a much later date.

When *London* reached Istanbul she anchored off the Dolma Batche Palace from which there is a tremendous view of the Seraglio (from which, on a tip-up platform over the fast flowing sea current, surplus slaves, wives and children used to be dropped into the water) right up to the entrance of the Bosphorus Straits which spread north to the Black Sea, and then, to the eastward, the Asiatic coast of the Sea of Marmara — in which direction the Turkish fleet could be distantly seen at anchor. As it happened they were all on long leave, but the minister for the navy recalled the admirals and captains to come on board to call upon the British. In conversation it was learned that they were furious at this interruption of their "visit to their wives", as they described it. Their uniforms looked rumpled and one or two had not found time to shave for the occasion. However, suitable liquid refreshments healed most of their wounds. The British personnel were interested to see the old German battle-cruiser *Goeben* which had been ceded to Turkey as part of the reparations exacted by the Allies after World War I; unfortunately no opportunity to go on board was offered.

At that time the hillside in Istanbul immediately opposite the *London* was closely packed with tall narrow wooden housing from the water's edge up to the skyline. The area had been burnt out more than once in past years and was destined to be completely destroyed by fire in the near future. It was most picturesque and the streets extremely narrow so that a car could not pass through some of them.

Hugh passed nearby and got out of his car to look into one or two of these alleys for a few minutes on a day when he was lunching at the British Embassy with Sir Percy and Lady Lorraine. The ambassador had recently arrived in Turkey after a long career as high commissioner in Egypt and had quickly made friends with

Kemal Ataturk, the president, who resided at the new capital Ankara in the interior. It was said that recently the two men, who enjoyed the same kind of drink, had played poker continuously for two days, several other participants having come and gone while a large fortune passed across the table. If that was true, then the ambassador showed no sign whatever of such a gruelling contest, and took some pride in describing to his guests how he had gone out into the country and purchased a young lamb which now lay roasted on the table. This is a special delicacy in Istanbul, and Hugh thought that it was the most delicious meat he ever ate. Lady Lorraine was a very beautiful woman and made every effort to arrange entertainment for these visitors.

The old Palace of the Sultans, now used as a museum, contains an enormous collection of treasures of every sort. One room is entirely lined with Chinese green celadon ware comprising a dinner-service of several hundred pieces sent in a sailing junk as a present from a Chinese emperor to the reigning sultan. In another room vast quantities of personal jewellery, and jewelled clocks, daggers, swords and other articles surround a large gilt throne almost completely encrusted with rubies, some being very large. This particular room contains wealth which must amount to hundreds of millions. In the seraglio (the women's quarters) endless rooms and corridors lead one into another and nearly all of them are richly decorated in arabesque style with original furnishings of mirrors, couches, chairs, and divans piled with cushions still in place. The tip-up platform over the waters of the Bosphorus is also displayed to the public and there surplus wives and attendants were disposed of.

There was another expedition to see the Cathedral of St. Sophia, originally the mother-church of Greek Orthodox Christianity, built by the Byzantine Emperor Justinian about the third century. Later on, when Istanbul fell to the Turks, they converted the cathedral into a mosque and plastered over the Christian mosaics and other symbols. Now, in these latter days, the plaster is being removed and the cathedral has been largely restored to its original brilliant appearance. Nearby is the "Blue" mosque surrounded by acres of courtyards, a very impressive and spacious building. Its foundations stand in underground water which absorbs earthquake shocks and lead sections in the pillars also have the same effect, so that it has never been damaged.

After about a week *London* went on to Varna in Bulgaria. By

s

now it was midwinter and very cold, the ground on shore being frozen solid, but with scarcely more than a dusting of snow. King Boris came down from his capital, Sofia, accompanied by his brother and attended by five cabinet members. There had been rumours of an intended coup to dethrone him and while on board at one point he was seen to be delivering — in Bulgarian of course — what appeared to be a first-rate dressing down to the ministers. They spent their time all through lunch in the admiral's cabin silent, looking apprehensive and nervous. When the king got to the wireless office while on a tour round the ship he asked if he might send a message to King George V in England, and, before lunch was finished, a reply was handed to him, and this obviously pleased him very much.

While *London* was at Varna her companion cruiser *Sussex* visited Constanza in Roumania, and the captain and one or two other officers were invited up to the capital to stay for a few days with the king and queen. Queen Marie, the king's mother who lived with him, was a granddaughter of Queen Victoria and was always delighted to make contact with visiting British people, and the whole visit developed into a cheerful, happy family party with fun and games for the children, one of whom later became King Michael of Roumania who was exiled from his country by the German Nazis and has not of course since been restored to the throne by the Russians who later took over the country.

Another cruise took the ship to Venice to represent Britain at the International World Motor Boat Speed Championship race for which the British expert, Scott-Paine was a favoured contender. They moored opposite the Doge's Palace at the entrance to the Grand Canal, and next above them was Mussolini's yacht *Aurore*, and beyond her Marconi's famous yacht *Elettra* on board which some of his most important experiments had been conducted. There was in Venice an exhibition of paintings of living artists from many of the civilised states. Hitler had already visited it and bought three small paintings which, when Hugh went there, he liked best of all he saw. The Russian section, mostly of very large landscape scenes, and the Spanish collection of strong, almost strident paintings, fascinated him, for he had never before seen current paintings from either country. The British section was modest, but included some very beautiful small etchings done by Mrs Leighton the wife of an officer in the ship, and of course they all went to see that section of the exhibition.

Scott-Paine came to live on board in the wardroom and his several mechanics were also accommodated on board. The day before the race he moved into a dockside shed where his boat, *Miss England III*, was housed, and he had two mechanics with him to make final adjustments. They all went off together to get an evening meal at a restaurant, and when they returned discovered that a determined effort to break into *Miss England*'s shed had been made, but Scott-Paine had strengthened the door hinges and the lock, and the would-be saboteurs had failed to get inside. During the night, through which the crew kept a continuous watch, a second attempt at entry was heard, and again the intruders failed to get in. Scott-Paine was well prepared because the same thing had been attempted when he was racing in the United States at an earlier date.

By nine o'clock in the morning of the race the course had been cleared of all boats and Hugh had taken out a large party of ratings in a cutter and anchored close to the finishing line. The racing boats started singly, a short time elapsing between each one so that they would be unlikely to hamper one another on the ten laps of a three-mile circular course. A tremendous cheer went up from each group of spectators from the various nationalities as their boat crossed the starting line, but *Miss England* did not appear until the first boat had completed two circuits. Then she seemed almost to explode like a rocket and overtook every other boat, finishing two laps ahead of her nearest competitor. Mussolini was in the Yacht Club when the race began, but vanished when it was finished, and it was the Commodore of the Yacht Club who presented the cup to Scott-Paine to the hesitant applause of some of the Italians present and the uproarious but distant cheers of the boat full of Londoners. Everyone in Venice had been sure that the Italian boat would win.

Mussolini arrived in Venice three days before the race and the ship had been informed of the time he was expected, but not the public, though they seemed to have guessed. He came at high speed from the railway station surrounded by police patrol craft in a small boat down the Grand Canal to *Aurore*, and a group of English tourists had gathered at the waterside in expectation. Distant cheering broke out and rapidly drew nearer. A young woman in the English group opened her handbag in search of a handkerchief, was seized from behind and rushed off in a police wagon, for they feared she might have had a gun. She was grilled for some hours and only released after the consul had been to the police station to guarantee her integrity.

Hugh was not far away in a shop bargaining for some small trinkets he wanted to purchase when the sound of distant cheers drifted in through the open door. Two or three saleswomen on duty rushed excitedly out of the shop shouting *"Il Duce! Il Duce!"* and vanished in the direction of the nearby canal. He waited for twenty minutes alone there, finally dropping whatever articles he had in his hand and returned to the ship. There was a sort of hysteria in the air, a hero worship that had gone beyond reason.

That night Princess Ruspigliosi, the American wife of a wealthy nobleman, gave a reception in the family palace on the Grand Canal. The officers from *London* were guests of honour and Mussolini, it was rumoured, would appear — but he didn't. The Royal Dukes of Aosta and Bergamo and their wives were present and Bergamo, who was a naval officer, spent much of his evening talking to the *London*ers, a young man of great charm and simplicity of bearing whom Hugh showed over *London* a day or two later on.

This evening when *London*'s motor boat arrived at the front door, they stepped off onto a marble platform and where ushered by a bewigged major-domo up a winding staircase where a footman in a red velvet coat and white knee breeches stood on every sixth step until they reached the reception-room two stories up, a splendid apartment off which led two or three smaller rooms. An orchestra played and introductions seemed to be almost endless. Probably everybody who was anybody in Venice was present. The members of the royal family seemed to stay most of the time in one of the smaller rooms, and Hugh hardly got out of there, no doubt because he could speak French, which they all understood. Late in the evening, and getting very footsore from long standing, a young son of the family took him off to a window embrasure overhanging a garden at the rear of the great house where they were still talking at one o'clock in the morning when Princess Ruspigliosi found them and sat down with them, equally tired, and they talked on for another hour after the last of the guests had left. It was a sort of fairy-tale experience — the canal reflecting the lights, the shadowed garden where marble statury and fountains could be dimly seen in the moonlight, and the magnificent rooms of the palace; no fairy princess there to be sure, but royal personages to whom one could talk on level terms because that was what they wanted, and at the very end the happy companionship of the heir to all the grandeur and his nice, almost homely, mother who knew people and places familiar to Hugh, and wanted to talk about them. He went home bemused, having through a long evening sat back, as it were, to look on life in one of its more gracious aspects.

Another day Hugh fulfilled an ambition to visit the famous Lido, a long stretch of bathing beach at the entrance to Venice which is several miles down the lagoon. Huge and expensive hotels line the shore along which are ranged rows of cabanas, luxuriously-fitted bathing tents where one changes and takes meals, for it takes a whole day to enjoy the expedition. The reigning beauties of most of the civilised world paraded along the sandy shore in costumes that would never enter salt water but were designed to ensure that press photographers would not miss them. It was crowded of course, but somehow it was fun and Hugh's Italian hosts were intent on enjoying themselves. It was only he who was stunned by the fashion parade, perhaps disappointed that the sea water was not very clean — not that it mattered because there was an efficient fresh water shower at the back of the cabana. Only three out of the party of ten people actually went into the sea and swam, and it was noticeable that very few of the many hundreds lying out in the sunshine ever went for a swim.

On another day Hugh went to explore St. Mark's Cathedral which had recently been flooded to a depth of about three feet and one could see the marks on the walls. This apparently happens quite often. He soon got tired of the guide, who collects his party at the front door, and, finding himself standing against a little low door, he pushed it open and climbed a circular staircase in complete darkness. Finally light above began to increase and he stepped out onto a wide balcony where the famous bronze horses of St. Mark's stand, and from which a marvellous view of the Campanile (recently collapsed and not quite finished rebuilding) and the huge square spreads out. He wandered on and found the interior of the cathedral was so dark that not very much of the decorations could be clearly seen. That night he attended an outdoor concert in the square at which Gigli, the great tenor of the day, sang for nearly two hours as flocks of pigeons fluttered round and round overhead, disturbed by the music from their customary sleep. It was a wonderful experience.

Some Italian friends took Hugh out to Murano in their motor

boat to visit the glass factory which has operated on that island for several centuries past. The chief glass blower was brought out and introduced to the party and then made for them two or three pieces which the ladies took away as presents. The sales room was lined with finished pieces, many of them being reproductions of museum exhibits famous all over the civilised world. The chief glass blower, a very fine-looking man of about forty years of age, was stone deaf, and, when he was actually working, had that absorbed look and total detachment from his surroundings which one sees in many artists. It was a memorable afternoon's excursion which millions must have made through the years.

One day Mussolini came on board to lunch with the admiral and was shown all over the ship, in which he took the greatest interest. The Royal Marines' eight-inch gun turret was manned for a demonstration drill, and the Duce spent almost an hour examining every detail right down to the magazines. Someone told him that in order to get from the right-hand gun operating platform to the left-hand one it was necessary to get out onto the deck. He cocked his head for a minute considering that, and then jamming his little black forage cap tightly onto his head started to climb upwards over the breech fittings, and a few minutes later was able to lower himself down onto the left gun operating platform. The Royal Marines were speechless. Nobody had ever before found a way to do this, and they believed it to be impossible. The little man with his enormously thick — but not fat — body was delighted with his visit, but when he was leaving could not reach up to ceremoniously kiss the admiral goodbye, and so he threw his arms around him a bit lower down and hugged him vigorously. That was a day to remember.

On the return journey to Malta the ship visited several of the small ports on the eastern shores of the Adriatic Sea. Dubrovnik, the largest place, in Yugoslav territory, was the most historically interesting and the first thing one sees is the large area of Tiberius Caesar's Palace to which he retired when Rome would no longer tolerate his excesses. The remains are extensive and well preserved. Makaska, a seaside resort on the shore immediately below a wall of mountains, was a place everyone enjoyed, for they quickly made friends with the people there. It was particularly noticeable that the local people were beautifully built and strikingly handsome. The whole length of the eastern coastline is interesting and much of it scenically impressive and has in later years become a busy tourist area.

The ship was now ordered to hurry to the island of Samos close to the Turkish shore where a forest fire had burnt out more than half of the island and it was feared that large scale evacuation might become necessary. As soon as they anchored, our seaplane was launched and Hugh flew over the island to map out roughly where the flames were still burning. A boat was sent inshore to find out what help was needed, and they later landed some foodstuffs. A change in the wind and a little rain soon brought the fires under control so that there was no longer cause for anxiety.

On a Sunday afternoon the torpedo officer, Maunsell, and the young doctor, went off for a picnic in the sailing dinghy, and a drop in the breeze caused the boat to drift with a strong current into the narrow straits which separate Samos from the mainland coast of Turkey. This strait narrows down to only about four hundred yards width in one part, and as the little boat, which had a white ensign displayed on a short staff, approached the narrows it came under rifle fire from trenches on the Turkish shore. Both officers jumped into the water; Maunsell was hit in the upper part of one arm, and the doctor swam alongside the dinghy and pushed it out of range of the gun-fire and they got back to the ship a few hours later without further incident.

The official view taken was that such an attack was completely unjustified and the British Government demanded an apology and financial indemnity. The Turks seemed hesitant, perhaps unwilling, to accept responsibility. *London* was ordered to go to the nearby provincial government headquarters, steaming through the straits where the incident occurred, and if any gun-fire was directed at her, to reply with her eight-inch guns. They went through the next day with main armament manned and HE shells fused at the ready, but nothing happened, though a few soldiers were seen watching their passage. At the port, Hugh landed in a boat armed with a machine-gun. A car, which had been requested by the ambassador at Ankara, met him and drove him to the provincial governor's office in the nearby town. He walked straight in and was told that the governor was not ready to receive him (although the embassy had telegraphed the hour at which the visit would be paid), so he sat down and waited for about twenty minutes. Then a servant asked him to go upstairs to the governor's lodging and after another short wait, an unshaven and rather dishevelled man came in looking thoroughly scared. He apologised for the delay and said that he had been asleep in bed; then he called for coffee which was so thick and sweet that the spoon could almost be made to stand up in the cup. A bottle of crème de menthe was passed round and Hugh began to read the British Government's demand from a paper addressed to the governor which he then handed to him. A suitable sort of apology was then offered — the soldiers stationed in the fortifications were militiamen under training and their officers inexperienced volunteers and the Turkish Government much regretted the incident and was fully prepared to negotiate the question of whatever damages might be claimed. Hugh made him write down all that he had said, and sign and date the paper, and then took his leave and drove back to his boat at the jetty. That seemed to be the official end of the matter, but Maunsell's arm was crippled for the rest of his life.

Eventually when it became apparent that Mussolini's Abyssinian War had become bogged down, the annual fleet rowing regatta was organised to take place at Argostoli. This is on every foreign station the major sporting fixture and source of entertainment. Officially, betting is forbidden, but during the preceding few days small boats could be seen pulling from one ship to another with money that was to be wagered. The larger ships in the Mediterranean congregated for this event at Argostoli which was almost ideally suited for the races which could be conveniently watched from almost every ship present. Crews had been training for weeks through the summer and the pulling boats were carefully prepared. *London* ship's company looked forward with special keenness, for they had to defend most of the major cups which their predecessors had won during the last commission. Hugh, as first lieutenant, traditionally held the position of Regatta Officer, and found little time for expeditions ashore during the summer cruise. Several other officers also trained crews and the captain took the officer's gig out at six o'clock every morning the ship was at anchor.

The great day came at last and dawned on a slightly choppy sea, and the starting gun for the first race in a programme of twenty-five events went off at nine o'clock. There were successes, a few failures, only one protest on account of an infringement of rules, and the day wore on with the Australian cruiser *Sidney* closely following *London* which, two races before the end, was just a single point in the lead. The seamen petty officer's fourteen-oared cutter was the competitor in the race preceding the last one on the programme. *London*'s crew was a good one, but some dispute over their coxswain had arisen a week ago and they had come to Hugh and asked him to replace the man with a much younger coxswain, who was a competent level-headed petty officer and seemed a suitable choice and would have sufficient time to get used to his special job — so Hugh made the change. A quarrelling crew was not likely to be a winning one. *London*'s boat was neck and neck with *Sidney*'s right from the start and looked like a winner when the final spurt came. Then without any reason that onlookers could see, they altered course rather sharply, losing ground, and came in second by a boat's length. *Sidney* won the Regatta by two points.

Hugh muttered to himself: "There goes my promotion!"

Later Vice-Admiral Horton tackled him:

"Why did you have a coxswain like that? He wasn't fit for the job!" Hugh told him what had happened and that in the last moments of the race the coxswain thought that he was going to be blocked by the boat next to him and so altered course. His mistake was to alter course so sharply. Hugh lamented that his last chance of promotion had slipped away.

The next year a French squadron comprising the flagship cruiser *Algérie* and four new destroyers paid an official visit to Malta and considerable preparations were made for their entertainment. Hugh, probably because he was a French interpreter, was nominated liaison officer for the visit. The *Algérie* was berthed next to the *London* in Grand Harbour and the four destroyers went to the crowded destroyer base in Marsamusetta Creek. The French had in advance particularly asked that they might lay wreaths on the graves of the French naval personnel which, it seemed, dated from the Napoleonic Wars, and it took Hugh some time to discover them, for they were almost buried in wild vegetation in some far corner of Fort St. Anton. A work party was soon despatched to tidy up the area, and Hugh accompanied Rear-Admiral Sir Lionel Sturdee in command of shore establishments (with whom he had served in *Colossus*) on an inspection tour before the French arrived. The usual round of sports fixtures and sightseeing tours for the ratings, and parties and games for the officers was easily organised, and it seemed as if they were somewhat overwhelmed when he took the programme on board as soon as they were berthed. Hugh had little time for sleep and less for meals during the ensuing week, but it became apparent early on that they were enjoying their stay. On the last night the commander-in-chief, Admiral Sir William Fisher, gave a dinner and dance at Admiralty House in Valetta, and it was a brilliant scene in the ancient Knights Templar's Palace which was his official residence. Hugh went on board to say goodbye at the last moment as *Algérie* was weighing anchor, and when he went down the gangway he found that his boat was completely filled with flowers and plants which they had used as decorations, and so he went straight across the harbour and landed the whole cargo at the hospital steps where orderlies came to collect them. He also brought away a silver cigar box and a signed photograph of *Algérie* which the French admiral formally presented to him on behalf of his squadron, mementoes which he greatly treasured. Later in the day the commander-in-chief made a general signal to the ships in the harbour thanking them for all that they had done and included Hugh's name — so he felt that the whole affair really had gone off successfully, and went off to the beach at Ghain Tuffieh at the far end of the island to catch up on some sleep and swim in the sea.

But not all was plain sailing for him. The vice-admiral in command of the cruiser squadron took a keen and technically informed interest in the catapult launching of the small seaplane carried on board, and often came down from the bridge at sea to watch more closely the actual drill for launching of which Hugh was in charge. On one such occasion the engineer officer who was responsible for the efficient working of the catapult machinery reported at the last moment that some valve was not working properly and Hugh at once aborted the launch. Such a technical fault could have resulted in a slow launch dumping the little plane into the sea, and the vice-admiral was asking all sorts of questions about this mechanical failure, and Hugh, somewhat flustered by the whole thing, answered without a thought in his head:

"I don't know, Sir! I am responsible for the safety of this plane and crew and will not allow a launch to take place until the engineer officer reports that the mechanical equipment is functioning perfectly."

"But do you mean to tell me you don't know what has gone wrong?"

"No, Sir, I don't. I have stopped the launch because I am not satisfied that the machinery will work properly. The lives of the two men in that plane are in my hands. The defect is under investigation now.'' The admiral was obviously furious, and told the captain so.

On return to harbour the captain told the engineer commander to investigate, and his report was that the procedure carried out at this particular launching was correct, and moreover that he considered that the young engineer lieutenant concerned was a brilliant officer. (His judgement was vindicated much later on when that young man became the chief engineer of the Navy.)

Such an incident does not do any junior officer any good, and later on there was another one. The vice-admiral had a white Persian cat to which he was much attached. Puss when let out on deck did exactly what one expects of cats, to the disgust of the petty officer in charge of the quarterdeck, who arranged a sandpit up above on the boat-deck near a small chimney that came from a coal-fired stove in the officers' mess. When it rained, coal-dust washed down onto the deck immediately below, and puss loved to lie against the chimney when it was warm — and thus became coated with soot, which did not make her welcome in the admiral's cabin. Hugh was ''mate of the upper deck'', and as such in charge of its general cleanliness, and now for a second time found himself confronted one day by an angry admiral. An able seaman had already been carefully instructed and visited the offending chimney several times a day, but failed to keep pace with the descending soot when there was rain. The cat continued to get black from time to time, and the admiral continued to be angry about it until the day came when puss went off her head and jumped into the sea in rough weather and was never seen again. But this she did too late to save Hugh's professional career.

Such trivial mischances can and do happen in the lives of all of us — but these were of the kind for which there is no remedy.

London was at Larnaca on the south coast of Cyprus on the occasion of the Jubilee of King George V which was celebrated with a twenty-one gun salute at noon, the ship being dressed overall with signal flags, and she also landed a large armed party to take part in a parade inspected by the Governor of Cyprus. At this time there was serious internal political tension between the Turkish population living mostly in the North, and the Greeks in the South, and the government feared that a riot might break out during this official celebration parade. The naval armed party was stationed close around the governor — who was accompanied by the admiral and the captain at the saluting base — and part of the armament on board was manned and ammunition prepared, Hugh being left in charge of the ship. Nothing happened, but the tension was so serious that ship's company leave ended at dusk each day and the men were only allowed to go out of the town on sightseeing trips in cars, and, even in Larnaca, were instructed never to move about the streets alone. There was one fracas in a bar, but the police moved in and quelled the disorder in a matter of minutes and nobody was injured. There was an "edgy" sort of feeling whenever one went onshore, and Hugh, out late one night with a party including the family of the chief of police, was told by that official that he would not be allowed to taxi back to the landing place, and when no police car could be made available the chief drove him back himself.

Happily other parts of the island were at peace, and half a dozen cars took a party from the ship on a day's drive to the top of Mount Troodos. They landed at six a.m. and drove first to the salt mines which were near at hand. There is an enormous deposit of white salt which has been mined for hundreds of years and when one enters one finds oneself on the flat glittering floor of an immense chasm perhaps a mile long with white vertical walls of salt on either hand. The glare even in the very early morning sunlight made it impossible to keep one's eyes open for more than a few seconds at a time, and they were told that through the years many of the convicts who had, it seemed, always supplied the labour force, became blind if their sentences were long ones.

The farming country through which they drove for twenty miles was rich and beautiful, but once they began to climb the steep-sided mountain, cultivation almost ceased. The road zigzagged about five thousand feet up to the snow-capped crest, and, for the first time in his life, Hugh became carsick — when they reached the summit he had to lie down on the ground for a while until his reeling senses became normal once more. In the winter there was good skiing up there and even now there was a large sloping area of unmelted snow oozing water into little streams on both sides of the crest. They drove down by a more easy road and stopped in Nicosia, the capital, to walk about some of its beautiful streets.

About this time a new admiral came to the squadron, Max Horton, a distinguished submarine commander of World War I, and one sensed almost at once a brisk change in the air. He was not a communicative type of man, but rather a supremely efficient professional officer for whom no detail in the daily routine was too small to escape notice. Everybody was very soon "on their toes".

Mussolini had, presumably with the object of extending Italy's colonial possessions, picked a quarrel with Abyssinia and invaded the country with a large army which soon became bogged down in the arrid hot wastelands of its northern and eastern fringes. The Mediterranean Fleet at once moved its base to Alexandria where Britain had rights of usage guaranteed by treaty with Egypt. And the Fleet was almost doubled in strength as quickly as possible, for it was feared that the Suez Canal route to India and the Far East might be imperilled. The harbour, enclosed by long breakwaters, was tightly packed with warships and their auxiliaries. After a while there were no less than thirteen admirals' flags flying there. War exercises of every description were almost continuously going on, and the first cruiser squadron, now increased to nine ships, was at sea exercising at least two days every week.

This was an interesting period when every aspect of a cruiser's wartime role was investigated; tactics were explored and, most importantly, defence against air attack and damage control were experimentally exercised. They did numerous anti-aircraft firings at sleeve targets towed by aircraft at about a hundred knots, shooting them down with ease, and at simulated bombing attacks by the Royal Air Force at much higher speeds which revealed that no gun could be trained fast enough to keep on target when a dive-bomber came hurtling in. In *London* they studied and trained for possible procedures to be followed in the event of damage. A anti-gas attack exercise led to the discovery that twenty-two thousand places existed where it was possible for toxic gas to enter the ship and a very extensive programme of work was undertaken to reduce as far as possible this serious danger, which was all the more appreciated when the Italians began using internationally forbidden poison gas against Abyssinian troops in the field. The air defence look-out organisation was under Hugh's charge and the personnel became so skilled that no aircraft could get inside twenty miles distance without being reported. At night exercise they learned to see anything that came within eight miles. Some who are experienced in such matters might dispute these figures, and indeed they are unlikely to be equalled in places where the atmosphere is not so clear. All this was of course about four years before the first radar came to sea. Indeed it was still a secret laboratory project far removed from the knowledge of ships' officers.

That year the Fleet spent at Alexandria was, as future events were to reveal, a providential working-up practice for World War II. Treasury purse strings became looser, flag officers exercised some of the functions which fall to their lot in wartime, and all ships had invaluable training in manoeuvring together at sea. Probably the most important aspect was the tuning of minds to active consideration of the effects which aircraft would in the near future produce on the operations of ships at sea. It is perhaps of interest that a simulated attack by only nine Royal Air Force Anson aircraft on the first cruiser squadron at sea was the largest air operation Hugh witnessed prior to the outbreak of World War II. Most of the cruisers carried a Walrus aircraft which was a miniature flying boat with maximum flying speed of about two hundred and fifty knots, and their reconnaissance exercises, or spitting fall of shot at gun firing exercises, was too often curtailed by unfavourable weather, for they could only safely land on water when it was almost flat calm. There was no aircraft-carrier at Alexandria because major alterations and improvements to this class of ship were in hand, and any one of them at that time capable of going to sea was employed on training aircrews.

One of the officers in *London* had a relative who was a director of the museum at Cairo, and Hugh flew up from Alexandria with him to the capital for a few days' leave. Staying at Mena House Hotel beside the pyramids they spent three days in charge of a carefully chosen dragoman seeing the usual — and splendid — sights in that area, and took half an hour to climb to the top of the Great Pyramid, having watched an Arab boy race up it in about two minutes. The huge stone blocks, the magnificent view from the top, then the Sphinx at sunset when the broken stone of the face disappears in some trick of evening light and this monument suddenly seems to have been built only yesterday, and then its expression of pride and nobility as it gazes out over the desert, is seen to perfection and leaves an indelible impression. Yet the most striking thing of all that one sees is, perhaps, the apparent freshness of the underground temple wall carvings. One looks on the ground and expects to see stone chips and dust not yet swept away.

A whole day in the museum was devoted to the Tutankhamun relics which occupy two of the floors. The small statuettes of the four young goddesses which guard the golden walls of the inmost sarcophagus, and also the small head of Nefretiti, must be amongst the most beautiful sculptures in the world. Indeed, the whole collection of relics discovered in the tomb by Lord Carnarvon is of the very highest standard of workmanship, and one moves from one glass case to another amazed at the perfection of workmanship, most of it done by only two or three hundred people segregated in a village in the Valley of the Kings where skills were handed down from father to son through hundreds of years. In fact the craftsmen were never allowed to leave.

Later in the day, at lunch in the director's home, the two officers met a family of five Coptic people just arrived from a far distant oasis in the desert where their ancestors had lived from time immemorial. It was astonishing to find their faces to be identical with the large-eyed peach-coloured skin of the faces of carved or painted heads among the Tutankhamun relics with which they had just spent a long morning. This family believed that they could trace their descent for four thousand years, which is not at all impossible in an isolated oasis at a great distance from any habitable place, and too, where the dry and almost unvarying climate would tend towards the preservation of whatever records each generation had left behind them.

Another day was spent in the "Souk", a crowded quarter in the heart of the city where the finest artistic work is concentrated in open-fronted shops lining both sides of the street. There one can see carpets by the hundred from all the eastern countries where they have been handmade for centuries past. Only Chinese carpets seemed to be unavailable, though these could, of course, have been hidden away elsewhere. It is more likely that the Chinese have found it impossible to conduct profitable business with the Caireans, who indeed have almost as long experience of trade as the Chinese themselves and are equally acute where money is at stake.

As part of the celebration of the Coronation of King George VI the Mediterranean Fleet came home to join up with the Home Fleet for a Royal Review at Spithead, and the largest concentration of warships ever to be held in this world moored in five lines over six miles in length. The two Fleet flagships headed two and *London* a third of these lines. Several notable merchant ships and ocean-going liners took part, and one of the former was chartered to take official guests, and another the general (and paying) public for tours round the warship lines. On the day of the actual Royal Review guests were entertained on board all warships, amongst those in *London* being the Lord Mayor of London and his family. Hugh, too, had invited several relatives and friends, so that it was not merely a Service exercise, but also a festive social occasion. Ships were dressed overall with flags and illuminated after dark with lights that outlined their silhouettes, and a searchlight display also took place. At one point in the programme all lights were switched off for a few minutes, and then suddenly searchlights and illuminations all came on together to make a brilliant display. Hugh was watching all this from a hilltop on shore when the voice of a television commentator burst out excitedly:

"The Fleet's all lit up!"

Millions heard it and laughed about it for a long time afterwards. To many this was the culmination of all the coronation celebrations that took place that year.

When the day came for ships to disperse and for the Mediterranean Fleet to return to its station, Hugh, in charge of the quite complicated and lengthy process of unmooring, found that one of the two anchors had hooked its projecting flukes under the narrow keel of the ship, probably a quirk of the strong current, and this was something that had never happened before. The flukes of the anchor usually slide along till they reach the stem and there they disengage themselves because they are able to rock to and fro if any pressure or weight comes upon them. On this day the capstan was winding in the chain cable at full speed because unmooring ship is always a competitive drill, and the anchor brought up so sharply under the narrow keel that the capstan jammed and its driving shaft bent an inch or two out of the vertical. Nothing that they tried would free either the capstan or the anchor, and *London* had to lie there wrestling with her problem while the rest of the Navy passed by on their way to their various destinations. Finally orders were given to cut the cable, and while the necessary blowtorches were being assembled an elderly ship's carpenter came up to Hugh and said:

"I've seen this before, Sir. We threw a bucket of paraffin over the cable and she cleared!" Hugh hurriedly ordered up a bucket of paraffin and threw it himself on the place where the cable was jammed on the barrel of the capstan. The cable freed itself a couple of minutes later. The anchor was weighed and the ship hurried out to sea to rejoin the Mediterranean Fleet.

A court of enquiry was of course ordered, and when Hugh told them what had happened and how the problem was resolved in the end, the president of the court burst out:

"I've never heard of such a thing before. Have any of you?" Members shook their heads. Their judgement was that "an accident not previously known to have happened had occurred and no blame could be attached to any person concerned". Hugh never heard the incident mentioned again and was greatly relieved, hopefully assuming that his name had been officially cleared.

A little later in the summer of 1937 the Spanish Civil War broke out and that whole country became locked in fierce fighting at a dozen different places at the same time. Russia supported the Communists, and Hitler supported the forces of the "Right", each smuggling in guns, tanks, a few aircraft, and military personnel. The small and not very efficient Spanish Navy went to the "Right" but had no noticeable effect on the internal struggle.

London had been sent to Malta to replenish stores and was speculating that she might be sent to Spain to guard British interests on completion of storing. They had left harbour to return to Alexandria when Hugh, whose cabin was immediately over the port propellor, was woken up in the middle of the night by a marked acceleration of the rhythm. He telephoned the bridge and learned that they were off to Barcelona in a hurry, and they arrived there two days later early in the morning.

As the coastal haze dispersed they saw tall columns of smoke ahead of them rising into the air, and when they got close to the harbour entrance no answer came to their signalled request for a pilot, although it was a compulsory pilotage port. After a long wait a little motor boat emerged and when it came alongside a pilot climbed out, but as he did not understand a word of English, and the only person onboard who had ever been to Spain and was reputed to have a smattering of the language, could not understand anything he said, nothing could be learned of the situation on shore, but when this pilot drew his hand across his throat and cast his eyes up to heaven — they realised that the situation was unpromising.

What the pilot did say was: "Full speed ahead!" — which, considering that that meant twenty-eight knots through a narrow entrance into a crowded anchorage, would have produced a considerable sensation. The captain, of course, ordered ten knots, and they berthed quite comfortably at the Yacht Club jetty where some club personnel connected up a fresh water hose. These men had a smattering of English, and it was learned that fighting in the city had produced heavy casualties, that looting and burning was in progress, and that anyone seen moving in the streets was likely to be fired at. All services, except the fresh water, had ceased to operate.

Hugh was sent off as officer of the guard (the official representative of his ship to whatever authority was present), and landed at the naval base a few hundred yards across the harbour, taking with him a machine-gun and its crew, hidden in the cabin, and a signalman. His orders were to find out whatever he could, especially about the British Consulate.

He was greeted by a lieutenant in uniform who spoke with a broad American accent and had been brought up as a child in Chicago. He could confirm what they already knew, and did not add much to it as he had not been allowed outside the high stone walls surrounding the naval establishment. Hugh sent off a signal to the ship to tell them what he had heard, and then got into a Spanish naval car and brought with him a white ensign on a short staff which he hung out of the window. The lieutenant sat beside him with a loaded revolver on his knee and beside the uniformed chauffeur sat a sailor with a loaded rifle. On each running board a uniformed sailor clung to the doors with one hand and carried a loaded pistol in the other one.

The dockyard gate clanged behind them as they set off for the consulate. The street was almost deserted, and a smell of burnt meat pervaded everywhere. It was a bright sunny morning as they turned into the main square of the city where armed soldiers were on guard at several buildings. The last embers of what had been a very big bonfire flickered beside a statue surrounded by formal beds of flowers. A bugle sounded and a moment later a large glittering open car bore down towards them from the raised back seat of which a general in gold peaked cap smilingly acknowledged the saluting sentries. Seated beside him a smiling blonde-haired woman dressed in bright colours gaily waved in the direction of the very few people to be seen on the pavments. They stared at Hugh's naval car but were gone in an instant, and his journey continued. They came to a wide road lined with shops, some with broken windows, and in front of one a small crowd milled around as a young man hurled a stone at a plate glass window which crashed onto the roadway; the crowd then rushed over the broken glass into the building. Further along a stream of people with various kinds of provisions in their arms were streaming out of the empty shop window of another foodstore. A woman stopped and dipped a hand into the large rectangular box of biscuits she had just stolen and pulled out one which she chewed for a brief moment, then dropped the box onto the ground and turned back into the store — presumably to get other biscuits more to her liking. All these people were quite well dressed and looked clean and tidy. Round another corner they came on a large and seemingly old stone church which had no tower. Flames were coming out of several windows and others were licking at the eaves of the tiled roof. In the garden in front stood a huge woodpile just beginning to flare up, and onto this a stream of people coming out of the church door carrying all manner of combustible objects, threw whatever was in their arms: curtains and hangings, a gilt-framed picture, splintered benches, broken chairs, and one of them, a quite beautiful, smartly-dressed girl, staggered under the weight of a wooden cross about eight feet high which she flung onto the bonfire which flared dramatically around the cross.

Such hatred of the church as this seemed to be was seen in many places in Spain in those days, yet the youth, the beauty, the elegant clothing of this girl seemed to Hugh to be proclaiming some definite message to the world which needed explication. He has for long wondered just what activated such action on the part of such a person.

The church was burning fiercely inside and nothing could now have saved it, nor did anybody attempt to do so.

They sped on down a broad tree-lined avenue where large houses stood behind high stone walls, each one surrounded by its own garden. Rifle fire suddenly broke out and the chauffeur drew in to the sidewalk edge and stopped the car, apparently with the idea that the passengers should get out and take shelter. There was a brief argument in Spanish with the lieutenant, and then the shooting stopped, and so they moved on to the consulate which was only fifty yards ahead. Hugh got out, knocked on the big door, and a little wicket side gate cautiously opened. He talked fast and pushed his way through, but it was doubtful if the porter would have understood English. Anyhow the uniform was sufficient to overawe the old man.

Inside the large and impressive building he noticed that no lights were burning anywhere at all and the window shutters were closed.

A small pale young man greeted him and identified himself as the acting British vice-consul, the consul-general being away on leave. A small group of Englishmen — heads of business concerns in Barcelona — were introduced and they all sat round a large desk in the consul's office. The fair young man flung himself down in a big chair and then opened a couple of drawers, searching for something, and finally triumphantly found one banana which he skinned and stuffed into his mouth. He smiled at Hugh:

"This is the last food in the house. I haven't had anything to eat since yesterday."

The vice-consul's wife had given birth to a child a week ago. The telephones had gone dead. Sporadic shooting was going on all over the city. Barcelona had been attacked by a Communist force four days ago which quickly overcame resistance from the garrison. Four thousand cavalry horses were reported to have been killed and fires had been consuming the carcases for the past two days. Casualties were thought to be in the thousands, and small pockets of resistance were still holding out in several areas. The naval units — three or four small gunboats and one old destroyer — had surrendered. Practically every shop had been, or now was being looted, but the invading Communists were by now in full control and only mopping-up operations were still in progress. They had not made any move to interfere with foreign business interests.

Hugh quickly ascertained that food was what the foreign community most needed. Their personal safety appeared to be more or less secure, and no threats had been made against them. He asked the vice-consul if he wished to send his wife and child to safety on board, and the lady, who had just come into the room, refused to leave without her husband — and he, too, said he did not intend to leave. So, still escorted by the Spanish naval lieutenant, whom he had left in the car outside the consulate, he returned to his boat and on the way arranged for a car-load of foodstuffs to be purchased from the Spanish naval stores and sent straight back to the consulate. He had also promised that other provisions from the ship would be sent ashore as soon as possible and arranged that the naval car would take them also to the consulate. The signalman in the boat sent a brief message to this effect to the ship, and after settling the last details with the Spanish lieutenant, he went back to the *London*. The Spanish Navy could not have been more helpful and placed all their transport and other services at *London*'s disposal while she remained in port.

They were obviously not Communists.

That evening the commanding officer of the Spanish destroyer who was the senior naval officer in the port still remaining at his post, came on board and wept as he amplified the story of the current state of affairs. Innocent people of Right Wing persuasion were being shot everywhere. He couldn't make up his mind whether he should put to sea and make for a foreign port, and anyhow he had very little fuel and could not get far. The Communists had not communicated with him in any way whatever. Later he found he really was out of fuel altogether and borrowed a small quantity of diesel oil to keep his dymanos going. A few days later he decided to leave, but had scarcely got clear of the wharf when a machinery breakdown occurred and he ran out lines to the shore and hauled himself back to where he had come from.

A day or two later communication was established with the embassy in Madrid where a senior office clerk had been appointed as temporary acting vice-consul in charge, the ambassador and his family being in France, and the secretaries all out of the country on summer holidays. The *London*'s wireless at Barcelona and an intermittent telephone to the British Consul at St. Jean de Luz in France across the northern frontier were, for the moment, the only lines of communication out of Spain. Foreigners all over the country were besieging their embassies to help them to get away, and it was quickly arranged that any who could get to Barcelona and come on board *London* would be transported by a shuttle service of British destroyers to Marseilles where the various foreign countries had set up a reception centre to deal with their needs.

London at once geared her organisation to serve as a refugee reception centre and established a sort of entry gate at the foot of the gangway on the yacht club jetty. At the other end of the jetty the Communists examined the credentials of all who came, and were glad to hasten the departure of foreigners after a brief scrutiny of whatever identification papers they possessed. In Madrid a daily train service to Barcelona was re-established and all embassies sent out their own nationals as fast as they could process the many hundreds of applicants, a large number of whom were tourists. The Communists reserved as much of the train accommodation as they required and seemed glad to get rid of as many foreigners as possible, and also to collect the cash they paid for their fares.

So it was that each day about two hundred and fifty foreigners arrived on board *London*, spent the night there, and sailed by destroyer at six a.m. the next day for Marseilles, where they arrived the same evening. On board the cruiser almost all officers cleared out of their cabins and ambassadors, ladies, seriously ill people or high officials slept there, and meals at separate times from those of the officers were served in the wardroom. There were two large recreation rooms for the ship's company where women could sleep in privacy, and all men joined the ship's company messes, which were made responsible for organising their meals and sleeping accommodation, sometimes in a slung hammock if they were young, but usually lying flat on the hard deck. Every blanket, pillow and hammock in the ship, and additional ones borrowed from the three transport destroyers, were utilised. The cooks, augmented by several assistants from the ship's company, worked round the clock so that some form of food was continuously available. The refugees co-operated splendidly in almost all cases, and in a way seemed to almost enjoy their unusual experience, for the help they most needed was always given with sympathy. No ship's company ever did a difficult job with more humour, understanding and goodwill.

People came in from the Balearic Islands where many British were permanent residents, others arrived at all hours on foot or in cars. One man swam across the harbour and was suddenly spotted naked climbing up the small ladder at the boom to which ship's boats were moored. He had been hunted through the city by a posse, climbed over the dockyard wall, stripped off his clothes and swam to safety. A Spanish lady, wife of an industrial magnate, arrived with her two small sons, and nothing whatever beyond the clothes they were wearing. Her family had been in the country house in which they lived some miles outside the city when a band of Communist soldiers suddenly drove up in a truck, jumped out and ran up to the front door. The husband saw them, told his wife to take the boys to the back door and go out and hide in the yard while he went to the front door to speak to the gang. She heard a single shot, ran back through the house and through a glass panel saw the soldiers climbing into their truck and her husband's dead body lying on the steps. She then took her sons through the fields to a friend's farm, and persuaded the man to drive down to Barcelona harbour.

A small British liner presently came into port carrying two

hundred and fifty British Young Communists who were to take part in a Communist organised International Games planned as a kind of opposition to the Olympic Games, and they had expected to hold their meeting at Barcelona. The ship was impounded by the Spaniards as soon as it berthed, and the athletes learned that the games had been cancelled. *London* found that she would have to evacuate the travellers. They came on board on a very hot and airless afternoon and were soon complaining about the lack of facilities. Some of them took off their shirts and were walking about the upper deck half naked to the horror and astonishment of a considerable proportion of Spanish women refugees who assailed any officer they could find and said that they were shocked, appalled, and that they must leave the ship at once unless shirts were put on straight away. Hugh went round to the few offenders he could see, and one group, truculent and disobliging, said they wouldn't be ordered about by any officer, nor would they put on their shirts. He led them to the gangway and then turned round and said:

"Very well. You will do as you please. So shall I. Put on your shirts now, and keep them on while you are on board, or else go ashore."

"You can't do that to us!"

"Oh yes I can! The Marine Guard will carry you ashore!"

Then they complied. This was the only unpleasant behaviour amongst the 3,400 refugees who passed through the ship.

A group of about a dozen nuns appeared one evening, dusty and very weary. They were the survivors of the staff of an orphanage housing two hundred children. They had been suddenly aroused during the night by crackling fires at several different points around the buildings. Communist soldiers had climbed over the high surrounding walls, collected garden rubbish and lighted the fires and were already inside several ground floor rooms shooting whomever they met. These nuns had quickly dressed and led whatever children they could collect to staircases that were not yet on fire, and escaped into the thick clumps of bushes which were growing in the garden. The screams of children and staff who had been shot were still in their ears. The soldiers had left while it was still dark, and the surviving score or more of children they led out into the country where they left the children in several different houses, and then made for the railway station and eventually reached the *London* two days later. They now found themselves surrounded by men on board, of course, and were most distressed about that, and when Hugh sent them to a seamen's recreation room on the boat-deck level, which was for the moment empty, they found a key and locked themselves in and refused to allow the men who brought food to enter. Hugh went up there to investigate, but he wasn't allowed inside either, although he did persuade them to stretch out a hand to take the dishes off the trays. When more women arrived quite late in the evening they were led up to the nuns' room to sleep there for the night, but nothing would make the nuns open the door again. Possibly they did not understand what was required; but time went on, and presently the new arrivals asked if they might just lie down on the deck and rest where they were. Blankets were brought up and they slept out under the stars. Fortunately through all those weeks of August, September and into early October the weather was calm, there were only a very few showers of rain, and the temperature remained high so that each night the several hundred people on board who had no beds were able to get some hours of rest. The destroyer passage to Marseilles was, too, almost always a flat calm, and although conditions on board were overcrowded, the passengers were able to look forward to restoration of the ordinary comforts of a normal life before the day was ended.

A few days after *London* reached Barcelona, the German pocket battleship *Admiral Hipper* anchored in the roadstead outside the harbour, and then still later on the Italian light cruiser *Monteciccouli* appeared. Official calls were exchanged and both ships seemed uncertain about what they were supposed to be doing. Some question of dispute arose about German business interests in the city and *Admiral Hipper* sent a message one afternoon to tell *London* that he would commence a bombardment with his eleven-inch guns next morning if by then the Communists had not agreed to the German demands. An officer was sent out hastily to tell them they must not do so because British property was sure to be damaged and after some discussion the German threat was withdrawn.

The captain of *London* felt that this success might be profitably followed up with friendly intercourse of some kind. So Hugh sailed out the four miles in his 14-foot international racing dinghy and boarded *Admiral Hipper*. They were astonished that such a small boat would dare to go so far from shore, and they welcomed him warmly. Although he did no more than walk from the quarterdeck down into the wardroom he noticed very extensive anti-gas fittings and other precautions at every turn. They were obviously concerned about gas warfare. He explained to them the old naval sea game of deck hockey, played with walking sticks and a small wooden block with almost no rules at all; and invited them to bring a team to *London*, which they did two or three times in the dog watches (4 p.m. to 8 p.m.) and some friendly relationships were thereby established.

A day or two later he sailed out to *Monteciccouli*, which was then the fastest ship in the world, having reached a speed of 38 knots. He noticed that the plating was so thin that it had wrinkled wherever it was rivetted to a beam; even the ship's side plating showed its extreme thinness in this unmistakable way. She seemed to be constructed to obtain a record, not for warfare. His reception there was a warm one, and he found that the Italians had no cordial feelings towards the Germans. *Monteciccouli* sailed away a day or two later, and was eventually sunk by our gun-fire at sea during World War II. Oddly enough it also happened that the British Navy caused *Admiral Hipper* to scuttle herself at the River Plate early in World War II.

Some weeks later *Admiral Hipper* was struck forward by a medium-sized bomb dropped at random off Palma in Majorca (in the Balearic Islands) by a Communist plane. She weighed anchor as soon as possible and made a fast passage through the night to Gibraltar where she arrived next morning with signs of scorched paintwork below the bridge, one of the boat booms still sticking out from the ship's side (and not housed to prevent damage at sea), and her starboard accommodation ladder not hoisted, but dragging in the water. This, for a warship, was astounding.

They had signalled briefly that they required medical assistance on arrival, and Hugh was sent over as officer of the guard and with a surgeon lieutenant to make whatever arrangements might be required. The officer of the watch on the quarterdeck was unshaven and seemed distracted and vague in his speech. Hugh told him to take him to the captain and the reply was that the captain was not well and couldn't see him. Nor indeed did he see any other senior officer, so he chatted to an engineer officer whom he had met earlier at Barcelona and who was standing by while the doctor had to go and search for the German medical officer. The two doctors eventually went off to the forward messdeck where the bomb had exploded about twenty hours earlier, and there he found some 240 casualties, sixty or more lying about dead, others with arms or legs blown off and no bandages in place. The whole compartment was a charnel house with blood and human flesh stuck to bulkheads, deck and ceiling. There was no evidence that any of the wounded had been medically attended.

A hospital lighter with a staff of nurses and orderlies on board was making fast alongside as the young doctor came back to the quarterdeck and he simply ordered the German officer of the watch to send a working party to the messdeck to help the British medical team disembark the casualties — which he obediently did at once. It looked as if nobody had given any order of any sort since the explosion had occurred, except to raise steam and put to sea. Hugh and the young doctor agreed that the officers had lost their heads, and appeared to be in a state of mental collapse, incapable of rational thought or action. Hugh believed that he had learned something of real importance about what really underlay the blustering Nazi claim to superiority over other nationals. It was incredible that no effort of any sort whatever had been made to tend the numerous casualties on the messdeck. Only a few rough and ready bandages had been put on by members of the German ship's company who chanced to be in the affected area but had not been injured themselves. The doctor reported that many able-bodied sailors were just sitting or lying about apparently in a state of nervous shock doing nothing to help the injured.

During *London*'s three months at Barcelona sixty-two foreign embassies were evacuated and some 3,400 refugees of all nations passed through the ship on their way to Marseilles. This must have been almost a peace-time record of rescue work completed by a warship.

As time passed, the new Spanish regime began to settle down, and the ordinary business of life was largely restored. *London* had reached the end of her commission and sailed directly from Barcelona to Portsmouth where the usual small crowd of wives and sweethearts welcomed them at South Railway jetty from which they had sailed two and a half years ago. The Admiralty had arranged for the Press to come on board on arrival to get their stories of the Spanish refugees' evacuation. About thirty representatives were assembled in the wardroom, and Hugh and two other officers handed out a written account of the facts of the evacuation, and then answered questions, all of which lasted until lunch-time. After lunch they were free to leave. However, Hugh, who was in charge of the arrangements, discovered that several journalists who had left the mess to go to the toilet had in fact slipped away over the forward bow where stores were being handled, and these civilians were not therefore being controlled. He telephoned the dockyard police at the gate, who intercepted five of these people and put them in the lock-up. The Admiralty order had been that no journalist was to be allowed on shore before 3 p.m., so that all newspapers would have the same opportunity to publish their stories at the same time and no one would be able to steal a march on the others. Hugh left the early starters where they were in the cooler until the hour of release at 3 p.m., and then walked down to the dockyard gate and released the five who had been detained. One or two were indignant, but he read again to them the Admiralty order, of which all had copies, and then politely wished them goodbye and a pleasant rail journey to London, and reminded them that the next train left in twenty minutes' time. He searched diligently to see if this little episode would appear in any newspaper — but it did not.

A day or two later the captain, who had just paid a visit to the Admiralty, sent for him and told him that the Director of Naval Intelligence had selected him for special duties in his department. A new section had just been established there to deal with certain types of foreign intelligence and a dozen officers were being chosen who would undergo appropriate training and then be taken on in the Admiralty on this new kind of employment until the age of sixty, and with additional pay.

"You haven't been promoted, as you know, Hugh, and I said I would ask DNI if you were willing to take on this job. It sounded quite a good thing to me. I told DNI I would let him know your reaction."

Hugh had made up his mind even before the captain finished speaking. The alternative was likely to be rotting away at dead-end jobs in ships laid up in reserve, or dull office work in shore establishments.

"I should be very glad to accept this offer, Sir!" And so his future was settled. It turned out to be something that no "passed over" officer could have imagined.

Chapter 12

Making an Intelligence Officer

Hugh finally left the *London* early in 1937, and went on foreign service leave for ten weeks, nearly all of which he spent skiing in the Tyrolean Alps where he joined friends at Lusens and, when walking home at dusk along the flat of the valley, escaped destruction by a sudden avalanche which stopped only a couple of yards from the pathway. The whirling snow blinded the little party for a few minutes while tree branches and small lumps of ice and rock struck them from all sides, doing no damage whatever. The local people said that no avalanche had ever been experienced in that valley before. A few days later, on a long day's climb through the high mountains, his party was overtaken by dark and found refuge in the Heidelberger Hutte at about six thousand feet. During the night and for the two following days a violent storm raged and twenty feet of snow blocked all passages. He had caught a severe chill and could not get out of his bed, which was a pile of straw spread over the floor immediately beneath the roof, shared with twenty-two other stranded people lying in a row covered by what few blankets were available and sleeping in their skiing clothes. The naval friends in his party had to rejoin their ship and, when the blizzard ceased, could not wait for his recovery, so that he now found himself alone, unable to speak a word of German, and also unable to stand up, for he was very weak. After some hours a German girl noticed his plight and, speaking a little English, alerted the hut-keeper, who by now had run out of all the food in the house and was waiting for a messenger he had sent down to the valley to bring up fresh supplies. However, water could be melted from snow and the German girl had one orange in her rucksack, and these things she brought to Hugh who felt a little better after two and a half days of total starvation. It was a further five days before he was able to put on a pair of skis and gently run down to the Niedertal Valley and rediscover the comforts of an hotel. There he had arranged to join a guide from Innsbruck with whom he had earlier made friends, and they went off on a glorious six-week ski tour.

At the beginning of April 1937, he took up his appointment at the Admiralty, which turned out to be a course of instruction in certain branches of communications which was conducted by a small elderly group of World War I experts. This was a minute nucleus of specialists retaining lessons learned in World War I, and just beginning to reach out to modern electronic developements which would soon revolutionise every sort of communication. The general plan was that, if Hugh turned out to be sufficiently bright, he could be trained to work in ships at sea and so make immediate reports to the admiral, which would be time saving and therefore of real value. That same summer an exercise in defence against invasion was staged on a large scale, and Hugh together with a couple of his instructors embarked in the *Royal Oak* for a week to see how their new skills worked out in practice. The result was encouraging, but it also revealed that the job could be better done on shore with results being sent to the flagship. Hugh, on board the flagship, would be able to advise the admiral at all times on the quality of whatever information was received, and that advice must be based on a complete understanding of the procedures being followed on shore which produced such information.

The practical point is, of course, that the factual accuracy of any sort of information is always open to question, to opinion, and to human error in appreciation. The evidence given in any police court by witnesses to a traffic accident almost never gives a true view of what really happened. The judge must make up his mind on how much value he can place upon each one of the different accounts he hears. This was well understood by Rear-Admiral Godfrey, the Director of Naval Intelligence (DNI) at that time, who created an Operations Intelligence Centre (OIC) in the Admiralty which later grew up to be a cardinal influence on the victorious prosecution of World War II. He was one of the few people in England who were convinced at this early date that Hitler was preparing to go to war to secure his objectives.

The two months Hugh spent under this professional tutelage proved invaluable to him. It directed his mind into channels never before imagined, and, probably most valuable of all, taught him what security really means and how frail a thing it is.

Then on 1st June in this same year he was appointed to the staff of the Commander-in-Chief (C.-in-C.) of the Home Fleet, Admiral Sir Roger Backhouse, flying his flag in *Nelson*, armed with nine sixteen-inch guns, the most powerful armament ever mounted at sea at that date. She looked magnificent and was maintained at the height of efficiency.

When he joined his ship the admiral asked him what he wanted, or expected, to do. He hadn't anticipated that sort of question, though he knew that the admiral had personally discussed his appointment with DNI. Hugh answered:

"I think, Sir, that the more I can learn about what goes on in wartime at sea the more useful I can become. The Russians and the Germans are fighting in Spain, and I have seen a little of that. I want to get out to the north coast of Spain where some of our ships are on the Noyon Patrol, in the middle of it all."

The admiral evidently liked that and told Hugh to go ahead with whatever arrangements were necessary. A cruiser and one or two destroyers were employed on that service, and when the next warship went out to North Spain, Hugh took passage in her.

An international agreement had been reached at Noyon (in France) that participating nations (of which Britain was one) would refrain from trading with either side in Spain, especially with regard to war supplies, and that they would set up a shipping control organisation to enforce this agreement. Russia and Germany did not join the other powers.

By September 1937, when Hugh arrived in a destroyer on the north coast of Spain, fierce fighting was in progress there, and the forces of the Right, led by Franco, were slowly driving the Communists westward. A major bombardment and then an assault on Bilbao was watched from the ship only about three miles away. Field gun crews could be seen working their weapons, and assault troops charging out of their trenches. The city, a major port for the export of iron ore, fell into the hands of the Right, and from then onwards the Left were in a slow, desperately contested retreat. The Basque population of the region were leftists, and, as towns and villages fell, quite large numbers of fighting men and their supporters escaped to the sea in whatever small craft they could find — motor boats, fishing trawlers, even a few rowing boats were picked up by the Noyon Patrol warships. Hugh witnessed some of these rescues where the escapees had been without food or water for several days, and wounded fighting men had received no medical attention. Without exception they came on board, thankful certainly to be alive, but also defiant and determined to get back into the battle as soon as they could. They had only put to sea to avoid being slaughtered, or often enough because their ammunition was exhausted. Many of them were miners, some were women, and they must have been among the toughest people on earth, for their physical endurance astonished all those who had to deal with them.

Franco's Spanish warships and auxiliaries were dominant in the area and made active attempts to capture these small craft, the occupants of which would mostly have been shot if they had been caught. On several occasions a British destroyer steamed between a Spanish warship and a boatload of refugees who, when they had been rescued, were taken into the nearby French port of St. Jean de Luz which the British ships used as their base. Overhead one saw single Russian and German aircraft firing at one another quite often.

Hugh had a small party of telegraphists who tried to monitor the wireless traffic of both sides and occasionally picked up intelligible messages, none of which were of much value. They usually recorded the events which he was watching through his binoculars. Nevertheless the war atmosphere of almost daily action, either of rescue work, or gun battles on shore, created a real feeling of tension and conflict that is characteristic of all warfare. On his own account he experienced the planning and execution of active operations, the sudden emergence of unforseen encounters at sea, and the complicated business of exercising control of trade, for this turned out to be much more tricky than he had expected. The warship must avoid infringing the rights of neutrals and at the same time be alert to appreciate violation of the rules that had been internationally set up. There was a small free-lance cargo ship capable of about nine knots speed that persistently tried to evade the Noyon Agreement. Her captain became known as "Potato Jones", for it was a notorious cargo of potatoes he attempted to land and that would have broken the Noyon Agreement. Hugh eventually got on board the ship with the official inspecting officer and had a quick look round to see if there were any stowaways and had some conversation with four passengers about whom suspicion had arisen. Jones, whom he briefly met, was a hard-bitten little Welshman who admitted nothing and disputed every point, but he was condemned and had his ship impounded. He didn't care; he sold the potatoes at black market prices in St. Jean de Luz and his ship was eventually returned to him.

When Hugh's various ships went into harbour to refuel and get provisions the officers went ashore to look at Biarritz, the famous Edwardian resort, and dine on shellfish in a little restaurant at La Rochelle on the harbour front. One of the officers chanced to stop at a tiny estaminet out in the country where he learned that some unlabelled local wines had been lying in a cellar for years past. He bought the whole lot, and all the officers took their pick, paying no more than two and a half shillings a bottle. *Southampton*, the cruiser then on patrol, was due to return to England to refit in a few days' time and carried out a full speed trial across a placid Bay of Biscay so that no rolling motion damaged the wine. No customs duty was payable, and when the cases were opened in various homes the invariable report was that the unnamed wine was of superb vintage quality. Hugh gave his quota to friends — who always remembered the gift — but he never tasted any of the wine because he had to hurry back to rejoin another patrol ship off the northern coast of Spain.

Next year the whole British Fleet was assembled in Weymouth Bay for the king's inspection. King George VI and Queen Elizabeth lived on board the Royal Yacht *Victoria and Albert*, and His Majesty came on board *Nelson* to watch exercises at sea which culminated in a sixteen-inch gun practice at a towed target. The day was cloudless and calm and the target and its towing tug came in sight at over forty thousand yards. Hugh, who was standing close to the king, spoke up and said: "The last time we fired I was blown off my legs, Sir. Would you please hang on to this rail." The king looked surprised, but took hold of the rail and as the first salvo fired he almost lost his footing.

"I didn't know it was as fierce as that!" he said smiling.

The guns opened at twenty-nine thousand yards, close to maximum range, and a second salvo went off before the first one fell. They both hit, and the target was demolished. The admiral turned to the king standing beside him:

"Well, Sir, that's finished us. It would take all day to get out another target. I'm afraid we'll have to go home."

"This has been a tremendous experience," said the king. "I had no idea that such accuracy was possible at such long range. I congratulate you, Admiral. Please send for the gunnery officer; I would like to have a word with him." The king had last seen a

U

heavy gun firing when he was a sub-lieutenant in the twelve-inch gun turret of his ship *Collingwood* at the Battle of Jutland.

In the evening there was a reception held on the decorated upper deck of *Nelson* which 1,200 officers attended. Prince George, a naval officer, and the king's youngest brother, accompanied His Majesty, and when they began to walk round the deck the young prince soon discovered familiar faces and broke away from the official party to talk with his own friends. At about ten o'clock the king said he would leave and he stood chatting on the quarterdeck while his barge came alongside. But: "Where is my brother?" He, and everyone around him, looked about, but Prince George was nowhere to be found. At last — and after quite a long time — he was discovered in the gunroom having a cheerful time with the sub-lieutenants and midshipmen, and when he joined the king he protested:

"But I don't want to go home yet. I'm having a great time and there are lots more people I want to talk to!"

This was disrespect to the sovereign, and the king went very red in the face. Though nobody heard what he actually said, his voice sounded like a fierce growl. Prince George seemed to fold up and almost scuttled down into the waiting barge.

The king went on board several ships to inspect them and while he was in *Nelson* a new sloop, fitted with underwater movable fins designed as an anti-rolling device, steamed past, and as she gathered way with fins spread she began rolling about twenty degrees in perfectly calm water and everybody was impressed, for none of the large group of senior officers around the king had ever seen this new gadget at work before. Although later on fitted in new ships, it was abandoned by the Navy, and soon discarded, though it is still in use in some large liners.

As the king stood on deck watching he seemed very young, and lonely. The dozen or so senior officers in attendance all appeared to stand at a distance perhaps expecting him to summon whomever he wished to speak to, and it was obvious that they were all much older than he was. His personal aide-de-camp, Commander Lord Louis Mountbatten, was in attendance and moved about taking one admiral after another up to the king who had so recently and unexpectedly come to the throne, and could not yet have grown used to chatting to strangers.

As it was impossible for the king to go onboard all the ships in the time available, it was arranged that those which had not yet been inspected would land every available man and line the half mile of roadway leading up the hill behind the harbour to the Asdic School so that the officers and men could at least see the "new" king, who had, as second son, seldom appeared in public before his sudden accession after the abdication of his elder brother King Edward VIII.

Hugh was told to make the arrangements, under the direction of the captain of the Fleet, who is the C.-in-C.'s chief of administration. He went ashore to see the captain in charge of the dockyard at Portland and discovered that they had about twenty small craft — tugs, motor boats, large launches, etc., and all were available, in addition of course to the ships' boats. There was transportation for 20,000 men and several convenient landing-places. The distance each ship's company would have to travel and the speed of all craft to be used was carefully worked out and the whole operation lasted exactly twenty minutes. It took another twenty minutes to get the men fallen in and sized for height and then to march to their allocated positions, which were marked along the roadside.

Hugh waited at the jetty with the C.-in-C. and the captain of the Fleet for the king to come ashore. On that jetty twelve hundred men from the aircraft carrier *Furious* were drawn up and a car was waiting to take the king up the hill. As he stepped ashore he looked up the roadway ahead where the dense ranks of seamen lined one side and, turning to the C.-in-C., he said:

"I watched these men leaving their ships. How did they get here in such a short time? I timed it; they started off only forty minutes ago. How many are there?"

"Twenty thousand, Sir. We borrowed whatever water transport the dockyard had, and of course used the boats from all ships present."

"Who was responsible?" the king asked.

"The Captain of the Fleet, Sir."

The captain of the Fleet, Captain Kinahan, spoke up:

"The Staff Officer Intelligence actually planned and organised the landing, Sir." The king looked straight at Hugh.

"I wouldn't have thought this possible if I hadn't seen it." Then he gave a royal nod and turned away to inspect the *Furious*' contingent, not merely the front rank, but the whole six ranks.

Then the C.-in-C. spoke up:

"I don't think there will be time to inspect every rank, Sir. May

I suggest that the front rank would be sufficient?''

"Oh no. They have turned out to see me." Every one of them did, too, at three feet distance, and found out what sort of man the king was. Not many would have done what he did that day.

Lord Louis Mountbatten intervened:

"There is a car here waiting for you, but you like walking, Sir."

"Send it away and tell them I shall be at least an hour late for lunch."

And so he plodded up the hill, walking past all of the 20,000 men, trailed by several elderly admirals who dropped out one by one and had to be picked up by cars, for they, too, were to lunch with the king at the Asdic School.

In the spring the Home Fleet went out to Gibraltar for exercises, joining with the Mediterranean Fleet for a period of about two weeks at sea.

There was some anxiety about getting *Nelson* safely out of Portsmouth harbour because just beyond the narrow entrance a submerged sandbank built itself up in gales each winter and she had grounded lightly on it a year or two earlier. Dredgers worked on it for some weeks, but up to the last minute it was uncertain if they could finish on time. They were still dredging away as she passed safely out.

Nelson called in at Lisbon for a few days and the ambassador brought his family on board to lunch with the C.-in-C. and Hugh was sent for afterwards to show the two children — ten and twelve years old — over the ship. He had guided many visitors before this day and took his charges to all the most interesting places, but they seemed thoroughly bored. Up on the admiral's bridge, from which a splendid view was to be seen, they scarcely bothered to look out of the windows.

"There was much more going on down on the carrier's flight-deck than here," said the twelve-year-old daughter.

"Well, I thought that submarine's engine-room was just wonderful," rejoined her brother. Then they said they didn't want to go inside a sixteen-inch turret; they had seen lots of guns; and would like to go back to their parents.

When they got back into his cabin, Admiral Backhouse said:

"Well, you haven't been very long. What did you see?"

"Oh, we've seen everything here. It's mostly the same as we saw last year."

Afterwards the C.-in-C. complained to Hugh that he hadn't

done very well, to which Hugh answered:

"No Sir. I haven't. It was a flop. They've seen a dozen other ships already this year. Before we were half-way round they asked to go back to their parents."

At sea, during the concentration of the whole Fleet, a cruiser squadron of four medium-heavy ships had to steam in from ahead and then turn round and take their place astern of *Nelson*. There were about twenty ships near the Fleet flagship which restricted the space in which the cruisers would be able to manoeuvre, and for this reason they steered a course which came very close to *Nelson*. As they got to a distance of only a mile it looked as if they would drive straight into her. It was too late to hoist any signal, and the rule of the road for a fleet at sea is that the Fleet flagship has absolute priority for her passage over all other ships in sight. The cruiser admiral did not seem to realise how close to *Nelson* he must pass on his present course, nor apparently did he allow for the uncontrollable suction which a very large ship would exert as she passed close at hand to another only a quarter of her tonnage. At the very last possible moment the suction effect began to operate strongly and the leading cruiser passed down *Nelson*'s side at less then fifty yards distance.

In the Fleet flagship we could hear the pipe: "Close all watertight doors, hatches, and deadweights. Hands to collision stations!" The three other cruisers following turned away a few degrees. The leader couldn't because *Nelson*'s stern would have struck her own stern.

A board of enquiry was held later but, as is customary in the Service, its findings were not published. Hugh, who watched the whole incident from the C.-in-C.'s bridge, believed that this was the closest shave of his life, for the combined speed at which the two ships would have collided was about thirty-five knots and a crash at such speed must be fatal.

On another occasion at sea it was obvious on the bridge that the admiral was extremely angry about something, though the officers on duty did not know the cause. Presently he exploded and told in turn the gunnery, torpedo, wireless and signal staff officers exactly where each had gone wrong on some highly technical matter concerning each one's speciality. He demonstrated an astoundingly detailed knowledge of every one of these highly complicated fields; he seemed to know more than the technical specialists did of their own trades.

The executive branch officers on the staff took round-the-clock watches in harbour and at sea as duty staff officer, and their chief function was to receive all incoming messages addressed to the C.-in-C. or which might concern him, and then filter out those which he ought to see at once, waking him up at night if necessary. Hugh was on duty in harbour one afternoon when the admiral sent for him.

"Is the so-and-so out of dock yet?"

"I don't know, Sir. There hasn't been any signal."

"But there must be. She should have come out two hours ago. Why haven't you checked this?"

"I didn't know she was in dry dock, Sir."

"You ought to have known. Her name is in the last weekly docking list we received from Chatham and high water there was two hours ago."

"How on earth did you know that, Sir?" Hugh evidently looked as astonished as he felt, for the faintest shadow of a smile flickered across the admiral's face.

"Don't you know how to use the Admiralty tide tables? She is one of our ships, and you ought to know what every one of them is doing."

"Yes, Sir."

"Make an immediate signal to the captain of Chatham dockyard and bring me a reply as soon as it comes."

Hugh scuttled out, and then returned with the Chatham reply upon which was printed all the relevant times. The C.-in-C.'s signal had taken fifty-seven minutes to reach Chatham. Another hour and a quarter elapsed before a reply was despatched, and that took over an hour to reach *Nelson* — "About three hours and a quarter to get information from only seventy-eight miles away," the admiral observed. He then sat down and wrote two or three blistering signals to the authorities involved, and thereafter transmission times began to be measured in minutes. Hugh was, a few days later, on duty again, and took the usual sheaf of signals in to the admiral.

"Have you noticed how long this message took in transmission? There has been a marked improvement. If there is a war we can't afford to waste unnecessary minutes!"

He was right — as always.

Another day Hugh took some signals to the admiral's house a few miles out in the country and found him slumped in a chair at his desk looking a very queer greenish colour, and speaking in gasps.

"Are you all right, Sir? Can I call someone?"

"No, no. It's only a passing thing. Now what have you got there?" He pulled himself together and dictated several messages, and then rummaged in his desk and brought out a half-opened parcel from which he fished the glittering star of a decoration — the Grand Cross of a Knight of the Royal Victorian Order which had just been conferred on him by the king. He turned it over once or twice in his hands and then looking up said:

"What do you think of it? A pretty sort of thing — more suitable for a lady, I should say!"

It is about the highest decoration the sovereign in person confers, all others ordinarily being given on the recommendation of other authorities, though the king must always approve.

As time went on the unprecedented and violent activities of Hitler began to affect the populations of all European countries, and after his alliance with Mussolini, he became an increasing threat.

In April 1938, Admiral Backhouse left the Home Fleet to become First Sea Lord and Chief of Naval Staff at the Admiralty, and was succeeded as C.-in-C. by Admiral Sir Charles Forbes with whom Hugh had come into some slight contact on the Mediterranean station where this admiral was second-in-command.

The two characters could not have been more different, the one, brilliant and difficult to get to know, the other eminently approachable, cheerful but never missing a point nor a detail. In each of these cases. Because of the unusual nature of his appointment, the C.-in-C. had told Hugh that he was to come directly to him with anything affecting intelligence. A staff officer ordinarily went to the chief of staff first, and then would be taken in to speak directly to the C.-in-C. if that was desirable. The chief of staff was not bypassed, and Hugh would always let him know what was happening and what had been discussed. It all worked smoothly because the three people concerned always knew what each had said or done.

In March 1939, a French Squadron consisting of the battle cruiser *Richelieu*, three cruisers and six of their newest destroyers, came to the Firth of Forth on a sort of "get to know one another" visit, and Hugh was put in charge of the social entertainments. He was fortunate in having friends and relations in the Edinburgh area, and through their good offices arranged that large numbers of French officers would be entertained in private homes. Every sort of game and activity was organised on shore, including fishing and shooting parties out in the country, and *Nelson* gave a dance for fifteen hundred guests. Cinemas, theatres and clubs were thrown open to French officers and men, and in the end a few would-be hosts were disappointed because the French Squadron just could not furnish at all times a sufficient number of guests. The whole visit was a resounding success, and the French admiral, when he said goodbye to Hugh, told him that when they had come to Britain they thought that the people were cold, stand-offish and inhospitable, but now he knew that this was mistaken. He said that in all his career he had never experienced such generous entertainment. On the last night *Nelson* dined about a hundred French officers in the wardroom and the hosts and guests exchanged photographs of their Fleet flagships which everyone present signed. It was an emotional moment, and everyone felt as if he was saying goodbye to a friend who would stand by him when war came.

Later in the summer, Colonel Beck, the Polish Foreign Minister, and also Minister of the Polish Navy, came to London to ask Lord Halifax, the Foreign Secretary, for guarantees of help if either Germany or Russia invaded Poland. He obtained nothing from Neville Chamberlain's government, which had no way of getting help into Poland, since her coastline was wholly inside the Baltic, and Britain had no cargo-carrying aircraft.

Colonel Beck then came down to Portsmouth and a day's outing at sea was arranged for him on board a new destroyer. Hugh, who was told to be his ADC, took him briefly round the dockyard and then on board the destroyer. They went almost at once into the captain's sea cabin where lunch was waiting and Colonel Beck lay back on the bunk pale and exhausted from day and night discussions in London. Hugh gave him some wine, and after an hour he went out on to the bridge to watch the exercises that were in progress at full speed. But he was exhausted and almost unable to walk, and went back to the cabin, where the two of them talked for two or three hours. Lord Halifax had offered to fly Mrs Beck immediately to London for safety, but she replied that nothing would separate her from her husband. He would go home and rejoin his regiment, and she, as a member of their Red Cross, would go with him to serve the wounded. Beck loved the sea and was proud of his ships, but must now go home bearing a death sentence for his country, for Britain's refusal of help sealed Poland's fate. No other country would lift a finger and Beck was certain that Germany would invade as soon as the failure of his mission became known. Hugh watched a tragedy in the making that afternoon, but Colonel Beck did not quail; his last word was:

"Tell your admiral we shall fight for as long as the ammunition holds out and after that while we are still alive!" — which is exactly what happened. After Poland was conquered and occupied he was heard of "somewhere in Hungary", and then vanished without any trace. His wife was still later reported killed in Romania. Neither Germany nor Russia wanted a man of his quality to survive the war in Poland. Hugh went back that evening to *Nelson* and told the C.-in-C. what had passed and said that on such evidence he was finally convinced that war was not far ahead, and he then wrote a very detailed report which the admiral read before he sent it off to DNI.

There was of course, a steady stream of indications that Hitler was completing his final preparations, and Neville Chamberlain's visit to him at Godesburg and his return to London waving a German paper promise of peaceful intentions failed to convince anyone in the intelligence organisation. Hitler had a long record of peaceful promises at the end of which was his signature; but the occupation of the Ruhr, and Austria and the Anschluss, spoke in a different tone. When Germany recalled her merchantmen from all over the world, the last doubts slipped away in August, 1939.

Hugh had some years before become close friends with a family living in the West of England. The husband was a retired major and his mother who lived with them was German. His sister was married to a cabinet minister in the local government of Prussia. This British officer took his wife and two young sons to East Prussia in the late summer of 1939 to pay a visit to his sister and her family and they all had a happy time together on the sea coast, the minister commuting to his office in the capital city. There was a coolness between the two English children and their two rather older German cousins, but the adults paid little heed to that, and supposed it was natural enough where the difficulties of an unfamiliar language were involved.

Then one weekend the minister did not return home to Danzig as he had promised, nor did he send any message. His wife telephoned the ministry and a secretary told her that her husband was under arrest. She immediately went off to the capital where the police refused to tell her where her husband was or what charges had been brought against him. She spent several days searching among influential friends for someone who could help, but they were all frightened of the secret police and refused to become involved. At last she did find her husband in a prison and learned that the charge against him was that he had been harbouring foreign spies in his villa at the seaside and that the information had been laid against him by his two sons, aged fourteen and fifteen, both of them being members of the Hitler Youth Organisation. When the lady got home the two boys proudly said that they had done their duty to the Reich. The English relatives flew back to England that same day.

Hugh, when he heard the story, cancelled a holiday visit he had planned to Danzig on the Baltic coast. He expected that it would be the initial point at which the Germans would attack Poland, for it was a threat to the security of the German Fleet. In the event, Danzig was the first point at which the Germans did attack Poland.

Somewhat later on he recalled a random general discussion in the *Nelson*'s wardroom five months before war broke out, when he said that he was certain that the Germans would go to war that year, probably in September, and was roundly condemned by everyone within earshot. They reflected public opinion in Britain at that moment; people were still clinging to the hope that war could be avoided; the opposite view seemed too bleak a prospect to be contemplated. He wrote the same thing to his father ranching in Canada, begging him to make whatever preparations might be needful. His warning was not wholly rejected, but neither was any action taken. Long-standing friends in London to whom he spoke in the same terms almost angrily charged him with warmongering. However some people in government shared his view, but the Chamberlain cabinet temporised and would not prepare on any large scale. Nevertheless the really vital naval preparations were initiated and the defence of the Home Fleet War Operations base at Scapa Flow were in place in the nick of time, and this was Admiral Backhouse's contribution from the Admiralty.

It would appear that Hugh sometimes strayed a very long way from his official intelligence duty — and indeed he did. On the other hand, the more he learned, even of the peripheral aspects of war, the greater would be his understanding of whatever actions the potential enemy might take. As time went on he gradually built up a considerable appreciation of German thought processes, and intelligence is, after all, aimed at discovering what the adversary will do in the future, and a great deal of that is foreshadowed by what he has already done in the past. He was steadily pursuing the course he had proposed to Admiral Backhouse, namely to learn as much as he could, which to him meant taking a personal part in whatever activities were within reach in the hope that experience would come in handy at a later date. In this way he was acquiring the faculty of judging the value of whatever intelligence came before him. He was also learning to understand the great responsibilities which must fall to the lot of a naval commander-in-chief in wartime.

Chapter 13

Outbreak of World War II

The short, almost triangular, quarterdeck of the Fleet flagship *Nelson* had seen many ceremonies and some historic events, but at a quarter past eleven on the morning of 3rd September 1939, it was deserted. Hugh had stepped out there immediately Prime Minister Chamberlain's announcement of war with the Axis Powers was completed. The battle fleet lay that day in the south-western corner of Scapa Flow in the Orkney Islands off the north coast of Scotland. An occasional flash of sun streamed through the low grey clouds to light up the great expanse of the harbour. In that corner lay at anchor lines of four other battleships, a carrier and half a dozen cruisers, while behind low heather-covered islands, to the westward one could see the dim smoke and white topmasts of some fifteen destroyers, two depot ships and, still further in the distance, a dozen small oilers, colliers, water boats, ammunition ships and oddments — the "Fleet Train".

This huge expanse of steel-grey water roughly nine miles from east to west by four miles from north to south, enclosed by the bald, low-lying dun-coloured islands, had already cradled the Grand Fleet of World War I and, at its termination, also the surrendered German High Seas Fleet, and now we were back again twenty-one years later on the same old job, blocking the German exit route into the Atlantic. In September the last heather is turning to deep purple and brown, giving the low rounded undulations of the several islands a silky sheen whenever a brief shaft of sunlight pierces the almost constant cloud cover that hangs above the Orkney Islands. Here live the hard-bitten islanders, descendants of Norsemen and fishermen, tilling their meagre sandy soil, and happy if once in five years a thin crop of oats can be saved from destructive autumn storms — this year the skimpy little sheaves were still lying in the fields black with putrefaction at Christmas time. An occasional black cow, tethered to a stake in the ground, seemed to be the only surviving animal, mankind being represented by an elderly gaunt figure cutting peat from the neat trenches that cross the heather in orderly rows. From the *Nelson* one could see but four works of man on nearby Flotta, the small dilapidated stone house with several windows gone or boarded up, inhabited by the solitary old woman eighty-one years of age; then half a mile further on farmer Sutherland's neat, cement-washed farmhouse on the skyline; the Kirk, a bleak barn-like structure without the "vain image" of even one cross; and eleven miles away at the eastern end of the Flow, St. Magnus Cathedral spire in Kirkwall town, the metropolis of the islands, a fishing village of about twelve hundred souls.

Such were to be the surroundings of the haven sheltering some twenty thousand seamen and shore personnel for the next five years.

Hugh walked up and down twenty-six paces — how often was he to count them on that cramped deck — and, today, heaving great sighs of relief. The release from apprehension lest the politicians should fail to comprehend the awful danger was almost overpowering. The slowness of public awakening, in spite of warnings from the Austrian *Anschluss* and the occupation of Czechoslovakia, had not inspired public confidence in government. And then as he paced, there floated out of the wardroom scuttle the thin wail of the first air raid warning siren from London.

Presently, a little calmer, he went down to the staff office, a small triangular compartment right in the stern of the ship. There was no room in it for a desk for him and he worked in his cabin close by. The place gradually filled up — the fleet gunnery, torpedo, submarine, wireless, signal, operations, planning, and other specialist staff officers forming the operational arm. All were of lieutenant-commander or commander's rank and amongst them were an RAF wing commander, an ex-captain of submarines and an ex-captain of destroyers, so that, with the later additions of a fleet radar officer and a fleet fighter direction officer, they formed directly under the chief of staff a widely experienced little crew available to supply the commander-in-chief at a moment's notice with informed facts and views upon most naval matters. The administration services of a great fleet were directed by a senior captain, under the title of Captain of the Fleet, and comprised engineer, constructor, accountant, education, medical and recreational officers, their work extending into the Admiralty and departments on shore.

Faces were glum, for everyone was thinking of his family and how a war would affect them and their safety. Hugh talked for a while with the "springer" (physical training officer). He had been in Germany among the British representatives at the Olympic Games in '36 and had stayed on afterwards for some weeks learning about German methods of physical and recreational training. He had known Admiral Raeder, and Ley, and Baldur von Schirac quite well, and had met several other prominent personalities including Goering and Goebbels; all had been charming and everything had been done in brilliant and efficient style for the entertainment of the visitors. Quite a number of German sportsmen and individual representative people had become very friendly; there had been merry parties and good fellowship. All that brilliance, ability and friendliness had come to this — he simply couldn't believe that he was now called upon to kill the good fellow whom he had marked on the hockey field in the great stadium outside Berlin — "Why, I spent the weekend with his family after the match and stood godfather at the christening of his boy!" The passenger liner *Athenia* was to change his bewilderment to disgust at ten p.m. this very night. She was torpedoed by a U-boat without warning fifty miles south of Rockall off the west coast of Scotland, and some hundreds were drowned.

Oddly enough today there was very little to do. A series of warning signals had been reaching the Fleet for the past couple of weeks, each bringing into force some more stringent preparation so that, with the lesson of Munich only a year behind, the Fleet was ready for whatever might come — but nothing did. The previous evening Vice-Admiral Max Horton had slipped out at sunset with five cruisers making for the northern patrol line which had been designed to cover the passage between Shetland and Iceland, some seven hundred miles. Under his command he had altogether twelve oldish cruisers and armed merchant cruisers, and about ten armed trawlers. Some of his force had already sailed from west coast ports where they had been completing last-moment preparations. Somehow nobody thought much about the Denmark Straits, that 240-mile gap annually closed by ice to less than fifty miles between Iceland and Greenland, and this was even less patrolled than the rest of these great spaces. It must be remembered that even on the clearest day a ship could only watch twenty miles of visible ocean on either beam; at night that distance shrinks to barely five, and in the bad weather which prevails in these latitudes more often than not, the patrol ship can see only a few hundred yards. Our object was, of course, to intercept raiders breaking out to attack the Atlantic traffic, and at the outbreak of war to capture the optimistic German merchantman who would try to get home with their cargoes intact.

Before lunch in the wardroom a few people — rather less than usual had a pink gin or two, but by now the Fleet had come to immediate notice for steam and the sea watchkeepers would undoubtedly miss out on their normal quota. The atmosphere was subdued. Hugh had encountered his marine servant while washing in his cabin and asked him what he thought about it all.

"Only to be expected is wot I says, but you could 'ave 'eard a pin drop on the messdeck when Chamberlain 'ad finished."

After lunch Hugh rang up the Admiralty (the Fleet flagship always lay at a buoy at Scapa connected by cable with the shore) to ask for any news there might be from the continent. Then a little thing happened which well illustrated the tone of the relationship between the Fleet at sea and the Admiralty. He was put straight through to Rear-Admiral Godfrey, the Director of Naval Intelligence, who at once said:

"If you want anything just give me a ring. I'm living in my office now and am always available. Whatever the C.-in-C. wants you let me know and we'll do whatever we can for you."

As one goes aft on the main deck past the range of staff cabins one comes to a lobby where there stands a Royal Marine sentry, very smart with pipeclay, knife-edge trousers and the front of his tunic closed at the bottom with a press button because he thinks it looks "tiddly". He is flanked by large glass-fronted cupboards of neatly stowed pistols and a great range of magazine and other important keys hanging beneath tallies. A whistle and chain round his neck could summon assistance in emergency — we hope he would remember to blow it. A second marine, just a fraction more glossy than he with the whistle, paces to and fro telling, if you had ears long enough to hear it, interminable stories about food, ditty boxes, his girl and the sergeant. He is the admiral's orderly and as such is in a position to be listened to and not interrupted. He will, from now on, be second only to the admiral's steward in passing along to the messdecks the latest news of when we're going to sea and all the other buzzes that colour the sailor's rather dreary life.

Hugh asked the orderly if the C.-in-C. was engaged, and he said he thought the chief of staff was still with him, so he hovered about, trying to peer through the half-open door. A moment later Commodore King, the chief of staff, came out, saw him and called out:

"Oh, here's Hugh! Perhaps he's got some news for us. Come on in."

So he walked quickly through the dining cabin which stretches the full width of the ship and beyond into the admiral's day cabin, a big triangular space with square ports, right in the stern of the ship. Admiral Sir Charles Forbes was standing beside an electric fire backed by a solid mahogany mantelpiece with a broad-cushioned fender around it. He was of medium height with a rather long Scotsman's head, hair thinning on top, iron grey at the sides, thick eyebrows and blue-grey humorous eyes, and with a tongue that could castigate with vigour — and a heart more generous and kindly than most.

"Well, what have you been up to now?"

"I've just been on to DNI, Sir. He says Canada and Australia have joined us with more to follow and the Prime Minister of South Africa seems unwilling to support us. Eire will be neutral. And this is some marked German Press news which has some bits we haven't heard before."

"Thank you. Let me know anything you pick up as soon as you get it. No news of German ships, I suppose?"

"No, Sir."

"Make sure that the Admiralty lets us have anything they've got about merchant shipping too. I'm going out anyhow tonight to see what we can pick up."

"Very good, Sir."

That was the end of his first wartime interview with the commander-in-chief, typical of so many at all hours of the day and night that were to follow during the next four years.

That afternoon at about three o'clock signals were hoisted ordering the fleet to sea, the first group passing through the harbour net defence boom at five o'clock; the rest following in small groups at safe navigational distances in accordance with a printed order which had been issued some days before. The fleet minesweepers had been out at dawn carefully searching the exit

v

channels and other areas which the fleet might use with a rather lower percentage of cover, the object being to escertain whether minefields had been laid by enemy submarine minelayers. We felt confident that surface movement would have been detected, for the weather was fine and the RAF coastal command was sending out patrols as far as the mouth of the Skagerrak at the northern point of Denmark and well into the Heligoland Bight, the two exit gateways the German Fleet possessed.

First the carrier got under way and went out, meeting her escort of three destroyers as she passed through the net defence gate. Although her full compliment of Swordfish aircraft (commonly referred to as "stringbags", because of their archaic structure) was on board they wanted to have time in hand to operate a dusk patrol. Flying off aircraft involves turning the carrier into the wind, and if it happens to be blowing up the tail of the fleet the carrier loses a lot of distance when she turns to the opposite course from that which the other ships are steering.

Then followed the cruisers — we had but three, and were always cramped for numbers. The estimated requirement of 70 had been reduced to 50 during the Washington Treaty negotiations.

Then came *Nelson*'s turn.

"Half ahead starboard, half astern port. Port twenty-five!" The captain's voice sounded hollowly up the copper voice-pipe from his bridge immediately below the admiral's, and we all felt that now we really were off to the war and there was a lift of spirits as the first tremor from the propellors rattled a loose pin in some fitting beside the compass. Hugh did not wait up there long, for he had the first watch — eight p.m. till midnight — and it would be almost an hour before they passed the boom gate.

That first wartime watch sticks vividly in mind. The high western cliffs of Hoy Island were reflecting the last red glow of the sunset as Hugh reached the admiral's bridge to relieve the duty staff officer of the last dog-watch. He turned over the course, speed, and disposition of the fleet and pointed out the nine destroyers on the screen fanned out ahead and on either beam at roughly a mile from the battleship line. They were headed to the westward to cover the Iceland passages through which German warships might sally. The North Sea has only once during this war been the scene of any major British sortie for the compelling reason that German airmen were bound to spot the fleet, bomb them and report their position, so that German ships would be enabled with certainty to avoid action. The only chance of a contact would be to steam to the westward, hoping to escape air searches, and to use our own submarines and aircraft to watch the northern end of the North Sea, and then, from a position well ahead of the enemy, to catch him outside the range of his own reconnaissance as was done with the *Bismarck* two years later. Sorties of *Deutschland* (later renamed *Lutzow*) *Admiral Scheer*, *Hipper*, the battle-cruisers *Scharnhorst* and *Gneisenau*, and the cruiser *Prinz Eugen*, were never detected early because they used the cover provided by the stormy Iceland passage weather.

One of the problems to which Hugh personally had given much thought since 1937 was the use of wireless at sea. There was an apparatus which could assess, with moderate accuracy, the direction from which a given transmission comes, and, with several stations scattered about, a number of bearings are likely to be found to intersect, and there, perhaps miles away, is your transmitter position roughly fixed. So it was resolved not to use wireless at all, or anyhow when only vital information must be sent out. Admiral Forbes was insistent on this precaution and it is not difficult to imagine that in the first days of the war his flag officers and captains occasionally differed from him in their interpretation of what was "vital information". Twenty-one peaceful years had blunted the judgement of some, and others took time to learn that the event which was giving them the thrill of a lifetime was not, perhaps, vital to the fleet. For instance, the happy captain who had just destroyed a Junkers dive-bomber could usually afford to keep it to himself until he returned to harbour, but in those early days sometimes he did not, and thus gave the occasion for some peerless admonition composed by the C.-in-C. so that the error would never be forgotten. It was said that the recipients commonly framed these notable signals and hung them in their cabins along with photographs of their wives and other treasured possessions.

So the fleet kept silent when they were at sea, and during those early days it was a great strain. We had to learn to depend on the Admiralty Operations Intelligence Section to send out automatically the information we were going to need and it was Hugh's special function to act as the link in that chain. It is a tribute at the outset of a war when one can say that failures from this source were unknown.

On this first trip, the admiral spread our forces somewhat, and three homing merchantmen were intercepted; all attempted to scuttle, one succeeding. The fleet flagship witnessed the capture of a small three-thousand ton cargo vessel by one of our destroyer escort — she must have felt very helpless, for she was right in the path of the fleet and at her eight knots speed could not hope to escape. However, she attempted to pass a wireless report to Germany, for which we were prepared, and we believed that we jammed her transmission successfully, though that in itself might give the enemy their opportunity to fix our position by wireless direction finder (D/F) and to set U-boats on to us. The one counteraction open to the C.-in-C. was to make a drastic alteration of course after dark, and this he did.

Amongst other ships on our list of possible interceptions was the blue-ribbon liner *Bremen*, a record holder of the Atlantic crossing, which had been reported leaving New York in a hurry on 31st August. The staff made a lot of calculations about her possible speeds and courses, for she was capable of mounting eight-inch guns and if detected would have been formidable, after conversion at home, as a carrier. We thought we might just catch her, but in the event she was already passing through the Denmark Strait when war broke out, and reached Murmansk and Soviet shelter on 6th September, though we did not learn this until some while later. Subsequently she slipped down the Norwegian coast and into the Heligoland Bight in which locality she passed the submarine *Salmon* on 12th November at eight hundred yards range. *Salmon* experienced perhaps the greatest temptation of the whole war as he watched this colossal target steam, across his sights, blotting out the whole sea and sky ahead of him. International agreement decrees that the crew and passengers of a merchantman must be put in a place of safety before she is sunk, and this the little *Salmon* could in no wise accomplish, and so he obeyed the law which, after all, he was engaged in fighting to uphold.

When the news of the safe return of this great ship leaked out there was some public clamour. People felt that such a large ship ought to have been easier to catch than smaller ones, and there was a school which thought that retaliation for unrestricted U-boat warfare was justified. The heartless destruction of the *Athenia* rankled in British minds, and it appeared to many that the government had been slow in paying back the Germans in their own coin.

A few days after the declaration of war a cruiser was sent with a small military force to seize the Danish Faeroe Islands to the west of the Shetlands. This was, of course, to forestall the Germans who could have used it as a fuelling base for submarines attacking Atlantic trade. We built a small airfield there, but the island group was never used as more than a staging post for aircraft or a haven for trawlers. The Danes appear never to have registered more than a perfunctory initial protest; in any case they had no weapons with which to defend themselves, and their homeland was overrun shortly afterwards by the German army.

By the evening of the fifth day it had become necessary to send our destroyer escort home to fuel — the Faeroes and Iceland were still neutral — or else to fuel them from the large ships, which involved a reduction of speed and holding a steady course for some while, thus offering a sitting target to a U-boat. We almost never took oilers with us; there were insufficient destroyers available to screen them; they were too slow to maintain fleet speed; and we operated in an area which produces some of the worst weather in the world almost all the year round, and that in itself would have made them usless most of the time. Various matters by now requiring the issue of instructions were accumulating and some had become urgent, yet we were, for our safety's sake, and in order to catch the homing merchantmen, tongue-tied. Messages for transmission were accordingly passed by visual signal to the carrier who ranged four of the new Skua fighter aircraft on deck. A search sweep was worked out for them, upon conclusion of which they were to land and deliver the messages in the north of Scotland — and so off they went. We reflected with some wonderment that their tea would be taken with fresh milk at an aerodrome while we, in ships, must plod on for three more days before making harbour.

It is curious to look back and reflect how this speed and facility impressed us at that time, and how we remarked on it almost with awe. We certainly wanted to be air-minded, but we were not air-experienced, and that was to be remedied very soon.

This was a period of shocks for the Home Fleet. On the 17th September the carrier *Courageous* (now twenty-three years old), screened by three destroyers, hunting U-boats out of Plymouth, had in the course of operating her aircraft turned away from her destroyer screen, which was some three miles distant, when at least two torpedoes struck her. She heeled over steeply. One officer known to Hugh was on the flight-deck when she was hit and he skidded down into the lee rail and was picking himself up, somewhat bruised and shocked, when the order "abandon ship" was given. The ship was settling rapidly and he jumped down ten feet into the water and swam away as fast as he could to avoid the suction. He was about two hundred yards off, amongst a multitude of bobbing heads, when she plunged, and as she went down Captain Makeig-Jones could be seen as he clung to the rail of his bridge at the salute, facing the disappearing ensign. He had been the captain of the *Nelson* for more than a year just before he went to the *Courageous*, and his loss was keenly felt.

The majority of the *Courageous'* company were picked up by the destroyers after counter-attacking the U-boat and their pursuit was so hot that it was thought that she was sunk, but that was not to be; in fact she escaped.

Towards the end of September the C.-in-C. felt that the time had come for something more lively than catching merchantmen, most of whom would have reached ports by now.

The submarine *Spearfish* reported damage and was about forty miles off the south-west coast of Norway, steering for the Firth of Forth. She had probably been sighted by the Germans and a light force was despatched to assist her. Rumours of a German counter-attacking force reached us and a sortie towards the Skagerrak entrance was accordingly planned for the 25th September. This would give us a chance to find out what protection our fleet could expect from our carrier-borne fighters. Some of us had experience with a miscellaneous assortment of Russian, German and Italian flying machines during the Noyon Patrol period of the Spanish Civil War in 1937, and Hugh had been bombed in a destroyer and missed once or twice by handsome half-miles; but there had also been the case of a destroyer who was caught stopped, with a boat lowered investigating a freighter, and the result had been something like a dozen casualties and a pepper-pot effect on the ship's side and upper works. Hugh's personal impression had been that anti-aircraft fire in Spain was ineffective.

By the morning of 26th September, the fleet was well over toward the German side of the North Sea, and at about 11 a.m. the first sighting of a Dornier flying boat was reported. Hugh was on the bridge at the time, and it was not many minutes before a second one was in sight. The fleet turned into the wind, the carrier *Ark Royal* flew off two sections of three Skua fighters and then our education began. The Skuas dashed off to the north. The Dorniers hurried along the horizon to the south and the halting and intermittently failing radio telephonic communicaton could not get the hunters turned to the correct direction before they had run out of fuel. It was an exasperating performance. A few minutes later a third Dornier appeared. These large aircraft looked for all the world like bumble-bees in a hurry. Off went the Skuas once more, and this time in the right direction. They went like three arrows straight for the flying boat who sighted them too late. He was about eleven miles from us when they reached him and in a matter of seconds he turned on his side as if one wing had gone, and flopped with a splash into the sea. The destroyer *Somali* on the screen was despatched to pick up a proud and rather insolent air crew of four. They had only twenty-three days of warfare and were to miss experiencing the bombing of Berlin and the German industrial centres, and perhaps may be accounted lucky.

Quickly the Skuas were turned towards yet another Dornier but once again communications failed and they ran out of fuel before they could be conned on to this next target. In the meantime *Nelson* fired a few rounds of anti-aircraft high explosive at the enemy when they came within range, but as soon as the shots fell close they turned away and it was not on that day considered desirable to try the longer-ranged sixteen-inch guns on them. One reason for this was that no guns of the main armament had been fitted with anti-aircraft sights, and in consequence the shooting would be largely a matter of guesswork. This is one of the legacies of peace. The gunnery department got busy with remedies as soon as the fleet returned to Scapa, but until the end, the experts opposed the use of the largest calibre guns, claiming that such firing was wasteful. Only two years later after the Japanese overwhelmed the *Prince of Wales* and *Repulse* in Malayan waters did the idea of a main armament barrage find official place in the measures proposed for combating air attack and then it took some time to procure the proper sights and fuses. The whole question was highly debatable.

By about 2 p.m. on this fine afternoon the first Junkers 88 bombers were reported approaching from the eastward. The fleet was then almost a hundred miles west of the southern point of Norway. At this time we were disposed in two groups and had just completed the turn to retire to the westward. Leading were a couple of cruisers; about five miles astern of them the *Nelson*, followed at a distance by *Ark Royal* and *Rodney* and surrounded by screening destroyers from one to two miles distant; five miles astern in a second group was the second-in-command, Vice-Admiral Whitworth in *Hood* with *Repulse* and a destroyer screen. This open sort of formation gave room for manoeuvring if that should be required.

Suddenly air alarm stations were sounded and everyone put on his tin helmet, anti-flash hood and gloves and hurried to his station. The admiral's bridge became jammed with staff officers anxious to see the anticipated air attack. All was well until the admiral wanted to walk from one side of his bridge to the other, and then, discovering that he could not, he ordered everyone to his proper action station. The C.-in-C.'s staff edged sheepishly this way or that, for they really had no action station. At this stage nobody quite knew just where the staff was likely to be wanted. The general instruction for the unemployed was to get under armour. The chief of staff quickly cut in and said he wanted the signal, wireless, aviation and gunnery officers to stay, and the rest could "get the hell out of it", which they did — more or less. Hugh couldn't think of anything useful to do and went down to an engine-room which was his harbour air raid station. It was a bleak experience; everything very shiny, slippery underfoot, and very hot. He looked at large hissing pipes and thought about bomb hits down here — there was only about six inches of armour overhead. The four-point-sevens could by now be heard firing, just a distant hollow metallic knock. There were other obscure bangs which one imagined as bombs, but were more probably stokers shutting steel watertight doors behind them as they moved about the interior of the ship. From a state of keyed-up apprehension the engine-room personnel gradually subsided into a sort of anxious inaction. Here was another lesson learned: that the ship's company wanted to be kept informed of the progress of the action, a policy adopted by all ships from that time forward.

After about twenty minutes Hugh returned to the bridge — there was little news to be gleaned. The enemy had scattered when gun-fire came close and then they bombed individually and inaccurately thereafter, and finally disappeared to the eastward. One of the bombs had come within two hundred yards, but that was the closest.

Discussion was still in progress when the next wave appeared, in two formations, each of about twenty Junkers 88s. They came straight in at 16,000 feet from the eastward, and at six miles distance started to glide down in increasingly ragged array as our shell bursts came among them, but, because of the concentration of gun-fire from several different ships it was impossible for control officers to spot their own shots, and the fire was ragged and ineffective. This was rather a blow, for we had imagined that our anti-aircraft batteries would knock down at least a proportion of attackers. We did not see even one destroyed by gunnery during this day. Our fighter aircraft numbered only nine, and of these, three were now caught refuelling on deck. Friendly aircraft in the air were directed to clear out of the zone of gun-fire for their own safety during this attack, and therefore gave no protection. This policy was thereafter revised and with great bravery the Fleet Air Arm fighters pursued their quarry right through defensive barrages anywhere, and, at a later stage, in order to secure the passage of relief ships to beleaguered Malta.

Ragged or not, the Junkers came on, and it was not long before they discovered the safety cone directly overhead within which our guns could not at that time bear because their elevation was insufficient. It was with some apprehension that Hugh gazed upward at one particular JU88 circling tightly overhead in a clear patch of blue sky, surrounded by dark smoke puffs. An instant later, this pilot put his nose down and dived at the *Ark Royal*, about four hundred yards astern. Almost at once the carrier put her helm over and slowly began to turn to port. The flash of the JU88 machine-guns was clearly visible as he aimed at the flight-deck and then, at about 3,000 feet, he released a large bomb — probably 500 kilograms — and then began to pull out of the sixty-degree dive. This was the first of an ambitious line of German pilots who claimed to have sunk the *Ark Royal*. Hugh saw the bomb strike the water in a white splash about thirty yards off her port bow. It is probable that the attacker believed he was going to hit, but while pulling out of a steep dive at high speed one travels too far and too fast to make it easy to observe a hit with certainty. He was about 1,500 feet up when he crossed their flight-deck and zoomed away and upwards as the puffs of explosive shells marked his track. *Ark Royal* collected and preserved a number of his machine-gun bullets as souvenirs of the encounter. Nevertheless it had been a close call, and we were obliged on this day to recognise that neither our guns nor our tiny fighter force were capable of adequately defending the fleet at sea.

A minute or two later, while still looking aft towards the *Ark Royal*, Hugh saw another dive-bomber attack the *Hood* about two miles away. As the clearly visible bomb came down, it looked like a certain hit, and when it struck there was a flash and a small puff of dark smoke, but the *Hood* forged steadily ahead. One could see a dark brownish stain down her port side to the waterline. The bomb had struck a glancing blow on the armour belt and exploded in the water alongside. She was claimed by Germany as sunk that day.

This 26th of September had furnished an illuminating lesson and it demonstrated the prescience of the C.-in-C. in a way which was to be repeated time after time throughout his tenure of the Home Fleet Command. He saw that there was much we needed to learn and realised that the whole fleet had received the finest form of instruction one could wish for. On the way home the admiral made a signal describing the shooting as the worst he had ever seen, and indeed it was a sorry spectacle; distribution of gun-fire was uncertain, sights and gun elevation and especially in the heavy calibres, not fully adequate to their tasks. Some, if not all of this had been realised and represented by ships during the Noyon Patrol era two years earlier, but very few of their experiences had been witnessed by qualified gunnery technicians, or by senior officers, and the lessons they had learned there did not filter through to the shore departments with the urgency that was now needful. Efforts to produce coloured bursts were in hand but did not achieve early success and that idea was later abandoned. It is true that a new and hopefully efficient apparatus for control was in the design stage, but it would take some time before the benefits were felt at sea.

On 26th September 1939, the most important lesson was in the realm of the air. This day demonstrated that voice communication with protection fighters was both inefficient and vitally necessary. As far back as 1918 we had been using a rather halting intermittent Radio-Telephone to talk to the balloon towed in ships for observation purposes, but shortly after the war it had been abandoned as inferior to a flashing Morse signal. In the spring of 1939 when a French squadron had visited the fleet in the Firth of Forth, many of us had watched their manoeuvring efficiently with Radio-Telephone, but this failed to impress our own experts — they thought our wireless was as quick and more certain. Radio-Telephone (R/T) did have, however, some disadvantage in point of security. Be that as it may, our wireless was not yet adequate for fighter direction and we were fortunate in meeting an inexperienced enemy on this occasion.

The loss of the SS *Clement* to a warship raider off Pernambuco was announced a few days later, revealing that something was afoot in the South Atlantic. The pocket battleship *Graf Spee* had sailed from Germany just before the war broke out and got clear away, though it was not until the River Plate Battle that her identity was finally established. Our cruisers began to vanish elsewhere and *Renown* and a carrier were detached into the central Atlantic.

The far northern autumn quickly changed to winter, and at Scapa, gale succeeded gale with wearing regularity, though most people were too busy to take more than passing note of the appalling Orcadian weather in those early stages. The first storm after the outbreak of war in September reached a wind speed of eighty-six miles an hour and eighty-three ship-borne Walrus reconnaissance aircraft were destroyed as Hugh stood on deck watching. Some had wings stripped off, others were torn from their platforms and fell into the sea. At Hatson Airfield near Kirkwall where many fleet aircraft had been landed for safety, whole groups moored behind banks for protection were torn from their moorings and rolled across the airfield in a jumbled mass of metal which fetched up in a deep drainage ditch a mile away. Small metal hangars to protect fleet aircraft were quickly constructed in the larger ships, but northern weather hardly ever allowed such operational flying.

The C.-in-C. timed his sweeps so that the Flow was as empty as possible during full moon periods, for our own anti-aircraft defence was in its early stages. The few guns and searchlights available seemed almost buried in a sea of mud and sodden peat and their crews spent much of that first winter under tents that sometimes blew away. Their inmates learned from the sheep where shelter could be found in a fold of the hillside. Occasionally the soldiers would come on board for a bath, hot supper or an evening at the movies — it was good for both to learn of the others' problems. The base at Lyness on Hoy Island developed rapidly from a few oil tanks and a concrete slab where boom defence nets could be ranged, into a cluster of workshops, huts and even roadways, down which inches deep of mud and water oozed to the sea. Everyone wore sea-boots and needed them. The Church of Scotland soon erected a hut at the head of the landing jetty and dispensed tea and kindliness, and this remained for long the only amenity available for some hundreds of shore and seagoing personnel, other than a rather cheerless beer canteen and three rough football grounds on Flotta. The weather was gales, rain and more gales, and had officers the leisure for shore-going, there were only a few days upon which the ship's boats could be safely used at the tumble-down little jetties, much eroded by time, relics of World War I. On Flotta, the nearest island, the fleet resurrected seven holes of the golf-course which had been constructed under Lord Jellicoe's direction during the First World War. Admiral Forbes was as keen a golfer as his famous pedecessor, and different ships undertook the reconstruction of a hole — *Hood*'s hole was her first memorial, and never lacked a volunteer party of greensmen when she was no longer there to carry on the work herself.

It was not only the thin anti-aircraft defences that gave cause for anxiety; we looked at the five gaps between the islands surrounding Scapa Flow. Three of these entrances could take the largest size of ships, and the two which were the most convenient were fitted with defensive netting plus a gateway which could be opened and closed to permit passage of traffic. The third deep passage between Hoy and Stromness was in the process of being netted, but there the gales and strong currents uprooted sections of netting more than once and this entrance was probably more continuously protected by physical conditions than anything else during the first year of the war. Two more entrances, passable only for small craft, existed at the eastern end. Block ships were being prepared to close them, but these were not yet ready, and two of them when sunk swung out of position in the sluicing tide. Trawlers were fitted as a standing patrol at every entrance, whether netted or not, a most soul-destroying form of sentry-go. Sometimes these small craft were forced off their beat by the weather and it then became necessary to replace them with hard-pressed destroyers who otherwise might have obtained a night's rest in harbour. There were also suitably placed guns and underwater sound detector defences, but even these were occasionally damaged by the fierce gales that prevailed during much of the winter.

Korvetten Kapitän Prein had been among the several German submarine captains who had visited Scapa Flow on a goodwill cruise two or three years previously, but nobody had taken much notice of this. The German air attaché's wife had been unwell in

London during the latter part of August, 1939, and her solicitous husband had sought and obtained permission to take her on an air trip northwards through the Orkneys and Shetlands for a breath of fresh northern air. The civil airline route to Norway also went that way regularly, and the convalescent lady and her husband only left Kirkwall for the south on the first of September. Another diplomatic visitor to the North had been Ambassador Grandi of Italy, who had been taking a motoring holiday in the John O' Groats region on the Pentland Firth as recently as 3rd September. Nobody, in time of peace, was able to think of a reason why these distinguished foreigners should not seek recreation in whatever part of the British Isles they cared to select. The air attaché could obviously have observed the state of the net and blockship defences, while Grandi, it is said, had watched with binoculars from Dunnet Head the fleet entering the Flow by the Switha and Hoxa gates a few days before war was declared. Prein's party could have examined the entrances and studied the tides which provided safe passages or impenetrable torrents at different hours of the same day. And, finally, the picture was completed for Grand Admiral Raeder by an occasional reconnaissance plane which after the declaration of war flew across the anchorage at a great height, undisturbed by gun-fire that never was able to get on to him before he was out of range. Radar detection was being erected, but it was still only of an experimental nature at this early stage, and gave our six Blenheim fighter defence force insufficient warning to take off and climb to twenty thousand feet where the enemy was flying.

Britain had not been at war since 1918 and that was before aircraft had become a recognised form of transport.

So the day came when, at sea with almost the whole of the fleet, a signal arrived to say that *Royal Oak* had been torpedoed and sunk in the Flow while anchored in Kirkwall Bay. This possibility had been half feared, but not seriously expected. A German reconnaissance plane had flown over the anchorage in the early afternoon and evidently spotted *Renown*, *Royal Oak* and *Albatross* (an obsolete seaplane tender) lying in the same part of the Flow. Near midnight, an hour before high tide, when the currents would be slack, Prein's U-boat dodged the two patrol trawlers at the eastern entrances, and slipped into the Flow through the hundred yard gap created by the displaced blockship and accomplished his brilliant and bold design, escaping by the way he came. If the sentries on shore close by were awake they were not very alert on this very black night, for the submarine periscope was no more than three hundred yards from them — the swish of submarine engines was probably lost in the lap of water stirred by the breeze, and a sentry look-out post, when nothing has been seen for a very long time, can become ineffective. The same sad facts apply with equal force to the patrol craft.

Hugh was given a vivid account of this disaster from a friend on board *Royal Oak* at the time. This officer had been turned in for about half an hour when he was woken from the first moments of sleep by an explosive noise which he judged to come from forward. His cabin was on the upper deck level, and it was the work of a moment to slip on an overcoat and slippers and run to the scene of what he imagined had been an explosion in the inflammable store right in the eyes of the ship. He had reached the fo'c'sle deck within a minute or two, enquiring of a miscellaneous group of officers and men who had got to the scene in much the same way as he had, when a shattering explosion and a sheet of flame burst from amidships roughly abreast of the funnel. The ship immediately took a heavy list and he slid down the deck on to the lee quard-rail in company with all the others, plus a miscellaneous collection of gear which had been lying loose about the fo'c'sle deck. No sooner was his slide checked by the berthing wires than he found his feet in the water and, realising that the ship was rolling over, he leaped clear away into the sea and threw off his coat. His bedroom slippers had already gone as he struck out away from the ship's side. Everything was dark and oil fuel seemed to be everywhere, some of it burning; a few shouts could be heard, and he saw the *Albatross* half a mile away lowering boats. There was a trawler at some distance which was picking up survivors and had bright lights shining. All this seemed far away from him, and catching sight of the low cliff of the adjacent land like a black line against a slightly less black sky, he struck out towards the shore. Apart from a little oil fuel swallowed and some more in his eyes, he felt he was in good condition and hardly noticed the cold. He reached the rocky beach without misadventure and there gradually collected in ones and twos about twenty other survivors, some blinded, or speechless and retching with the oil, and mostly naked or smothered completely with the smelly clinging mess — a condition that was to save them all from perishing of cold. They clambered up into a heather-choked ditch twenty feet above and huddled close in its scanty protection, the more fit ones pulling tussocks with which they covered their exhausted shipmates. None of them were sure about which part of the coast they had landed upon, nor in what direction to look for help, and they agreed amongst themselves that it was wisest to huddle together to get what mutual warmth was possible until dawn. For some six hours they lay shivering in this plight until morning revealed a little peat-thatched cottage and the means of rescue half a mile distant.

This disaster shook us considerably — for a ship without a base is likely to become as helpless as a snail without his shell. Londonderry, Loch Ewe and Loch Eriboll on the coast of Scotland were mooted as alternative anchorages, but all lacked any air defences. Loch Ewe was chosen as the most northern anchorage in which relative safety might be found.

In the early part of October there had appeared in *The Times* a fine half-page photograph of the *Nelson* lying in calm harbour surrounded by smaller craft and auxiliaries in a framework of steep and rocky hills. The C.-in-C. sent for Hugh shortly after the newspaper came on board. He was fuming; who had taken the photograph? How had it got past the censor? Who was the censor? Go and find out all the details. Quite simply it was a very fine picture and the censor passed it because it did not betray a single confidential feature of any ship or other visible object. A little while later a shipmate told Hugh that he had just received a letter from his mother who was delighted to find from that lovely photograph in *The Times* that he was at Loch Ewe. She recognised the place at once as she had been motoring up there last summer.

A couple of weeks after this the fleet was coming into Loch Ewe from a patrol, *Nelson* leading with other ships astern. A mile from the little island which divides the narrow entrance, the destroyer screen turned to make an Asdic search of the coast on either side and astern. Ahead the fleet minesweepers were steaming on either side as they swept out the entrance before we went in. Speed was reduced to about eight knots to ensure that the sweepers would be clear of the course in time, and the great ship slowly moved ahead. At 7.50 a.m. precisely the admiral's bridge clock left the peg on which it customarily hung and, flying through the air, was fumblingly caught by Hugh standing directly behind the compass in the middle of the bridge. The gyro compass sprang out of its gimbals and shattered itself on the deck beside him, and he saw a bluish flash down on the starboard side of the fo'c'sle just before

320

the breakwater, and felt a mighty jerk as if the bows had suddenly jumped several feet out of the water and then a sickening sort of slump as the fo'c'sle plunged again and sank fourteen feet in the water so that everybody was tipped forward.

The admiral immediately said:

"Did anyone see? Mine or torpedo?"

They looked over the edge of the bridge at a frothing circle of dull brown water sliding along beside them as they moved ahead and then passing away clear astern. They could feel the ship as though it were a live thing stricken beneath their feet.

There was no torpedo track but that was no guarantee, for there was room for a U-boat to lie close to the beach; yet they were up-sun from him and his periscope should have been seen. Beside that, there were two asdic-fitted trawlers patrolling, and also listening posts and look-outs on shore, and the sweepers had been working in the channel for the last hour or more since break of day. If it was not a torpedo then it must be one of the new magnetic mines about which reports had been coming in from the shallow waters of the East Coast. They were in more than forty fathoms, but *Nelson*'s great bulk would create a strong magnetic field and the touch of these infernal machines could detonate when the small bulk of trawlers and sweepers might not cause a detonation.

The captain immediately stopped engines and they drifted gently ahead. The ship seemed to be sinking gradually forward and on the bridge there was some discussion about beaching her on a sandy strip just to starboard, but there soon came reports from the engine-room that the main machinery and pumps were undamaged and that the flooding was no longer increasing, and so they went ahead to their usual berth with a couple of minesweepers and a destroyer ahead and a tug standing by to tow.

It was a sad tale forward on the messdecks. Every movable fitting — light brackets, shelves of crockery, mess tables, everything — was fractured and flung in a senseless jumble on the deck. The barbette of the forward 16-inch gun turret showed cracks in its paintwork where the immensely thick armour plates had been fused together during construction. In Hugh's cabin, six hundred feet away from the scene of the explosion, the iron frame of the bedspring was broken and had leapt from the solid iron fitting in which it normally rested, and it was flung with the bedding on the deck. An electric overhead light fitting swung gently from a single wire, its broken securing screws like old teeth gaping black from the white paintwork of the steel ceiling. Eleven men were seriously injured and almost seventy were cut and bleeding. The seamen's living spaces were most severely affected and for the next three hours reeked with splashed blood as the five doctors and dozens of helpers worked to tend the injured and clear up the mess. The shock effect on some was noticeable for two months afterwards.

We were short on battleships at that moment and it was necessary to keep this disaster secret. Every possible step to that end was taken straight away. Nevertheless the wife of a senior officer stationed at Portsmouth 600 miles away welcomed her husband to a late tea that afternoon with the shocking news that the Fleet flagship had been severely damaged by an underwater explosion. She had heard it from the children's nanny. The girl had met her policeman friend during her afternoon outing with the perambulator. The policeman's brother home to lunch, told how the head of his department in the dockyard had sent for him privately in his office that morning and told him to prepare the chocks in the bottom of the great dock in a certain way, the way they must be placed when *Nelson* came in. And the story was all over Portsmouth that night, although the Germans did not apparently learn of their success until five months later.

In due course several more magnetic mines were detonated at Loch Ewe by newly-invented sweeping devices, and, as their positions were plotted, one could see on the chart how a U-boat must have approached the narrow entrance, laid her cargo of about twenty as she turned across it in a wide curve, and went out to sea again close to the opposite shore.

This coming night four light cruisers were due to sail for the Northern Patrol which we dared not leave empty. These ships cleared all hands out of the forward part and steamed out — perhaps the most uncomfortable journey, short though it was, that any of them was asked to undertake during the whole of this war, for there was not yet any certainty that all the mines had been detonated. Mathematical calculations of magentic effects indicated that they should be safe, but it was with great relief that we saw the cruisers clear without mishap.

The following morning the staff, numbering about one hundred officers and ratings, boarded three large buses and drove off to Inverness from where a special train conveyed us and the office

W

equipment and records to Greenock on the Clyde. We arrived there on a bitterly cold and rainy night and went immediately on board *Warspite* lying in the stream. The C.-in-C. had gone down by car and arrived a little ahead of us.

This incident, of course, meant that we were denied our second base, and hereafter the main fleet used Greenock for some weeks to come.

Hugh felt sad at leaving the *Nelson*. He had got to know her very well. Although *Warspite* was fitted as a Fleet flagship with the necessary staff accommodation and offices, she was an old ship and cramped for space. At sea the quarterdeck was awash with hatches battened down and occupants of cabins had to be evacuated; yet time and again these cabins got flooded in rough weather. Some found places to sleep on the bridge structure. On their first trip at sea in *Warspite*, Hugh's bed was made up on a table in a small interior compartment above the crew's smoking room. The atmosphere at night was thick. As the ship rolled the mattress slipped and it was not long before it slid with him onto the deck, fortunately on top of the Fleet gunnery officer who had chosen, as he thought, a safer billet, but he did not complain too unkindly. They soon settled down amongst what proved to be a very fine ship's company which later on earned the great reputation which she achieved in the Mediterranean. In these northern latitudes she was cold and wet, ploughing into the steep seas with much of the living space between decks constantly slopping salt water to and fro, and almost incessant trickles leaking through hatchways and ventilators, so that everyone clumped about in heavy damp sea-boots while at sea.

Most of the fleetmen were delighted to see the modest civilisation of Greenock after many months of complete isolation from almost all amenities, and the dank fog and piercing cold of the Clyde seemed a very welcome easement from rigorous Scapa.

The fleet sweeps to the westward continued through the winter, usually nine days out and three days in, and the capital ships piled up a considerable mileage. They did not entirely desert Scapa, for much small ship training continued there and it was only the capital ships and carriers that avoided it entirely until the blocking of the entrance was completed.

The First Lord of the Admiralty, Mr Churchill, was an early visitor. They had gone into Loch Ewe to refuel after one of their sweeps, and in great secrecy he suddenly appeared on board. He went into the wardroom and other officers' messes each evening to have a drink before dinner and talked freely to everyone. Hugh recollects that, later on, one evening he came up to the wardroom and a few officers sat chatting with him till after midnight. The question of the use of deception in wartime arose and his dictum was:

"It is very wrong to tell lies, and I would never countenance that. But where the country's interest is at stake — ah! that is a different matter. I would not like it, but I regard it as a part of the tactics of war and we must use every weapon; neglect nothing!"

Churchill was very keen on the idea of having a war room, an institution which served him efficiently in the conditions obtaining at the Admiralty. Something of the sort had been tried in the *Nelson* in the early days, and charts, signals and records for reference were laid out in a screened off part of the admiral's dining cabin, but the scheme proved valueless to either the C.-in-C. or the staff, and it had petered out by a sort of unspoken agreement. Apparently the first lord had heard of this war room and now asked to see it, and so the staff were directed to produce one forthwith for his inspection. The midshipmen's study was hastily cleared and the staff routed out charts and stuck them on the bulkheads and brought in files of references, masses of signals, and books from the staff office, so that within a couple of hours a not very convincing imitation had appeared. Mr Churchill gave it a quick appraising glance when he was brought along to see it, asked one or two questions, sniffed somewhat derisively, was not favourably impressed, and had walked out again within three minutes. It was a poor effort anyhow, and after a few weeks of uneasy uselessness, accompanied by much subtle propaganda on the part of the midshipmen, it achieved its permanent demise.

Mr Churchill's visits — and Hugh witnessed four of them — always followed the same plan. He would be ready for the fray with a large glass of brandy in hand and a cigar between his teeth by about half-past nine, at which time there would be a staff conference and the admiral would run through the situation at the moment and the latest developments since he had left London, probably the day before. Then he would have the ship's company mustered and make a speech of about fifteen minutes' duration. On the first occasion he recalled how, as first lord during World War I, he had visited the Grand Fleet under Lord Jellicoe in this selfsame anchorage of Aultbea on the shores of Loch Ewe. It made one realise something of the vast stores of experience which he had to draw upon. He would usually speak without a microphone, and it was amazing how, without any lifting of the voice, he made himself audible to perhaps twelve hundred men, mustered on the upper deck in the open air. His theme was always the same: the country depended in the last resort on the Navy, and he believed their confidence was justified. He said this in a way that made every stoker go below and keep his monotonous watch with alert purpose for the next six months. He would move from ship to ship, walking round some part of each, and delivering his speech. On one occasion he spoke eleven times in one day; he had a heavy cold at the time, and every speech was different, and to every ship he brought some special reference to her recent work or activities — it was a tremendous performance. Among Hugh's jobs was looking after the Press and with them he witnessed it all. The effect on the whole personnel from the admiral to the side boy was electrifying — he exalted monotonous daily work into a great and glorious endeavour in which each one shared in a personal measure, and after he had left everyone felt that in London, whatever lacked, and much did in that first year, it was not for want of will and effort, and if they needed something it would be supplied as soon as possible while Winston Churchill remained alive.

He usually arrived sallow and dead tired, so that everyone was anxious for his health, and when it was suggested that the programme of inspections and speeches should be cut short or that he should go and rest in his cabin, his answer was always the same:

"No, No! Certainly not. It refreshes me. This is a different air from London. No; we will go on!"

And he was right. Twenty-four hours later pink had come into his cheeks and a flash into that pale blue rolling eye and his step was more springy than it had been.

Later on, after he had become prime minister, he came into the wardroom late in the evening where a handful of officers were still talking.

"Ah! I see you are having a nightcap. I wonder if I might have a little brandy?"

He chatted away and presently said:

"I would like to have a look round the messdecks; could someone show me the way?" And he was looking straight at Hugh, who happened to be standing nearby. Nobody volunteered, and after an embarrassed silence Hugh said:

"Of course, Sir, if you wish!" and wondered with a moment of horror what on earth the captain of the ship would say about this night-time inspection that was bound to reach his ears, but he dared not desert Churchill and run away to wake the captain.

They went off forward, banging their heads into hammocks slung overhead, and of course encountered sailors at every turn. Winston stopped to talk to all whom he met, spending more than an hour on his midnight round. He wanted to know what they were feeling about things in general, and to be caught by the prime minister at one o'clock in the morning clad perhaps in a pair of underpants, or half an overall, ensured informality and an absence of priming — what he learned there came straight from the horse's mouth. Admiral Forbes dealt with the captain next day, but nobody knew what was said, and Hugh kept quiet about this "inspection".

On another occasion they took the first lord up to Scapa — just a night's trip through the Minches, and on arrival off the entrance a signal was flashed to inform them that German aircraft had been over in the dark and there was a suspicion that mines had been laid in the anchorage. Sweeping would not be completed before late afternoon. This would, of course, disrupt Mr Churchill's timetable and his special purpose this day was to inspect the shore defences. They steamed into sheltered water, lowered him in a cutter, a twelve-oared lifeboat, always ready rigged at sea, and the midshipman of the boat steered him over to a small dockyard launch which conveyed him ashore. He was delighted with this little adventure, and carefully adjusted his cork service lifebelt with a happy grin just before climbing into the boat which was lowered to the upper deck level to make it easier for him to get in. Normally the lifeboat's crew races over a wire netting to man the lifeboat.

It was during this visit that a movement of German warships was reported in the Skagerrak and the fleet immediately raised steam. A further report decided the C.-in-C. to put to sea and while (in Hugh's presence) he was drafting the signal ordering the fleet to sail, Mr Churchill suddenly burst out:

"You won't put me ashore, will you, Admiral? I shall come with you. This is a great opportunity!"

"Oh, no, First Lord. We can't take you along. I'm not going to be responsible for that."

"But you could put me down below under armour if anything really happened."

"I could, but you wouldn't stay there. Besides, you would be needed in the Admiralty if anything happened."

Mr Churchill looked very crestfallen. At that point Hugh left the cabin and never knew how the argument ended. In the event the Germans quietened down, so they did not go to sea that day.

The German airmen displayed right from the start a curiously timid attitude towards Scapa. They were rightly cautious about the weight of the defences, but a bold test would have confirmed the weaknesses which aerial photographic reconnaissance might have indicated. It may well be that the shocking weather which was our constant bane in the anchorage, and which severely hampered the development and strengthening of the defences on shore, often served as our protection in keeping the Luftwaffe grounded at their coastal airfields.

Eventually that first autumn they undertook a minelaying expedition at dusk. About a dozen planes glided in from all directions with engines shut off, and although they were located a couple of minutes before they released their parachute mines — several of these were actually seen falling — only one or two shots were fired by the guns which were unable to see the planes in the hazy conditions overhead and the fading light. This was, of course, in the very early days of radar, which was still an uncertain though potentially powerful aid. That night the C.-in-C. considered our position very seriously, for the main gate was blocked. We could still get out by the Hoy and Switha gates, if we could reach them without being mined, and some ship could have been sent ahead as a precaution to act as mine-bumper had it been necessary to put to sea in a hurry. The minesweepers, of course, went to work at once, and next morning at daylight were all over the Flow. Watching from his cabin scuttle after breakfast Hugh saw three mines detonated in quick succession. The explosions gave a loud metallic knock on the bottom of the ship. The nearest one was about four hundred yards away. The great column of water thrown into the air in the comparatively shallow sea looked as if it could swamp the little sweepers, but they were having the time of their lives, and after weeks of monotonous tramping up and down the tracks without a sniff of war, here they were with their teeth into the real thing, and, later in the day when Hugh visited one of them, he found them all as pleased and excited as a bunch of children at a party. A safe passage way out of the Flow was reported within a few hours, and the whole Flow was clear at the end of the day. The attack was repeated a little while later on, and these attacks left an anxious feeling behind them — it was clearly possible that we could be bottled up if only for a short while at a critical moment.

This situation occasioned a visit from the new First Lord Mr A. V. Alexander, and the First Sea Lord Admiral Pound. For the best part of two days the Admiralty view that Scapa had now become a trap was pressed upon Admiral Forbes, but he would not accept it. He believed that three exits would not easily be closed at one fell swoop, and that the right course was to fight back with more suitable types and numbers of sweepers, and to increase the anti-aircraft gun protection. Again, in a fundamental strategical argument time proved him right. The German Air Force was very powerful, but he did not overestimate that power. His was the view of the man who lived constantly within the conditions of visibility and weather which the attacking airman must meet. Smartness of lookout would best help us in this type of emergency.

There had been much talk in the days of the Munich agreement before the war, and it reappeared from time to time during the war, of the isolation of the C.-in-C. when at sea, and how useless he became when wireless silence might interfere with his taking charge of affairs. Surely, the Admiralty asked, he could only control effectively from a position in which he was able to communicate freely with all his ships at all times? Apart from operations, many administrative matters must be left undecided while he was at sea and out of wireless touch, and this was inconvenient, though not necessarily seriously injurious. But such arguments, sound in themselves, leave out the human element. The sailor who knows his admiral is plugging along in filthy weather with the rain running down his neck for days on end and exposed to the same dangers from U-boats as every man in the fleet, feels rightly that his leader appreciates the reality of the conditions, and the very sharing in those conditions creates an important human bond at the very core of British naval strength. One had heard soldiers of all ranks say time and again: "But of course your admirals are with you at sea"; and to them this amounted to a whole world of difference where a general must be placed beyond the likelihood of sudden destruction.

Admiral Forbes let everyone have his say and listened to all attentively and then spoke out one day at a staff conference:

"No. It would never do. The men would not like it. I could never be in touch with them. While my flag flies it will be in a seagoing ship. If they want the Commander-in-Chief on shore they will have to get another one." And that settled the argument for the time being.

We had, of course, expected heavy air attacks on Scapa. It was within reasonable bombing range of some German airfields, but no really heavy attack was ever delivered. Two attacks conducted by perhaps a dozen machines, were made on the Lyness base installations while most of the fleet was at sea. In the first of these one or two vessels sprang leaks and two or three trawlers and barges were sunk. The *Iron Duke*, Lord Jellicoe's old flagship (long since demilitarised and turned into an accommodation vessel for harbour personnel) received a near miss which fell close alongside and started the plating so that she quickly flooded and took on a heavy list and settled to the bottom.

From the Fleet flagship buoy in the southwest corner of the rectangular Flow they had a magnificent view of the shore guns and searchlights surrounding the anchorage on all sides, and of the ship-borne anti-aircraft guns chiming in. The effect was as of an immense amphitheatre walled by searchlight and tracer beams and the flashes of guns, and accompanied by the orange explosions of shells inside, above and below the clouds. Hugh claims to have seen aircraft illuminated on only a few occasions and even then had no idea whether they were enemy or our own fighter defence. Only once was a major warship hit, and that was the cruiser *Norfolk* which was pierced by two bombs aft, part of a stick which straddled the *Repulse*'s quarterdeck and missed her by fifty yards. Tugs were always on duty, and at an air raid warning were prepared to get under way at immediate notice. That night they were alongside *Norfolk* within half an hour.

These attacks were worrying because it seemed clear that gun-fire did not knock out even one of the enemy, and nobody could guess what deterrent effect, if any, it produced — one could only crowd in more and more guns as they came from the factory and cultivate a hopeful frame of mind. We knew of about three certain enemy aircraft shot down out of all these raids.

By the end of the year considerable irritation had arisen amongst a section of seafaring Americans at the interference which our control of contraband caused to their trade, particularly in the

Mediterranean. There were specific complaints of delay and of search of mails. We received specially strict instructions to avoid bringing American merchantmen into Kirkwall where real danger of attack always existed and would inevitably have aroused hard feelings had it occurred. It was no part of our policy to antagonise the source from which we always hoped to draw our main bulk of supplies.

Sweden had for some years manufactured the highest quality of ball bearings, and when these were required by British industry they usually bought them from the Swedes. Now, because of the great increase in the production of tanks, stocks were running out and it might take up to two years to build a plant in Britain capable of meeting the demand. It therefore became critically important to get increased supplies from Sweden, a country wholly contained within an area controlled by the Germans, who, if they knew of the situation, would surely take steps to prevent export.

Sir George Binney produced a plan to run cargoes from Sweden to Britain by breaking through the German blockade. He mustered twelve Norwegian ships which had escaped into the neutral protection of Swedish territorial waters, and, collecting volunteer crews of some very brave Norwegian and British seamen, and even some machine-guns and ammunition for defence, he sailed the whole convoy loaded with ball bearings from Goteborg. Two vessels reached the east coast of Scotland, seven were sunk by German gun-fire and air patrols with great loss of life, and three turned back into Swedish waters to escape from air attack. Before the operation he came to Scapa to solicit the help of the C.-in-C. for this venture. It had earlier been rejected as an impracticable operation of war when he proposed it to the Admiralty for consideration. The most our fleet could do was to send a couple of destroyers half-way across the North Sea to meet the ships. Even Coastal Air Command would do no more than strengthen their thin patrols over the route. The plan was that these merchantmen, moving at about nine to fourteen knots, would escape in the frequent foggy weather, and avoid the most dangerous part of the voyage near the coast.

Hugh later on had the good fortune to meet one or two of our representatives in Sweden and learned from them a little of the history of these matters. Sweden was no match for Germany and could never be expected to face a threat of force from that quarter.

1939 seemed to be producing nothing but bad news at sea until,

330

on 12th December, three cruisers found and engaged the pocket battleship *Graf Spee* which had been raiding commerce in the South Atlantic. Hugh had an account of the action from a friend who was in *Ajax*. *Ajax* knew the day before that they were close to the *Graf Spee*, and at daylight flew off their Seafox spotting plane which quickly sighted the enemy, and on this report the three cruisers fanned out and closed at full speed. The *York*, an 8-inch cruiser, fired first at maximum range, and the others with their 6-inch guns as soon as they came in range at about 15,000 yards, but only the forward guns were bearing. *Graf Spee* fired at all of them in turn with her 11-inch guns, and *York* was twice hit with severely damaging shots. *Ajax* was also hit and suffered some damage. At one moment it looked as if *Graf Spee* might knock out all three of them one after another. The Seafox spotted fall of shot and when it ran out of fuel it was hoisted on board to replenish and then flew off again during the action. They eventually noticed that the enemy firing slackened, and although they had not seen any positive hits, *Ajax* began to hope that she was damaged. She seemed to be making for territorial waters and entered the deep-water channel amongst the sandbanks that lie off Montevideo. Our ships ceased fire when she crossed the three-mile limit, and the Seafox followed her into Montevideo harbour reporting the exact position of her berth. *York*, who was in some danger of sinking, managed to make temporary repairs which proved sufficient to keep her afloat. The sequel is well known. The *Graf Spee* was given the legal twenty-four hour time limit for her stay in port, and knowing that the cruisers were waiting outside for him, the captain transferred nearly his whole crew to a German merchantman and then steamed out of port and scuttled his ship just outside the channel, the few hands on board leaving in the ship's boats and returning to harbour. Captain Harwood in command in *York*, whom Hugh had known when he joined the *London* in 1937, was knighted for this cheering success which gave a tremendous boost to British morale both at home and abroad.

Christmas 1939 was spent at Greenock in a muck of fog and smoke that would sometimes have prevented the fleet sailing. Hugh recalls witnessing the arrival of the first Canadian troop convoy in the Clyde. The visibility varied from a hundred yards to half a mile as one liner after another slid past the Fleet flagship at her buoy. They berthed alongside jetties all the way up the river and the Navy admired the job done that day by the pilots, no less than the captains of those huge ships. One or two berthed close to the Fleet flagship at the Albert Dock — a grim and grimy region of soot-ridden red brick sheds.

On the wharfside to give an official welcome was a little group of bowler hats and dark overcoats from London amd some khaki and gold braid as well, but it was utterly dwarfed and overpowered by the immensity of the great liners, and then by the Canadian troops, as they streamed down the gangways in a solid khaki river with bags over their shoulders and the drizzle darkening their greatcoats more and more every minute. A shout went up: "The Canadians have come!" A thrill ran through the fleet at that name! They had built their reputation in World War I and here they were back again, tall, red-faced, rowdy, so that the speeches over the loudspeakers were drowned out. We were at that time facing formidable odds and these men of us, yet not belonging to us, had come from a great distance of their own freewill — we would never forget this.

In peace-time the lightly built aircraft-carriers were always involved in major fleet exercises, but as these took place in the early spring when the North Atlantic is stormy, they were frequently a cause for anxiety rather than a strong factor influencing those exercises. More than once a carrier was severely damaged in rough weather and finished up in dock for several months thereafter. Moreover in rough weather consideration for the safety of air crews quite often prevented whatever flying had been planned. In early days the overriding problem had been to check the speed of aircraft after they had landed, and dependence rested upon the strength of the head wind. But now a hook trailed by the landing aircraft was used to catch in wires stretched across the flight-deck and this brought them to a standstill in a remarkably short distance. Carriers remained extremely vulnerable to fire damage because of the widespread distribution of aircraft fuel lines, and this remained a carrier's chief weakness.

In 1939 we had no previous war experience in carrier operation and whatever functions had been visualised for them had scarcely yet been fully tried out. Most of their time had necessarily been spent in experimenting with a series of new aircraft, and in training aircrews. The number of aircraft suitable for landing on a carrier at this time was about one hundred, and all were light-type machines. The German invasion of Norway soon provided a very wide variety of targets and every possible complication of air navigation for our pilots and the aircrews performed magnificently, but the casualties were heavier than we could safely support.

Very shortly after war broke out *Ark Royal* was sent to the west coast of Scotland where on 14th September 1939, two U-boat torpedoes were fired at her which missed. Her destroyer screen sank the U-boat. On 17th September, as has already been recorded, *Courageous* was sunk by submarine torpedo, and we realised how vulnerable these valuable ships really were.

It was in October 1939 that direction finding equipment (known as RD/F) began to be fitted in ships. The instrument enabled the ship to measure with accuracy the range and direction from which a wireless transmission was coming and, as U-boats almost always notified one another of the position of any quarry they sighted, our RD/F ships could, if there were a couple of them, at once plot the position of the transmitting U-boat and move to attack it. Since U-boats could at best only hope to sight a ship at about twelve miles, a convoy escort had not far to steam before developing its attack. Hugh, from his experience of using this instrument during the Spanish Civil War, early realised its value in the protection of convoys. He discussed the use of RD/F with the Fleet wireless officer and then went to the C.-in-C. to propose its use in convoy protection. Admiral Forbes took this idea up at once and a few days later the carrier *Furious* with a strong screen of destroyers three of which were fitted (as was the carrier) with RD/F, sailed to the western approaches and quickly found U-boats who were making sighting reports. Aircraft fitted with depth charges and bombs were flown off in the direction of the transmission and attacked if they sighted a U-boat, and destroyers too were directed to the position, and, with the help of asdic sound equipment, they depth charged whatever contacts they made. Several submarines were forced to dive and abandon the attacks they were planning and one or two kills were claimed by our ships and aircraft. But the carrier was a too attractive bait, and on two occasions *Furious* dodged torpedoes by a hair's breadth. The C.-in-C. considered that the carrier was too valuable to be risked deliberately in such a way and she was withdrawn from this particular type of operation. However, as quickly as RD/F sets could be manufactured they were fitted in convoy escorts and eventually in most other surface craft, and RD/F became a principal instrument in the detection of U-boats. Later on some merchantmen were fitted to carry aircraft to be used as *Furious* had shown the way. Shore stations, expected to be far more accurate than the small instruments fitted in ships, were built in many parts of the world; and even an approximate bearing obtained from a shore station was of value in estimating the position of a transmitter.

The flag had now shifted to *Rodney* because *Nelson*'s steering gear had become defective. On 12th December 1939, Hugh landed after lunch to walk in the hills all frozen and brown that shut in Greenock from the south, putting up several coveys of grouse and thinking about Captain Harwood's brilliant action against the *Graf Spee*. The anchorage was easily visible — in fact had never been out of sight for more than a few minutes, when in the gathering gloom of the dying day *Rodney's* masthead suddenly displayed a string of red lights, the immediate recall signal. He belted down the steep heather slopes and through the narrow grimy town to Prince's Pier where a little flight of steps was reserved for the officers' boats. The coxswain of *Rodney's* boat said that they were raising steam and that was all he knew. A few minutes later on board he learned that the armed merchant cruiser *Rawalpindi* on the Northern Patrol had reported sighting two German warships south-east of Iceland. And that was the last we were to hear of her. Survivors later told of some of her guns frozen under thick ice and immovable, and hardly a shot fired before she was in flames and sinking.

While steaming down the Clyde at a speed which must have made the ferry steamers packed with homing workpeople curse our apparent carelssness, a signal came in from the cruiser *Newcastle* that she had sighted *Rawalpindi* burning fiercely and stopped, and that she was engaging an eight-inch cruiser at long range and that a second German warship in sight was much larger. Later reports showed that *Newcastle*, steaming at full speed, had lost contact when she turned away from this superior force·in a rain squall and in the event she never re-established contact.

The fleet went at high speed towards the reported position in the hope of intercepting what was evidently a battle-cruiser and an eight-inch cruiser. The sweep was a forlorn hope with only six hours of daylight. The normal stormy weather helped the two raiders to get clear away.

The great liner *Queen Elizabeth* had been launched by the Queen as war's shadow was shutting down on the country. The immense hull had been rising in a builder's yard for a couple of past years amongst a green and pleasant stretch of fields while the muddy Clyde swept past her stern, and we heard the queen's silvery voice over the air speaking words of hope and encouragement, while the drag chains skidded down the slipway and unleashed the ship into the river. As the Fleet flagship lay in the Clyde this war winter we saw the completed *Queen Elizabeth* come down from the builder's yard, grey and enormous, to take up a berth half a mile from us at the Tail o' the Bank. A few officers went onboard and walked about the empty areas of deck and looked inside the unfinished cabins — everything seemed to be there but the passengers. A directors' dinner with speeches was given the same night, and the Admiral attended. Then the next day she went down river to do speed trials and soon after disappeared to commence her troop-carrying career. Hugh was not alone in his feeling of pride as he watched all this. The speed of these "monsters", as they became known, was able to defy U-boat attack and contribute an important element to our eventual victory.

At the outbreak of war the Polish submarine *Orzel* was at Gdynia, and she put to sea on 1st September to patrol in the Gulf of Danzig where German aircraft bombed her and she was also harassed by their surface patrol craft, so that the narrow waters became dangerous and the captain decided to make for more open parts of the Baltic. On his way out of the Gulf he twice ran into mines and their mooring wires were heard scraping along the hull. Another submarine was in distress in the area and appealed for help — but nothing could be done in view of his own hard-pressed situation. Patrol was continued in the open water but the captain, who had been unwell before they left home, became worse. He insisted, though only with the aid of a rope's end to haul him up through the conning tower hatch, on keeping bridge watches. Eventually the first lieutenant took over command and decided that he must get medical aid for the captain. Accordingly he put into the neutral port of Talinn in Estonia on 15th September.

The little harbour basin has two entrances about a hundred feet wide; in the centre is a rocky shoal. Along the dockside walls were moored two German merchantmen, a small oiler, several destroyers, and a gunboat, and *Orzel* was placed between the warships with a hauling-off wire laid out to an anchor in the harbour. They were hospitably received and the captain was immediately taken ashore to hospital. *Orzel* wished to leave as soon as her captain was safely ashore, but the Estonian authorities made difficulties because the German cargo boat had already been granted clearance and they wished to give her a clear twenty-four hour start and so preserve their meticulous and nervous neutrality. The first lieutenant did not protest overmuch because it gave him time to ascertain his captain's condition and make all possible arrangements for his welfare, and also to despatch some messages to his own and his ship's company's families who had, of course, been left without notice when the ship put out to sea.

At the end of the twenty-four hours, *Orzel* was preparing for sea when civil and military officials came on board and announced that since *Orzel* had exceeded the time limit allowed in a neutral port by international law, she was under arrest. German power was indeed felt forcefully in this diplomatic trickery.

The breech-blocks of the guns were removed, charts, small arms and torpedoes had to be landed, though the Poles noted curiously that no parole was exacted. They at once began planning an escape and every man on board was quickly made aware of the acting captain's intention. One Estonian military guard was placed in the control room and another ashore at the end of the single gangway. The German oiler's crew watched these proceedings with glee and ribald and threatening shouts and fist shakings. The torpedoes, of course, took some considerable time to hoist out — the crew saw to it that everything went wrong as often as possible. The second lieutenant finally contrived to file through the hoisting wire which left five torpedoes still on board, and, as it was Sunday, the Poles pleaded weekend indulgence which the Estonians were ready enough to accord. Tomorrow the wire must be spliced and the remaining torpedoes hoisted out. As dark closed in, the mooring wires to the jetty were secretly half sawn through with a hacksaw; blades broke and finally the last one in the store was fitted, and it held. Friendly conversation and the beguilement of cigarettes distracted the rather bovine sentries' attention, but there were one or two tricky moments since all must be done on the upper deck in full view of the surrounding ships. The gyro compass must be started some hours before sailing, and its motor in the silent ship would immediately attract attention, so they decided to find their boat insupportably hot and started up the ventilation fans and then turned in.

In the middle of the night two reliable men went on deck for a smoke but they found the guard at the shore end of the gangway chatting inconveniently with a friend who did not clear off till two o'clock in the morning. Then the two Poles walked down the gangway, and offered the guard a cigarette. No; he wasn't a smoking man, but they held him in conversation and, by attracting his attention to some fitting in the submarine, they decoyed him to the head of the gangway, grabbed him and hustled him up the short distance to the conning tower hatch and popped him down inside, though not without some noise of scuffling and several lusty though half-muffled shouts for help. An officer slipped ashore and cut the telephone wires and others leading to a big arc light which illuminated the jetty. The last strands of the shore wires were cut with an axe, and then the hauling-off wire brought to the capstan. The noise of this winding in immediately made their intention clear, and there were shouts and the noise of running feet in the adjacent warships where the possibility of an escape must have been much in mind. The capstan clanked on as the bow swung out from the wall and the gangway collapsed and fell with a splash into the widening gap of water that soon separated *Orzel*'s bulging saddle tanks from the low stone dockside wall.

Destroyers' searchlights switched on and wavered about sometimes blinding the captain on his bridge, sometimes helping the men on the fo'c'sle to finally free the last wire. Then machine-gun and light automatic fire began to splatter about. It must have been inefficient, for in spite of the mounting fusillade not one casualty occurred, and only a few bullet marks showed on the hull when *Orzel* was examined carefully some weeks later. Perhaps some of the Estonian sailors were less neutral than their brow-beaten government.

Slowly *Orzel* moved ahead, and then the captain, blinded by a searchlight at the critical moment, ran onto the rocky shoal close to the entrance. Full speed astern cleared her, and they slid out through the narrow way leading to relative safety in the dark night, and to freeedom. They spoke, too, somewhat wistfully of a plan to torpedo the German oiler, but this had been abandoned out of consideration for Estonian neutrality, and in addition because of a desire to conserve their last five torpedoes for delivery to a more important target.

Within a very short time the shore defence searchlight and guns found them and they were forced to dive. They crept along blindly through surrounding islands until destroyers and light patrol craft caught up with them and then they dropped quietly to the bottom and lay listening all through that Monday to the tapping of propellors and innumerable jarring depth charges, fortunately few of which were at all close. By dark the uproar was dying away and at midnight *Orzel* rose for a cautious look round, and also to freshen the air, and decided to make for open water.

They hoped they were at the mouth of the Gulf of Finland. The Estonians had removed every chart in the ship, for unfortunately they were stowed complete and together in one place and it was impossible, surprised as they had been, to secrete anything at all. However, a navigational light list, which prints the geographical positions of various navigational marks, had been overlooked, and it contained a diagram on a tiny scale of most of the Baltic. From this the engineer officer plotted out onto a large sheet of a squared paper which, though lacking much of the meticulous calculations of Mercator, was nevertheless to serve *Orzel* as her only chart for some weeks to come through a hostile Baltic only partly governed by neutrality and blocked by shoals and minefields.

None of these impediments weighed against the acting captain's determination to search out the enemy shipping while his fuel and his five torpedoes should last. The immediate necessity was to find a quiet spot to recharge the depleted batteries and if possible to seize some charts. A course for the Oland Islands was guessed and in that region he cruised, without finding any ship from which he could procure a chart. It is a treacherous sea and the *Orzel* struck rocks on at least five occasions, denting her plating and holing some of her tanks, but always escaping major damage.

The Poles were genuinely distressed by radio broadcast news about their alleged cruelty in murdering their neutral Estonian guards, and these two worthies themselves maintained a ceaseless flow of complaint and lamentation so that their presence on board became burdensome to the entire ship's company. Moreover some water tanks had been holed and a shortage was making itself felt. They therefore made for Gotland and one fine evening they got out their collapsible berthon boat, furnished the two Estonians with money, a bottle of spirits, and some cigarettes, and pushed them off for the shore a thousand yards away, and then made a wireless signal, risking their chances of survival in so doing, to tell the Estonian government where their missing men were to be found and, as they put it, "to ease the minds of their families who must have been very anxious for their safety with all those German lies flying about on the air''.

For the next fortnight they watched German and other shipping while they moved carefully inside neutral territorial waters, and, still chartless, obeyed the international law to which their now defeated country was a party, and left this commerce unmolested. Often they were sighted and chased and several times suffered depth charge attack. Washing, except with salt water, had come to an end. There was insufficient water for cooking and little enough for drinking. The cook developed blood poisoning from a cut finger and grew worse as the days passed. On the 38th day they decided that they would make for England and accordingly, having identified Bornholm lighthouse, they followed the Swedish coast westward towards the Sound.

At the entrance, a German torpedo boat division was patrolling. As they were in only seven fathoms of water they decided that an attack was too risky. They lay at the bottom listening to the propellors of the enemy all day, and then at dusk rose to the surface with conning tower awash and made it off to the north. They grounded twice. While stuck on a sandbank on the second occasion a sweeping searchlight from a vessel thought to be a destroyer passed to and fro ahead of them but always missed them. They guessed that they were out of the proper channel and that for this reason their position was not being searched. Then they blew all ballast tanks and floated off the sandbank.

Making their way back, as they hoped, into the main channel they found the varying densities of fresh and salt water, plus the current which in places runs strongly, rendered navigation most difficult — at times the *Orzel* was not properly under control, for she was running on only one motor to reduce noise. To regain control at one point they had to go at full speed ahead on the diesel motors. The noise raised an alarm and so they had to dive and lie silent on the bottom. For two hours the echoes of the hunt up above rattled to and fro. At last the sound of searchers died away and they rose to the surface again and pushed on till dawn when once more they took to the bottom for safety and sleep.

It was an anxious day for the captain because water was now very short indeed and the cook was delirious. He decided at all costs he must push on. In the night they encountered two destroyers at a point where the channel is only a quarter of a mile wide and a lightship marks one side. It was a critical moment.

They chose the shallow side of the lightship and submerged all but the last couple of feet of the conning tower and went ahead at half speed. Perhaps the lightship look-out's attention was distracted by the two German destroyers. Signalling projectors were flashing to and fro and at any moment they might be illuminated. Just as they slipped past the lightship a small beamed light swung round and wavered uncertainly about them and then died out in a diminishing orange coloured glow — its carbon burner had failed. There was some shouting as they increased speed, but they were safely through the narrowest part of the Belts and away.

Up the Kattegatt they sped and on into the Skagerrak, submerging by day and going near top speed by night. Unidentified shipping was encountered, but their look-out always spotted the danger first and each time they dived without apparent detection. As they got out into the North Sea, aircraft made dives at them, and they had no visual recognition signals. They made wireless signals to England although knowing that their apparatus was damaged and that they might not be heard. But they were heard, and met by an escort and arrived at Scapa Flow late one afternoon. Hugh went on board at once and got this whole story and some other useful information from the captain.

His first remark when they sat down together in his little wardroom was: "Can you please take my cook to a doctor; he is poisoned in his hand. He is very sick." Then: they must have water for drinking. They could not fire their guns because the Estonians took away the breech-blocks, but they still had five torpedoes. They could go to sea as soon as the water was on board since they still had plenty of fuel, and "Could we please have some fresh food?"

Neither officers nor crew appeared unduly fatigued by their cruise. They were hollow-eyed and hollow-cheeked from lack of water, but had had sufficient food. All were very oily and longing for a shave and a bath. Inside the boat there was much superficial dirt and some sea water which had leaked in. The bow had a considerable dent on the starboard side caused by the nearest of all the three hundred depth charges that they had counted exploding about them and there were several bullet marks all over the upper works. The port anchor had been slipped at Talinn, and Hugh was proudly shown the axe by the petty officer who had cut the after wires that night; the inboard ends of the wires were still wound round the bitts. The Polish ensign at the stern floated spotless and proud. Surely the nation which can produce men of such quality as this will never die.

The C.-in-C. invited the captain of *Orzel* to lunch and sent his barge to fetch him the next day, and afterwards went up on the quarterdeck to say goodbye. Turning to Hugh he remarked:

"I've never heard the equal of his story. I doubt if it will ever be matched! You make sure that whatever they want is supplied."

They did not ask for publicity, though they received a modicum. The details here recorded were written down by Hugh in the *Orzel*'s wardroom. He could hardly believe his eyes when they showed him the chart constructed by the engineer officer. The next we heard of *Orzel* was on 8th April 1940 when, now back at sea after major refit, she torpedoed a German merchantman off the Norwegian coast.

A glance at any North Atlantic map calls to mind that the world's most busy trade route is bounded to the north by Greenland, Iceland and the Faroe Islands, all Danish territories at the outbreak of war; and, too, Spitzbergen, a Norwegian possession, had to be considered as soon as Russia became a belligerent. To the west one sees Martinique in the West Indies and St. Pierre & Miquelon at the entrance to the Gulf of St. Lawrence, and because of the collapse of France and the subsequent co-operation of the Vichy government with Germany, all these obscure and distant outposts became unexpectedly points of concern. A French cruiser had escaped to Martinique with the whole gold bullion reserve of France, where it remained as a source of influence on American financial dealings with the Allies, and as none of them trusted one another to be custodians of so great a treasure, Martinique remained wholly unmolested throughout the years of warfare. On May 29th 1940, a Dutch warship intercepted a Vichy merchantman bound for Martinique and found 300 Germans on board presumably intent on seizing that island. On December 24th 1941, Admiral Muselier, head of the Free French Naval Forces (which were very small indeed) landed in Miquelon and presented the people with a plea to declare adherence to the Free French, and the next day they did so with an overwhelming majority of votes. The Germans would have liked, if they could have managed it, to make use of both these potential supporting bases for their ocean raiders and U-boats.

The vast icefield which is Greenland had two or three very sparsely inhabited little settlements on its southern shores where fishing trawlers could call for supplies or repairs, but the rest of the sea coast was choked with ice almost all the year round. Its geographical position now made it a place of interest as early as June 1940, when the British became anxious about the German supply of cryolite, a rare element used in the manufacture of aluminium, the interruption of which would have been serious. In August 1940 a small allied Norwegian vessel, *F. Nansen*, visited Myggbuckta in Greenland where they were surprised to find newly landed stores. The only person at the wireless station was a pro-Nazi Norwegian and so they sent in an armed party to take charge there. The area around was found to be about 50 square miles of flat land naturally suitable for an aerodrome, and it was ice-free from mid-July to early September. The *F. Nansen* went off southwards to capture the enemy Norwegian sealer *Veleskari* which had lately landed the stores at Myggbuckta (undoubtedly sent by the Germans).

F. Nansen went north again to Eskimones to search for a consort sealer, *Ringsal*, which had originally sailed in company with her. While she was away another sealer arrived at Myggbuckta with more stores, and this ship was manned by loyal Norwegians who, after they had landed their cargo, waited for *F. Nansen*'s return. On 25th August a long-range Fokke-Wulf 200 appeared and attacked the W/T station and put it out of action. A few days later the *F. Nansen* in company with the two sealers sailed for Reykjavik in Iceland, taking with them the disloyal W/T operator. No doubt our loyal Norwegian friends had got wind of a German project to establish some sort of base at Myggbuckta and it would have been useful to them if they had succeeded. These minute settlements are desolate almost beyond belief. Sedges, moss, some prostrate shrubs are the only sparse vegetation that exists amongst the rocks.

Later the USA signed an agreement with a pro-ally Danish minister "to help Greenland to maintain its present status until the present dangers to the peace and security of the American continent have passed", and subsequently the Americans established an air base in the territory with modern communications. Also a British D/F station was set up which supplied valuable bearings for the rest of the war. Some aircraft and convoy escorts fuelled occasionally at Julianehab in Greenland.

Spitzbergen also came into our orbit at about this time and a cruiser was sent to reconnoitre. They found and rescued a small party of Norwegian coal-miners who had set fire to the large coal mine at the southern end of the island in order to deny its use to the Germans. The fire was still burning four years later. Unfortunately the place was too close to German air bases in Norway to be used by us.

By the end of 1939 we had developed a realistic perception of the influence which air power was exerting over the sea. It had become a governing factor in Home Fleet operations. Attacks by marauding Heinkels and Junkers upon East Coast convoys had now become a regular feature at dawn and dusk; torpedoes, bombs or mines took a toll of almost every convoy and the small ports became congested with damaged shipping. The small numbers of our aircraft available to go out to cover the convoys were sometimes unable to find the adversary or might arrive too late or too early and the results were reflected in the East Coast shipping casualty list. Convoy escorts put up a plea that they should be allowed to direct the aircraft since they usually knew more about the exact position of their assailants than anyone else. This request was duly forwarded to the Air Ministry but the reply was that the Air Force could not surrender its right to direct its own forces. This brick wall of misunderstanding persisted for some months. Eventually the Navy discovered that in Air Force parlance the word "direct" means "to exercise the function of command". The Navy had used the word to mean "point out a target". The devoted RAF officers in operations rooms struggled with this difficulty for some time, but they were not happy people. However, the personnel of both services who were actively engaged in East Coast operations soon found a way round the official block. The captains of the ship escorts began inviting the young pilots and observers for weekend convoy trips along the East Coast and the airmen were as keen as mustard to see the game from the other side. Within a few weeks the men on the job had fixed up between themselves exactly how they would tackle the next Heinkel that glided in at sundown. Some of their schemes were of course failures, and ended in our ships shooting up our own aircraft, but others were successful, and it was not too long before (quite unofficially, but nonetheless efficiently) members of the two services doing the actual fighting had evolved a workable co-operation.

During the critical first three days of our invasion of Norway, the fleet obtained the use of two Sunderland flying boats. Their scouting found the German battle-cruisers *Scharnhorst* and *Gneisenau*, but ran out of fuel at the critical moment and no relief patrol was available.

On 12th January 1940, the lightship at Smith's Knoll (a sandbank off the East Anglian coast) was machine-gunned from the air. This felt like the torpedoing of the *Athenia*. These lightship men pursued the most hard and dreary of callings and every ship of every nation owed them gratitude. A flame of indignation swept over the country. This was to be followed by air attacks on fishing craft off the East Coast and in the Orkney — Shetland region. One trawler near Fair Isle was approached by a Heinkel towing a three-hundred-foot length of wire ending in a large canister of explosive which was apparently designed to entangle itself in masts or superstructure. Fortunately the little craft's machine-gun spat with such effect that the German pilot was put off his aim and his fantastic missile struck the water a hundred yards ahead and exploded harmlessly. But there were other grim tales of little dories machine-gunned while rescuing crews from foundering fishing boats, and the civilian casualties mounted. The large ships of the fleet stripped themselves of their light automatic weapons and sent them to the small craft plying along the South and East coasts. Between 29th and 31st January, 1940, as a result of sixty-eight air attacks six ships were sunk, five damaged and driven up on the beaches, twelve others damaged and one escort minesweeper damaged and subsequently lost in a gale while in tow.

Christmas had seen the onset of a cold spell which persisted for the next two months. The Belts leading into the Baltic were frozen and Danes went visiting their Swedish friends on skates. The Kattegatt was partly frozen and partly covered with ice-floes and one of our submarines had a very anxious time trying to get to the surface for air. Another had periscopes put out of action and another found his hatches frozen open so that quick diving would have been impossible. The Heligoland Bight was almost solid as far out as the island itself, and one evening a reconnaissance aircraft reported a pocket battleship, three cruisers and seven other lesser craft all jammed in a line about seven miles to the eastward of Heligoland. This opportunity could not be immediately seized, and a bomber force next day found the German squadron had escaped. From Iceland came reports of fiords blocked with heavy ice and the Denmark Strait reduced to a thirty-mile gap.

It was while patrolling north of Iceland that the 8-inch cruiser *Berwick* gave us a nasty turn one day by sending an emergency signal that she had sighted a convoy of more than a hundred ships to the westward. Was it, we wondered, an invasion of Iceland, or an expedition to establish a base on the Greenland coast? Later she reported that reflections from Greenland ice cliffs had deceived her. The echo of those fears persisted for three years, and we repeatedly discussed the practicability of such an enemy undertaking. Consultation with the Admiralty Pilot, however, revealed that the ice edge had sometimes been mistaken for shipping, due to the shadows cast by indentations in the face which might be as much as a hundred feet high. Hugh saw that same effect of a group of shipping another winter when the Fleet flagship closed the edge of these floes to within a couple of miles. There were great humped piles of creamy white ice with gleams of green and snow and again a wall reared up exactly like the chalk cliffs of Dover. Overhead the sky was a pale greenish blue, shading down to a faintly yellow tinge at the horizon.

U-boats also were now operating within sight of our coasts. In Kirkwall Bay the Danish cargo ship *Ingeborg* was torpedoed and broke in two. At first the presence of a submarine in what we had supposed was an effectively patrolled area was not credited, but divers found large unmistakable pieces of a German torpedo inside the wrecked hull. The destroyer *Exmouth* disappeared off the Moray Firth one dark windy night while on escort duty. There was not one survivor.

The presence of neutral shipping round our coasts gave rise to considerable misgivings as it afforded the enemy a means of spying on our convoy routes, swept channels and patrol boats. In one or two ports seamen from neutral ships were heard expressing very anti-British sentiments over dockside bars. From Iceland came a steady stream of trawlers laden with fish which fetched enormous prices. Few cleared less than four thousand pounds on a round trip and one of them made fourteen thousand. Coal, purchased in England at a few shillings a ton, filled their holds for the return journey and fetched 120 shillings in Reykjavik. At a somewhat later stage when export of goods was more strictly controlled, expensive wireless sets, cosmetics and silk stockings found passage to Iceland on the return voyage where cod and herring had lately crammed the holds. The existence of a Nazi Party in Iceland and reports of German agents in the Faeroes made these neutral fishing craft an embarrassment in the immediate vicinity of Scapa Flow. Many were stopped and examined, but there was no case in which suspicion of unfriendly activity arose; they proved themselves honest fisherfolk.

Germany's armament industry depended to an important extent upon the importation of some seven million tons of Swedish iron ore, mostly through the port of Lalea. By Christmas all Baltic ports were freezing up and in early January the last ship sails out with the aid of ice-breakers, but the southern Swedish ports, which are not always frozen quite solid, provide a strangled outlet until the thaw comes in March. To maintain the continuous flow of this important traffic, the Norwegian port of Narvik had been developed and connected with neighbouring iron ore mines by a narrow gauge electric railway across the Norwegian border to Sweden. The winter was, therefore, bound to see an increase of German shipping traffic along the Norwegian coast and it was a continuing preoccupation of the Home Fleet until the end of the war to frustrate that trade. In this first winter the ore ships sought shelter of the passage (known as the Indreled) inside the islands which fringe the coast for all but short stretches and even there a safe passage within the three-mile territorial limit usually exists, so that without violating Norwegian neutrality we were in effect powerless. Small sweeping forces were sent along the coast but found little to pick up.

It was in February that an aerial reconnaissance confirmed the suspected presence of the tanker *Altmark* in the Indreled. This vessel had acted as auxiliary to the *Admiral Scheer* in the South Atlantic. British prisoners of the *Scheer* landed at Montevideo had recounted how the *Altmark* had supplied fuel and stores at sea to the *Scheer* and other raiders, and that she also carried replenishment stocks of ammunition and torpedoes and that a part of her officers and crew were German naval men who wore the proper uniform of their service and who were readily distinguishable by their use of the naval salute as opposed to the merchant seamen who used the Nazi upraised arm and "Heil Hitler" form of greeting. Moreover *Altmark* now carried on board about three hundred British and neutral seamen, survivors of ships sunk by various raiders. The Admiralty regarded this ship as a warship and accordingly rejected her claim to sanctuary in neutral

Norwegian waters for more than twenty-four hours, which was the international limit for a warship.

The small cruiser *Arethusa* with the destroyers *Ivanhoe* and *Intrepid* proceeded to the neighbourhood of Haugesund where it was hoped to catch the *Altmark* in an area where her size would force her for a mile or so beyond the three-mile limit.

No doubt the presence of the British squadron was reported to the local German naval authority at Bergen, where the *Altmark* had to stop on the 15th February to pass through a control post, and from then onwards she was furnished with a Norwegian torpedo-boat and aircraft escort. While she was stopped two Norwegian gunboats and two Norwegian destroyers circled about her, one approaching within a few yards. The prisoners, watching through a small hole in the hatchway, saw three uniformed Norwegian officers come on board. This was the signal for a sustained outburst of shouting and banging and whistling of the SOS, but although they were bursting their lungs, neither the boarding officers nor the torpedo-boat which was fifteen yards off showed any sign of hearing this unusual and surely suspicious uproar. The prisoners belted the hatchway until it almost burst. One of them climbed up to an overhead ventilator and yelled and whistled SOS through it, but still no reaction could be seen — except, of course, on the part of the German crew. These, unaffected by deafness, stuffed up the ventilator with rope and canvas and then started up the capstan engine and made it rattle its loudest; finally a hose was played on the bursting hatchway door — yet neutrality noticed nothing untoward, and *Altmark* was allowed to proceed southwards on her way.

Early next day *Arethusa*'s little force made contact with the German SS *Baldur* which scuttled off Stavanger, and then, later, sighted their real enemy, the *Altmark*. The destroyers prepared to board, but *Altmark* did not stop when ordered by international signals, although she was for a short space outside the three-mile limit. The destroyer *Ivanhoe* went inshore to cut her off and *Intrepid* fired a warning shot across her bow. At this the Norwegian torpedo-boat lowered a boat and sent a protesting officer to our force. While argument was proceeding, *Altmark* persistently moved ahead and toward the coastline. *Intrepid* lowered her boarding whaler directly ahead of *Altmark* and the torpedo-boat quickly steamed between the whaler and the big tanker, and then headed off each destroyer in turn as it attempted to close *Altmark*. Meantime, of course, a stream of polite protesting signals poured forth from the small Norwegian warships, and so tender were the British for the sanctity of the last letter of international sea law that the *Altmark* was enabled to slip away into Jossing Fiord.

Just as this was happening a reinforcement arrived on the scene in the shape of Captain Vian in *Cossack*, with the Tribal Flotilla of destroyers, the most powerful ships of their type afloat, and calculated, we hoped, to shake the tough neutral confidence of the diminutive Norwegian warships. Despite still more international conferring, this time on board *Cossack*, the Norwegians maintained their determination to fire on whoever molested *Altmark* while she remained within Norwegian waters, and night fell with still no answer to the riddle. In reply to a request for the necessary authority the Admiralty instructed Captain Vian to go into the fiord and get the *Altmark* prisoners.

The little Norwegian warship had his searchlights sweeping the narrow entrance and illuminating our darkened ships from time to time, but he did not observe that *Cossack*, assisted by the others, was gradually nudging him out of the narrow passage. It was so gently and so skilfully accomplished that in the dark he failed to appreciate what was happening. Slowly *Cossack* increased revolutions, gained headway, swung round in the darkness to an easterly course, and then with a sudden burst of speed shot into the fiord and out of sight, an uncertain searchlight flickering across her stern and coming to rest on the wrong destroyer as *Cossack* disappeared from the view of our flotilla.

The famous dash alongside through broken ice-floes, the leap of the first boarders securing the mooring lines under a hail of shot, the rush of the armed party and overpowering of the German crew hidden about the deck were audible minute by minute to the three hundred anxious prisoners battened down in the hold. And then the muffled shout came up: "The Navy's here!" They flung themselves at the hatchway door and very quickly the securing irons were burst by the naval party on deck and the prisoners freed. They climbed up the ladder from the hold in perfectly disciplined order.

Meantime *Altmark*'s manoeuvres into the head of the fiord in an effort to thwart *Cossack* had led her into trouble. The rudder pin had fractured as she struck the rocky shore and the rudder broke off and a propellor was also severely damaged. Observers on the *Cossack*'s bridge watched the boarding party as they jumped onto the *Altmark*'s deck and saw most of the brief struggle in the glare of their own searchlights. Some of the Germans fled over the *Altmark*'s side and, leaping from one ice-floe to the next, made a dash for the shore pursued by a few desultory bullets. A few were wounded or killed and their dark forms could be seen stretched out against the white surface of the ice. Two men fell into the water and their splashing about and cries for help so moved one of *Cossack*'s company that he climbed down onto the ice and with the aid of a rope's end rescued the drowning Germans whose own companions gave no heed to their shipmate's appeals.

As soon as she had all the prisoners onboard *Cossack* withdrew. *Altmark*'s manoeuvres had placed *Cossack* in a precarious position and there was not a moment's delay to be risked, for she was very close to dangerous rocks and found herself in no position to torpedo *Altmark*. Such action might have infringed the neutrality of Norway, and in any case Captain Vian was anxious about his flotilla which had been lying outside for many hours affording an excellent target to any U-boat that might have come within striking distance.

When the liberated seamen and the German prisoners were later landed in the Firth of Forth, it was found that the latter were in a very dirty condition, several suffering from contagious and other diseases which indicated a lack of proper medical care and effective supervision by *Altmark*'s officers.

Russian reactions to the progress of the war were a matter for much speculation in the early days. They had swiftly seized half of Poland as soon as Hitler's intentions towards that country were declared by his invasion of Polish territory, and then a German trade treaty was signed, but curiously enough very little trade ensued. Stalin attacked Finland and the Russian armies had suffered a notable defeat there, which in turn resulted in a Russian purge.

But by the first days of 1940, it had become evident that Finland was collapsing. The Norse powers would not, and the British could not bring effective aid, and the Finns capitulated on 13th March to Russian peace terms, which seemed stiff but not too harsh.

One evening at about this time Hugh was sitting in the staff office in the stern of *Rodney* at sunset when quite suddenly he was bounced upwards from his chair. Several electric light bulbs burst and a cascade of books and files from the surrounding shelves descended. For an instant it seemed like an internal explosion, but he felt that it had not been violent enough for that. He hurried on deck and found someone who had seen a Junkers 88 dive out of a cloud to about fifteen hundred feet, release two large bombs and climb across the ship before any shot could be fired. From this it was apparent that our air raid warning system was inadequate and thereafter a proportion of the close range armament was kept at immediate notice for action at Scapa, but it never had to be used there. Fifty and one hundred yards astern he saw two boiling greenish pools in the clear water where the bombs had fallen. From the nearer one bubbled up a succession of gobbets of oil which burst on the surface into an iridescent ever-widening circle. This manifestation puzzled us all for a while until the C.-in-C., who had been commander in the *Iron Duke* in Lord Jellicoe's day, recollected that one stormy night an oil barge had drifted across the ship's bows and foundered. A diver subsequently confirmed that it was indeed this oil barge lying forgotten for twenty-three years which had been rediscovered by the Luftwaffe.

On 5th April 1940, the Allies presented a firm notice to Norway complaining of the unusual advantages which accrued to the Germans through the use of the Indreled inshore sea passage for their importation of contraband iron ore from Narvik. There was a veiled threat of countermeasures which perhaps provided Hitler with the final push that precipitated him upon the invasion of Norway.

When that invasion began in early April we were slow to appreciate its significance. Hugh later on discussed this brief phase of the war with acute neutral observers who were in Berlin at that time and they, too, had failed to discern the German intention, although there had been rumours of troop movements towards the Western Baltic and the Danish frontier. We had heard such rumours before and a report of the assembly of transport vessels was a recurring theme of neutral seamen. On 7th April, a movement of U-boats and surface warships northwards out of the entrance to the Baltic was observed. Vice-Admiral Horton (now in command of all British submarines) had disposed his submarines about the entrance to the Kattegatt and by the 8th more and more definite proof of a major move of naval forces northwards was forthcoming.

On the night of 7th — 8th April, our minelayer squadron laid minefields at two points within Norwegian territorial waters chosen to force shipping from the Indreled out beyond territorial waters. A third minefield had been planned but the eight-knot converted merchantman which was to accomplish this task was delayed by bad weather, so that she could not reach her assigned position in the dark, and accordingly stood off the coast ready to lay on the morrow. The next few days of her career were hectic. There they sat on a thousand tons of explosive, too slow to escape pursuit, backing and filling amongst a milling throng of enemy aircraft and warships of all classes. It was due to a considerable degree of foresight favoured by a measure of good luck, that the C.-in-C. succeeded in rerouting this very vulnerable ship clear of all trouble. She probably only guessed at the narrow escapes which she had on several occasions and will never know what anxieties she added to an already critical situation. She returned home in the end intact.

The remaining minelayers punctually reported completion of their tasks and at a quarter to six in the morning of 8th April the British diplomatic representatives at Oslo presented a note to the Norwegian government informing them of what had been done. At the same time notification of the dangerous areas was broadcast to neutral, and inevitably of course to German shipping.

The Home Fleet had put to sea to cover the withdrawal of the minelayers, and we were off the north-east corner of the Shetlands when the report of completion of the minelaying task came through. Hugh well remembers the tense couple of hours that passed as our minelayers withdrew, and then the signal from the Admiralty warning neutral shipping was published. We all felt keyed up expectantly as a grey cloudy dawn broke over a troubled sea.

Then a few days later a military expedition sailed at the invitation of a divided Norway to assist in her defence against Germany, and a naval operational base was set up at Harstad in northern Norway under the command of Admiral of the Fleet Lord Cork and Orrery. This early part of 8th April was to be the last comparatively quiet moment that Hugh was to enjoy for many weeks to come, and it ushered in such a pressure of events as none of us had ever before experienced. The admiral had trained his fleet, as far as resources permitted, to meet what they must now face and the test was upon us.

The previous afternoon, when we were about thirty miles to the north-eastward of the Orkneys, one of the screening destroyers,

Glowworm, reported "man overboard". She immediately turned to search for her man, but owing to the high speed at which the fleet was moving, was quickly lost to view, and it seemed probable that, with the headwind prevailing, she would not be able to catch up before dark. The C.-in-C. accordingly made a signal to her that if she was not able to regain station before dark she was to make for a daylight rendezvous in a position which he gave her. This kind of thing happened occasionally in northern waters. It was always dangerous to permit a night meeting where indentification procedure might not work smoothly and where a mass of darkened ships, possibly manoeuvring, would present the chance of a collision. Destroyers did, in spite of all precautions, lose men overboard from time to time, or occasionally they would be delayed by some temporary mechanical breakdown, though such misfortunes decreased in frequency as the war went on and efficiency and experience increased.

One of the saddest wastages at sea is the loss of men washed over the side, for there is always the feeling that it might have been prevented.

At one minute before eight *Glowworm*, whose captain was an old friend of Hugh's, reported by emergency procedure the sighting of four German destroyers. One or two more reports came in, over the next fifty-six minutes, and then silence. Each German destroyer had 5-inch guns. *Glowworm* had four 4-inch. There was never a possibility of survival, for she was more than a hundred miles from the nearest chance of help. We could do nothing for her. Her loss was a sad and bitter one to us, arising as it had from her devotion to a shipmate, and it cast a gloom over us. A carley float with a handful of survivors was picked up the next day.

At three p.m. a battle-cruiser, two Koln Class cruisers and five destroyers were reported on a northerly course in the Kattegat — a puzzling piece of information; for we could not believe·that small divided forces would seek action with us. Their role could only be to attack our light forces and Hugh's feeling was that this sortie indicated that our main fleet had not yet been discovered. The idea of a major German invasion of Norway had not yet lodged firmly in our minds. The risks seemed enormous to their seaborne forces and Germany's air power would be operating in a mountainous country with very few airfields.

The only obvious advantage to be reaped from that lean country was a winter security for the iron ore trade when Swedish ports were closed by ice.

Acting on our submarine reports of shipping movement in the Skagerrak a division of destroyers had been detached in that direction and in the latter part of this afternoon came action reports from this force. They had run into a convoy and sank four merchant ships. This was something substantial on the credit side, but we hardly felt its impact, for events were beginning to crowd in upon us with the thickening effect of a storm.

At 5.50 p.m. a force of ten U-boats was reported steering north through the Great Belt, a concentration such as had never before been reported. A few minutes later a surface force, whose composition was not specified, was reported passing the Skaw westwards, and at 6.15 p.m. the heavy cruiser *Blucher*, two other cruisers, and one destroyer were reported north of the Skaw, steering north by east which was the direction of the Oslo Fiord. We did not know whether these two latter reports, so close together in time, referred to the *Blucher*'s squadron only, or to another separate one. The courses were divergent, but zigzagging might account for that difference. This squadron pointing for Oslo raised in our minds the strong suspicion that some action against Norwegian neutrality was contemplated. Hugh said at a staff conference that he thought that Norway would grant any and all demands and would never fight. The rather nervous and colourless socialist ministers then in office seemed to him to be a portent of capitulation, and in particular the loyalty of Colonel Quisling (one of the Norwegian ministers) was highly questionable, and there was other evidence of widespread Nazi activity all over the country.

As dusk closed in at about 6.50 p.m. the fleet was disposed for night emergency with the heavy 8-inch cruisers to the north-westward and the 6-inch cruisers to the eastward of the battle fleet. The *Warspite* and *Renown* had already been sent off to the north at high speed to block the entrance to the Vest Fiord leading to the ore-loading port of Narvik. The C.-in-C. felt that that would be a magnet which might be expected to draw German naval forces.

Between 8 p.m. and 10 p.m. Scapa anchorage was raided by a fairly large but scattered number of German planes. Some bombs fell on shore and also upon Wick aerodrome, about twenty miles away on the southern side of the Pentland Firth. One of the two enemy aircraft known to have been destroyed fell on the runway there. The night was becoming rough and any injured planes would have a hard struggle to get home.

During the night our submarines in the Skagerrak had a great time, contact after contact was made and a considerable execution recorded. *Trident* intercepted the tanker *Posidonia* which was scuttled. The *Rio de Janeiro* was sunk off Kristiansand South by the Polish submarine *Orzel*. The *Kreta* sank off Oslo Fiord and an unidentified vessel off Lillesand. Just after 11 p.m., seven German ships were reported steering westwards, twelve miles off the south-west coast of Norway. By now we had no doubt that something big was afoot, but until more precise information of the German heavier ships was available the battle fleet was very well situated where it was.

There was no question of rushing in at night — the advantages of our superior gun-fire would all be placed at the mercy of chance. Both star-shell and searchlight control were less than reliable, and a big ship was likely to be hit by submarine or destroyer torpedoes before it even sighted its smaller enemy. Our night exercises, though much practised by all ships, seemed chiefly to teach us that blind-man's buff in the dark was a game of chance with a bias against the battleship because its great mass made it more visible than anything else on the ocean.

It will be remembered that in the Mediterranean, Admiral Cunningham did not hesitate to hunt the Italians by night, but there the conditions were different in that visibility is often very good. Furthermore in the Mediterranean, Italians were the enemy and neither their fighting efficiency nor their morale compared favourably with the Germans.

At 3.10 a.m. on 9th April, a report came from Oslo that one large warship, three cruisers and some U-boats were entering Oslo Fiord, and a little later that landings were being made at Oslo, and then also that Denmark was being invaded.

Later on a Norwegian naval commander who was in charge that night at the Naval Headquarters at Horten, on Oslo Fiord, told Hugh of his experiences during this hectic period. The Norwegians had for the past couple of days been expecting a German invasion and there was feverish activity at Horten naval dockyard getting warships filled up with their war crews, stores and fuel, and moving them to their stations. A defensive mining plan was put into operation and fields were layed in the Oslo Fiord, at Bergen and one or two other places. Because of the reports of German

Y

warship movements which had been pouring in during 8th of April, the Horten fortress commander had decided to sleep in his office, close to his telephone and communications control. He was anxious about the cable wires, for during the last twenty-four hours suspicious breakdowns had occurred in different parts of the country including communication with higher command in Oslo. They were too numerous and too frequently on key lines to be accidental. He had a sickening apprehension that the enemy was already within the gate, that people inside the naval organisation must be implicated, that not all officers could be trusted. He had with him a little band of messengers and his own office staff who he knew were not traitors and that was all that he could rely on. He could not sleep for these thoughts racing through his mind, and still dressed he lay down on a sofa.

During the day orders had been issued that navigation mark buoys must be removed or sunk in Oslo Fiord, but just before dark he discovered that certain important marks had not yet been removed and some lighthouses on shore which should have been extinguished were seen to be flashing after dark. He sent off patrol craft to enforce the orders but reports were not yet to hand that all the lights were in fact extinguished, and while going the rounds at midnight he saw one particularly important set of navigation lights still burning. He sent off a steamboat to attend to this but, in spite of the fact that they were only a mile or two distant, the lights did not go out. He now had no other reliable person remaining whom he could send, and feeling that something sinister was afoot he finally communicated with the police, who promised to investigate at once.

He had been lying down for an hour when the telephone bell rang. The fortress commander on the eastern side reported a number of darkened warships steaming up the fiord. They did not answer the challenge, and they refused to stop when signalled. They were only two hundred yards off the shore while his men were hailing the leading ship, a very large one with turrets trained on the shore. German voices shouted back something unintelligible which ended with "Heil Hitler!"

In another minute an immense explosion rent the night as the large ship (later identified as the cruiser *Blucher*) passed into the minefield. Within half a minute came two more detonations and, as the fortress searchlights switched on to her, she rolled over and sank. In the meantime bedlam had broken loose but the commander's telephone was already dead. It told him nothing more.

In the darkness some German warships opened fire and only a few of the fortress guns answered them. Some hundreds of *Blucher*'s crew swam ashore. Meantime German soldiers were swarming ashore from the remaining ships and when daylight came the defences were overwhelmed and German troops were moving into Oslo city.

The German invasion of Norway came as a shock to her people who were, for a short time, unable to believe their eyes. A peaceful country that had never known warfare in modern times, Norway possessed a very small army trained for little beyond garrison and ceremonial duties, and a fleet of lightly armed mostly aged coastal craft, none of which was designed to go out into the open seas, and no effective air force existed. The country traded to all parts of the world, but her main traffic was through the Indreled, that inshore sea lane of pilotage waters winding along the whole coast inside innumerable islands. The Norwegian public did not yet know that the country had been infiltrated by pro-German agents, and that even in the cabinet there were Nazi sympathisers. Germans were everywhere, tourists in summer, commercial representatives, contractors, owners of mines, timber resources and other business enterprises. So much was this the case that during the last week or two of peace about 8,000 German troops, some in disguise, mostly concealed in the holds of merchantmen, or hidden in mines or factories during dark hours, were in fact now ready to seize control points on the declaration of war. The German plans were fully detailed, well thought out, unexpected and completely successful. The strong points had already fallen before any German military attack had occurred. The private citizens were utterly bewildered. Colonel Quisling and others on radio publicly urged the nation to support the Nazis.

As the Norwegian people came slowly out of their state of shock they began to plot the sabotage of German enterprises and a steady trickle of fishing boats slipped away to Britain bringing information and suggestions for points of attack. In quiet country places men were forming themselves into bands of saboteurs who were determined and skilful.

At this point Britain decided to support every possible indigenous effort so that a series of small destructive raids and attacks were planned wherever opportunities presented themselves and the Fleet Air Arm and our small ships principally were directly involved, with our main fleet taking a covering position to seaward ready to counter any major German naval sortie.

Early in March 1941, we mounted a raid on the Lofoten Islands off the Norwegian coast, the objective being to destroy a fish-oil storage depot, and also to encourage the local Norwegians. A fishing boat had reached Britain and a young Norwegian of the resistance movement was able to give very complete details of the area. The attack was made on a moonless night and a patrolling German trawler was sunk by gun-fire. A landing force of 500 troops, 52 Royal Engineers, 52 Norwegian troops, a naval demolition party about 20 strong from the fleet, and several Norwegian guides who had escaped to England were all embarked into fast cross-channel passenger steamers, escorted by five destroyers, the leader, *Somali*, carrying the headquarters staff party. The landing, timed for 6.45 a.m., was brightly illuminated by an unforeseen display of Northern Lights, but there was no opposition; indeed the arrival was enthusiastically welcomed by the local inhabitants, especially when food, cigarettes and clothing were distributed. A 10,000 ton fish refrigerator ship and five other merchantmen and two trawlers were sunk, and the storage depot on shore containing 800,000 gallons of fish oil was destroyed. A small military control post nearby was taken and destroyed and its garrison of twenty-five captured. The invaders re-embarked at 1.00 p.m. and brought back to Britain 188 escaping civilians, twelve quisling collaborators, and 314 Norwegian volunteers, including eight women. As they departed one German patrol aircraft was seen and fired at.

On 30th July 1941, aircraft from the carrier *Victorious* attacked shipping at Kirkenes and the cruiser *Bremse* was hit, and also four merchantmen. An attack by aircraft from *Furious* raided shipping at Petsamo, firing torpedoes at jetties, setting fire to warehouses and hitting an oiler.

Some echo of the desperate resistance of small groups of Norwegians reached us on board *Rodney* in which the C.-in-C. flew his flag at this time, and it was not long before we had the cheering reassurance that all the Norwegians who could do so were going to fight and that a passive resistance was rapidly building up all over the country. They earned respect and indeed popularity within the hour. Many fleetmen had visited their ports in past times and been charmed by their hospitality and they had seemed the most akin to us of all the European peoples. Denmark, which seemed very Germanic, we regarded on a different footing. Their subsequent history of indomitable individual resistance has won back for the Danes a full measure of the respect due to honest men. Certainly their personal bravery cannot be questioned.

At daylight, *Renown*, in which ship the second-in-command, Vice-Admiral Whitworth, flew his flag, reported being in contact with one large ship, thought to be of the Scharnhorst class, and one 8-inch cruiser. *Renown* had cruisers with her and a destroyer screen and so our spirits rose. The position was somewhat to the westward of the Lofoten Islands and seemed to leave the Vest Fiord entrance to Narvik unguarded, but we felt that a successful action at sea would soon settle the fate of any German force that might be creeping along the coast inshore. The next report was not so good. The weather was rough and the destroyers could not keep up and had been detached to patrol off Vest Fiord, and the two large enemy ships were gaining ground away to the north-westward, which drew *Renown* still further from Narvik. The action, such as it was, developed into a stern chase, with *Renown* gradually losing ground. *Renown* could not stand the seas that her twenty-four year younger rival bucketed, and when the forward turret became submerged so that the guns filled with water and could not fire, the vice-admiral decided that nothing more was to be gained and returned with his squadron to the Vest Fiord. A couple of hits had been given and received, and *Renown* picked up part of an eleven-inch projectile and suffered some superficial damage. But by now our people were a long way from Narvik and daylight was drawing on.

These reports of *Renown*'s engagement were interspersed with other action messages arriving every hour. At 5.30 a.m. the submarine *Triton* had scored four torpedo hits on a fifteen-ship convoy in the southern area. Word came that German landings were in progress at Lillesand, Kristiansand South, Stavanger, Bergen, Trondhjeim and Narvik. A forenoon air reconnaissance of the Norwegian coast reported one Koln-class cruiser, the *Emden* and two destroyers off Egersund; a destroyer and two large seaplanes at Stavanger; two Koln-class cruisers at Bergen; one 8-inch cruiser at Trondhjeim; and a number of unidentified warships at Narvik. This left us at midday with two pocket battleships and one battle-cruiser unlocated out of the whole German seagoing fleet. The Oslo, Kristiansand South and

Stavanger airfields had been occupied and German aircraft were operating from them. Every one of these reports, except those from our submarines, was a blow against us. If we went into the coast there would be waiting concentrations of U-boats, and it was already certain that heavy air attack could be delivered. It would have been easy to rush in and have our main fleet crippled that day; it was an immensely hard decision to hold off and watch Norway go down.

The fleet was now spread in an immense line with the battleships farthest to westward and cruisers and destroyers disposed closer to the Norwegian coast sweeping northwards in the hope of catching the large enemy warships which had not yet been located. In the late forenoon one or two German shadowers appeared in the sky and we were therefore not surprised when at 2.30 p.m. the first JU87 dive-bombers and JU88 high-level bombers appeared from the eastward. They came over in formations of about thirty machines seen in a clear blue sky in which floated occasional white puffs of cloud at about twelve thousand feet. It looked like a fleet exercise, and what Hugh saw is recorded in this way:

"Then our guns barked. *Rodney* was armed with three four-point-sevens, two eight-barrelled two-pounder pompoms and two five-barrelled half-inch machine-guns on each side, and about a dozen Vickers and Maxim machine-guns scattered about in charge of selected dead-eye Dicks. Mostly the Germans kept out of range of the smaller calibres. As they came in to about five miles distance, our gun-fire appeared to get close to them and their attacks turned away, or split up into small groups or individuals by the time they had closed to three miles. Two or three high-level and dive-bombing attacks were usually in progress at one time and the plan seemed to be for any formation which ran into close gun bursts should turn away and distract attention from the other approaching formations. This game went on for three hours. Closer inshore to the eastward our lighter ships were getting the bulk of the dive-bombing attacks. *Aurore* was directly attacked five times and dodged it all by well-timed manoeuvring."

It will be remembered that after the 2nd Destroyer Flotilla had been detached by Vice-Admiral Whitworth when they could no longer keep up in heavy seas with *Renown* in her chase of a German battle-cruiser and an 8-inch cruiser west of the Lofoten Islands. This flotilla had received orders to patrol off the Vest Fiord and was hardly in position when Captain Warburton-Lee, their leader, was ordered to proceed to Narvik and investigate. Less than half of the German destroyer force had as yet been accounted for, and it seemed probable that a strong division would have gone to Narvik, which was, supposedly, a principal objective of the German attack on Norway. By 4 p.m., our flotilla had arrived in the vicinity of Narvik and learned from some Norwegians that the place was held in force, that German destroyers in unknown strength were in the harbour, and also that one or more U-boats were present and minefields suspected. Vice-Admiral Whitworth had transferred at sea to the battleship *Warspite* and was now closing Vest Fiord. The C.-in-C. considered that the officers on the spot were in the best position to judge what action should be taken and he felt that there was sufficient force available there to deal with any likely German concentration. Somewhat later Captain Warburton-Lee in the *Hardy* signalled his intention to attack at dawn on the morrow — the 10th of April. The Admiralty's reply was couched in noble terms:

"You alone can judge, we will support whatever decision you take." This sounded like Churchill's voice.

As I read through these entirely personal notes of information given me by several friends, I am struck again and again with the complexity of the events which flooded in upon the C.-in-C. during these few days. In presenting them to the reader I am endeavouring to recreate something of the atmosphere which we breathed on the bridge of the *Rodney* as cypher officers came up in procession from their code room three decks below armour, or the small sliding trapdoor which separated the admiral's plotting room at the rear of the glassed-in bridge from the wireless receiving room, each in a seemingly endless procession disgorging little thin slips of message paper bearing the clipped language of naval signals announcing event piling upon event. In these days, too, I learned how real is the advantage of taking the offensive; but we were on the defensive. If the reader's mind is overwhelmed with detail, stretched with the compassing of great distances, or possibly critical of the action taken, let him reflect that we, too, suffered all these processes of the mind, sharpened with the keyed-up tension of sleeplessness, intermittent action and the unknown. Most of our meals consisted of corned beef sandwiches, odd cups of soup or cocoa taken as we stood on a gently heaving deck, unshaven, unbathed, often cold and sometimes wet, looking out over a widespread ever-changing web of ships zigzagging on the steel-grey sea. The sun seldom gleamed through the prevailing low cloud, and when every few hours our radar reported approaching aircraft, ships assumed the first degree of readiness and fired at the shadowers or bombers when they came below the clouds. At this time the ship's company was closed up at action stations for several days and nights semi-continuously, mostly shut down in cold steel compartments where globules of sweat steadily trickled down the bulkheads with only the whirr or click of machinery to assure them that they were still in contact with fellow men. An occasional BBC news bulletin would be announced over the ship's loudspeakers, and when we could, we supplemented this with some snippet of information directly concerning our own forces, but it was little enough the sailor knew of what was going on around him, and that little was a grim tale of German advance scarcely interrrupted by the small successes our utmost effort had so far achieved.

At early dawn on the 10th April, we learned that the Germans were invading Holland and Belgium. Since midnight reports had been coming in of an extraordinary wireless beacon activity audible all over the western end of the battle line in France. This had warned us that something unusual was about to occur in which aircraft and probably mechanised divisions would have a major part. The Germans invariably provided these navigational aids for the Luftwaffe.

But our hearts were at Narvik where the destroyers would be attacking a target of unknown strength in narrow and possibly mined waters as soon as early daylight permitted.

Shortly after 5 a.m., some of our destroyers' wireless signals were intercepted during the course of the developing action and from these we learned that *Hardy*, the flotilla leader, *Havock*, *Hostile*, *Hotspur* and *Hunter* were steaming up Ofort Fiord when they overtook the German ship *Ravenfels* which they immediately enagaged and drove ashore. Fire quickly got a grip on her and she blew up with an almighty explosion which left some who were close to it quite dazed. Then we heard that someone had counted five or perhaps six German Maas-class destroyers in the inner harbour. These were formidable adversaries, for they were considerably larger and more heavily armed than most of our destroyer force. We consoled ourselves with the hope that *Warspite* might by now be in close support astern of our flotilla, but, as we eventually learned, this was not the case, because Vice-

Admiral Whitworth considered that the submarine and minefield dangers were unacceptable for a large ship, and our destroyers therefore did their own work unsupported.

Scraps of action signalling came through — orders to engage this or that target, to fire torpedoes, to alter course or speed, and then the *Hardy*, who as senior officer was naturally the most prominent in this traffic, disappeared altogether from it. The signal officer, Lieutenant Cross, had been a close friend on the C.-in-C.'s staff over the past year before he left to join *Hardy* a few months ago. We thought of his bustling energy and technical efficiency wrestling with smashed wireless gear and shot-away aerials and felt that he would continue to get *Hardy*'s signals through one way or another. But he was already dead, killed instantly at his place on the bridge by the same shell that wrecked the whole of that structure and mortally wounded his captain. There were many of us who felt this loss all too keenly when we learned of it a little later.

A friend of mine who was on the *Hardy*'s bridge throughout this first battle of Narvik gave me his account of his experiences at a later date. I knew his ship well, for that flotilla had formed part of the main fleet screen for a considerable period and not long before that *Hardy* had come alongside to take on oil from us at sea. The method used was that in which the destroyer steams alongside at about fifty feet distance, secured by ropes while an oil hose is passed across. As this was in progress I had carried on a conversation with Cross, and other people I knew in *Hardy*, and they had asked me for fruit. A marine servant and I burgled the wardroom messman's cupboard and threw over one by one about fifty oranges, which was all that we could find. I was unpopular with the messman at the time, but my only regret then was that I could find no more.

As daylight came *Hardy* led the flotilla up Ofort Fiord. The destruction of the SS *Ravenfels* was a momentary incident. Farther in they sighted five or six German destroyers who behaved like trapped rats, dashing here and there without sign of a plan, though firing effectively with broadsides and launching torpedoes whose tracks were generally visible and could usually be avoided. Three or more of these enemy destroyers were on patrol outside Narvik Harbour entrance and off the narrow passage leading into the adjacent Rombaks Fiord. Our ships were compelled, owing to the narrow width of the Ofort Fiord, to approach end on so that generally only the two forward guns would bear, and our leading ships frequently masked the fire of those in the rear as they dodged about. It was a case of firing as hard as you could with whatever weapons would bear. *Hardy* fired on seven different targets at one time or another. They soon disposed of the patrolling Germans; one was sunk, three driven ashore in flames, and another disappeared into Rombaks Fiord apparently in a sinking condition, though still firing one after gun as she disappeared round the point. Then the harbour entrance opened up. Only one, or at most two of our destroyers at a time could bring guns to bear through this narrow entrance, and some defending field guns on the spit to the north proved very troublesome until knocked out by the fire of several of our ships. Through the entrance could be seen a confused mass of merchant hulls, funnels and masts, and alongside the jetty one very large ship and also one destroyer. Later two other destroyers became visible among the merchantmen. There was in fact a solid wall of vessels from amongst which gun-fire spurted quite wildly. A later count estimated five British, one Swede and eight German merchantmen in harbour. In this situation an efficient defence should have been able to concentrate on our ships cooped up in the narrow entrance, and to destroy them one by one as they appeared; at this same time our gunners were trying to pick out the German destroyers and to avoid the merchantmen.

But there were other German destroyers and several individual battles raged all over the outer end of Ofort Fiord. *Hunter* had by now been very badly damaged and was unable even to make a grounding on the beach. She sank in the fiord and her flotilla mates could rescue only a part of her company, for the ice-cold water quickly numbed even those who were still in a position to struggle. *Hardy* herself had been hit many times and was limping down the fiord with silent guns and machinery in a bad way when a salvo caught her, cutting a steam pipe, smashing the bridge and doing other damage.

Paymaster Lieutenant Stanning, the captain's secretary, suddenly found himself flat on the bridge deck, his captain dying beside the compass, and everyone else in sight already dead. His one idea was to get to the steering-wheel on the deck below. He managed to struggle down there and found the quartermaster apparently dead lying on the deck, and quickly took the wheel, steering the ship in a westerly direction towards the fiord entrance.

The torpedo officer dashed up to the bridge from his station aft, having appreciated that severe damage had occurred there, and, finding that the ship still answered her helm, told Stanning to carry on steering westward while he went off to see what other damage there was. A minute or two later Stanning felt the ship settling and noticed that she was losing way. He felt dazed and one foot had begun to hurt excruciatingly. He looked down at it and saw that it was twisted in a right angle, and he almost lost consciousness — but not quite. He kept enough grip on himself to put the wheel over, and turn the sinking ship towards a nearby beach where she ran up on the shelving stony shore a few minutes later.

Meantime the firing was dying down. Seven or eight merchantmen were sunk in Narvik Harbour and one destroyer there was considered to be very heavily damaged as well. Out in the fiord at least two enemy destroyers were sunk and another possibly sunk, and others had been damaged. Amongst our flotilla *Hunter* and *Hardy* were lost. *Hotspur* had sustained seven hits but could still steam, and *Hostile* had a few chips, but nothing to impair fighting efficiency. *Havock* had come out untouched.

There was a general lull next day (12th April) while British forces regrouped, and *Furious'* aircraft reconnoitred and bombed Narvik, reporting five German destroyers still present.

On 13th April, *Warspite* was attacked early by twelve aircraft as she moved up Ofort Fiord to bombard whatever remained at Narvik. She was now in company with nine destroyers (*Cossack, Punjabi, Bedouin, Eskimo, Forester, Foxhound, Hero, Hostile, Icarus* and *Ivanhoe*). *Furious'* aircraft attacked shipping in snowstorms as soon as daylight permitted. Those destroyers fitted with minesweeping gear were deployed ahead of *Warspite*. On the way in, *Eskimo* depth-charged and destroyed a U-boat. *Warspite*'s aircraft was flown off at noon and reported "German destroyers ahead". Half an hour later *Bedouin* reported "Enemy destroyers in sight", and the minesweeping destroyers hauled in their sweeps. Shortly after that both sides began firing at each other whenever the snow showers permitted. By 2.15 p.m., *Punjabi*, with all guns out of action, one boiler dead and many shell holes in the hull was withdrawing. *Cossack* grounded but got off next day, and *Eskimo* had been damaged by a torpedo. At 3.30 p.m., *Bedouin* reported no opposition from Narvik Harbour and then, as she looked into Rombaks Fiord: "One enemy destroyer aground out of action. More round the corner out of sight. If they have torpedoes they are in a position of great advantage." *Hero* and *Bedouin* reported ammunition almost exhausted. *Bedouin*'s forward gun mounting was out of action.

The vice-admiral signalled: "The torpedo menace must be accepted. Enemy must be destroyed without delay. Take *Kimberley, Forester, Hero, Punjabi* under your orders and organise attack sending in the most serviceable destroyers first. Ram or board if necessary."

Just then *Warspite*'s aircraft returned, was hoisted in and reported bombing and destroying a U-boat in Harjangs Fiord not far away.

Hero, Icarus and *Kimberley* gingerly entered Rombaks Fiord, and as they rounded the promontory at the entrance experienced no gun-fire at all. Three abandoned, smoking and beached German destroyers lay there, one of which was immediately scuttled by its crew, another sank as they advanced, and then *Hero* and *Kimberley* boarded the third one, *Hans Linderman*, and found one lone and wounded — and evidently abandoned — officer still on board. *Hero* sank her with a torpedo as soon as the boarding party had returned. *Foxhound* had collected some prisoners who said that several U-boats were in the area and that the German garrison was estimated at 2,000. The vice-admiral decided to withdraw as his total landing party was only 200 and inadequate for an attack, and also all German shipping had now been destroyed. About this time twelve German aircraft arrived and bombed ineffectively. As the squadron withdrew down Ofort Fiord to the westward, *Foxhound* depth-charged a submarine contact.

Looking back with after knowledge, I remember how this news filled us with all the joy of a victory gained. We had lost a good deal, the Germans much more, but they still held Narvik. Their later final destruction in that trap did not seem so important as this first attack. Perhaps the true explanation is that at last we had been able to hit them. I had not yet learned that mostly one waits and keeps one's weapons ready in sea warfare, and that to use them is a rare event.

Later on we were to hear from German prisoners and from British merchant seamen who were caught in the fighting at Narvik, a few more details of the actions and events which surrounded it. Nine Maas-class destroyers had left Germany loaded to capacity with soldiers and weapons four days previously.

Four of these had been delayed by the encounter with *Glowworm* so that their force had arrived off Narvik in two waves. The latter part of the passage had been rough and most of the soldiers reached port in a state of exhaustion from seasickness. In fact, had the place not already been surprised by soldiery hidden in merchantmen waiting in the port, it is doubtful if the German commander would have risked a landing so early. The only opposition was from a few policemen and some civilian snipers, and that was ineffective.

The German destroyers had found their seasick passengers a great trial and were glad to be rid of them, for they were eaten out of provisions and very short of water and, of course, oil fuel. When *Hardy*'s flotilla appeared, some of the German destroyers had not yet refuelled and this early interruption scared most of them out of their wits. They had no aircraft warning of the approach of British forces.

Inside the port, indescribable confusion reigned. Some British merchantmen had been sunk by our own gun-fire, which was inevitable in such a congested space. One German destroyer alongside the jetty was so severely damaged that her crew abandoned her and rushed ashore. She lay half submerged through the night until they were persuaded to return next morning and commence salvage operations.

The German destroyers which beached themselves out in the fiord had some terrible experiences, much the same, indeed, as those of our men in similar plight. Their vessels were blazing hulks with many dead and wounded. It was difficult to escape from the imminent danger of exploding magazines except by taking to the icy water and swimming the few yards to the shore. Once the shore was gained the sodden and exhausted seamen had to make their way in bitter cold and recurrent snow showers across considerable distances to whatever habitation could be found. One German has related how they sank into the deep snow at each step and when they eventually reached the shelter of a farmstead discovered that their trousers were frayed to ribbons and their legs horribly lacerated up to the knee where the ice crust had cut in at almost every step.

Further down the fiord, survivors of *Hardy*'s crew had ferried themselves ashore in a dinghy and in Carley life rafts. They made their way to a farm where the good woman of the house heated all the food she possessed and gave them all the clothing and bed coverings in her house while they stripped off and dried the stiff frozen garments in which they had struggled ashore. Some had collapsed and lain down in snow heaped up by companions to provide a sort of shelter from the biting wind, and these, too, were dragged out and eventually, supported by their more robust shipmates, reached the shelter of the farm through intermittent snow showers.

While Narvik and our battling destroyers in these icy fiords held our hearts, other events were claiming at least some part of our minds.

A squadron of twelve aircraft from the Fleet Air Arm station at Hatston in the Orkneys made a successful attack on German shipping in Bergen and hits were claimed on a K-class cruiser lying close in under a cliff in the outer anchorage. It had cost us some planes, and in one of those shot down was a midshipman pilot who, finding his engine suddenly dead, pointed his nose to the west and glided for several miles out of range of the pursuing shell fire. He spotted a quiet-looking island with a sandy beach, and the wind being in a favourable direction, decided to land in the water close inshore. His petty officer observer was warned and down they went, making a fair landing about fifty yards from the sandy shore. The plane sank as they struggled clear. Their lifebelts floated them successfully and in spite of the coldness of the water they got ashore. Within a few minutes two small Norwegian boys came out of the adjacent pine scrub and beckoned them to follow. They struggled along numb with cold, but realised that they must at all costs keep moving until shelter could be found. Twenty minutes' walk brought them to the country house of an elderly English-speaking doctor who was alone there with his wife and an old servant. They were immediately taken in and tended and carefully guarded from any chance of discovery for several days.

Their host had only come down from Bergen the night before. He was in practice there, living in a large house in the middle of the city with two servants and his assistant and a secretary. The German invasion had come as a complete surprise to him. He was woken suddenly in the middle of the night on the eighth of April to find his bedroom full of German soldiers with guns pointing at him. A short conversation reassured them that he was in fact what he purported to be and, with threats to ensure his good behaviour, they soon left the house, having first stripped the kitchen and larder of all the food they could find. Shortly thereafter, while he was hurriedly dressing, firing broke out in the direction of the docks, and he decided to quit the town and join his wife who was virtually alone at their country house on an island about twenty miles down the By-Fiord. He was puzzled beyond measure to explain why the German soldiers had come into his house and, before leaving, he searched every room in the building. In the cellar lay the clue. There he found all the evidence of occupation by a numerous body of people, and stumbled over a hiding servant who confessed that he was German and told him how some twenty men had come from a cargo vessel in port about eight nights previously and that he had successfully concealed them since that time. His duty in the household was to keep the heating furnace stoked and nobody else ever went into the cellars. He had bought food in town and attended to the soldiers' needs throughout the waiting period without detection. The dumbfounded doctor fled. This sort of thing repeated many times — with variations — explains how Norway was cut down with hardly a shot fired; these days were congested in ways that had never before been paralleled.

In due course the midshipman and his petty officer were smuggled on board a friendly fishing boat. Dressed in the guise of Norwegian fishermen they were passed from boat to boat up the coast until, about two weeks later, they were finally landed near a British strong point into which they made their way, and were then flown back to England.

Now that the Germans were established along the whole length of the Norwegian coast it became at least possible for them to seize Iceland and use it as a U-boat base. Before the war two U-boats had cruised to Reykjavik and a German scientific expedition, including aviation experts, had made a survey in the area of Reydar Fiord on the eastern coast where a sizeable harbour exists. There had also been a considerable drift of young Icelandic students to German universities, and partly as a result of this cultural link an Icelandic Nazi party had emerged. Although its numbers were not large, they included a number of highly intelligent and active citizens, and so now Iceland was going to be added to our responsibilities. A U-boat in the North Atlantic which had an appendicitis case on board had put into Reykjavik some months back to land the sick man, and the occasion had been used by the local Nazis for a propaganda drive. To these straws must be added an important commercial consideration: the Icelandic fishing industry was in a serious state of disruption due to the British action, and it was the only source of income to the territory. Before the war, fish and a large amount of valuable fish oil had been sold to Germany, and this trade was now stopped by the British blockade. Britain, it is true, was willing to receive these Icelandic products in the place of Germany, but the prices offered were considered inadequate in view of the risks of the voyage which lay directly across the U-boat route into the Atlantic; and the British had not sent any coal or fuel oil for many months and stocks were now so depleted that trawlers and fish carriers had been obliged to lay up. The shortage of available British shipping coupled with the Nazi tone audible in Icelandic public life explained this British neglect, but the fishing population was displeased with both British and Germans.

When, therefore, on the morning of 10th April 1940, a large transport escorted by British cruisers and destroyers arrived in the roadstead at Reykjavik and armed troops began to swarm ashore and to seize the key government offices, they were met by gloomy, hostile faces. Radio propaganda accompanied the landing of this force. The newly-appointed British Minister Mr Howard Smith, who accompanied the expedition, made an immediate call upon the regent, Svinn Bjornsson. He tried to explain the temporary and defensive nature of the invasion. The women of Iceland shut themselves within doors, and when their household duties obliged them to go out into the streets they averted their heads in passing a uniformed Britisher. One day Hugh walked out from Reykjavik along a country road and, coming to a gang of men doing repair work, saw that as soon as he came within about forty yards of them they all cleared off the roadway and walked down the hillside presenting their backs to him as he passed by. The same gesture was repeated an hour later on his return along the same roadway.

As there was only a token police force in the barracks at Reykjavik and no other armed force in the country, the occupation was a bloodless one. A little later on the British government, desirous of making every possible gesture of friendship, sent a number of Canadian army units recruited largely from logging camps where Icelandic and Norse emigrants mostly worked, but this was not a success, for these troops disliked the awful monotony of garrison duty in that bleak region and presently began to kick up their heels. There were some fights in bars, and what was more serious, one or two cases of rape, the news of which spread all over the island like wildfire. The garrison was changed and as time passed a more friendly frame of mind eventually developed.

The occupation of the country was undertaken in order to provide a staging place for aircraft coming from North America, and also as a refuelling base for convoy escorts — both vitally important for Britain, but the Admiralty feared that this might provoke a German counter-invasion.

At a later date when Rear-Admiral Dalrymple-Hamilton had taken over command of the British naval base which was established at Reykjavik, his wife, who was an expert Scottish weaver, started up a factory for weaving Scots tweed material which was readily sold to visiting warships, aircrews and the military, and this helped local people to supplement their incomes and to establish cordial relationships through some of the Icelandic women who staffed this new enterprise.

On at least two later dates the first sea lord telephoned the C.-in-C. to express anxiety over the security of Iceland. At the usual morning staff conference in the admiral's cabin the C.-in-C. informed the staff of a renewed message of warning which he had just received. He asked Hugh what evidence existed and Hugh detailed such meagre information as there was; he said that the Admiralty Operations Intelligence Centre did not think any serious threat existed, and added:

"I hope they do invade. It would give us an opportunity to get at the Germans." There was an electric reaction all round, and the admiral replied: "I don't agree at all. You've no business to say such a thing!"

Hugh recalls the first occasion in 1941 when the Fleet flagship entered Akyureiri Fiord in the evening and, as they turned round a point and came in sight of the little town on a hillside, the street lighting was suddenly switched on and the whole ship's company came up on deck to gaze on this lovely Christmas card sight, now so long passed into a fading peace-time memory. Seidis Fiord was used more often for large ships, being more commodious, and it was, like all the other fiords, bleak and uninhabited except for a scattering of tiny farms at the base of the high rocky sides where nothing but great tussocks of tough grass could grow, many of the clefts being filled with snow all the year round. On these small patches Hugh tried to ski, but found that the hard labour of carrying a pair of skis up the steep rocky hillside was not worth the trouble when only a fifty-yard long patch of melting but usable snow was all that he was able to reach in the time available before the ship's boat would leave the shore.

It was in this fiord that he went on board his first and only U-boat. The *Burwell* (an ex-four stack American destroyer) from Reykjavik was steaming to the eastward along the south coast of Iceland quite close inshore when one of our aircraft passed her a message that a U-boat a few miles ahead which it had bombed was waving a white flag, adding this tailpiece: "Bring him back alive. Good night." The weather was bad and the U-boat was only sighted at 4.30 a.m. the next day, now surrounded by four trawlers which couldn't lower their boats to board it. *Burwell* decided to put men on board and by threats make the German crew keep their boat afloat. The U-boat signalled: "Please save crew", and there was much signalling to and fro to try to discover just what damage had occurred. In the midst of all this a Norwegian manned float plane suddenly appeared and straddled the U-boat with two lightweight bombs, and then asked permission to sink her as soon as the destroyer had saved the crew. The bombs stirred up the Germans who had previously refused to be taken in tow, and they got out a hemp rope but couldn't manage a wire. The hemp parted and one of the trawlers attempted to pass a tow wire as the weather was slowly moderating. At half-past ten, the U-boat signalled: "Afraid we cannot float. Please come in and pick up crew." *Burwell* closed and fired a few machine-gun bursts across the bows, but then the machine-gunner misunderstood the "cease-fire", order and began to fire bursts into the conning tower where five of the crew were huddled, three being wounded seriously. This produced an immediate reaction. The Germans pumped out some oil and the bows rose visibly. Then about noon the Germans asked for an engineer to come and inspect their engines. A trawler then passed a Carley life-saving float across and took off the wounded and also passed a tow rope. At this point the U-boat signalled that she was filling up with chlorine gas, and so the remainder of the crew were taken off and the hatches were battened down. When the trawler moved ahead at eight knots speed the tow parted; they passed another tow-rope and recommenced their journey, but in the dark they could not see the U-boat and decided to beach her. Later on a party came overland and refloated her. Inside they found a mess: scattered about they saw flour, dried peas, scores of black bread loaves, bedding, and knee-deep oily water. And so they brought her into Seidis Fiord, pumped her out and cleaned up the mess, and later a British crew was put on board and she was taken to England, where whatever technical secrets she held were soon digested. Hugh went on board to find out whatever he could about her, but the boat was not a recent type and of no great value to us.

Nothing ever held the centre of the stage for long, however, and in Norway early in the morning of the 11th April 1940, the submarine *Spearfish* reported making two torpedo hits on the pocket battleship *Admiral Scheer* off the Norwegian coast, a very welcome bit of news, for it put a most troublesome antagonist out of business at an opportune moment. The submarines were indeed active, *Sunfish* the previous night sinking one ship and *Snapper*, *Triad* and *Sealion* others the same day.

The Naval Air Arm was now increasingly coming into action and every naval plane had targets awaiting it. A carrier-borne attack from *Furious* was staged in the early morning on Trondhjeim where reconnaissance reported a number of important targets. Our Swordfish and Skuas got in without interception, although the port is sixty-five miles up the fiord from the coast. Their effort was, however, abortive. Gun-fire forced them to discharge torpedoes outside Munklhomen bank, over a mile from the targets lying alongside, and several crews saw their torpedoes exploding on the shoal which lay between Munklhomen and the dockside. It cost us several crews and machines; one or two doubtful hits were all that could be claimed. The journey home was a nightmare experience for all concerned, pursued as they were by numerous infinitely faster German fighters. Our Skuas, however, found themselves able to drive off the German fighters with decisive mastery when they could contact them, and this was a geat encouragement to the carrier's aircrews. But we were very thin in the air and casualties were mounting faster than replacement.

Stavanger was attacked by RAF machines at dusk and they sank a ship in the Great Belt a little later in the evening. We counted aircraft in tens where the Germans were reckoning in hundreds, and we knew that such pinpricks were having no serious effect on the occupation of Norway.

News came that the small cruiser *Penelope* had grounded heavily in Vaags Fiord, a little to the north of Narvik and then, later, that she was off, but her bottom was ripped open in several places and had to be laboriously patched by divers working in the intensely cold water outside, and plugged with cement from within. She was, however, to become a most useful depot ship for all our forces up there. Her artisans repaired and maintained many different small ships. She loaned stores and ammunition, canteen gear and provisions to all comers. She distilled fresh water when there was need and her cooks baked all night long for those who could not make their own bread. She did a magnificent job of work for the ships in that area, and, though bombed intermittently, maintained a standard of air defence that came to be feared by the local Luftwaffe. Later on she was to become more famous in the Mediterranean, but never more valuable than now, when a ship with less spirit might have lain impotent in that Norwegian backwater.

During this early stage of the Norwegian campaign the Fleet Air Arm carried out over twenty attacks on coastal targets with the inevitable loss of an increasingly high proportion of air crews. Air personnel strength had been small to begin with and its principal task was originally considered to be anti-submarine patrol, spotting for fleet gun-fire, and also a modest role in bombing and torpedoing naval targets. Its strength now became so reduced that the training of new squadrons was imperilled through lack of sufficient numbers of experienced instructors. Admiral Forbes was to some extent blamed for too profligate a use of the Fleet Air Arm, but he was at this time under pressure from the Admiralty — and probably particularly from Mr Churchill — to take offensive action to hinder what seemed to be a German walk-over. Narvik had shown that ship intervention close inshore could be a costly business.

Meantime we, in the main body of the fleet, were sweeping northwards after covering the carrier raid on Trondjheim and were sighted and shadowed. Although *Furious* was with us it must be remembered that the direction of fighters by means of radar, and their control in the air through radio-telephone, was as yet in a primitive stage and we didn't have any radar. Shadowers were hardly ever shot down. German control was, fortunately, as ponderous as our own, and although we were no more than a hundred and fifty miles from their shore-based bombers, they did not begin attacks until about half-past three in the afternoon.

One day we were trying out a scheme of having the battleships and carrier in the middle of two circles of warning vessels, the outer at twenty miles range and the inner at about four miles distance. Cruisers took the van positions and thinly spaced destroyers covered the rest. The theory was that the outer ring would not only provide warning but disrupt flying formations and thus reduce the efficacy of bombing. Squadrons of nine or eighteen JU88 bombers came over for two hours at about quarter-hour intervals, and irregularly single machines would slip in to attempt an unobserved attack during the advance of a major air formation. Broken clouds at about five thousand feet helped these tactics. The outer ring of destroyers gave us a good warning on the whole, but their fire was too light and dispersed to be effective. The inner screen, reinforced by cruisers, made a better impression. Yet the large formations of bombers came steadily on until the heavy gun bursts got amongst them and at times they appeared to be uncomfortably close to what would be the dropping point, and that is when your neck begins to get a crick in it when you look up at them. Nevertheless the nearest bomb was five hundred yards away, and most fell a mile off and were probably aimed in desperation at the inner ring of cruisers and destroyers.

Presently however the destroyer *Eclipse* "bought it". She had been with us since the outbreak of war, and, like all our screening destoyers, came to occupy a special place in our hearts — for she had helped to keep the U-boats at bay for seven long months. As Hugh watched her he could see a JU88 in a shallow dive. She put her helm over and increased speed, for the white plume of water under her stern suddenly rose higher. A near miss amidships caused flooding of her machinery spaces and she heeled over about twenty degrees. A second bomb exploded on the fo'c'sle while she was still steaming at about twenty-five knots and she quickly sank. Survivors were, however, saved. Presently the bombers went home, as always did happen at about 5 p.m., presumably to be in time for supper, and after this we never had another large air attack on the main fleet at sea, perhaps because we stayed mostly outside normal bombing range.

It was just at this time when the Fleet flagship was in harbour at Scapa Flow that the Chief of Staff Commodore King, who had contracted influenza, went away on leave for a few days. Admiral Forbes sent for Hugh in the middle of a quiet afternoon and when he entered the admiral's cabin the latter said:

"Oh, stoke up this fire, will you. I want to burn some papers. Then come along with me to the chief of staff's cabin."

When they got there the Admiral produced a bunch of keys and unlocked a large safe bolted to the deck in one corner, out of which poured a quantity of files — for it was tightly packed to its limits.

"Now, we'll carry all this stuff into my cabin and put it on my fire!" He was smiling brightly, almost like a schoolboy. There were masses of gunnery reports which had come in from ships doing their working-up practices, all of which came into the C.-in-C. for his comments, and no doubt he had already glanced at those which were of special interest. But now nobody had the time to go through them in detail, least of all the chief of staff, who had to handle an ever-increasing volume of action material. Admiral Forbes well knew that the Gunnery Division at the Admiralty would also be swamped with war action material. The admiral had an uncanny knack of distinguishing between essentials and the unimportant.

On 14th April, a major landing under General Carton de Wiart was made at Namsos, and five smaller ones at other points, including Narvik, all places where German shipping could be obstructed. A French squadron of three transports, one carrying a thousand mules (who were to haul mountain guns), and a substantial military force trained for mountain warfare, joined with an equal force of British troops, all assembled at Scapa beforehand. As the French squadron had been at sea for five days, the first thing they wanted to do was to put the mules ashore to get exercise, without which they would shortly become useless and die. The landing on Hoy Island was undertaken from large flat-bottomed boats carried by the French transports and as soon as these grounded and the ramps were lowered the mules made a wild rush for the shore, some of them falling into the water, though there were no casualties. When the time came for re-embarkation it was a different story. Three days elapsed before the recapture of the last unwilling mule. On 14th April, General Carton de Wiart and some of his staff flew over in a Sunderland flying boat which was shot down just as she was preparing to land in Namsos Harbour. The ADC was badly wounded but the general was quickly rescued unhurt by a dinghy sent from a nearby trawler. Stiff fighting was going on, for there was determined opposition from a small German garrison equipped with field guns, and German bombing during daylight hours became incessant so that allied troops were compelled to keep under cover and could only move about, dig trenches and set up their guns after dark.

Convoys were organised to bring in supplies, and they came under such heavy attack that ninety per cent of the ships and their cargoes were lost before they reached Namsos. The rate of loss was so high that it quickly became obvious that the force ashore could not long be maintained. In a period of fourteen days, our ships suffered sixty-two bombing attacks and claimed twenty-three aircraft shot down.

On 28th April, our air reconnaissance reported two large ships and three cruisers in Trondhjeim Harbour. The C.-in-C. (now returned to the *Nelson* because the *Rodney* had gone away for repairs), accompanied by the carrier *Furious* and *Warspite* and the usual destroyer screen, was within immediate striking distance. *Furious* flew off aircraft which dropped some light bombs and confirmed the presence of these warships and pin-pointed their exact berths. Air opposition was not heavy, but one Skua fighter was shot down.

Hugh, who was on the admiral's bridge when this report came in, handed it to the C.-in-C.

"Now we've got them in a hole they can't escape from," he said, "and the local air opposition seems to be unusually light. It would take some time to reinforce their air strength, and their main forces have always gone home about five o'clock in the afternoon. If we went in now and lost a battleship, or even two, we would still have seven left. They have only two, both still building."

"What shore defences are there?" the admiral asked.

The naval intelligence report on Trondhjeim Fiord was produced and revealed that nine years ago Austrian eleven-inch torpedoes were mounted in the cliff face on one side of the very narrow entrance, and possibly also on the other side, but their actual whereabouts was successfully concealed. There were also movable field gun positions on both sides. Four of our destroyers had mine-sweeping equipment and minefields were to be expected either in the approaches or within the fiord.

An immediate signal was sent to the Admiralty asking for any more recent information and the reply came back in half an hour that nothing more was known. Meanwhile the ships had turned to a course for Trondhjeim and were ordered to prepare to go in and attack, *Furious* being sent off to a suitable flying-off position. The captain of the *Nelson* was sent for and he asked some hard questions but did not oppose the suggestion that surprise would be on our side. Thereupon the C.-in-C. made another signal to the Admiralty reporting his intention to attack the warships in Trondhjeim Harbour. It was now mid-afternoon and German bombers would soon be on their way home to their bases to refuel and bomb up. Some at least would be immobilised during that process. If we could get in, the sixty-mile passage up the fiord and quite a short action should see us on our way out again before complete darkness — which is late in that northern latitude. And then an Admiralty signal came forbidding us to enter the fiord.

Hugh turned to the admiral and said: "But Sir, we are already committed, and I remember Nelson put his telescope to his blind eye at Copenhagen. We can say that the signal came too late to stop us!"

The admiral pondered this suggestion for a brief moment.

"You would do that, would you? No! We can't do that. Hoist the signal to turn 180 to starboard."

And so we reversed course and no later opportunity ever occurred to deal a really heavy blow against the invasion of Norway. It was a pity, for Nazi morale was a fragile thing incapable of standing up to real adversity.

To Hugh this incident was a hard blow. He was convinced that success was within reach. The defences at the entrance were probably antique and would almost certainly be taken by surprise, and in any case the *Nelson*'s battery of nine 16-inch guns mounted forward could deliver a tremendous weight of high explosives, and this ship was built to take up to nine torpedo hits. The German bomber force would be surprised at a moment when most planes were without fuel or bombs, and the local air defence around the port area was not large and its reinforcement was unlikely to be immediate. Remembering the *Admiral Scheer* at Gibraltar he also knew that a German ship taken at such a disadvantage could panic. Their whole force was only lightly armoured, so that a single salvo from *Nelson* would certainly cripple any ship it hit. Additional light forces, if any were present — and there was no report that any were — could not manoeuvre freely in the inner harbour and the Munklhomen bank across its approaches would probably prohibit them from making a torpedo attack; and if any did come out into the fiord while we approached we had the power to destroy them with ease. Hugh's regrets remained with him for life, though at that moment they were swamped by the flood of other events taking place over the whole Norwegian coast area.

In the far north, Harstad had been seized on 15th April and a naval base was established there with a small garrison. It was hoped that it would be relatively free from heavy air attack so far north and the retired Admiral of the Fleet Lord Cork, familiarly known in the Service as "Ginger Boyle", was appointed in command there. Perhaps this move was made by the government in order to have a base from which we might operate against the Russians steaming from Murmansk out into the Atlantic, for they had recently signed a treaty of friendship with Germany and it was obviously possible that they might become an active enemy in due course. But the appointment of this officer — who was much senior to the C.-in-C. in whose operational area he would exercise his command — was a surprise, and it quickly became apparent that he did not recognise that he was in any way "under" the C.-in-C., for normally he communicated only with the Admiralty, even though the Home Fleet must obviously be responsible for covering convoys to and from Harstad. This uneasy — and also unnecessary — complication was later on to produce disaster.

On 27th April, one of the convoys to this far northern region had 125 bombs dropped on it without a hit, but it alerted us to the fact that already at this early date the German Air Force was able to reach in strength our most distant garrison on the Norwegian coast.

By the first week in May, it had become apparent that, with France collapsing, and Italy and Turkey preparing to declare war on us, we could no longer afford to continue much active support for Norway. On 3rd May, Namsos was evacuated by night and about 2,700 to 3,000 French troops were re-embarked there. The escorting French destroyer *Bison* was bombed and sank and, while going to her rescue, a British destoyer was also hit and sank, but all the troop transport ships survived. The other small garrisons along the coast were also evacuated by warships at about the same time.

On 10th May, Prime Minister Neville Chamberlain resigned in face of widespread criticism of his handling of the war and had, in the House of Commons during a debate, heard the voice of Winston Churchill interjecting at one point the famous angry exclamation: "In the name of God, go! For God's sake, Sir, go!" Churchill succeeded him that same day. Only a very short while later, when we were lying in the Clyde, he came aboard unexpectedly in the darkening evening to stay for the night. Early next morning the ship's company was mustered and he addressed us quite briefly:

"I do not want you to think that I have deserted you — by no means, indeed! My new office is only two or three hundred yards away from the Admiralty across the Horse Guards Parade, and from my windows I can see into my old office. Be sure that I shall keep a close watch on all that you are doing and I want you all to know that, whatever it is, I will be helping you in every way that lies within my power! I wish you Godspeed and good luck!" We didn't doubt him and felt encouraged and much relieved that a new direction and greatly increased energy would now be installed into the whole British war effort.

The C.-in-C. received information from the Admiralty that our remaining forces in the far north were to be evacuated shortly, no specific date being given, and the carrier *Glorious* and a destroyer escort were sent to cover that operation, though the actual date and composition of the evacuation convoy were not known to us. A chance radio interception revealed that the King of Norway was leaving in a cruiser for Britain. Recently the battleship *Valiant*, newly fitted with a tremendous anti-aircraft armament, had joined the fleet, and, as time passed, the C.-in-C. became increasingly uneasy about this northern evacuation, and eventually the fleet left Scapa for a general sweep to the northward and finally *Valiant* was detached to proceed to Harstad. Then on 8th June, a signal from *Glorious* came saying that she was sinking. She was two hundred miles west of Vest Fiord (which leads into Narvik) when she sighted the *Admiral Scheer* and a cruiser, in company. They opened fire at 20,000 yards range and hit *Glorious* with the third salvo and she sank an hour and a half later. Meanwhile the escorting destroyer *Ardent* closed the enemy to fire torpedoes but was sunk on the way in, while her mate *Acasta* laid a smoke screen to cover *Glorious* and then in turn went in to attack with torpedoes and was also sunk. Only thirty-seven survivors from this action were rescued by small Norwegian craft. Had the officer in command at Harstad made his evacuation plans known before, or even during their execution, the fleet could have provided strong support. Harstad was finally evacuated on 15th — 16th June. The "Norwegian Campaign" had come to an end, and hereafter only small harassing raids were launched against that long coastline.

This tragedy followed closely upon the much more grave news of the collapse in France. On 2nd June, it had been announced that a total of 335,490 troops had been evacuated from Dunkirk through the efforts of 222 warships and 665 other craft, a tremendous national effort rightly named "The Miracle of Dunkirk". "And now," as Winston Churchill remarked, "we stand alone, and I cannot but feel that this unsought freedom confers certain important advantages upon us!" He went to Paris with a small staff to offer a union of nationalities which the French rejected on 16th June. As the little British group stood on the station platform awaiting their train, Churchill noticed Captain Lyons from the Admiralty Plans Division, and said to him: "Well, Captain Lyons, you always have a plan ready for the next thing. Pray what plans do you have for this situation?" Marshal Pétain asked Germany for an armistice the next day.

Throughout this period both the Fleet Air Arm and the RAF were launching daily attacks on the Norwegian coastal ports and shipping, incurring a steady drain of losses but also hitting a satisfactory proportion of targets.

On 3rd July, a naval force from the Mediterranean Fleet attacked the large concentration of the French Navy at Oran on the Algerian coast and destroyed everything except the battle-cruiser *Richelieu* which escaped to Dakar on the West African coast where subsequently she was attacked and damaged beyond repair. The French naval commander would not guarantee that his ships would not fall into German hands, nor would he neutralise them.

This was for Hugh, and probably some others, the saddest and most bitter memory of the whole war. It will be remembered that Hugh had acted as liaison officer during the visit of a French squadron to the Firth of Forth in March 1939, and at that time the two services had been of one mind where the Nazis were concerned.

Six months after the holocaust at Oran a parcel reached Hugh containing the fire-damaged photograph of *Nelson* with many of the signatures blurred by water. Across it was written with a very thick pen: "We return this souvenir to you who we believed to be friends but now know have turned out to be enemies and stabbed us in the back."

The destruction, ordered by Churchill's government, was believed at that time to be essential because, had the French Fleet come under German control (which was a clear possibility), it would have given that country command of the Mediterranean and the war could have been lost.

Chapter 14

The Sinking of the Bismarck

A German — apparently officially inspired — newspaper report just prior to the outbreak of war said that "only the heaviest ships could get the Atlantic striking force through," and Hugh's assessment (for he was convinced by facts he had unearthed as early as 1938) that war with Germany was certain, and the German paper went on to say that their two fast battle-cruisers *Scharnhorst* and *Gneusenua* would spearhead that force and that the fast new battleships *Bismarck* and *Tirpitz*, now being built, would support them. That seemed to him to be the German naval plan. *Bismarck* was still fitting out in the summer of 1940, and in due course went to the Baltic for trials which were likely to last six months and were due to be completed about the spring of 1941. Hitler inspected her at Gotnhafen (Kiel) on 5th May. The crew numbered 2,350, and just before she sailed on her first expedition, Hitler ordered the embarkation of 500 naval cadets under training. Rear-Admiral Lutjens and staff embarked on 18th May. Shortly afterwards exceptional minesweeping activity was taking place in the Kattegat, through which she must pass on any voyage to the Atlantic. On 23rd May came a report from Copenhagen that a very large warship under escort steaming westwards had passed a point in southern Sweden. By now our fleet was at short notice for steam, and we were anxiously awaiting the arrival of the· new carrier *Victorious*, which had just completed her trials but not yet embarked her complement of aircraft. At 8.42 p.m. on 20th May, *Bismarck* had sighted a British aircraft off Bergen on the Norwegian coast which was in fact an RAF photographic reconnaissance sortie. *Bismarck*, evidently nervous of an air attack, spent the night in Bergen fiord at action stations. The next day visibility on the Norwegian coast was about nil, and our usual reconnaissance aircraft could not get into Bergen fiord.

Commander Rotherham, an experienced air navigator, in command of the Naval Air Station at Hatston, near Kirkwall at the eastern end of the fleet base at Scapa Flow, climbed into a somewhat elderly little machine and into bad weather, judging by his drift by the breaking seas, and made his landfall only 50 feet above the sea when he sighted the lower part of Marsten lighthouse, hidden in fog, on a small island at the entrance to Bergen fiord. He flew up the fiord scanning the whole of it carefully under sporadic fire, made his report that *Bismarck* was not there, and flew back to Hatston with little fuel left. He was at once brought on board the Fleet flagship, where Admiral Tovey questioned him carefully, Hugh standing by to take notes. This reconnaissance proved to be a key factor in the later sinking of the *Bismarck*. Rotherham's flight was hazardous, and his close inspection under fire was exhaustive and complete. A few days later he was awarded the Distinguished Service Order for this very fine feat of airmanship.

When *Victorious* arrived earlier that day the C.-in-C. had sent for her captain to ascertain the exact state of her readiness. The captain considered that if he could get his aircraft on board in time — they were flying up to Thurso from southern England in poor weather that day — then *Victorious* would be ready to operate. The C.-in-C. was doubtful if these aircraft would be fit for action, since they had not done any flying-on practices nor communications exercises. The two lieutenant-commanders in charge of the two air squadrons were sent for and stated very firmly indeed that they were confident that their aircrews were fit for action at once because they had done the necessary practices on shore.

"But," said Admiral Tovey, "that isn't the same thing as doing your stuff operating from a ship at sea, is it?"

"No, Sir, it isn't, but most of us have operated from carriers before this."

"But *Victorious* is a new carrier, and that makes some difference. You have never landed on her flying deck, have you?"

"No, Sir, we haven't, but we shall get our initial practice tonight when our squadrons fly-on to embark."

The speaker was Lieutenant-Commander Esmond (who later on was awarded the Victoria Cross for his outstanding air attacks in the Dover Straits area). He looked a tough and determined sort of person. The admiral told the captain that he would take *Victorious* to sea in pursuit of the *Bismarck* but that no risks were to be taken. As they left with their captain, Admiral Tovey turned to Hugh: "Well, if anybody could do this those fellows look as if they would bring it off!"

Victorious was under way within the hour, and the two new squadrons had flown on before dark, though there was not time for all their baggage and equipment to reach the carrier, and they spent half the night equipping their aircraft with torpedoes.

Hood, flying the flag of Vice-Admiral Holland, and *Prince of Wales*, a new 14-inch gun battleship, had already sailed for a position south of Iceland, and the cruisers *Norfolk* and *Suffolk* were well on their way to patrol the northern entrance to the Denmark Straits between Iceland and Greenland. The flag-officer at Reykjavik had reported that the straits were about fifty-four miles wide with loose ice-floes on the Greenland side. The 700-mile gap between the Faeroe Islands and Iceland was already watched by the Northern Patrol consisting of armed merchant cruisers and trawlers, eight strong at sea at the moment. This was always the weak link, but mines had been laid across the whole of this vast gap, though these constantly broke adrift on account of the very rough weather so often prevailing in the area.

King George V (*K.G.5*, colloquially), *Repulse* (an elderly battle-cruiser), and a destroyer screen put to sea at dusk, and *Victorious* joined them an hour later, the fleet steaming at twenty-seven knots toward a position somewhat to the eastward of *Hood* and *Prince of Wales* so as to cover a possible break back for home which *Bismarck* might make if she were sighted early in her passage into the Atlantic. Some air patrols were being flown from Iceland, but in the prevailing condition of patchy fog and snow showers in the Denmark Strait not much hope lay in these. Other long patrols to cover the gap between the Faeroes and Iceland were also ordered, but these were few and far between, and again, weather would make a sighting difficult. At 4 a.m. on 23rd May, *Bismarck* and the light cruiser *Prinz Eugen* were 181 miles north-east of Iceland.

At 7.22 p.m. on 23rd May, *Norfolk* and *Suffolk* reported sighting *Bismarck* and *Prinz Eugen* steering southwards near the ice at the northern end of Denmark Strait in patchy fog and snow showers with visibility varying from one to ten miles. *Bismarck* fired three salvos and the two cruisers turned away. Her speed was twenty-seven knots, and the two cruisers spread and followed astern on either quarter, *Norfolk* using her new radar with great advantage. *Bismarck* made sudden turns and fired whenever a cruiser came in sight — but there were no hits, though some shots fell close. Both *Bismarck* and *Prinz Eugen* made occasional smoke screens. Later *Bismarck* reduced speed to twenty-five knots. *Hood* and *Prince of Wales* set a course to close her.

At about this time, Hugh, who had been almost continuously on the C.-in-C.'s bridge awaiting an enemy report or whatever other information might affect the chase, went down to the wardroom for a cup of tea and fell asleep in his chair, where for eleven hours he was undisturbed.

Meanwhile all through that night, *Norfolk* and *Suffolk* were transmitting enemy reports at frequent intervals recording each alteration of course and speed. Vice-Admiral Wake-Walker in *Norfolk* and the captain of the ship stood watch and watch on the bridge, but neither got more than a few minutes of sleep throughout that period. *Norfolk*'s radar operator crew stuck to their instrument and refused all offers of relief until at long last after thirty-two hours of continuous alert operation they lost contact with *Bismarck*.

By now the Admiralty had summoned the old battleship *Ramillies* near Newfoundland. They also (at 10.22 a.m. on the 24th May) ordered *Rodney* the 16-inch gun battleship, who was just sailing from the south of England for a refit in the United States, as well as the five Tribal-class destroyer group in mid-Atlantic, to join the C.-in-C. At 2 a.m. on 24th May, Admiral Somerville in the carrier *Ark Royal* with the cruiser *Southampton* and a destroyer screen sailed north-westwards from Gibraltar.

At 5.25 a.m. on 24th May, *Hood* and *Prince of Wales* sighted *Bismarck* and *Prinz Eugen*, the latter leading because *Bismarck*'s radar had broken down. Hugh being duty officer on the admiral's bridge took their signal to the C.-in-C. The enemy was ahead and Vice-Admiral Holland made a signal to turn so that all guns could bear, but they were "over the horizon" and still out of range. As range closed both sides opened fire, *Hood* on *Prinz Eugen* (supposing her to be *Bismarck* as she was in the lead), but corrected her mistake after the third salvo. Her first shot on *Prinz Eugen* was over, but the second shot and the third made three hits, one on the bows which didn't explode, though water flooded two compartments. The second shell hit the armour on the port side below the waterline which sprang a plate but did not enter, though two compartments were flooded. A third shell, believed to be from

Prince of Wales, wrecked the boat-deck but didn't explode. In all five men were slightly injured. Her speed was reduced to twenty-seven knots and the forward oil tanks were isolated and could not be used. The first shot to hit *Hood* was an 8-inch shell fired by *Prinz Eugen*.

Prince of Wales had not completed gun trials when she went to sea and had forty-three dockyard workmen on board, but five of her ten 14-inch guns could not fire. Before Vice-Admiral Holland had sailed, he and the captains of the two ships had been sent for by the C.-in-C., who gave a clear instruction that *Hood* was not to close to a damaging range and that *Prince of Wales* was to keep clear of gun-fire as far as possible and that their role was to attempt to inflict damage, but primarily to maintain contact and report *Bismarck*'s position so that *King George V* and *Victorious* could intercept. *Prince of Wales* was obviously not fit for serious action, though capable of doing appreciable damage at maximum range. *Hood*, a World War I battle-cruiser, was about twenty-five years old and had not been constructed as a heavily armoured ship, though a quantity of armour plating had been added from time to time. Her underwater protection was out of date and a careful study of her construction had been made as soon as she joined the Home Fleet at Scapa, with the result that it was reported by inspecting officers that a single torpedo striking in the favourable area (which was very large indeed) could sink the ship. She was therefore the object of anxiety rather than a valued reinforcement. Still, her speed of thirty-one knots gave her a special importance, for no other large ship afloat could match that, and she was an ideal opponent for the German battle-cruisers *Scharnhorst* and *Gneisenau*.

Hood had just completed the turn when (probably) two of *Bismarck*'s shells hit her amidships at a range of about 19,000 yards, which gave them a very steep angle of descent. Watchers from the *Prince of Wales* saw a tremendous explosion amidships; the bows and stern lifted and then disappeared beneath the water. There must have been a magazine explosion. Seconds later a shell exploded close to the bridge in *Prince of Wales*, the captain being knocked senseless and the navigator beside him being seriously wounded, and everyone else, except the signal boatswain, killed. Fortunately the captain quickly regained consciousness, dragged himself to his feet and gave the order down a voice-pipe to the quartermaster to put the wheel hard over, for he had seen that his ship was just about to run over the centre of *Hood*'s wreckage, and his first thought was to avoid possible survivors — of whom there were in fact only three. One thousand four hundred and sixteen officers and men were lost. Of the only two shells that hit the *Prince of Wales*, one failed to explode. *Prince of Wales*, who now had only two guns firing, withdrew beyond gun range and continued to shadow *Bismarck*, who was now seen to be alone, as *Prinz Eugen*, with a heavy list, had just been detached to make for, presumably, Brest. Evidently, *Bismarck* had used this moment of confusion to despatch the cruiser, short of fuel and leaking as she was. *Bismarck* had by now fired forty shells in all at the two ships.

The loss of "the mighty *Hood*", as she was known world-wide, was a shock to the ships at sea — not unforseen, but still, unexpected. We had thought that with luck her speed would save her, but she could only have been saved by retreating and keeping out of range, and that has never been recognised as a wholly correct action in the face of an enemy who, on this occasion, was an unknown quantity. She could only have been certainly saved by keeping her in harbour, and she was not built for that purpose. The risk was recognised — and had to be accepted.

Once again it was Hugh who had to take the fatal signal to the C.-in-C. who was, when it arrived, in his sea cabin a few feet away from the bridge. He immediately ordered *Prince of Wales* to disengage and shadow.

Meanwhile *Norfolk* and *Suffolk* had joined *Prince of Wales* in shadowing, and at 7.15 a.m. on 24th May, *Suffolk* reported a fire blazing at the fore end in *Bismarck* and that her speed was reduced, and at 12.35 p.m. an aircraft from Iceland reported that *Bismarck* was leaving a considerable wake of oil, which we in the Fleet flagship hoped might indicate a shell hit. At 2.20 p.m. the C.-in-C. ordered *Victorious* to prepare a dusk attack. She was to be escorted by four cruisers and after the dusk attack, timed for 10 p.m. on the 24th, she was to return to Scapa with the last cruiser which had sufficient fuel to escort her. The destroyers and the cruisers were to fuel in Iceland when this became necessary.

At 9.57 p.m. on 24th May, the C.-in-C. made a general signal to the Fleet: "Hope to engage *Bismarck* from eastward about 9 a.m. on 25th May." At fifteen minutes past midnight, *Victorious* reported that an air torpedo attack had been completed and one hit was claimed, though not certain. A German prisoner of war later said that "There was a hit and a column of water shot up as high as the masthead, but the hull was not penetrated, and a petty officer nearby suffered a fracture of the skull."

Three of *Victorious'* Swordfish aircraft were lost, and those returning on board reported very heavy anti-aircraft fire, though their attack, in two waves, was pressed home, and they said that they might have failed to find *Bismarck* altogether until her guns started firing. Later, a Swordfish aircraft that had been in the attack took off about 8 a.m. on reconnaissance and got lost. He landed at 1.15 p.m. alongside an empty lifeboat and found sails, water and some brandy, and set sail north-westwards "for America". After some days they observed that the gunner's feet had become badly frozen, so they altered course to north for Greenland. Presently they met a boat full of Danish survivors from a merchantman, who advised a north-easterly course for Iceland which was nearer, and on 3rd June, after nine days at sea in mostly bad weather, they were picked up by a small Icelandic ship. The air pilot was well on arrival at Reykjavik, but the other two spent some weeks in hospital.

At 2.45 a.m. on 25th May, the Admiralty signalled two D/F bearings of *Bismarck* transmissions obtained by a Greenland station: at 0148/25 D/F bearing was 320°; at 0159 it was 327° — this spread of seven degrees in only eleven minutes indicated that they were not very reliable. Greenland bearings we knew were sometimes 20° in error, probably due to Polar electrical disturbances.

At 3.06 a.m. on 25th May, *Suffolk* reported that radar contact had been lost. *Bismarck* was now lost. At 6.16 a.m. Vice-Admiral Wake-Walker in *Norfolk* reported that he believed *Bismarck* had turned eastward, but gave no hard evidence to support his view. At 9.06 a.m. *Repulse* was detached to Iceland, short of fuel. At 9.19 a.m. *Victorious* reported her aircraft were searching, and also her escort of four cruisers. About the same time the force from Gibraltar under Admiral Somerville reported that he was on a course to intercept and assuming *Bismarck* was going to Brest — again an opinion but no concrete evidence.

The C.-in-C. had also received a report saying that a heavy mooring suitable for a large ship had been laid in Brest harbour a few days previously. The opinion now offered indicated Brest as the destination, but on the admiral's bridge in *King George V* other possiblities were explored. She might have turned north-westward to disappear into the Hudson Bay area to refuel from an auxiliary. There would be ice-floes, and probably fog or snow showers up there. Japan was also an outside possible destination. The South Atlantic, too, we knew to be harbouring a number of supply ships to supply lone raiders. St. Nazaire, on the west coast of France, had a large dock which might be able to accommodate *Bismarck*. Vigo in northern Portugal, is a deep-water anchorage and virtually undefended, and could possibly supply repair facilities and fuel oil. On the bridge, they discussed all these possibilities.

The C.-in-C. decided to turn to the north-eastward, which would bring them nearer to Brest, and also nearer to fuel coming from a British port (and *K.G.5* was beginning to get low on this), and also nearer to an intercepting position should *Bismarck* decide to turn back to Norway. He felt doubtful of Brest as her destination because of the very heavy bombing that harbour had been receiving from the RAF when other raiders had sought refuge there. He took this course as a sort of optimum waiting position pending any further information of *Bismarck*'s whereabouts.

Then at 9.27 a.m. D/F bearings from two stations in Britain at 270° and 299° were received. Hugh's special wireless party had listened to *Bismarck*'s long cyphered transmission, and he was expecting to get bearings from some of the shore stations he knew would be listening. These D/F bearings gave a spread of 27 degrees, which is enormous, and when placed on a Mercator's chart, where the two earlier D/F bearings of *Bismarck* had been plotted, produced a vague triangle of over 300 miles broad within which *Bismarck* would probably be. He took this immediately to the chief of staff who was in the plotting room at the rear end of the bridge. Then it was shown to the C.-in-C., to whom he explained the above details.

"Well, that doesn't get us anywhere, does it? I think we must hope for a sighting by one of the long range air patrols who will be getting into the area now."

Two days before leaving Scapa a new form of chart for plotting D/F bearings more accurately had reached Hugh. He began to study the procedure, discovered that he could not understand some of the printed instructions, and took the whole package to the Master of the Fleet (Commander Lloyd, who was both the navigating officer of *King George V* and also the navigation specialist on the C.-in-C.'s staff). The two of them pored over the instructions for a while and then Commander Lloyd was called away, and neither of them spent any more time to obtain an understanding of the procedure before the flagship sailed, since there was a great deal going on then, because *Bismarck* was on the move. The chief of staff now told Hugh to plot the bearings on the new chart and see if any better result emerged. After about twenty minutes wrestling with this he found that he was still unable to understand the procedure — and these bearings that he had tentatively laid off on the new chart he left lying on a table in the plotting room when he was called away to attend to other matters, and, as he left the plotting room, told the chief of staff that he hadn't been able to work the thing out by the new procedure. He alone had, however, observed the vitally important point that the latest two D/F bearings showed that *Bismarck* had not moved to the northward from her last known position, and this she must have done if she was breaking back to Norway or going off to Hudson's Bay. He went back direct to the C.-in-C. with the Mercator's chart in his hand and stated this conclusion which he had reached. The admiral examined the chart, checked that the bearings were correctly laid off on it, and then accepted Hugh's conclusion; and immediately altered course to the south-eastward, which was a course that would intercept *Bismarck* if she were proceeding to Brest or elsewhere to the southward. This was the crucial move which would either lose the *Bismarck* or else catch her, and Hugh felt certain that the C.-in-C. had made the correct decision.

On 26th May, at 9.30 a.m. the 8-inch cruiser *Dorsetshire*, *en route* to England from South America, reported her intention to join in the search. At 10.30 a.m. a searching RAF Catalina flying boat sighted *Bismarck*, course 150° (which made Brest her probable destination), speed twenty knots. The last previous sighting report had been made thirty-one hours ago. At 10.47 a.m. the C.-in-C. made a general signal estimating *Bismarck*'s position at 8.52 a.m. as 57N, 33W, and that all Home Fleet forces should search accordingly. Then at 11.14 a.m. on the 26th, *Ark Royal* flew off a torpedo attack force in very bad weather. Later at 3.44 p.m. *Rodney* joined *K.G.5* and they all heaved an enormous sigh of relief. She carried ten 16-inch guns. At 5.15 p.m., the C.-in-C. signalled to *Rodney*: "Have reduced to twenty-two knots to economise fuel. Our main hope lies in *Bismarck* being slowed down by aircraft." *Rodney* was also told not to keep accurate station but make the best speed she could, and not to lose sight. Her best recent speed had been twenty knots, for she was long out of dry dock. This afternoon she made twenty-one knots, and at 5.35p.m. *Rodney* signalled: "Conditions in engine-room are very severe but I do not wish to reduce speed in case you go on and I get left behind." In fact a steady stream of men were collapsing from heat and exhaustion down below and her fuel position was so critical that a large volunteer crew including some officers off duty were bailing oil out of the last corners of compartments in buckets and transferring it to other compartments where suction had not yet been lost. They did a wonderful job that day. Nobody wanted to be left behind. At about this time, a destroyer five miles astern reported sighting a submarine.

At 6 p.m. *Ark Royal* reported that her first striking force had scored no hits and that aircraft shadowing had lost touch with *Bismarck*; and furthermore a second striking force would take off at 6.30 p.m.

What had happened was this: the cruiser *Sheffield* had gone ahead towards *Bismarck* to act as a guiding radio beacon, when the first wave suddenly appeared out of low clouds and, mistaking her for *Bismarck*, fired nearly all their torpedoes at her, which fortunately missed, some exploding when they hit the water. A new magnetic pistol was defective. Later *Sheffield* at nine miles range was fired at by *Bismarck* and a near miss caused eleven casualties but only slight material damage.

At 7.30 p.m. *Ark Royal* aircraft reported: "Enemy laying smoke screen." At 7.45 p.m. *Sheffield* (who had radar) reported: "Lost touch with *Bismarck*." Then at 10.25 p.m., *Ark Royal*'s second wave attack reported : "Scored one torpedo hit. Possible second hit on starboard quarter."

Later Admiral Somerville reported that in very rough sea *Ark Royal*'s flight-deck had been rising and falling twenty-six feet, in spite of which the second wave landed on in semi-darkness with only three aircraft slightly damaged. Experienced fliers commented that such a feat had never before been attempted, and that they would have declared it impossible. It was but one more example of the exceptional quality of the airmanship of the Fleet Air Arm. They did, of course, have the alternative of the storm-tossed Atlantic waves to spur them on!

At 10.51 p.m., a destroyer reported sighting *Bismarck* nine miles distant, but she had little confidence in her estimated position, for the bad weather had prevented taking star or sun sights for four days past. She attacked with torpedoes and then shadowed. By this time, and for the same reasons, the master of the fleet had told the C.-in-C. that his estimated position would be a circle with a diameter of sixty miles, and so everyone was equally uncertain of our position. At 10.51 p.m., the C.-in-C. told the destroyer *Zulu* to fire star shell, but these exploded above the low clouds and were not seen by anyone. Then the admiral ordered another of our destroyer screen to fire star shell, but the cloud base was only about 300 feet, and no one saw those bursts either. The tribal flotilla of destroyers were closing in on *Zulu*, and *Bismarck* fired at several of them at ranges of 20,000 yards while each destroyer closed independently and fired torpedoes as opportunity offered. One report indicated that *Bismarck*'s steering appeared abnormal and irregular. They began to believe in the reality of *Ark Royal*'s aircraft torpedo hit in *Bismarck*'s stern and suspected that her steering gear was damaged.

Captain Vian's destroyer *Cossack* was ordered to transmit wireless signals on full power so that *Rodney* in their company could take a D/F bearing, but *Rodney* never heard the signal. As this destroyer was approaching *Bismarck* to fire torpedoes a shell exploded close alongside without causing any visible damage, though a few pieces of metal fell on board and were quickly collected as souvenirs. Quite a large piece was given to the admiral when they returned to Scapa. At daylight next morning, someone happened to look aloft at *Cossack*'s foremast and noticed that a wireless aerial was broken and hanging down, swinging with the motion of the ship. This meant that no signal that she had transmitted during the dark hours could have been heard. A shell fragment had cut the aerial wire.

At 11.45 p.m. *Ark Royal* reported: "Dawn attack by twelve torpedo aircraft planned." And then at nine minutes past midnight the C.-in-C. signalled *Ark Royal*: "Enemy appears badly damaged, intend engaging from westward at dawn." And then thirty-seven minutes later *Ark Royal* came back with: "After torpedo hit *Bismarck* reduced speed and made complete circles," and that confirmed the guess that her steering gear was damaged. At 1.45 a.m. on 27th May, *Zulu* reported one certain torpedo hit and also a fire seen on *Bismarck*'s fo'c'sle.

At 2.10 a.m., *Norfolk* signalled: "Intend to keep to northward to flank mark for you," which meant that she would take a position from which to report the fall of shot so that the two battleships could correct their aim and be more likely to obtain hits. At 2.34 a.m., *Sikh* reported "Enemy appears stopped," and at 2.36 a.m. the C.-in-C. made to *Cossack*: "Fire star shell every half hour to indicate *Bismarck*'s position." Again, these star shells also burst above the low clouds and were not seen. Twenty minutes later *Cossack* reported: "*Bismarck* still capable of heavy and accurate fire," and fifteen minutes after that, *Maori* reported "Possible submarine". This is what was now feared: that a U-boat might torpedo our two battleships and so prevent them from making contact, a possibility that was very real, especially during the dark hours. Shortly after 6.00 a.m., *Maori* reported "*Bismarck* on the move again. Course 160°. Speed 7 knots."

A little later they knew that *Ark Royal* would be flying off her air dawn torpedo attack and that the cruiser *Sheffield* would be steering for *Bismarck*'s last known position to act as a radio direction beacon. Then presently, in the early grey dawn, a black shape appeared, nobody in the flagship being sure that it was not *Bismarck*. Two or three tense minutes passed as our battleship's guns trained on the dark object, and then Hugh yelled out: "It's *Sheffield*. She has two funnels and *Bismarck* has only one." Recognition signals were of course exchanged, but this takes time, and in such dusky and stormy conditions signals are not always clearly distinguishable. They had scarcely caught their breath again when, with a roar above the wind, torpedo-carrying aircraft were diving in to attack our two battleships and nobody could identify them with certainty. None of us had, in fact, actually seen German torpedo-carrying aircraft, and it was known that on the East Coast of England they had sometimes used the British red-white-and-blue roundel identification mark. Hugh had binoculars trained on them, but rain splashed into the eyepiece and he could see nothing for what seemed an age. The admiral demanded "What are they, Hugh? You ought to know!" There was a prolonged pause while he mopped the rain out of the binoculars, and then at last, "I saw a roundel! They're ours!" The admiral ordered down the voice-pipe to the captain's bridge: "Hold your fire! Don't shoot!"

The aircraft were now about 500 yards away when their squadron leader fired a red Very's light indicating to his squadron not to fire as the ships they saw were friendly. This time it was a little more difficult to catch one's breath again. It was a call much too close for comfort.

Next a signal came in from the Admiralty (at 7.07 a.m.) that two, possibly five U-boats might be in the area, and immediately afterwards *Cossack* came up with: "*Bismarck* continually altering course. Speed 8 knots." This did not sound like ordinary zigzagging; *Cossack* would have recognised that and would have said so. By now, though, no ship after four days of cloudy skies knew her geographical position within a radius of probably fifty miles, yet they felt certain that *Bismarck* must be very close. Our ships had closed up at day action stations just before first daylight a couple of hours ago and breakfast in the form of corned beef sandwiches and thick cocoa had been distributed through *K.G.5*. Hugh had now been continuously on the bridge for twenty-two hours and kept going with small packets of dates in his pocket and sundry cups of cocoa. From time to time the admiral's steward had been appearing on the bridge with large trays stacked with this welcome cocoa. Hugh noticed that the C.-in-C. didn't take anything when the tray was offered him, and so quietly took a cup and half a sandwich in his hand and offered it to Admiral Tovey at an opportune quiet moment. The admiral looked at it, and then at Hugh: "No, I can't eat now." Hugh answered: "You're going to need it presently, Sir! Try the cocoa; it's hot." And he did, and gulped down the sandwich as well a little later on.

If they thought at all at this time, probably all of them feeling a little shaky inside, they wondered how things were on board *Bismarck*. Perhaps she was feeling much the same. And who would have to swim today? Perhaps both of them?

Prisoners from the *Bismarck*, and there were 247 of them out of a total of 3,350 persons on board, later gave their story.

To begin with a German gunnery officer recorded that *Hood*'s gun-fire had been very accurate. Action had commenced at 4.42 a.m. on 24th May, and *Hood* blew up at 4.58 a.m. Hitler had sent him an Iron Cross — by wireless of course. The hit by *Victorious*' first aircraft torpedo attack had cut off fifty per cent of the oil fuel by breaking a main oil line connection running from the forward tanks to the after tanks which they could not repair with their own resources. At 11.50 a.m. on 25th May, about nine hours before the first sighting of the Catalina aircraft (at which they fired), Rear-Admiral Lutjens addressed the ship's company on a loudspeaker. He hoped for aircraft and also U-boat assistance, but the best he could expect was "to take one or two opponents with him to the bottom". His speech caused the deepest depression. Some friction then arose between the admiral's staff and the ship's officers as a result of the speech. False information received from German aircraft at this time caused half a day's loss on their planned course. By evening, however, spirits had begun to rise again as *Bismarck* entered the U-boat zone, and expectations of aircraft and U-boat support revived.

Bismarck, facing fuel shortage, was obliged to reduce speed, and in some measure therefore, manoeuverability. *Ark Royal*'s first air torpedo attack in the late afternoon had not secured any hit and one or two aircraft had been shot down — which was not very encouraging. But the second attack, when it was very nearly dark, was mortal. One hit forward caused some damage, but a second hit on or near the rudder resulted in the rudder being jammed in the "hard over" position. The captain tried to steer with varying propellor speeds, but found that the jammed rudder prevented him from keeping the ship on any course, so he stopped and sent down divers who worked for about three hours, twice placing explosive charges to blow off the rudder during the night. These attempts failed, and the project had to be abandoned.

By now our six Tribal-class destroyers (the latest and most powerful in the Royal Navy) were in contact, sometimes making smoke screens, circling round to fire torpedoes. In all they fired sixteen and got three hits. *Bismarck* fired at most of these, though none was hit, and the flash of her guns enabled one of them to get into 3,000 yards range. The longest range shot was only 7,000 yards. The Polish destroyer *Piorum*, who sighted *Bismarck* momentarily at 10.38 p.m. was with this flotilla but very low on fuel, and the flotilla captain ordered her to Plymouth to refuel when she failed to make further contact in the dark. He knew that the Poles intended to close in to use their armament and he wanted to prevent the certain loss of a valuable ally. Twice during the night, perhaps from our destroyer gun hits, fires on deck flared up on *Bismarck*.

Bismarck got under way as soon as the divers were up and yawed to and fro in a way that was uncontrollable and occasionally made complete circles while waiting dismally for air or submarine support, and this went on until her end. A few Heinkel 111s were sent out, and one of these reported hearing a U-boat homing beacon signal, but cloud at 900 feet and poor visibility prevented him from finding *Bismarck*. Commander Rotherham, flying from Hatston, and the rest of the Fleet Air

Arm, had been trained to succeed in these quite customary weather conditions.

Through all this long ordeal, *Bismarck*'s ship's company were kept closed up at action stations, and for three days and three nights suffered intense discomfort and scarcely had more than momentary intervals of sleep. Perhaps too, the reader will experience something of the pressures and confusion that fall upon a Commander-in-Chief in sea warfare.

The final action was a nightmare, with heavy shells constantly exploding inside the hull, and within minutes communication lines failed in all directions so that orders could only be passed by messenger, and these mostly failed to reach their destinations. The interior of the ship became a series of jagged iron wells out of which nobody could climb. Wounded and dying could be heard yelling, but were left where they fell; no rescue, no help was, or perhaps could be, offered. It became a place of "each man for himself". The guns fired while they could, but after the first few minutes the control apparatus broke down and one sort of explosion seemed much the same as another. Men were losing their minds, running about aimlessly, screaming. If you tried to stop one he would probably attack you like a wild animal. Gradually a sort of mass urge to get out onto the deck developed, and when men managed to reach it they ran through exploding shell fire quite blindly following others ahead of them, and if they got as far as the stern jumped over the side into the sea, some of them just blown into the water in the blast of an exploding shell. Almost the last sight recorded was that of the captain, whom they admired, standing out on the fo'c'sle, apparently waving to some men in the water while they waited to go down with the ship. The talking survivor rambled on and on, and one wondered if he had really yet recovered his mind — or ever would.

But we have left Admiral Tovey eating half a sandwich from one hand and taking gulps of hot cocoa from a thick white cup held in the other, dressed in a very old cap with its deeply tarnished heavy gold oak leaves on its peak, a sea-worn knee-length dark blue British warm overcoat with collar turned up and a muffler round his neck, trousers stuffed into his sea-boots, his usual destroyer captain's sea rig. The chief of staff and plotting team — about a dozen in all — are crammed into the little plotting room with its charts, radar screen and maps covering two or three small tables at the rear of the bridge, all visible through the open door. On the bridge, about eighteen feet wide by twelve feet fore and aft, stand at the sides Pat Matheson, the fleet signal officer, with his inseparable telescope under his arm and a signal book in one hand, the skin of his freckled Scots' face tight drawn; and the signal boatswain, a short square hard-bitten elderly warrant officer, with his cap jammed well down over his ears, for he will spend his day out in the wind supervising the dispatch of signals by semaphore, flashing lamps, or flags from the small signal deck immediately below him at the rear end of the bridge. The only other person there is Hugh, also muffled up in a British warm overcoat and sea-boots, with enormous heavy binoculars slung round his neck, in one hand a small board with a clip fixed on it to hold the steady stream of signals he receives from a little tube and shows to the admiral as they reach him. These were fourteen inches deep by the end of the day. He measured them just to see.

It must have been about 8 a.m. when the C.-in-C. called up the captain of the ship by voice-pipe and said he would like the chaplain to say a prayer over the loudspeaker. A few minutes later the familiar voice came over the air, calm and controlled, with few words but meaning just what it said. It seemed so very right, and it relaxed the tension.

Shortly after that the admiral's steward came up from his sea cabin with binoculars which he handed to the admiral.

"Hugh, I want you to use these on the *Bismarck*. You are to tell me everything exactly as you see it. They are the latest thing; only about a dozen of them have been made. I got them just before we sailed, but they are too heavy for me and would get in my way." So Hugh put the leather sling over his head and when they settled on his chest they were indeed heavy. At once he put them to his eyes and adjusted the focus on a distant destroyer. The image was incredibly clear, and he said:

"They are terrific, Sir!"

"Don't forget; everything you see; and don't expect an answer from me. Keep your eye on that range recorder dial as well, and let me know whenever the range changes." So those were his "battle instructions".

The destroyer, *Maori*, had been passing enemy position reports since 6.08 a.m. *Ark Royal* signalled at 7.07 a.m. the cancellation of further air sorties "due to indentification difficulties", so evidently *Sheffield* had told Admiral Somerville of the hazardous moments we had just experienced from this very thing. While landing-on, several of our own bombs fell close to the carrier *Ark*

Royal but did not do any damage. No enemy aircraft attacked her.

Then at 7.50 a.m. they sighted *Norfolk* about sixteen miles to the north as a passing squall unveiled her, and in a very good position for flank marking, too. Five minutes later she and *Suffolk* were firing with their whole armament to the southward of her, so we knew that they were steaming straight at the *Bismarck*, who ought to have been silhouetted against the eastern sky but was invisible. *Norfolk* zigzagged widely to avoid *Bismarck*'s return fire, but they only saw very few shell splashes around her, and as there was no sign that she was hit they supposed that most splashes were below the horizon, and also frequent passing rain squalls could have hidden many of them. This went on for fifty minutes, and one felt the tension growing.

About 8.46 a.m., *Rodney* was ordered to open her distance to half a mile and manoeuvre independently to keep guns bearing. Since her 16-inch nine gun armament was all on her fo'c'sle, this meant a head-on approach. *K.G.5* had six 14-inch guns on her fo'c'sle and four aft on the quarterdeck. *Bismarck* had four 15-inch guns forward and four aft all mounted in twin gun turrets so that she would try to keep beam on to us if all her guns were to bear at the same time. What was not yet known was that a shell from *Norfolk* had hit the main gun control position at the top of the tower and killed the whole team of forty-three men; that would be the "first eleven" gun control experts.

At long, long last out of a rapidly moving thick dark rain squall appeared a huge ship's bow, pointing at us with a great wide tower about 100 feet high with a very fat funnel behind it, larger and more solid-looking than anything we had seen before. Later on it transpired that she was a 56,000 ton ship, not the 44,000 tons which the Washington Arms Limitation Treaty had specified and which Hitler had signed and immediately betrayed.

It was instantly apparent that she must be a much larger ship than any known antagonist. But we counted her guns unconsciously yet again and wondered if she also intended to engage bows on, forgetting for the moment that she could not steer a steady course — could not steer at all, in fact. And she only had the second, less expert gun control crew to direct her fire, and from a second-rate position in the conning tower.

At 8.48 a.m., *Rodney* fired a ranging salvo of five guns and Hugh watched the diminishing black footballs that were her shells soaring up in a great arc until they vanished in the low grey clouds.

Then *Bismarck* fired her four forward guns, and their shots at the present 23,000 yards range would reach us in about forty-five seconds. *K.G.5* fired an instant later and her four shells were again visible. A long time seemed to elapse before Hugh saw a tall splash shoot up close to *Rodney*'s bow, much of the water falling on her fo'c'sle deck. (This in fact cracked a ship's side scuttle and some water flooded into the adjacent compartment, and that was the only damage she suffered that day.) A moment or two later a three-gun salvo fell close ahead of *K.G.5*, 1,000 and 400 yards short and 200 yards over. *Bismarck* spun round and seemed to be zigzagging on enormously wide changes of course, sometimes firing from both turret groups, but within a very few minutes reducing to only one or two-gun salvoes, and then Hugh knew that, whatever else might yet happen, she was beaten.

K.G.5 and *Rodney* kept their bows pointing at the target and the occasional splashes of their shots were unmistakable, *Rodney*'s being a tall white pillar sixty feet high and *K.G.5*'s like a broad low puff of cotton wool, so that gunnery officers always knew exactly where their own shells had landed. But that was not quite true, for, although both ships kept firing at about forty-five second intervals, only very occasional splashes were visible. Our armour-piercing shells were certainly hitting, *Rodney*'s the largest, at that date, ever fired in sea battle. *Rodney* also had a new type super-large torpedo firing ahead, and during the course of the action fired nineteen of them. It was never known if she obtained any hits, because shells were continuously exploding on the target. When she got home a report of this filtered through to some civil supply department, and they arose in wrath and demanded justification for such a "grossly extravagant expenditure", since each torpedo cost over twenty thousand pounds. The angry letter reached the C.-in-C., and Hugh happened to be with him when he read it.

"Look at this!" he exploded. "What do they expect us to do with their torpedoes! Fetch me the War Manual over on that shelf!" Hugh gave it to him.

"Yes. I thought so. Here it is!" and he read out the paragraph which ordered commanding officers of HM ships to "use every weapon at their command as circumstances permit".

"That will fix them!" the admiral said. A lifetime in a civil service department is really no preparation at all for warfare; nevertheless they supported the Fleet with their utmost efforts throughout five long years, and there were very few failures, even while they lived under heavy and continuous bombing conditions.

Hugh's eye was turning with increasing frequency to the range dial which he could hear ticking its alterations: 17,000 yards, 16, 15. Then the C.-in-C. reduced speed to fifteen knots. 14,000 yards, 13,500, 13, 12, until at 8,300 Hugh could bear it no longer and walked over to the admiral, stood directly in front of him and said:

"Range 8,300, Sir. The range is 8,300 yards!"

"Yes; yes, I've got that." For a fleeting moment he wondered if the admiral intended to ram *Bismarck*! She showed no sign whatever of sinking as yet.

As the firing went on and on, cruisers and destroyers closed in and opened up, and at one moment Hugh reported eight flaming orange explosions along the whole length of *Bismarck*'s superstructure — probably a broadside from an 8-inch cruiser. Then came a brief sound of cheering, almost, one felt, light relief. *Piorum*, the Polish destroyer, who had been sent off to Plymouth to refuel the night before, suddenly appeared from nowhere, belching funnel smoke at apparently full speed, a large Polish ensign streaming out from the stern, with every gun blazing furiously at *Bismarck* — and she would have been a difficult target to hit as she zigzagged into about 3,000 yards range in broad daylight. One wondered if *Bismarck*'s guns could depress far enough to hit her, for she got so very close at the end of her run before she turned away. The admiral watched her, smiling:

"Well, she doesn't intend to miss a chance!" He spoke of this later on with admiration.

And then on board *Bismarck* an upper deck ready-use anti-aircraft ammunition locker got hit and small shells flew up in the air in all directions and exploded like a firework display. But the now almost silent turrets were the most impressive of all. The lower fo'c'sle turret had its rear end plate stripped off, perhaps sixty feet long and twenty feet high, and it bounded across the deck and came to rest against the superstructure in the rear. Then, at a later stage, when only 4,000 yards distant, the right fifteen-inch gun of the upper turret was seen to be bent upwards at a 30° angle half-way along its barrel. Later a photograph taken by a doctor in a destroyer confirmed this extraordinary fact. Until then, Hugh had been loath to speak of it, for one would have judged it an impossibility. A shell presumably hit it at an enormous velocity. After about fifteen minutes of action the very large and high bridge tower structure suddenly began to glow a dull cherry red, the colour spreading rapidly up to the very top. All personnel stationed there must have been incinerated. A heavy gun salvo had obviously detonated at its base. Hugh could see that the heavily armoured conning-tower structure was separated from and slightly before the bridge tower, and this did not change colour.

The author wonders, why recount all this horror story? There is only one justification: that people should know what really happens to the men who do the actual fighting.

The battle is not over — the last range at which we (the two battleships) fired was 3,300 yards on the bridge dial, and Hugh saw great black holes dotted about *Bismarck*'s side plating. Quite early in the action, he noticed along her upper deck first a little trickle and then a solid stream of white-clad men running or walking towards the stern where almost all of them paused until the next shell exploded, obliterating some or all of them even before they leaped into the stormy sea, and drifted away astern, while *Bismarck*'s propellors kept revolving steadily at a slow speed.

The admiral was repeatedly asking Hugh: "Can you see her colours?"

"Yes, Sir. The naval ensign is at her stern." Then a little later: "The stern ensign is gone, Sir, but there is a small one flying at the mainmast-head."

"Are you sure she hasn't hauled down her colours? Check it again."

"No, Sir. They are still flying at the mainmast-head."

"We ought to stop firing but I can't while she is still in action. Are you sure you can see her colours flying?"

"Yes, Sir. They are still flying."

This must have gone on for another ten, perhaps fifteen minutes, until in a desperate sort of voice he ordered Pat Matheson to hoist the "Cease Fire" signal. This was followed by a general signal: "All ships having torpedoes fire them at *Bismarck*." A cruiser and several destroyers closed in and fired. *Bismarck* looked to be a little lower in the water and she was very sluggish in rising to the increasing seas. Then her engines appeared to stop. *Dorsetshire*, an 8-inch cruiser, appeared from somewhere in South America and the admiral ordered her to close and "Sink *Bismarck* with torpedoes". She steamed down the starboard side at a distance of about 500 yards and fired six torpedoes, rounded the stern and fired another six into the port side. *Bismarck* seemed even more sluggish to rise to the seas but very little if any lower in the water. A signal had been made to the Admiralty: "I can't sink *Bismarck* by gun-fire." We did think, however, that in time, if only we could have time, she ought to go down. A German aircraft and then a U-boat were reported in the vicinity, and the Admiralty signalled that Heinkel bombers had taken off from a French airfield. *Dorsetshire* now went alongside the starboard quarter and rescued about 75 men, but had to move away, for she made a sitting target for U-boats, one of which had just been sighted.

There came in about now (presumably Churchill's) famous signal: "*Bismarck* must be sunk at all costs." The C.-in-C. looked furious when Hugh handed it to him.

"All very well, but if I stay here and keep on firing, these Heinkels and the U-boats will get at me, and if I don't leave now we shall run out of oil on the way home."

He made a signal to the Admiralty asking for tugs and an oiler to be sailed to the westward, reporting our fuel shortage at the same time. That seemed to quieten them down.

At last he sent *Rodney* off to refuel and onwards to the United States for her refit, and *K.G.5* turned to the course for home. A signal came in reporting that half a dozen fishing boats flying the Spanish flag had been sighted in the area, which was some consolation to the admiral, who said he hoped they would manage to pick up survivors. As they steamed away *Bismarck* was wallowing in the seas, not rising or falling at all, and she disappeared astern, blotted out by the hazy smoke from *K.G.5*'s funnels. The Royal Marines manning the turret on the quarterdeck aft were ordered to keep a sharp lookout on *Bismarck* and report any changes in her situation. Hugh was told to go to some place where he could watch her and he found a place on the signal deck below and behind the bridge where he was underneath the funnel haze and able to see her clearly. He watched only for a few minutes, and then through his big binoculars saw at 10.26 a.m. the stern slowly disappear beneath the water and the very long pointed bow rise almost vertically in the air and then slide downwards out of sight. The whole thing lasted hardly more than one minute. The marine's turret telephoned and he dead-heated on the admiral's bridge with the report that *Bismarck* had sunk, and a signal informing the Admiralty was immediately dispatched. Some of the crew were rescued by destroyers, including *Maori*, who picked up twenty-four. The total was 247. A German engineer officer was found to have a plan of the ship on him, which was a valuable source of information. By now Mr Churchill was making his famous announcement in the House of Commons in London: "The *Bismarck* has sunk!"

Everybody was low on fuel, but most ships were able to join the C.-in-C., and presently a destroyer screen was formed and they went on at an economical speed towards Northern Ireland in a rising wind and sea with frequent rain squalls. The engineer commander of the ship came up with the captain to confer with the C.-in-C. about the tight fuel situation and in the end they got into the Clyde with just 340 tons left out of a normal full cargo of a little over 4,000 tons.

When the fleet turned for home, Hugh had been on the bridge for twenty-six hours and was due to take the afternoon watch at 12.30 p.m., but someone came along and offered to substitute for him, so he went to his cabin and to sleep.

Later on when they rounded the northern coast of Ireland, German reconnaissance aircraft were reported, and for a couple of hours sporadic bombing attacks occurred. One of these hit and sank a destroyer on our screen, but fortunately the weather had calmed down and she floated long enough for a nearby destroyer to pick up the whole of her surviving crew. Hugh was watching all this from the quarterdeck right aft when, with a loud roar, a large Heinkel bomber with Iron Crosses on its wings broke through the low clouds with its small guns firing at the *K.G.5*. As he watched their flashes he suddenly became aware that splinters of wood torn up from the deck were flying all about him. A Bofors anti-aircraft gun mounting struggled to swing round on the target, but only managed to get off a very short burst before the Heinkel vanished into the cloud again.

So *K.G.5* made the Clyde in the end — but only just. It was a critical situation for a battleship of 44,000 tons, and she stayed there long enough to fill her tanks, and then sailed immediately for Scapa Flow.

The normal entrance into Scapa Flow was by the Hoxa Gate, a boom defence of wire nets supported by floating buoys stretched between the islands. In the centre one section of netting attached to winches on board a trawler moored at each of its ends could be lowered to allow traffic to pass through, and then immediately be winched up again into its normal position. The trawlers' crews had been there for almost three years watching ships enter and leave, lowering their net and then heaving it up again, and must have suffered from one of the dullest jobs to be found anywhere afloat.

As *K.G.5* passed in through the net the whole crew of each trawler rushed out on deck and cheered like mad, waving shirts, towels, anything that came to hand — a tremendous enthusiastic welcome home that came as a complete surprise, for they had never before been seen to cast as much as a glance in *K.G.5*'s direction. The C.-in-C. moved out from the cover of the bridge and stood up on a little platform and saluted first one and then the other, and the cheering followed us half a mile into the Flow. This, for Hugh, was the most splendid moment of his service in the war, and the moment at which he suddenly realised that something really great had been accomplished for Britain. Everyone on board was talking about those two trawlers for some days to come; no trawler had ever behaved like that before.

The Admiralty asked the C.-in-C. to send somebody down to the BBC in London to make a broadcast on the action, and Hugh was told to prepare a script as soon as possible. It was vetted by the chief of staff and one or two small alterations were made, and then together they took it in to the admiral.

"Hugh has got his broadcast script ready. You would probably like to see it, Sir, before he leaves for London?"

"No, I don't think so, thank you. They will let me know when you are going on the air and I shall hear it then!"

Hugh's knees wanted to knock. He would greatly have preferred to hear the admiral's comments before, and not after, and was in a sort of suppressed panic until he got back to the ship a few days later and learned that there was no comment, that it was "alright".

The BBC offices had recently been bombed but when he got there the mess had been cleared away and sandbags and boarding hid nearly all the damage. Upstairs a smooth and decisive young man offered a chair and asked him to wait. In another chair sat Professor Harold Laski, a prominent publicist of the day and a very able man. They stared at one another in silence until the man in charge returned and asked Hugh to follow him. Laski sprang up angrily: "And am I to hang about waiting for this officer to finish?"

"I am afraid so, Professor Laski. He has a train to catch to rejoin his ship." The professor looked angrier and flopped back into his chair again. "Really, this is intolerable!"

They took Hugh into a little glass box, adjusted the microphone on the desk, tried out a paragraph and made another adjustment, explained the red and green light drill, and then they left him, closing the glass door carefully. He set his manuscript out, raised a hand, and the green light came on and he couldn't speak for a few seconds, but then plunged into his script. It must have lasted about fifteen minutes. Two of his friends wrote later to say that they had listened to the broadcast and immediately recognised his voice. Nobody ever did say whether they liked it or not! The broadcast was translated into fifty-eight languages and presumably heard over most of the world. The BBC sent him a cheque for eight pounds "for out of pocket expenses"; so they must have made a handsome profit on the business.

This was not, in fact, Hugh's first broadcast. About ten months after the war began, while he was talking to his special petty officer telegraphist in their own minute wireless room about the war news, the man said: "I wish you would explain that to the ship's company, Sir. None of us understands about what is going on. You hear something in the news, but it doesn't make much sense. It's only a little part of what is going on. You could use the ship's broadcast circuit so that everyone could hear."

Hugh thought this over. One of his concerns was the morale of the fleet, and he lost no opportunity of talking with lower deck ratings, and on such occasions quite often noticed that a little group had gathered round. They knew, of course, from his special wireless party that he had access to a great deal of information. Finally he spoke to the chief of staff on this matter and it went on to the captain of the ship and to the C.-in-C.; and all of them liked the idea. So, after all that, usually once a week in the evening, he broadcast a twenty-minute commentary on the current news, and it met with approval in all quarters. It took him eight hours to prepare the talk, but the expenditure of time appeared to be well worthwhile. Other ships did from time to time organise a similar sort of internal news service to suit their own needs. But of course the *Bismarck* broadcast remained for him his star turn.

Chapter 15

Sea War in the North

With the completion of the evacuation of Norway, the war, as far
as the Home Fleet was concerned, took on a new aspect, for action
was not demanded from us minute by minute, but rather it became
a matter of planning ahead. There was still plenty to do, but we
now had time to consider, assess, to balance up the pros and cons.

The absorbing immediate thing was the war in the air, the
"Battle of Britain" as it has become known, in which both sides
extended themselves to the limit of their different possibilities —
and Germany lost. Had this not been the case, an invasion of
Britain would have been attempted. An official estimate issued in
London on 18th August 1940, stated that the enemy had lost 636
aircraft, and probably 260 in addition to that figure, with 244
known damaged. British losses amounted to 164, the figure for
damaged was not published, and 66 downed pilots had been saved.
On 15th September, air reconnaissance showed 2,500 landing
barges mustered on the continental coast in Channel ports. It was
known that plans for invasion definitely existed, and at one
moment, just after Dunkirk, exactly four tanks were available for
defence in the whole territory of Great Britain. Land Defence
Forces (LDV), men over military age, were armed — where they
had any arms at all — with old discarded Territorial Army drill
rifles and bayonets, and a wide variety of shot-guns and rifles
donated by sportsmen all over the country. In central Scotland,
where Hugh spent a few days' leave at that time, the LDV had no
arms whatever beyond a few personal sporting weapons, and they
were drilling with roughly fashioned wooden imitations of a
Service rifle. He asked one of these men, who was in uniform and
on his way to drill, what he was going to do if German parachutists
came down around him.

"Weel ye see, m' wife has a long butcher's knife she uses in the kitchen, an' we keep it hung on a peg on the back door these times!''

The personal safety of the King and the heir to the throne became a matter of public concern. We learned that a submarine was earmarked to go to some obscure west coast harbour where the royal family could secretly embark and proceed to Canada. The story went round that when the king heard of it he flatly refused to go, but would approve of the two princesses being sent out of the country. Then of course the queen heard of it too and tackled Mr Churchill the next time she saw him, and their conversation was reported in this way and, though it may not be authentic, it does serve to illustrate what people were feeling at this critical time:

''I know of course that the king is constitutionally bound to accept the advice of his prime minister. But I am not the King and I shall refuse to leave England no matter what you say!''

So Churchill left the scheme in abeyance, if indeed it ever had been more than a planner's suggestion. Hugh tried once to get him to say what had really happened about this, but he wisely brushed the question aside and didn't answer it; neither did he deny the story. However, the German landing barges steadily increased in density in the Channel ports for many months to come.

On 22nd September, General Decoux in command of French Indo-China, agreed to the Japanese occupation of this French colony, and on 18th October, Japan officially joined the Axis powers, so we were now at war with them too, and the safety of Singapore and Australia came prominently into question.

Far north of Iceland there lies the little island of Jan Mayern, and to which country it belonged appeared to be in dispute, but it had no permanent inhabitants and was only visited occasionally by fishing vessels seeking shelter or replenishment of their fresh water supplies. On 28th September, a trawler sent there to reconnoitre, reported that aircraft could land on a dry lagoon bed, and seaplanes on another wet one when or if it was not frozen.

Towards the northern end a mountain several thousand feet high had its peak almost continuously shrouded in clouds. In due course a small British weather recording station was established in a tent encampment carefully camouflaged and sited near the landing grounds. Weather data from this position was critically important to forecasters for the far north Atlantic area, and the Germans sent a daily long range Fokke-Wulf aircraft to the island to obtain their own weather data, which it reported back. Twice the F-W plane flew into the mountain and exploded, but they never attacked our little weather station. It looked inexpressibly bleak and frigid the only time the Fleet flagship approached it closely; nothing appeared to grow but scattered tussocks of dried-out grass, and of course waterfowl and some sea-lions.

Presently information came to us that one of the German raiders, possibly the pocket battleship *Lutzow*, might be returning home. Most of the Home Fleet was at sea at that moment, and the C.-in-C. quickly organised a line of about fifty ships outside air reconnaissance distance, which covered an area through which the enemy was most likely to pass. The line was seventy miles long and ships had taken up their positions before dark. Nothing happened that night, and Hugh had come up to the admiral's bridge to keep his watch as duty staff officer at 4 a.m. An hour later, just as the first sign of dawn was breaking, a distant ship on the line signalled: "Emergency. Suspicious ship in such-and-such a position." The flagship went to action stations and Hugh had called the admiral before the end of the signal had been read. It turned out to be an Icelandic fishing trawler on its way home. Nothing more happened. Later in the day he was with the admiral and said:

"Well, that was another flop, Sir. I can't think how she missed us. We've tried to catch them so often!"

"Don't be so impatient. We will be lucky if we catch one at the fifteenth shot." As it turned out, the battleship *Bismarck*, which we sank later on, was the fifteenth shot.

Later on we learned that *Lutzow* was fitted with radar, and no doubt this enabled her to escape the net we had spread. The "Northern Patrol" operated between the Faeroe Islands and Iceland, with about eight armed merchant cruisers and a dozen ocean-going armed trawlers, none of which then possessed radar. Their operation was interfered with by the almost constant stormy weather. Any other class of ship would have suffered from much the same disability, and only occasionally could a cruiser be spared to strengthen the patrol.

At this period we were obliged to mount a series of Fleet Air Arm attacks on the Norwegian coast, which were little more than pinpricks, though costly in personnel casualties. The training of new air crews became seriously endangered through the shortage of experienced officers to carry out the training.

With the Norwegian coast freed of British obstruction and now fully open to them, the German submarine attack on the Atlantic shipping steadily increased in spite of the institution of universal convoy. On 2nd September, the USA had agreed to "lend" fifty obsolete four-funnel destroyers for convoy protection in exchange for a ninety-nine year lease of bases in Newfoundland, Bermuda, Jamaica, St. Lucia, Trinidad, Antigua, and British Guyana. This was an invaluable reinforcement even though some of the ships were well worn, but it was, of course, purchased at a considerable cost to us. It was very welcome news on 5th November that American electors voting for President Roosevelt formed a certain majority and that he would be returned as President in January 1941, for there was still a strong Nazi voice to be heard in the United States, and we would not be able to continue the war for long without substantial American support. The industries of Britain were now under daily bombardment and shipping bringing in essential supplies was being sunk at an increasing rate, which new tonnage now building could not fully replace. We had already lost 508 ships of two million tons, and also 253 neutral ships of 800,000 tons had been sunk.

To replace some of these losses an immense increase in merchant tonnage was initiated in the United States and at the same time a new class of ocean-going escort corvettes was begun in many small ports. By the end of the war Canadian naval forces had so greatly increased that their warship tonnage reached third place in world national tonnage — a record not exceeded by any nation.

Atlantic convoys were disrupted early in December by one of the worst Atlantic storms experienced in recent years. The escorting destroyer *Hurricane* in company with *Hesperus* reports as follows:

"Shortly before dawn on 5th December hove to in position 56 N, 18 W, course 290°, speed 7 knots. No barometer on board and difficult to estimate gale intensity but until 2 a.m. on 6th December seas were mountainous and spindrift reduced visiblity to about 500 yards. An officer who had experienced two typhoons in a destroyer in China said they were preferable, for here it was impossible to plot the centre of the depression but wind force was 9—10, direction west. At 2 a.m. wind eased slightly and then increased even more strongly than before. Up to this time there had been no serious damage except gyro compass upper suspension broken and No. 1 dynamo flooded. At 8.30 a.m. a giant wave higher than the bridge broke on machine-gun platforms both sides. Platforms buckled and from there aft the decks were swept practically clear of all fittings and many depth-charges were released from the quarterdeck. At 8.50 a.m., a second wave broke on the bridge structure smashing all window shields. The fo'c'sle was swept clear of all fittings and an inflow of water put the finishing touches to No. 2 dynamo. The diesel dynamo was ordered to be started and the electric load to be taken off the ship. When "B" gun's (the upper gun above the fo'c'sle) protective flare doubled back it put thirty-five degrees deviation into the magnetic steering compass so that the quartermaster now paid off to starboard thinking that he was off course and, before this was spotted, the ship was already 50° off the wind. At this point the dynamo finally stopped and the diesel dynamo had not yet been connected. The ship was in danger of rolling over but "half ahead 130 revolutions" on the outer screw and "slow astern" on the inner screw slowly brought her up into the wind and steering by engines continued until the diesel dynamo was connected. Water was now pouring into the messdecks under the fo'c'sle but was stopped by stuffing clothing and other materials into the ventilation apertures. The ship's company resolutely plugged the leaks so no serious flooding occurred though some stores and provisions were damaged.

"All remaining depth-charges on the quarterdeck were damaged and hatches and guard-rails were rolled backwards out of their traps on deck. On passage home *Hurricane* attempted to escort SS *Arundel Castle* but on certain legs of the zigzag she flooded again and had to leave her and go independently to Liverpool arriving on 9th January." Private conversation at a later date added little to this official report.

There is no doubt that the Atlantic convoy escorts experienced the hardest naval service of the whole war.

At the beginning of the war an Admiralty order had been issued forbidding the presence of women on board warships under any circumstances whatever. It was thought that in the event of a sudden emergency — such as bombing — their presence would interfere with the defence organisation. They were still, in the eyes of 'their lordships', perhaps (to quote Sir Walter Scott) "uncertain, coy, and hard to please". The men's attention to duty at a critical moment might have wandered. Only three years later some of them in the uniform of the WRNS were regularly embarked as telegraphists and coders in the motor torpedo-boat patrols in the Channel and along the east coast, and on several

410

occasions their ships were in action. One or two were wounded. In London women were, of course, the backbone of the Air Raid Emergency Ambulance Service and a number were killed during raids.

Even at Scapa this sort of ice began to melt, and it happened in this way. An agency known as "ENSA" had been developed with the intention of providing all the Forces with live theatrical entertainment wherever they were stationed. Frances Day, a leading London musical comedy star, came to the Orkneys in the autumn of 1941 to do a show for the Army and Royal Air Force personnel manning the shore defences which consisted of anti-aircraft batteries and barrage balloons. Apparently, when she saw the fleet at anchor out in the Flow, she asked the commanding general if she could not go out to at least one of the ships and give her show, and he did not know of any prohibition. One day shortly after lunch Hugh and several other officers, including the C.-in-C. and his chief of staff, were walking up and down the quarterdeck. Hugh observed a signal lantern flashing irregularly from the direction of Stromness, almost eight miles distant. Within a few minutes his binoculars identified for him the general's launch bobbing about in the choppy water and a signalman came to him with a message which briefly stated that Frances Day was on board the launch and was coming to the Fleet flagship. He took the signal to the chief of staff, who showed it to the admiral, and they wrote out a message in reply to say that women were not allowed on board. A winking light replied that they couldn't read the message owing to the violent motion of the steamboat — adding that they would be getting alongside in about twenty minutes' time. The admiral dived down to his cabin and, after a few minutes discussion between the chief of staff and captain of the ship they decided that since they had no way of preventing Frances Day from arriving, she would have to be allowed to come on board, and Hugh was ordered to greet her and tell her that women were not allowed on board. By now snow was beginning to fall, and, as the general's launch came up to the gangway, a minute figure shrouded in a leopard-skin coat with a hood over her head stepped smartly out of the boat and ran laughing up the ladder. She looked simply lovely, and the quartermaster and his side party of bugler and messenger boy, Hugh himself, and indeed the captain of the ship and the chief of staff standing at some little distance all found their faces dissolved into the brightest of welcoming smiles. The two senior officers hurried forward, shook hands warmly and swept the lady off down the admiral's hatchway to his cabin.

It was not long before the bandmaster had been summoned to the admiral's cabin, and half an hour later the concert began under an awning in the waist of the ship where several hundred men off duty were happily gathered.

Hugh had already seen Miss Day's current revue in London, and all England knew the songs she sang out on that deck for the next hour or so. Thereafter ENSA personnel were permitted to do their shows on board warships at Scapa — and in due course elsewhere — with slightly hesitant Admiralty approval. This gift of the theatrical profession to the fighting services became perhaps the strongest support to morale that developed during the war. In the course of time almost every star visited Scapa and, for a curious reason, Hugh soon found himself in official charge of their activities, although this was the proper province of the physical and recreational training officer on the C.-in-C.'s staff.

The "Springer", as he is known in the Service, went off on short leave and, while walking along the bank of a canal, saw a small boy tumble into the ice-cold water. He dived in and rescued the boy, but developed a severe attack of pneumonia and was unable to return to the Fleet flagship for several weeks. Hugh was put temporarily in charge of his department, chiefly because it was felt that he didn't have very much to do anyway — indeed nobody ever had defined his duties, most of which he invented himself as he went along. So it fell out that he was to welcome such great stars as Leslie Henson, Phyllis Monkman, Gracie Fields, Noel Coward, Evelyn Laye, and shepherd them through their programme of performances at Scapa.

Of all the troupers Gracie Fields was the most popular — and also the most distinguished amongst our theatrical artists. When she came to Scapa she appeared at the large canteen on Flotta where about 1,400 sailors managed to squeeze into the crowded seating. She sang her famous songs for two and a half hours with an interval of a Service band concert. Hugh, who was on duty, slipped into the backstage quarters at half-time and found her deadly pale and lying on a camp-bed in apparent collapse and asked her dresser if the concert should be ended. The woman said no, she was tired but would go on with the second half of the programme, which she did, he thought by a miracle. After it was over she walked a quarter of a mile down to the jetty to go off elsewhere, and the whole audience formed a huge lane of cheering fleet men while she talked to those who were nearest. It was the most splendid reception to an artist that he ever saw anywhere. That day she gave five performances, four of them being about fifty minutes long.

During the two days of her visit she spoke of the very large sums of dollar currency she had raised through concerts in the United States in order to help the flagging sterling exchange balance, and was indignant with some press complaints that she was having a "good time" while everyone else was working — a charge that was false in face of the published figures. She had founded an orphanage near Brighton and had christened a Liberty ship in the Kaiser building yards at Seattle and proudly wore a jewelled brooch displaying the name flags of the SS *Gracie Fields* which Mr Kaiser had presented to her.

Hugh reminded her of a concert at Cambridge University many years ago where, as a young girl, her performance had drawn boos and catcalls. Suddenly she stopped singing, and burst into tears of rage.

"Why won't you give me a fair chance, you so-and-so's?" And that drew a roar of cheers. Then she suddenly caught fire and sang as nobody had ever heard before, and the audience wouldn't let her go.

Another very famous player was Noel Coward. Hugh had met him long ago while he was in Singapore on a cruise. The small touring company there had gone bankrupt when Coward heard of it. He went to see the play "Journey's End", took over the lead, advertised his name and of course filled the theatre immediately, abandoning his voyage for the remainder of the run so that the players could earn enough money to get themselves home again.

Now in the middle of the war he had come up to Scapa to collect material for a propaganda type of movie called "In Which We Serve". The story told of the heroic captain of a ship sunk in naval action and the reaction of members of the crew. Hugh was told to "look after" him, but Coward seemed intent on talking all of the time, and always about himself, so that after a couple of days it became increasingly difficult to persuade members of the wardroom mess to meet him at all. Hugh arranged for him to go off in different ships on different journeys and he ended up in Iceland and then flew home. A few months later the movie appeared on board and was screened two or three times. When the officers saw it, the C.-in-C. could not stomach it and quietly slipped away in the dark. Other senior officers — almost to a man — felt the same way about the picture and silently walked out. Hugh and those who were younger than himself were enthralled and many of them saw the film a second time.

There was an interesting age division over this, and when Hugh spoke to Admiral Tovey about it he frankly admitted that he loathed the whole sentimental thing. It became widely popular in Britain in due course.

A little later on a nephew of Hugh's was at Manston Aerodrome near the east coast when a heavy air attack developed. Buildings were in flames on all sides and there were casualties all over the area, including the slit trenches in which off-duty personnel had to take shelter. At the height of the bombing a wooden shed containing the communications centre was set on fire, but the WRAF personnel who manned it stuck to their telephones and wireless sets as the burning roof began to fall in. The woman officer in charge ordered as many as could be moved from their normal desks to get under the tables where they continued their decoding or whatever it might be. Finally the last telephone line went dead and then she ordered the staff outside where bombs were still exploding. She took a quick look round to see where they might go and noticed heads popping up from the slit trenches.

"Girls, follow me — and walk! I'm not going to have all those men watching us from the trenches saying that the WRAF ran away from its job!"

The legend of the delicate frailty of women was one of the war casualties. They turned out to be as tough and served as selflessly as any man.

On 2nd December 1940, Sir Charles Forbes was replaced by Admiral Sir John Tovey, recently Second in Command of the Mediterranean Fleet, who had fought with great distinction in two actions with the Italians and was an old destroyer officer. Hugh had known him well in the Firth of Forth in the late 1920s. Everyone regretted the departure of Sir Charles Forbes, but he had flown his Union Flag in the rank of Admiral of the Fleet at Sea for more than two years (probably an all-time record), and, though he showed no sign of it, was of course ageing and had borne a heavy burden of responsibility for a long time. When the staff lined up on the quarterdeck of *King George V* to which new battleship the

Flag had just been transferred, Admiral Tovey, when he came to Hugh, smiled, and said to Sir Charles Forbes:

"Oh yes, of course, I know Hugh. We were shipmates some time ago," and then to Hugh, "You're staying!" He never did waste words. Hugh was highly pleased and had thought it likely that the new admiral would bring in someone from the Mediterranean in his place. He loved his job and wanted no other. He felt that, though only a very junior officer, he had reaped a unique variety of experiences which could nowhere else have been matched in the Service, and that in some measure, such long service under the conditions in the Home Fleet area might well be a continuing useful contribution. On the debit side was the realisation that he must brace himself to spend still more months — years perhaps — at Scapa, geographically almost the bleakest assignment that the Service had to offer. Then he suddenly thought: "Now I make a new start!" And that carried him cheerfully along for two more years of service in that foul northern weather.

Almost the first thing that Admiral Tovey did was to make an exhaustive examination of the present state of German warships. The new battleships *Tirpitz* and *Bismarck* had now left their builders' yards, *Tirpitz* being six months behind *Bismarck*, and in mid-March they disappeared into the North Baltic, which was too distant for photographic reconnaissance. That they were larger than the Washington Treaty limit of 44,000 tons was almost certain, and the first completion date was not due for at least another year. The two battle-cruisers *Scharnhorst* and *Gneisenau* had a speed of twenty-eight knots, eleven-inch guns, and were very good sea boats, and both in service. The three "pocket battleships", *Lutzow*, *Admiral Scheer* and *Hipper* were good for about twenty-two knots and carried eleven-inch guns, and they had excellent underwater protection and had aleady survived single torpedo hits. They had an abnormally long range of action. The exact number of cruisers was always in some doubt, but there were at least two eight-inch gunned, and probably four six-inch gunned of these, and about eight large destroyers; and over one hundred submarines with at least a hundred more building. There was also a numerous force of small torpedo and motor gunboats and other light torpedo armed craft. Landing barges were counted at three thousand, with more being added in the Channel ports every week. About ten armed merchant raiders and at least an equal number of supply and oil-carrying ships were at sea in the more distant oceans at any one time. It was a well-designed and balanced fleet for the purpose of attacking trade. Though the Italian fleet had been severely mauled in the Mediterranean, it was still afloat, and required a strong force to contain it. There still remained a small but quite modern French fleet in their ports and we felt an abiding anxiety that their government would find means of turning these warships over to the Germans — which never in fact happened. To face all this we had nine battleships, with three more due to commission during the next few months. There were also four carriers. As in every other war the government had never provided sufficient small craft to protect our trade at sea and we were continuing to face a very severe loss of merchant ships which could only be replaced from American sources upon which, therefore, our national survival in reality ultimately depended.

Admiral Tovey already knew that in Admiral Sir Andrew Cunningham's hands the Mediterranean would be as secure as anything can be in war. In the Home Fleet area his task would be a continuation of Sir Charles Forbes' work, and perhaps his Mediterranean experience would give new insights and a fresh outlook. The crucial fight lay in the hands of the North Atlantic convoy escort forces operated by Admiral Sir Max Horton, who was recognised as the Navy's most able and experienced submarine officer, and he was surely the right officer in the right place to deal with the increasing U-boat attack.

But what of Japan? We had little to spare with which to reinforce the Far Eastern area. In his own mind one felt that Churchill had already decided to leave the Far East to its own slim devices and hope that America would not take too long to meet the threat in the Pacific which faced her. President Roosevelt was fully alive to the Japanese danger, but the American public mind at that time was turned in the direction of Germany, and the president faced an uphill task in persuading both American military and civilian opinion to face the danger in the Pacific in addition to the highly visible menace on his continent's Atlantic shores.

The entry of Russia into the war now made a very great difference to our hopes of victory, and both Britain and the USA at once began to build up direct and close relationships with this latest associate — for Russia never became an ally, which is the name given to one who shoulders mutual responsibilities. Russia accepted help but left herself singularly free of obligations, though the attrition of very large German armies was in itself of the greatest value to the allies.

On 22nd June 1941 — as has already been noted — Germany attacked Russia. On 7th July, Mr Harry Hopkins arrived from Washington in London and flew on to Moscow a day or so later, returning to Scapa on 30th July where he waited in the Fleet flagship for the prime minister, Mr A. V. Alexander (First Lord of the Admiralty), General Dill (British Military Adviser in Washington), and an American minister, who all arrived on 4th August, the whole party sailing in the new battleship *Prince of Wales*, which conveyed them to Placentia Bay in Newfoundland to meet Mr Roosevelt, who arrived there on 9th August in an American battleship; the two delegations hammering out a document of mutually agreed intentions that came to be known as "The Atlantic Charter". Stalin was, of course, the notable absentee, but the Russian army was already reeling backwards under the heavy armoured assault of the Germans.

It is interesting to reflect upon the almost forty years of mounting rivalry and increasing tension that have persisted between the USA and Russia, both great countries in acreage, population and natural resources, yet both lacking in some basic human understanding, perhaps in sympathy and in consideration for the other's point of view.

Mr Atlee, the deputy prime minister, announced the signature of the British-American agreement in the House of Commons while Mr Churchill was still at sea. They steamed between the lines of a seventy-two ship convoy and spent a day inspecting the base in Iceland, and *Prince of Wales* delivered her passengers safely back at Scapa on 18th August. Mr Hopkins immediately flew off to Moscow yet once more, presumably to tell Stalin all about it.

For the Home Fleet there now commenced a new and different style of campaign because, although a steady stream of pinprick raids continued to be mounted against enemy shipping and bases along the Norwegian coast, our main preoccupation and task had become the organisation and protection of convoys of supplies to Murmansk on the northern coast of Russia. The first PQ convoy approaching Murmansk became entangled in ice-floes and a thick fog for some days, and there was doubt if fresh water and provisions would hold out, some ships reaching port with scarcely one day's supplies remaining on board.

The convoys were routed far to the westward beyond air

reconnaissance observation for their long slow voyage, usually at eight knots. Escorts were detached to top up fuel in Iceland, but by the time they reached the 200-mile gap between Spitzbergen and the Lapland coast the convoy was within easy range of German air attack. These waters could be mined, but in fact few if any losses were attributed to mines. A U-boat patrol, seldom in great force, was always a menace, and by the time a convoy reached Bear Island in the middle of the narrow waters separating Spitzbergen from Northern Norway, the escorts were very low on fuel and frequently had to leave the convoy and push on ahead in order to make port before they ran dry. The losses of merchant shipping were heavy and steadily increased.

The most devastating assault came when about fifty torpedo-carrying aircraft attacked in three waves. The first wave sank the nearest column of five merchantmen at a single blow; many of the ships in this convoy were loaded with explosives and blew up with tremendous force. In later convoys some merchantmen were fitted to fly off aircraft, and when these were present, both U-boat and air attacks were partially frustrated and losses proportionately reduced.

An accurate and well-presented account of the adventures of convoy "PQ 17" has been published, and some of the extraordinary sufferings of the crews can be well understood. It was the most disastrous of all these convoys, but they all had somewhat similar experiences. Just after PQ 17 had passed to the east of Bear Island, the first Sea Lord became convinced that the battleship *Tirpitz* was at sea, contrary to the opinion of the operations intelligence centre, and at 2 a.m. after senior staff had gone to bed, Admiral Pound personally despatched a signal from the Admiralty ordering the already decimated convoy to disperse, which deprived the merchantmen of whatever protection surviving escort warships might be able to give. When he read this message the C.-in-C. said to Hugh that he could not understand why this signal had been despatched.

Those in close contact with Admiral Pound at the Admiralty had at about this time noticed that he was absolutely unable to keep awake at the frequent midnight conferences which Mr Churchill insisted on personally conducting into the often minute details of current operations — for which of course as minister of defence he was ultimately responsible to parliament. The first Sea Lord did not seem always to grasp the purport of a conversation.

Some time later it was found that he had a tumour of the brain, which ultimately caused his death.

By now escorts were becoming well-armed with anti-aircraft weapons, and properly equipped to pick up survivors from sunken ships. The captain in charge of the PQ 17 escort force, disobeyed the disperse order, gathered together a little group of half a dozen merchantmen, all that he could find, and conducted them without any further casualties to Murmansk. Hugh well remembered the feeling of warm approval which was evident on the bridge of the Fleet flagship at that time. The heavy ships could not go into the narrow waters where they would have exposed themselves to bombs and torpedoes without being able to give much enduring protection to the slow-moving convoy. The battle fleet's job was to fight off surface ship attack and in fact on only one occasion did a large warship, a pocket battleship, get close to a convoy, and then was driven off by escorting cruisers, and it did not actually sight the convoy. On one other occasion a determined attack was made by a German destroyer force, but by skilful manoeuvring amongst ice-floes, the escort forces drove them off.

It came as no real surprise when one of the PQ convoys assembling in an anchorage on the west coast reported that the crews of some merchantmen had mutinied and told their captains that they would not sail for North Russia. Some American personnel thought to have come from Costa Rica and Mexico were principally involved, and the actual number was in fact quite small. The matter was "amicably settled", the commodore of the convoy eventually reported. There was also one other instance of reported "reluctance to sail" in a few crews, but that also was settled in the end. Knowing as we did the exceptional dangers and privations unavoidably associated with the three-week passage through icy waters often exposed to enemy attack, it was, though a matter of serious concern, not easy to condemn those few merchant seamen who quailed. Rather the fleet felt admiration for all who sailed; they were courageous seamen.

Hugh was to see for himself in the Denmark Straits later on the dried husks of five men frozen to a lifeboat's thwarts as she floated by, bent grotesquely grasping with frozen hands the looms of their oars that paddled aimlessly with the rock of the boat. We didn't know it when the first liner *Athenia* was torpedoed in 1939, but these men were to sail in convoys that lost twenty, fifty, even ninety per cent of their ships, and then to sail again — and yet again. They were to wear down the implacable attack of bomber and U-boat alike. They were to lay the foundation of victory not only for Britain, but for freedom. These brave merchant seamen should not be forgotten.

The PQ convoys coincided with the completion and entry of *Bismarck* and, six months later, *Tirpitz* into active service. These ships were kept in distant Baltic waters during the year their acceptance trials and then working-up practices lasted. Their preparation for warfare was lengthy and thorough. Hugh had (as has already been recorded) a small group of W/T operators who transferred with him to the five Fleet flagships in which he served. It is interesting to recall that *Nelson*, the first one, struck a magnetic mine at Loch Ewe; *Rodney*, the next one, was hit by a large bomb off the Norwegian coast; *Warspite* was of short duration only; *King George V* cut the destroyer *Punjabi* in half off Iceland and sank her in a fog and was damaged by her depth-charges which exploded alongside; *Duke of York* was sent away to fit heavier anti-aircraft armament; and then the C.-in-C. went back to the *King George V* again. Special W/T operators were trained to study German wireless traffic and easily found the *Bismarck* while she was working up in the Baltic, and she was evidently fitted with the most modern transmitters which sounded a soft but unmistakable musical note. Unfortunately those of our battleships that were fitted with D/F (direction finding) equipment were unable to discover a suitable position and the few bearings they did obtain of enemy transmissions were virtually useless because our ships were of such large metallic mass and contained a great quantity of electrical apparatus.

Experiments with midget submarines and "human torpedoes" were undertaken and were spurred on when the Italians launched about forty midgets at the entrance to Grand Harbour in Malta, all of which were either destroyed or captured.

Presently a young American journalist named Comer, attached to the Home Fleet, appeared in Hugh's cabin with a press article for transmission describing in considerable detail a plan which he had evolved for a submarine attack on one of the large German battleships. His description was so factual and so vivid that Hugh at once realised that this man might easily raise a serious alarm in Germany should his manuscript find its way into enemy hands, so he temporised while he quickly arranged to despatch the journalist to Iceland, and a little later on to Greenland, where he was effectually muzzled by the lack of communications in any direction for some considerable time.

But Comer was an unusual young man whose articles were of a penetrating kind that placed him in a class well beyond the usual half dozen British pressmen who moved to and fro between London and the Home Fleet, and Hugh much regretted his forced absence from the scene of real action.

Our own versions of our miniature craft were treated as top secret, and one day Hugh was surprised to see Admiral Tovey accompanied by a single staff officer go ashore early in the morning, climb into an inconspicuous elderly car and drive off — without telling Hugh (the duty staff officer) where he was going or for how long. Hugh had, ever since the attack on Malta, been trying to gather all the information he could about miniature submarines and had met with a sort of universal stonewall which increased his suspicion that some such attack was being planned. The admiral returned on board late in the day and as he walked towards the hatchway to his cabin in conversation with his staff officer, Hugh, following with a sheaf of signals to show to the admiral, heard the staff officer say:

"Well, the only thing I saw was the bubbles rising to the surface alongside."

This was, of course, enough to assure Hugh that a miniature submarine was being prepared to attack one of the big ships.

On 14th February 1941, the US Congress passed the Lend-Lease Bill, which ensured continuation of supplies to be paid for on easy terms. That payment, though its terms were generous, beggared Great Britain.

Lord Halifax, newly-appointed ambassador at Washington, came up to Scapa late in December, in company with Mr Churchill, who saw him off in the newly-commissioned battleship *King George V*. She was the first of her class to get to sea, and appeared to be well designed and formidable with six of her ten 14-inch guns mounted on the fo'c'sle, and she had twenty-eight knots speed. The ambassador's mission to Washington was of course of cardinal importance to Britain, for upon him depended the proper regulation of the main war supplies to the European theatre.

From the outbreak of war, Hugh had been going down to the Admiralty in London every two or three months to keep in close touch with the latest naval intelligence and to hear the latest views upon the ever-changing situation at home and abroad. His special "contact men" were Paymaster Commander Denning and Harry Hinsley, who between them assembled the operational intelligence available on the Home Station. The one later became the head of his branch in the Royal Navy, and the other the head of his college at Cambridge University, and Hugh was able occasionally to arrange for both of them to pay short visits to the commander-in-chief at Scapa, which were of practical value to both sides.

Fortunately it was always possible to find a reasonably quiet time when Hugh could get away from the sea, but not always was there quiet under the bombs in London. On one occasion when he was in a hurry to reach London in time for a conference it happened that Mr Churchill, accompanied by his wife and also his Chief of Staff General Ismay, Sir Charles Wilson, who was his doctor, and Professor Linderman his scientific adviser, were visiting the fleet at Scapa and would be leaving from Thurso on the north coast of Scotland by special train in the late afternoon. Mr Harry Hopkins, President Roosevelt's personal representative, had arrived at Scapa in a flying boat from Russia a few days earlier in a collapsed condition after protracted and exhausting negotiations and a dangerous and very long, rough flight. He was a small man and in frail health and the doctor ordered him to stay in bed to rest and recuperate on board the Fleet flagship until he should be fit to continue his journey back to Washington. It was now decided that he should travel to London comfortably on Mr Churchill's special train. Hugh, who had an urgent meeting to attend at the Admiralty, after consulting his chief of staff asked Mr Martin, the prime minister's secretary, if he might travel on the special train, and was passed on to General Ismay, the prime minister's chief-of-staff, who by now had, after several visits to the fleet, become a friend, and the general went straight to the prime minister, who at once approved.

That day at Scapa saw a rising storm developing and during the forenoon a new multi-barrelled pompom mounted on the upper 16-inch gun turret of the *Nelson* above the fo'c'sle deck was to fire a demonstration salvo from its twenty small barrels. The rounds flew off alright up to about a thousand feet and then a small white parachute opened and a little contact bomb dangled below it and would explode whenever it touched anything.

The PM and his party, including Mrs Churchill, climbed up to the C.-in-C.'s bridge to witness whatever the results of a demonstration firing might turn out to be. Mr Churchill thought it a valuable defence against dive-bombers, but the fleet gunnery experts did not like it at all. The ship's captain gave the order to fire and everyone pressed forward to the bridge windows, except Hugh, who had been told to "look after Mrs Churchill and see she doesn't get in the way", and so he guided her to the open rear end of the bridge where she could really see better than from the congested space inside. Everyone held their breath, and then with little flashes the white parachutes popped open and, looking rather like a flight of seagulls, descending slowly with their dangling bombs below, a couple of which exploded modestly when they chanced to touch another in the air.

Then it was noticed that the wind was carrying the whole flock down towards the bridge, but they all missed it and fell harmlessly into the water alongside — except one. This one wrapped itself round and round the wire jackstay running from a point above the bridge right out to the eyes of the ship on the fo'c'sle head and the bomb was drawn closer and closer towards the jackstay so that it finally touched the wire and exploded only twenty feet away from the glass windows. For an awful moment everyone feared the glass would shatter and blind the prime minister. The admiral whipped off his cap and held it in front of Mr Churchill's face. Nothing happened, and the small puff of smoke quickly dispersed in the wind, leaving a slight acrid smell behind it. Churchill swung round furious, partly because he didn't like the admiral's cap squashed over his face, partly because he was scared about Mrs Churchill's safety, and also because the demonstration had supported the gunnery expert's condemnation of this unusual sort of mortar, which evidently was unlikely to bring down many dive-bombers — it was visibly a flop as far as ships were concerned.

"Oh, Clementine! I see you are unharmed!" And then, looking round to see who was responsible and could be roundly cursed and finding no one in particular:

"This is disgraceful! I must know who is responsible! We might all have been blinded! Admiral, let me have a full report on the whole thing! I am most displeased!"

In the silence which fell over the bridge Mrs Churchill's tinkling laughter was all too audible as she broadly winked at Hugh and said:

"I bet they never thought it would work out like this!"

"Clementine, be silent! This is no laughing matter! Something is gravely at fault!"

She composed her face, but her shoulders were shaking with concealed merriment.

A destroyer had anchored about 300 yards off in preparation for the twenty-mile passage across the Pentland Firth to Thurso on the mainland. A signal was sent to her asking that a cabin be prepared for Mr and Mrs Churchill and a swing cot in the sick-bay for Mr Hopkins, who would have been given a sedative and was unlikely to be able to walk. After lunch the whole party embarked in the C.-in-C.'s large motor barge, Mr Hopkins heavily wrapped in blankets and the PM well padded against the cold in several extra sweaters. He had a heavy cold on his chest at the time.

As the barge approached the destroyer it could be seen that the high wind caused her to yaw widely over an arc of quite 70°, so that the approach to her small wooden gangway aft was difficult and taxed the skilled admiral's coxswain to the limit, while Hugh stood beside him at his steering-wheel on deck. After a couple of attempts the barge finally got alongside and a boat rope was secured in her bows. As the destroyer yawed to and fro the waves alongside subsided momentarily at times, and then a moment later, heaved up and down again about eight feet, the result being that the barge was level with the little platform on the gangway for only a few seconds at a time. A large hefty sailor darted down the gangway, jumped into the stern and whipped Mr Hopkins rolled up in his blankets into his muscular arms, stepped lightly onto the wooden gangway platform when it was level, ran up the dozen wooden steps and quickly disappeared along the ship's deck forward to the sick-bay with his bundle still in his arms. The whole thing lasted less than a minute.

Mr Churchill helped his wife towards the stepping-off point and the barge rose and fell a couple of times while he alternately tried to push her forward or pull her back. She carefully watched the waves and then, detaching the PM's arm which was half-way round her waist, stepped lightly off on to the gangway platform at exactly the right moment when it was level. Hugh was half-way down to grab her if she faltered, and heaved a sigh of relief, remembering that she was an old-time yachtswoman.

The PM came next, and Hugh came down almost to the platform, observing that Mr Churchill made slow heavy movements to step across and always at the wrong moment. Finally he gave a little jump just as the barge struck and shattered the gangway platform and woodwork below it, only the two stout planks forming the sides of the ladder remaining undamaged. He fell between these two side planks and his thick voluminous clothing jammed and held him there with his feet almost touching the water, which was just for that moment almost calm because of the yaw of the ship. Hugh thought: "If he goes, I ought to jump in after him, but in this icy water I can't last long. He moves too slowly to grab a lifebuoy or a rope's end if we throw it to him. What will England say if I lose the PM?" On deck a seaman had a lifebuoy on a line ready to throw. Mrs Churchill's frozen face was close behind the man. A seaman leaped down the broken ladder with a stout rope's end in his hand and together they got it round Churchill's torso beneath the armpits. Then they and others above them on the ladder hove and hove until he suddenly popped up like a cork out of a bottle and fell on some of the upper ladder treads, still untouched by the waves.

There were four more to come: General Ismay, Martin, Sir Charles Wilson and Lindermann. The general looked alarmed but determined and stepped across at the right moment and fell on his face, firmly grasping the ladder treads. A seaman was now standing as far down the ladder as he could get, and roping each one of them in turn. Martin got away alright. Then Wilson and Lindermann could be seen gesticulating in hot argument. Hugh went down and firmly ordered Wilson to do as he was told and pass the rope's end round his chest beneath his armpits. He was so astonished that his mouth opened while he actually did just that; and he got away alright. Lindermann began arguing but Hugh jumped into the boat and quickly passed the rope's end round him and knotted it and got back on the ladder in readiness to gather him up when he got there. But the professor just couldn't measure wave movements, made two false starts and then flung himself wildly in the direction of the ladder at a moment when the barge was rapidly falling far below it. He managed to get a tenuous hold on the ladder with one hand and a seaman eventually hove him right up on deck on his rope's end. Hugh left them and hurried aft, and pressingly suggested to the tensely watching Churchills that they should go down to the captain's cabin which was prepared for them.

The PM said:

"No, no! I want to see everything that's going on. How can the barge get away from this swinging ship when she is moving so fast?''

Hugh suggested that with his heavy cold the icy wind could be doing him no good. He grunted angrily, turned his back and walked away, so Hugh turned to Mrs Churchill and asked her if she could persuade her husband.

She answered: "Where is the hatchway?" Hugh showed her which one it was, and as she reached it she called out brightly: "Oh dear, please give me a hand with this awful hole!" Winston hurried to her side and thus the problem was resolved in the best possible way.

The Pentland Firth crossing was not so very rough after all, and when Hugh went down to the Churchill's cabin to see if they were all right the captain's steward met him at the door.

"Yes, Sir, they are quite comfortable. The captain told me to have a glass of brandy ready for Mr Churchill and he says he thinks it is a very good brand." They were each lashed into an armchair which was bolted to the deck and were reading the papers.

Still, this day was by no means over yet.

At Thurso the tide was out and they berthed outside a pair of large highly-smelling fishing trawlers and found that no sort of gangways across these two boats had been provided and, as their gunwales are about four feet above their decks, a complicated climb was involved. It was 6 p.m. and not a soul in sight, the trawler crews evidently having gone ashore for the night. The general and Hugh found several large rope fenders and stacked them so that the travellers could get up on the gunwales, step across the foot-wide gap between the trawlers, and finally scramble up the steep and fishy iron ladder leading on to the jetty about twenty feet above.

Meantime a loud sound of laughter and voices came from the upper deck of the destroyer where Mr Hopkins, in boisterous company with the sick-bay attendant and several capless ratings in singlets, were bidding one another a happy and rowdy farewell. Someone must have appreciated the steeplechase course across the trawlers and up onto the jetty, and suddenly the president of the United States' personal representative to Russia was swept up into the arms of one of his sailor friends, who carried him triumphantly across the two trawlers and up on to dry land. The two of them spent several minutes there in a positively loving farewell, Harry's face beaming with his particularly sweet smile. Hugh walked the few yards with him to the waiting special train and he could not stop talking of "those lovely boys. They've looked after me like a mother. They've made this whole tough trip just worthwhile after all for me!" He thought that the story would surely travel round Washington in due course and could do nothing but good for the edgy relations prevailing at that time between the United States of America and Great Britain.

At last the train puffed out of Thurso as dusk became night. There were four carriages, one fitted as a dining-room with small tables and some lounge seating accommodation; an adjacent one fitted with cabins and bathrooms for the Churchills and the lady secretary, the famous Rosie being the only one on board this night. A third carriage had ordinary sleeping accommodation for male guests and the staff, and the fourth was the kitchen store-room, and stewards' quarters. As there were only the senior staff, plus Mr Hopkins and Commander Thompson, the PM's personal adc, and Hugh, everyone had a whole compartment to himself. At eight o'clock, Thompson came along and carried Hugh off to the dining-lounge car for a drink, where later on Mr Hopkins joined them. The others trickled in one by one and finally about nine o'clock Harry Hopkins asked when dinner might be expected. Thompson said briefly that nobody ever knew. Then the PM appeared bright and smiling and ordered drinks all round. Rather later he sent for the steward and asked what there would be for dinner and was told that a salmon had been sent by Sir Alexander Sinclair from Thurso Castle, but Winston burst out:

"But that won't do at all! You've got that pheasant I gave you, and Mrs Churchill will be expecting it." The steward answered that the salmon was cooked and ready, but the pheasant would take at least another hour to prepare.

"We will eat the pheasant!" He went to see how Mrs Churchill was getting along and presently returned ruefully to say she had gone to bed and eaten only a sandwich and was very tired.

"But we are not altogether desolate! Here's Rosie!" and in walked a rather bulky woman in her middle years wearing thick glasses, and looking shy and nervous. Everybody got up to offer her a seat. She drank half a glass of sherry and then sat herself down between the professor and the doctor. She was famous in Whitehall as the most efficient, devoted and loyal secretary in the whole fabric of the government. If Rosie said something, it was a fact and you could stake your life on it, but she had the wisdom to say virtually nothing at all. That night she didn't go far beyond "Yes" and "No", except to tell Hugh that she would be typing despatches until 2 a.m. for him to take to London.

Somewhat after 10 p.m. Mr Churchill summoned Hugh to the table at which he was sitting with General Ismay, and then got up and brought Harry Hopkins over to complete the four places. A very good dinner with some strong wine presently followed and the general conversation was about everything on earth except current affairs and recent war news. Harry Hopkins wore out before the meal was quite ended, and, as he excused himself, sighed and said: "Gee, I wish I was tough like some of youse guys!" and tottered away with his wonderful smile on his face. The three who remained surely had the same thought in their minds: "No wonder he is the president's closest friend."

At about 11 p.m., the prime minister disappeared and Hugh started saying "Goodnight" all round, but General Ismay intervened:

"You needn't think you are going to get away yet! The prime minister wants to talk to you about so-and-so." So he waited around until Mr Churchill reappeared wrapped in the famous brilliant coloured silk dressing-gown, smoking his usual cigar and calling for "a little brandy if you please". He didn't leave again until well past midnight — and at last this day really was over and done with.

The prime minister's party was detached during the night to go to Glasgow, while the rest of the train went direct to London, arriving next morning, Hugh having been given two of the Downing Street red leather despatch-boxes which he was to deliver personally to Mr Jarrett, secretary to the first lord, Mr A. V. Alexander, at the Admiralty. Next morning Hugh discovered that in the bustle of departure he had forgotten to bring either his National Identity Card or his Operations Intelligence Centre special pass. He climbed miserably and apprehensively into a taxi at Euston Station and paid off the cab at the Whitehall main entrance to the Admiralty, where he stepped boldly forward brandishing the two red boxes and demanded to be taken at once to Mr Jarrett. The security guards, who of course knew what the boxes were and might possibly have recognised Hugh's face as a familiar one, ushered him along the corridors from one checkpoint to the next until he reached his destination. He knew Jarrett slightly and having delivered his two boxes, of which Jarrett had received prior warning from Martin, he sat down and confessed his sins. Jarrett laughed and rang a bell, and had a clerk make out duplicates of the two missing passes, and Hugh went on his way rejoicing.

One of his friends working in the Admiralty lived in the Carleton Hotel on Pall Mall very close to Trafalgar Square, and only a few minutes' walk from his office. The noise of an air raid woke him late one night and he automatically switched on the bedside light, which revealed to him that the foot of the bed was on the very edge of a black smoking precipice. There had been a direct hit and half the building had collapsed. He got gingerly out of bed and walked out of the bedroom door in shock and shoeless, down some surviving stairs and out into the street. He was dazed and bewildered but remembered his club, the well-known "In and Out", some distance away in Piccadilly, and set off to walk there. Presently he bumped into an air raid warden in the pitch dark and the man asked him brusquely what he thought he was doing out on the street in pyjamas, and as he flashed his electric torch on the culprit he exclaimed:

"And just look at your feet, will you!"

He had not thought to put on shoes and his feet were cut by broken glass and bleeding. His club looked after him splendidly and even borrowed clothes so that he could go to work next morning. Everything he possessed, except the pyjamas, had been destroyed.

The Admiralty was not to escape harm from the intensive bombing of London which was steadily building up. On 17th April, the first sea lord's office was completely demolished. No disruption whatever occurred in the normal flow of Admiralty business. They had prepared for just such an experience. Heavy bombs in the close vicinity on another night fractured a water main near the Operations Intelligence Centre (OIC), which was buried deep beneath a heavy concrete structure, nicknamed by Londoners "Lenin's Tomb". It is still there, but somewhat improved by an extensive covering of Virginia creeper. As the evening wore on water flooded into ventilation shafts and the whole personnel began to pack up and move their records to other quarters. The water-level rose to within a couple of inches of complete flooding before it was finally got under control.

Nearby was emergency bomb-proof living accommodation for the cabinet, and Mr Churchill usually slept down there during air raid nights. He was normally called quite early in the morning and from his bed dealt with paperwork while consuming his breakfast. By 10 a.m. he was dressed and receiving a stream of people. Lunch was a business affair after which he went to bed and to sleep at 2 p.m., and got up at 6 p.m. and worked again until 2 a.m. the next morning after having often enough changed into his gaudy dressing-gown. Frequently, accompanied by his chiefs of staff, he would visit the war map in the nearby Operations Centre, and any time after midnight the Fleet flagship at Scapa would receive a stream of important signals from the Admiralty which were the product of these consultations. Unfortunately the C.-in-C., who kept normal service routine hours and went to bed about 10 p.m., sometimes had to be awakened when such messages arrived. It was invariably an awkward decision for the duty staff officer to make, whether or not to call the C.-in-C., or leave the signal until the next morning, for the Admiral needed sleep more than anyone else in the fleet. Hugh found that none of the three Home Fleet C.-in-C.s he served at sea during the war even once complained that he had been called unnecessarily. The utmost that was ever said was that the matter could be "left until morning". Each of them showed great consideration for their staff officers.

During these periodic visits to London, Hugh either stayed with friends or slept in a wartime club for officers in Piccadilly in cubicle accommodation. One night he was dining with friends in Queen's Gate on the western edge of Hyde Park, when an air raid warning sounded, to which no one at the table paid any attention. Londoners no longer moved until they "could see the white of the enemy's eyes", as it were. Then there was an almighty explosion and all the cutlery and glass on the table leapt into the air and the salt cellars upset their contents on the polished mahogany surface. Hugh sprang to his feet ready to do he did not know quite what. The general conversation didn't stop, and his hostess, Lady Robertson (the World War II Field Marshal's widow), next to whom he was sitting, looked up smiling and said:

"One can always tell who is a visitor. Londoners don't notice these things any more!"

Later on she told him that she had a compact with an elderly man in the flat opposite to hers by which they mutually agreed that if either one thought things were getting too hot, that one would ring up and say so, and both would escort each other down the several flights of stairs to the basement air raid shelter. Only once did they decide to go down. They missed a turning and found themselves out under the stars in a little backyard with bomb splinters and debris dropping around them. They mutually agreed that their flats were much safer and went back to bed.

It happened that during the very first raid of the war on London, Hugh was having tea with friends in Roehampton, an inner residential suburb. The printed instructions ordered everybody not on essential duty or work to go to the nearest air raid shelter. The sirens sounded and while they were arguing about the obligation to comply with the regulations, the sound of heavy explosions in the direction of Croydon drifted in with the summer breeze. Then they went down to the shelter, which was a deep hole dug in the garden, roofed with heavy timber beams and an oozing mud floor. The bombers went on to Hendon flying field and dropped a few more bombs which they also heard. Then it was decided that the aircraft couldn't possibly have any more bombs left, and so they went back to their tea, which was now cold.

On another occasion Hugh was in a taxi at night during a raid when a small splinter fell through the roof. He wanted to have it as a souvenir but couldn't find it on the floor in the dark. When he asked the cabby if he would like to go to a shelter the man said no, he couldn't be bothered, and anyhow he had never been in one of those places and didn't like the idea of being buried alive.

"Wot I says is if yer number's up, that's it; and yer won't 'ave to worry about it no more!"

A few people who were scared, or perhaps ill, did leave London and take refuge away in the country. Hugh only ever knew one; and at a later stage when mass evacuation of women and children was ordered nearly all had filtered back again within a few months. They hated life in quiet country places and the country folk upon whom they were billeted never forgot the dreadful experience — as they regarded it. The refugees never forgot the "'orrible 'ush"!

Scapa had an undeniably deleterious effect on everyone who had to spend a prolonged time there. It looked depressing. The dun-coloured islands with their deep covering of heather offered a tedious repetition unrelieved by notable physical inequalities of level or shape. The low hills were smooth and rounded and just simply dreary. On the north shore there was a little ancient oak

wood with trees perhaps twenty feet high, the tops of which were
bent horizontal by the incessant gales, and they could be seen
from the fleet anchorage as no more than a small black gash in a
narrow cleft in the hills. At Kirkwall, to which hardly anybody
ever went, except the messman to buy fresh food, there were some
minute gardens and a scattering of small stunted trees, but by the
time you got there it was time to start back, for the only jetty
where the ship's boats could land was nearly two miles away. And
then one day, probably in September, there would be a blue sky,
calm water and the most lovely soft lights and colours one had ever
seen anywhere. Moreover it is a cold climate so far north. From
the very beginning of the war Hugh decided that it was going to be
a long war and that the art of keeping fit was a necessary pursuit.
He made a firm habit of landing in the officers' shore boat in the
afternoon whenever there was one, and it always went to the
nearby island of Flotta. In the course of time he discovered that
the southern shore — mostly deserted rocky cliff about 30 feet
high — was the most attractive place for a walk. If there was
sunshine in summer months Hugh found that it enabled him to
swim in little rocky bays, and a late discovery was a circular muddy
inlet choked with seaweed from which the water could never
wholly escape, and there he would swim or rather struggle against
the seaweed for a half an hour in water at about 60°F. He
managed to continue into the autumn until the temperature fell to
56°, but he was blue when he came out and had to run as fast as he
could to the boat jetty. This was all the recreation ashore he could
find, though there was an eight-hole officers' golf-course where he
worked at upkeep jobs, but not being a golfer he never played
there.

At about this time Commodore Egipko of the Russian Navy
appeared on board in response to an Admiralty request that some
senior Russian officer should join the C.-in-C.'s staff to represent
the interests of Russian warships — and in particular of Russian
submarines — operating from Murmansk along the Lapland
coast, and then round North Cape and southward along the
Norwegian coast. British convoys were now travelling to
Murmansk about once a month.

Egipko spoke good English and was decorated with the Red Star
for some undisclosed service. The Russian submarines were few in
number, old and not very efficient. They lacked modern attack
instruments and had apparently only got as far afield as North

Cape. The small torpedo craft operating out of Murmansk turned out to be unable or unwilling to venture much beyond a single night at sea, so that there was going to be work for Egipko to do. He was a pleasant man to talk to, but when it came to discussion of the employment of Russian warships centred on Murmansk the conversation veered away from facts and figures and into the vaguest of generalisations. He had been assigned to Hugh to assist him in every possible way and had asked that he might be messed in the wardroom where he would get to know British officers. He went out on one or two trips at sea but didn't appear greatly interested in what he saw there and spent most of his time reading a variety of Service manuals on all sorts of technical matters.

After a month, quite suddenly a tremendous row blew up. The staid, elderly and experienced Royal Marine servant allocated to the commodore had been found searching Egipko's personal possessions; he was a spy! The charge was plainly ridiculous in face of the man's excellent service record, and he had been carefully selected by his officers because he was exactly the type who would be wholly reliable. Egipko went off raving to the chief of staff.

Then Hugh discovered a copy of a long out-of-print war manual of some sort in the commodore's bag which he extracted while he was checking the commodore's disputed possessions. Egipko snatched the book away, locked himself in his cabin, and refused to communicate with anybody for the next two days, while he furiously copied the book and stacked the sheets of paper in his pockets and then demanded to be sent at once to his embassy in London; and that was the last anyone saw of him. He evidently supposed the old book was a valuable source of information. The C.-in-C., when it was all over, said:

"I thought that manual was dull stuff and anyhow it was years out of date, and I only read the first chapter!"

There never was a genuine liaison with the Russians. A sloop was sent to Murmansk to act as a wireless link and to handle the convoy traffic. At Christmas time the young Russian local liaison officer was invited on board for dinner, got very drunk and fell asleep, and later when he regained conciousness, went quietly ashore. He was arrested and shot by the commissar that same day, so the Russian admiral at the base said when he was asked if the young man was all right.

The splendid resistance of the Russian Army at the gates of

Moscow aroused much enthusiastic praise among British workmen, and Mrs Chruchill raised a fund to aid the provision of comforts for the Russian Army. Packing cases of goods hoisted out from convoy ships' holds were plastered with messages for "Good Old Joe" and "Down with Hitler" and so on, and as they landed on the dockside small parties of women with paint pots and brushes quickly obliterated all the messages of goodwill, including Mrs Churchill's specially labelled packages.

When our sloop's doctor visited some of his men who had become ill in the local hospital he noticed that old people and sick people were separated and treated differently to other Russian patients. When he enquired about them the Russian staff explained that they were not an asset to the war effort and that they were denied ration cards and medical treatment — and in actual fact sent away to die or to survive on family charity. When the doctor protested, the commissar did his utmost to get rid of the doctor and to confine him to nothing beyond the actual treatment of the handful of Service patients ashore.

The PQ convoys struggled doggedly on to and from Murmansk in what seemed to be endless gales and the Home Fleet provided escort destroyers and a covering force of heavy ships, occasionally fuelling in Reydar Fiord or at Akuyeri in Iceland, and Hugh twice got as far as Reykjavik for an hour of two. While walking out in the country one day he followed a path which divided two streams of water, one steaming with volcanic heat and the other ice-cold. They were so close together that it would have been possible to catch a fish in one and cook it in the other, but he never succeeded in catching anything there. It was a bleak country, almost treeless, and only inhabited close along the shoreline. The Icelanders understandably resented the foreign presence on their territory, and most of those one met turned away their heads and refused to answer when spoken to. In distant places where there were small farms along the shoreline the sparse population were more friendly and would talk in a natural way.

The great day came when the *Bismarck* broke out, and was eventually sunk, but the full details of that episode are recorded elsewhere.

Meanwhile the sister ship *Tirpitz* became fully operational and it was generally supposed that she would put to sea when chance favoured her. For a short time she vanished from the usual Baltic areas surveyed by our long-range reconnaissance aircraft and then reappeared in Alten Fiord on the Norwegian coast. The RAF sighted her moored close to a high vertical cliff, surrounded by anti-torpedo nets, and with a couple of small launches in attendance. From then on she was under almost daily surveillance, but she presented a real menace for she was in a difficult position to bomb and of course had formidable anti-aircraft defences, and her anti-torpedo nets would be expected to protect her against torpedo attack. But she was in a favourable position to attack Atlantic trade.

It was in fact from a news broadcast that Hugh eventually learned that a "successful attack" had been made upon *Tirpitz* and we were left wondering for some time what that might mean. What actually happened appeared later on. A mini-submarine wormed its way through the torpedo net defences and placed several "limpet mines" on the underwater hull of *Tirpitz* before discovery. He then scuttled his little craft and floated up to the surface and was carried up onto the quarterdeck where the German officers would not believe him when he told them that his mines would explode in a few minutes time. He was ready to jump when the first one detonated, and the others exploded in due course, according to plan. *Tirpitz* sank to the bottom with a slight list to one side. The Royal Air Force had been equally diligent in their studies of the problem and sent a number of heavy aircraft to attack *Tirpitz*, making several hits. A second heavy bomb raid caused the ship to capsize and photographs showed only a small part of the ship's side plating still left above water.

The battle-cruisers *Scharnhorst* and *Gneisenau* had earlier broken out into the Atlantic and sunk some thousands of tons of merchant shipping, and we organised an extensive search which included the Fleet flagship; this took us far to the south where everybody went out to enjoy the warm unfamiliar sunshine — but it was a profitless search, and one felt how large and wide a space is occupied by the Atlantic Ocean and how relatively small an area can be covered by a single ship, and too, how limited is the range available to a heavy battleship. Aircraft have since changed all this radically. The two German battle-cruisers made their way safely into Brest, which quickly became a priority target for the RAF. A tremendous anti-aircraft attack was mounted over the harbour and twice our aircraft attacked with torpedoes in most gallant and partly successful raids. Both these big ships were repeatedly hit, but *Gneisenau* received the greater damage and they spent a year there before they escaped.

Finally they made use of patchy foggy weather to make a dash through the English Channel for home. *Gneisenau* had certainly been hit by torpdoes once and by bombs on at least three occasions at Brest, and was thought to be in poor condition. The two ships had almost reached the Channel entrance before air reconnaissance sighted them, and thereafter they were heavily bombed without being obliged to reduce high speed, and *Scharnhorst* escaped while *Gneisenau* struck at least two mines, but still continued her progress northward past the Dutch coast. This we thought confirmed what we had already suspected, that German warships were better constructed below the waterline than our own. In the event *Gneisenau* was so badly damaged that she never put to sea again, but was broken up at a Baltic port.

On 7th May 1943, Admiral of the Fleet Lord Tovey of Langton Maltravers (to give him the full titles which he so brillantly earned) was relieved by Admiral Sir Bruce Fraser. He had been offered the position of First Sea Lord and Chief of Naval Staff in succession to Admiral Pound, but refused, probably because he felt that he did not want to cope with Winston Churchill who, as Minister of Defence, would have been his "boss". By now Churchill had achieved a position of such dominance that nobody in Britain was able to put a curb on him, and, like other human beings, he could not invariably be right. Even away back when he was the captain of the *Colossus*, Admiral Pound had been afflicted with quite severe deafness which may well have been of real help to him in times of stress.

Admiral Sir Bruce Fraser, the succeeding C.-in-C., had come from an important post at the Admiralty, and at once took the fleet to sea, as he said, to get his sea-legs again. Hugh admired his quick grasp of every detail and his cheerful good humour, but knew from the director of naval intelligence that he himself was shortly to be moved to the Far East, and he left the Home Fleet four months later, after six years and four months in the appointment as Fleet Intelligence Officer. On his last periodic visit to Scapa the King had asked some question at the morning staff conference which Hugh had to answer, and when the king saw him he said:

"Surely you have been here a long time, haven't you? I have seen you before."

"Yes, Sir, I have; about six years."

The King turned to the admiral:

"This must be about the longest appointment on record, isn't it?"

"Yes it is, Sir; but they have a change of scenery in store for him, I believe."

That same evening the C.-in-C. gave a dinner party to which one officer of junior rank from every branch of the Service was invited — about 20 in all. A young Royal Marine subaltern fell into the water when his boat came alongside and his friends on board were able to muster sufficient garments for him to appear — a little late, but also quite unperturbed, though he did go a little red in the face when the King asked him about his misadventure. After dinner the new war medals that were shortly to be issued came under discussion, and the King said:

"I have with me some sample strips of the ribbon that were sent to me for my approval."

Everybody wanted to see these, of course, and he went off to his cabin to fetch them. Then Hugh piped up:

"I am sure the ship's company would be delighted to see these, Sir, if it is at all possible?"

Admiral Fraser at once intervened:

"I have scissors in my desk here. Could I cut off a little piece, Sir, do you think?"

The King looked dubious. "I am not sure what the official position is about this, you know."

"Oh well, Sir, of course they won't go out of the ship," and with that the admiral quickly snipped off a couple of inches of each of the strips, which were later put in a glass case on the ship's company notice-board, where for several days thereafter one would find a little group of interested crewmen gathered.

One sensed that during these royal visits to the fleet, the King felt that he had "come home". He was an eminently simple man and obviously idolised by the personal staff who always attended him — his valet, private secretary and the equerry.

The next day the several ships at Scapa put to sea and joined with others out at exercises in the Pentland Firth in a royal review line that steamed past the Fleet flagship at high speed, each one cheering the King as they passed. It was a bright and calm day, and the King mounted a little platform at one side of the admiral's bridge to salute each ship from a place where they could see him. Hugh was on duty on the bridge and, as the leading ship of the line approached, the King turned to the equerry and spoke to him. He came across to the admiral and said the King wanted Hugh to come to him and so he went and stood close by to answer whatever questions might be asked. *Eagle*, the new aircraft-carrier, had come in late the previous afternoon, but as she passed the whole ship's side gleamed with fresh paint.

"How did she do this?" the king asked.

"Well, Sir, everybody off watch got onto stages with a paint brush and they finished by moonlight at about eleven o'clock last night. I saw them unrigging the stages then."

The King made a signal congratulating them on their appearance and added: "I trust a make and mend may be ordered." Thus was the Service phrase for a "Half holiday".

At one point His Majesty, as he watched his warships passing by, said:

"You know this is the life I always wanted: to be at sea." It was from his heart; he sounded as if he would have given almost anything to come back to the Navy.

Hugh said a few words about how much more he could do for the country where he was. This little experience was something Hugh greatly treasured.

That evening a concert had been arranged for the fleet in the large canteen on shore and when Admiral Fraser asked the King if he would attend, telling him that Leslie Henson, the leading comedian of that era, could probably be flown down from the Shetland Islands in time to appear, the king said that he should be asked to do his act about "Rumblebellypore" (which had recently been delighting London audiences, though the King had not seen it). All was quickly arranged and the concert was a riot of fun. At the end a roar of "Speech, speech, speech!" went up and Admiral Fraser went up on the stage and said a few appropriate words, and then invited the King to speak, but no, the King shook his head, and in spite of the tremendous cheers would not budge. Then Hugh remembered that in his younger days he stammered badly and would never risk a public speech. His Christmas broadcasts were rehearsed and may have been pre-recorded, but nevertheless there were some slight hesitations. Nobody minded; their content was always a superb uplifting kind of thing. In ordinary conversation he had conquered this disablility almost completely.

Hugh's final exit from the Home Fleet was quite spectacular in a small way. The chief of staff gave a farewell luncheon for him which the operations' staff (about ten) attended, and they had decorated the cabin with sinister cartoons of "cloak and dagger" characters, while the menu made references to "Blackbeard", which was the nickname he had been given long ago. It was all humorous and delightful. The Second in Command of the Home Fleet, Vice Admiral Moore, who had been the first chief of staff under whom he had served in *Nelson* way back in 1938, also invited him to a farewell lunch party, and on the last day the Press representatives — about eight of them — whom he had shepherded and censored for so long — organised a drink party. When he finally went down *King George V*'s accommodation ladder, he found the chief of staff's barge waiting to take him to Gutter Sound to board the ferry *King Orrey* which would take him across the Pentland Firth to Thurso, and the train for London. The same vessel had brought him across to join his first ship *Colossus* in 1917. But now he was seasick; the last time that happened had been in a destroyer in 1918, due to a sufeit of Scottish oatcakes, and now it was due to all those farewell drinks. He was struggling not to be too downcast at leaving such a rewarding appointment, which he had enjoyed for so long a time. Distinctions had been officially conferred upon him, but the one thing he truly wanted was another seagoing appointment and this indeed had been twice offered him in the form of a destroyer command by two of his C.-in-C.s. But it was not to be; he could not be spared. His seafaring career was to end on this 13th September 1943 at this very place — Scapa — where it had begun on 26th November 1917. His feeling on this last day was that, for him, the prime objective of his life had ceased to exist. Whatever future prospect presented itself looked bleak. The war was, of course, not yet over, and so he would go on to serve wherever he might be sent, and it was only some rumour he had heard that he might be going abroad that gave him a gleam of encouragement.

Chapter 16

SEAC

When he saw the Director of Naval Intelligence in London he learned that he was to join the Supreme Allied Commander's staff at the South East Asia Command Headquarters in Delhi and would once more be the vehicle for high grade naval intelligence. A day or two later he learned that Lord Louis Mountbatten would be Supreme Allied Commander (SAC). He had been an acting rear-admiral in charge of Combined Operations, an organisation which he had created, and would be promoted to the rank of acting admiral. It all felt rather "up in the clouds" after the solid regularity of life in a ship at sea, but it also sounded rather an exciting, new and unfamiliar prospect, and — a real plum — he was promoted to acting commander and hurried off to buy his first "brass hat", the one with gold oak leaves on its peak, and then had his photograph taken and circulated amongst his sisters.

He was to fly out to India and went down to Port Reith aerodrome in Cornwall a few days later, where he had to wait five days for fine weather. General Smuts, the South African leader, was also there, but they only saw him at mealtimes. At last they were ordered to be ready to embark at 11 p.m. There was ice on the ground and they heard landing aircraft coming in, and presently saw an enormous red glow in the sky. Some machine had crashed due to the ice. The couple of hours they waited seemed very long, but eventually the twenty or so passengers, including an enormously tall, beautiful and robust "Wren" (Women's Royal Naval Service) officer climbed aboard. They had false passports (in case they should be forced down in neutral territory) and a package of most excellent chocolate and canned fruit from Australia for "iron rations". The flight to Gibraltar was near the limit of the DC3 aircraft's endurance, and it was not pressurised. The pilot kept them well-informed — five hundred miles to the westward of the French coastal air bases, not above 18,000 feet which most people can at least endure, and, when battering noises on the hull became loud and continuous, they learned that they were lucky because the heavy coating of ice was breaking off, and that would ensure that they would really reach Gibraltar. They did so just after daybreak, but as they circled round to approach the runway north of the Rock, a violent air eddy pushed them down to within a few feet of the sea. The aircraft turned on its side; every movable object flew into the air; and at the last possible moment the aircraft righted, hit the runway in three bounces and came to rest very near the far end, beyond which is the Bay of Algeciras. Everybody gasped for a few moments, and Hugh, who was the senior officer on board and therefore the first to disembark, saw the group captain in command of the RAF station standing in front of a small group of airmen, his face a yellow-green sort of mask. He stepped forward to shake Hugh's hand but couldn't speak for a minute or two. The passengers went off to a nearby hut to wash and have breakfast, and the almost unbelievable sight of baskets of oranges, bananas and grapes, long unknown to ration card holders at home.

Later in the morning they flew on eastward, marking the tracks of army vehicles and seeing the burned-out remains of tanks and a few aircraft in the desert from time to time, and, too, the harbour at Oran choked with the hulls of the sunken French fleet. A night was spent in Tripoli in a vast tented camp where Italian prisoners of war did all the domestic service with skill and happy faces. Next day as they approached Cairo West Airport, traffic was congested and permission to land was delayed. The pilot sent off a quick message that this was a VIP plane, and immediate landing was granted. As the plane came to a halt Hugh saw a line of seven very senior officers standing at attention. Then as he staggered rumpled and unshaven out of the aircraft door the "reception committee" broke up and hurried off to a row of glossy limousines, obviously realising that a mistake had occurred. This was the day that Chiang Kai-Shek and Stalin were expected to arrive to attend the top-level Cairo Conference. Stalin, of course, never came, but all the other leaders of the allies arrived in due course.

Hugh could not get a room at Shepherd's Hotel and so stayed at another one a few doors away where he found Mary Churchill and Harriman (the American statesman) were already seated at lunch. He had been told to contact a Royal Marine major-general who had been sent out to control intelligence at the conference and also to advise on the set-up which would be established at SEAC Headquarters in Delhi. They had some interesting conversation which revealed to Hugh that nobody in authority knew how to cope with a Supreme Allied Commander; such a thing had never before existed, so that Mountbatten could in reality build up his own job in whatever way he thought would best serve the needs a Supreme Allied Commander might have. Nobody in Whitehall appeared to know how such a command would be organised. Fortunately Admiral Mountbatten did know, and, having got a Cabinet order which in effect gave him a free hand, he established his position with regard to the Viceroy of India and the Governor of Ceylon, and took command of the whole of the British and also the Indian fighting services in his area, which extended from Aden to Malaya. There were about three million service people under his command.

Hugh flew to Karachi and then Delhi, where he was accommodated at The Maidens Hotel, arriving rather late at dinner-time. He hurried down to the restaurant which was crowded, and the head waiter said he would have to wait, which he could not do because he had an appointment to keep. He looked anxiously around and spotted a small table with an Indian gentleman sitting alone and told the head waiter he would go there.

"But, Sir, there is already an Indian at dinner at that table!"

"Well, what of it? I don't think he would mind."

"But Sir, you couldn't sit down with an Indian gentleman!"

"Why not? I will ask him if he objects."

And he hurried across the room and asked permission to sit at that table. The Indian looked very surprised, but at once made him welcome, and they had a very interesting conversation. The Indian was a secretary in the Calcutta Chamber of Commerce and a delegation of its members had been summoned by the viceroy (Lord Wavell) in order that he might persuade them to release their large stock of rice to the now starving populace, which they had refused to do unless he would authorise them to charge a greatly enhanced price. The viceroy told them he would not agree to that sort of a squeeze, and would order the Army to seize the rice and to distribute it. They replied that if he did they would sabotage the single railway line to Imphal in Burma, where a desperate and critical battle was being fought with the Japanese Army bent on invading India. The viceroy backed down and the famine continued — he had no other option, for India could well have been overrun by the Japanese, and they would have been welcomed by at least some of the leading people.

Next morning Hugh saw the Director of Intelligence (India) at the headquarters offices which were adjacent to the Viceregal Palace, and told the major-general what he had learned at dinner last night. He also arranged to fly on to Burma to visit the front on the Arakan Coast. They stopped at Comilla, the depot of the military forces in Southern Burma where cholera and typhoid were rampant, and got the necessary injections, which took a few days to settle down. At Chittagong, the next stop on the way, an army jeep with its crew of two drivers from the Signal Corps awaited him, and almost wherever he went people mistook him for Mountbatten, as he was of course wearing the khaki jungle uniform which had been established for all personnel in SEAC, and probably nobody in that command had seen a naval uniform so far from sea water before.

Chittagong is sited upon a large river and a high iron bridge carries the railway line across. Loose planks of heavy wood rattled about between the rails and there was no sort of side railing. The whole supply of the army then fighting a hundred miles to the south had to cross in trucks which were crewed by African drivers not long since inhabiting jungle villages in their own country. The swirling muddy water a hundred feet below, the noise of the rattling planks and the absence of any protecting side rails somehow mesmerised the African drivers and almost daily whole convoys lost their heads and drove out of control over the side and into the river where they drowned. The day Hugh's jeep crossed, sheets of coconut matting had been stretched along the two sides of the bridge, but a gusty wind was tearing them away, and as he looked back from the far side two large lorries lurched to one side and drove off into the thin air, hit the water with a big splash and vanished in the liquid muddy flood.

The Arakan Mountains at this point seemed to be twenty miles away to the eastward, but as they drove southwards the heights approached slowly towards their road until at their destination (the Japanese front line) at Razabil the rise began at only two or three miles from the sea coastline — that is, if you could discover where the coast really existed, for the rice paddy-fields, each enclosed in its little two-foot high wall, merged into lagoons joined to one another by endless narrow sea inlets, or perhaps they were river outlets, for the rainfall along those mountains is about 146 inches a year, one of the highest in the world. As soon as one leaves the narrow coastal verge of rice paddy, one climbs amongst endless thickly treed hills which soon merge into precipitous rocky mountain sides, and over the whole area lies a jungle so thick that daylight is shut out. Through this jungle wild tribesmen have cut what are almost tunnels, at best perhaps five feet high, and so narrow that it is usually impossible for one European-sized man to squeeze past another. Whatever jungle animals live there will be visible on very infrequent occasions, and it is well to avoid an encounter with snakes. Some of the pythons are thirty feet long.

There are only three or four villages along the way — small shanty towns with perhaps a couple of mud-brick buildings to house government offices. The last of these was Cox's Bazaar where the African Service battalion was based, and they occupied acres of mud-coloured tents. Curiously enough all those men suffered severe sunburn when they first landed in the Arakan — a problem which confounded the doctors, who were unable to explain the reasons for this unforseen dilemma. Reason or no, whole battalions were laid up and hospitalised for a week or two very shortly after they reached this area, even though they had been born and lived all their lives close to the equator.

Because of the heavy rainfall, and now, in these latter days, a lot of wheeled army traffic, the narrow roadway at a level of about twenty feet above the fields was rapidly disintegrating into dust, and traffic moved in convoys with lights on at full brilliancy so that one could see where the next ahead was, even though visibility at the sides would be no more than a couple of yards. Often they were held up for an hour to allow northbound traffic to move past them.

At such moments one could get out of the jeep and move to the roadside. The whole thing was a simple heap built out of the fine dusty soil nearby so that a deep wide ditch full of water ran along both sides of the highway, and tramping up and down to that one could see gangs, mostly of women and children, with water pitchers on their heads, pouring their pitchers out on the dusty track in a vain hope of laying the dust and preserving the powdered surface.

Occasionally they passed a newly-built mud brick factory, and from there streamed an endless line of coolies carrying on their heads bricks in straw baskets, to be used for repairing the road surface. 20,000 people worked at the maintenance of that vital roadway. Incredibly it was in fact kept open for the heavy army supply traffic right through the campaign.

They had taken sandwiches and water-bottles for the day-long drive southwards, and about noon stopped in a wooded area where there was no dust. The drivers fell asleep after their lunch, and Hugh, hearing the sound of a saw, wandered off into the jungle to find out what was happening — a thing he had been warned was risky because of the extreme difficulty of finding a way back to the road in the thick undergrowth. He found two men standing on a ten-foot high platform sawing down an immense tree, the top of which could not be seen. It would take them at least a couple of hours to complete the cut, and so, after a vain attempt at conversation, he turned away to walk back to the road. He had come along a little hesitant jungle pathway but now found two or three of these wandering off in different directions, and after half an hour began to fear that he was lost, so he lifted up his voice and yelled and yelled, but it was twenty minutes before he heard an answering voice, and then a gunshot from the jeep which enabled him to locate the roadway.

After that the road began an endless zigzag, crossing little streams on loose log bridges, half a dozen of these to each two hundred yards. Then they reached a straighter track and stopped to catch their breath and rest their eyes for a few minutes. Hugh spotted a dark hole in the jungle at the roadside and walked into it to find out what it was. It was a track right enough, but only about four feet high so that he had to crouch down on his haunches, making very slow progress indeed. As he got back to the jeep he saw a sizeable log lying across the road ahead and was pointing it out to the driver when, as his eye was on it, it seemed to slide gently into the jungle at the roadside. This was of course a giant python. Thereafter he stayed on board the jeep and made no further expeditions of discovery.

At General Christison's headquarters he was warmly welcomed by the Signal Section and installed in his own tent, and too, with a native batman locally recruited, who filled a large round tin bath with hot water into which he gratefully sank — but not for long. An air raid siren began to wail and people could be seen scurrying into safety trenches in all directions. He heard the droning noise of the approaching aircraft and realised he couldn't reach a safety trench in time, and so raised the back end of the canvas tent and began to push into the jungle. The little plane flew only a couple of hundred feet up and its machine-guns could be seen flashing as it sprayed the encampment, and the spatter of bullets seemed to be all around him. He redoubled his efforts to get into safety — all to no purpose. The jungle consisted of millions of small tree trunks as big as a man's wrist and so tightly grown that nothing could separate one from another — there was scarcely even an air gap between them, and later, when Hugh attempted to cut a way in with a machete, its blade just bounced off the tough wood, hardly even scratching the surface.

Next day at the general's morning staff conference, he was led forward and introduced to him, and after it was over he called to Hugh and explained the whole position on a large scale display map of the area. The Japanese had tunnelled into the three hundred feet high Razabil hill which blocked the road to the south, and there were no heavy guns to blast them out, and a careful telescope watch had been set up and their gun flashes plotted. Then our guns would lay down a barrage on each position of a gun flash. They had already spent three weeks at this slow and unrewarding attack because an assault across a couple of miles of open level paddy-fields would have involved impossibly heavy casualties. Could Hugh produce a naval bombarding force to plaster Razabil from its rear? No, he could not. Ships could not get closer than ten miles from it, and if small vessels penetrated the endless "chuangs" they could lose their way and would be blown out of the water travelling at slow speed long before they got within range.

Then he noticed marked on the map a small pathway coming from the south and passing only a mile or so from the headquarters. He asked if the Japanese could come up that way and attack the headquarter's position. The general said they could, but he had insufficient forces to patrol that path, and even if it should be used to mount an attack, only very few men could move on it, and they would be able to provision themselves for no more than two or three days. The general had also prepared a sort of "strong point" in a hollow place not easily attacked by gun-fire, into which his personnel could retreat and defend themselves, and, he hoped, feed themselves for a longer period than the Japanese could manage. Only three days after Hugh's departure the Japanese did in fact stage exactly such an attack and, although the fighting was extremely hot, their ammunition and food did give out and they had to retire by the way they had come. It became known as "the Battle of the Box".

Next he visited Calcutta, a vast crowded city on the distant outskirts of which the headquarters of the Army Signal Corps was located, and he was assigned a lodging at a commandeered block of apartments eleven miles distant from the signalmen with whom his business lay. A car took him off each morning at eight o'clock and he noticed horse carts collecting bundles of rags from the monsoon flood ditches that bordered the roadway almost everywhere. When he asked the Indian driver what was going on he learned that four thousand people perished every day because of the rice famine. Their corpses were being collected for burning. At an intersection where a dead dog lay at the side of this busy roadway, nobody removed it during the four days of his visit to Calcutta.

His army hosts organised a dinner party for him at the Calcutta Club — an almost legendary establishment in the Far East. There were a dozen guests, including a few business and Civil Service men, and each guest had a tall turbanned personal waiter standing behind his chair to serve the ten courses and several different wines that accompanied them. He never saw a more beautifully presented and elaborate meal — not even in China. By the end of the long-drawn-out feast he was almost at the point of explosion, for he could think of nothing but the meagre rations he had been served so recently in London. He felt so wrought up about this that as soon as they got up from the table he made his departure, pleading that urgent Admiralty business required his attention at his lodgings. On the long way home his taxi passed a shopping area where several sailors conspicuous in their white uniforms were noisily and rather drunkenly staggering out of a restaurant. The driver spat out something about "bloody Englishmen we won't have here much longer," and Hugh felt somewhat alarmed about his own safety, for he had no idea where he was, and a disaffected driver could have driven him anywhere. When they reached home Hugh did not know what money should be offered for the long journey, and the driver created quite a scene, demanding an outrageous payment and once again volubly cursed the English.

But there was more to come. Next day he was to attend the racing at the Calcutta Jockey Club, an exclusive place where only recently had very rich or very highly placed Indians been admitted.

Amongst the sights was the line of Rolls cars drawn up at the entrance and then, in the Members' Stand later on, a young and somewhat tipsy Indian with a diamond aigrette in his felt hat was behaving badly with friends including Indian women in saris. They all placed their bets at the pari-mutuel windows with thousand-rupee notes. He left this affair as early as he decently could do so without discourtesy to his hosts. It was not his idea of how a country in desperate danger should behave in wartime.

Calcutta was just recovering itself from the shock of one or two Japanese air raids which were unexpected and for which no sort of preparation had been made. Not even was there a warning siren heard. It was said that they had all been disconnected for their usual Saturday cleaning. A few scattered bombs hit the docks area, and several ships were damaged. About three million poor people in that area simply fled helter-skelter out into the open country beyond the last city streets, and marine traffic came to a standstill for a week or two.

As he flew back to Delhi, Hugh saw a tiny white blob at a great distance which he was told was the Taj Mahal, and also, floating away high above the clouds on the horizon the glittering snowy peaks of the Himalayan range of mountains.

When he reached his office he learned that SEAC Headquarters was going to move to Kandy in Ceylon very shortly, a place with which he was already familiar. He was able to get an appointment to report himself to the Supreme Allied Commander, but twice when he got to the office Admiral Mountbatten had been called elsewhere. Then the third time he was lucky. The "Supremo" (as he was nicknamed) was in excellent form and jubilant because Imphal, from which he had just returned, was still intact, and had even started an offensive to drive the Japanese back. He had decided to get out of Delhi as quickly as possible because, as he said: "I have become a Ministry here, no longer a Commander, and I have eight thousand headquarters people hanging around here doing nothing as far as I can see!" He was going to Kandy the next day to hurry the necessary preparations on their way, so Hugh arranged to go to Colombo to the Naval Headquarters where he had his main business to attend to. He told Mountbatten he felt that India was going to burst into flames fairly soon and Mountbatten replied that the possibility was an additional reason for getting away from Delhi. The old city had been the centre of British government for two hundred years past, and it was deeply entrenched in its past and perhaps not able to move out into the urgent business of making modern warfare. On his way to HQ, Hugh had been held up by the street police for twenty minutes because his car must not disturb two enormous Brahmin cows who contentedly chewed a truss of hay some devoted believer had scattered before them, and he had been in fact late for his appointment to report to the Supremo.

Ceylon felt tense and bewildered. A Japanese squadron including a carrier had some weeks earlier come into the Indian Ocean and destroyed the only British carrier and some other warships who were taken by surprise. They had then moved on and bombarded Colombo lightly, but this terrified the Ceylonese who had fled out into the countryside bringing government and business to a standstill. Admiral Somerville, who now commanded scarcely a token force, withdrew his ships to East Africa, where he became ill and was invalided home. In order to stiffen up the position in Ceylon a senior admiral had been appointed as governor and the naval C.-in-C., also a very senior admiral, had established his headquarters at Colombo. The Legislative Council, a partly appointed and partly elected body which formed the parliament of Ceylon, was extremely frightened of the Japanese and hesitant — almost obstructive — about taking proper defence measures and showed signs of imminent disintegration. The new governor summoned a meeting which he intended to address and took the precaution of placing British military personnel at every exit to the Chamber. When he did speak he told parliament exactly what measures they must take, and when some members appeared to want to run out of the Chamber he told them that the sentries had orders to arrest whoever attempted to leave the building. Thereafter everything calmed down and government began to function again in a normal and eventually efficient manner. The Ceylonese whom Hugh met seemed to be rather pleased about the re-establishment of ordered public affairs, and the business community began to realise that the SEAC Headquarters would bring them considerable prosperity.

This small incident of the war seemed to indicate that a certain amount of firmness in administration can pay good dividends in a "free and democratic" society. It has always been true that not all men know how to use freedom aright, nor can democracy work unless there are sufficient honest and able men to lead it. Freedom would seem in practice to be a fragile sort of a benefit hedged about with numerous conditions required to prop it up if it is to prosper.

By the time Hugh reached Kandy up in the hill country of Ceylon, SEAC had moved into a veritable town of palm-leaf thatched huts, and all was organised on a "combined services" basis. The chief of intelligence was a major-general, his deputy an American brigadier; the Royal Air Force had an air commodore, and the Army a brigadier in charge of their intelligence departments. Naval intelligence was to be supplied as necessary from Naval HQ at Colombo, and Hugh began to wonder where he came into the picture. He never did find out. There was a captain designated as Chief of Naval Intelligence Eastern Theatre who established himself at Colombo, who had a roving commission anywhere between Aden and wherever General McArthur's HQ happened to be as he moved from one Pacific island to another in his steady advance towards the Japanese homeland. Hugh fetched up in a very junior little group called the Inter-Service Target Section, where air reconnaissance and other intelligence material was digested and resulted in suitable targets being recommended for RAF bombing. Perhaps it did help them a little.

In fact the only naval matter of any interest was the movement of small store-carrying fishing craft out of Singapore to Burma where the Japanese were making a desperate stand and being slowly pressed back. There were usually about ten of these craft moving on the coast. The only Japanese naval force was kept at Singapore and consisted of about three cruisers and a couple of destroyers which had probably brought convoys down from Japan.

After a while Hugh was sent to Melbourne as liaison officer with an American Naval Intelligence unit. The air journey was an interesting experience. Two passengers only took off in a Catalina flying boat fitted with extra fuel tanks and reached Exmouth Gulf 3,400 miles away in Western Australia after a twenty-nine hour flight. They passed far to the south of Cocos Island where there was a Japanese base from which fighter aircraft endeavoured to intercept this traffic, and for some while were able to listen to the patrol pilots' Japanese conversation. At one point they saw five rainbows simultaneously in an immense pillar cumulus cloud formation at 18,000 feet and similar cloud masses were ranged in orderly lines across the ocean, looking in the bright moonlight rather like dancers in a ballet. They were warmly welcomed at

EE

Exmouth, for it had been the longest flight in the world at that date. The seashore was thick with flocks of white pelicans, green parrots, pink parrots, and a larger white variety.

After a few hours to rest the aircrew, they flew on to Perth, where Hugh was accommodated at an hotel and walked into the dining-room as the doors were being shut. Nobody came to his table, so he went over to the head waitress and asked if he might be served. No; certainly not; dinner was at six and service ceased at seven. Hugh saw that it was now four minutes past seven and said that he had just flown in from Ceylon and was hungry. She looked him up and down with marked disapproval. Who was he, anyway? That wasn't an Australian uniform. So he told her exactly who he was — and that he was still hungry. She went off and brought whatever food she could still find in the pantry. Every other person had vanished from sight. He learned that mealtimes obey iron rules, not to serve the customer, but to suit the trade union. Well, he thought, Australia is something different; I ought to have expected it.

He flew on to Melbourne next day and found his American unit a very agreeable crew. They, rather like himself, were alone and out on a limb. McArthur's command simply did not "play with" Washington. They made their own rules as they went along. However, one almost would have supposed on a clandestine sort of basis, this unit communicated directly with Admiral Halsey who was in command of the seagoing fleet, and so did fulfil an important purpose. Hugh simply acted as a link with the similar British naval group at Colombo and that turned out to be an edgy sort of business where both sides tended to exhibit a spirit of rivalry even though they did co-operate extensively.

He had a lot of spare time and led quite a busy social life in Victoria, for he had friends and distant relatives in that state, and was the only British naval officer anyone had seen for years. The Americans would not "play with" the Australian Navy, so that he arranged only a minimal official contact there which the few senior officers concerned fully understood. It seemed to be more a diplomatic sort of post than a naval appointment. And in the end it all worked out very well.

Australia emerged as a fascinating and admirable country and people. They are generous to a fault; they have a marvellous dry sense of humour; and they have brilliantly intelligent minds, and a dynamic energy and strength of purpose.

Early in the Pacific part of the war they found themselves cut off from the supply of most drugs which they had hitherto purchased from abroad, and so they sent off a practical chemist to find out how such drugs were actually produced. Seeds of plants were purchased; minerals were mined; appropriate factories were built, and within eighteen months they were manufacturing a sufficient supply for their needs. Then they ran out of high-grade optical glass. Somebody from Bohemia (Czechoslovakia) was found and taken on an exploratory tour of Australia to find a suitable climate for glass manufacture, and a year or two later top quality optical glass needed for many war purposes was being produced. They ran out of fighter — and other — aircraft. Someone was sent to England to study manufacturing procedures, and the latest thing — a Beaufighter — was flown to Australia. Two years later Australian-built Beaufighters were being tested in the air and some fell and were destroyed, but the Australian Air Force was re-equipped. All this Hugh witnessed for himself, and in many other areas of human endeavour parallel wonders were being produced. The ten months in Melbourne were amongst the most productive Hugh ever experienced in his long life. Oddly enough he chanced to meet General Blamey who was the C.-in-C. and had conducted the brilliant fight and then retreat and evacuation of a small force sent to Greece by Britain in fulfilment of treaty obligations when Germany overran that country. But now here, in his own country, he was almost universally unpopular, although it was he who had raised and trained the Australian Army that was fighting in New Guinea and elsewhere with great courage and skill, though lacking modern equipment in some respects. He was the sort of man who would never have tolerated inefficiency or slackness of any sort and no doubt his inspections were conducted with rigour and without mercy on shortcomings. He led in New Guinea some of the finest fighting forces ever seen on any field of battle.

Evidently the general had become isolated in his position at the head of the Australian Army and he seemed to find in Hugh, who was a complete outsider, but also a quite widely experienced officer, someone he could talk to with freedom, though he never discussed official military matters. Hugh was invited to the Blamey's house, and went with them to occasional functions. An accurately representative statue of him has since been erected near the War Memorial in Melbourne, and when Hugh saw it several years later he felt that he was standing in front of this very distinguished man.

In due course Hugh flew to Auckland in New Zealand to have a look at their intelligence set-up, for they had contributed some valuable information when he was in the Home Fleet. During the eleven-hour flight from Sydney in a flying boat, he found the print in a book he was reading had become invisible. He chanced to brush a page with his hand and thick dust fell to the deck. This was silt blown from irrigation areas in the Murray River region, and later he saw photographs of orchard trees standing high above the hard pan ground on their network of roots which had been unable to hold the soil in place once it became dry, which happened when some of the holding tanks became filled with silt.

He was accommodated at the naval base at Auckland for a few days and then went by train to Waiouru which was a principal Service communications centre, and amongst other activities was taken to fish the Taupo River where he nearly got drowned when his waders filled in a sudden flash flood. Fortunately the hook on his line got caught in the bank and he was able to pull himself ashore out of the flood water. From the camp at Waiouru one could see a nearby volcano erupting from its snow cap, and this one had some years ago produced a major explosion when red hot rock had fallen among the trees and set the whole countryside on fire so that numerous people were trapped, and a few had lost their lives.

He went on by train to Wellington to report to the Chief of New Zealand Naval Staff, and from there they gave him a personal small plane to fly to Invercargill at the southern tip of South Island, where a particularly successful wireless station operated. There were only eleven men there out on a bleak sandy spit, and when he told them that the Home Fleet had been receiving their signals and using their information they were incredulous, and of course highly delighted, and so Hugh felt that his trip was indeed worthwhile. If it was possible to improve their lonely, isolated performance he felt they most certainly would do so.

New Zealand seemed curiously remote from the world. They had sent troops and ships to fight, but they could not comprehend what war was like — the sound of an exploding bomb had never been heard. He was particularly glad that he had been there; they longed to hear what the reality was like even if they could not quite understand it.

Back in Melbourne again, it was becoming clearer that Admiral Halsey's victories at sea and General McArthur's steady advance towards Tokyo were going to bring Japan to defeat. The Germans had been thrown out of the Middle East as well, and preparations for D-Day were advancing. Italy was invaded as a first step. After ten months the time came for Hugh to return to SEAC where he felt that some more worthwhile work should come his way. When D-Day came they held their breath — but the great landing on Normandy beaches was accomplished, and a slow advance into Europe began, leading as we all know to the capitulation of Germany.

VE day came to SEAC HQ at Kandy as a sort of distant, not wholly relevant, end of a war which was not our Far Eastern conflict. Japanese troops in Burma, though now hard pressed and very slowly giving ground, every inch of which was costing the lives of our men, showed no sign whatever of breaking. They would go on toughly fighting to the last round of ammunition. Our minds were set upon the eventual landing somewhere near Malacca with the objective of cutting their remaining tenuous lines of supply.

It was at about this time that the small group of naval officers of SEAC Headquarters decided to form their own mess in a large house on the lake shore at Kandy — a situation that offered some pleasant surroundings, and even a frequent evening breeze unobtainable in the cramped central camp. Hugh hesitated about joining because he well knew that the Supremo wanted everything to be run on inter-Service lines. However he did decide to join, and Lord Mountbatten did not seem to be annoyed when he learned of this. On the contrary, he said he would like to come and dine in the mess a few days hence and the evening went off very well indeed. While he was talking with Hugh he presently said:

"You know sometimes I feel it is all wrong that I who am really only a junior captain have to get up and give all sorts of orders to people who are senior generals or air marshals!"

He quite genuinely did feel embarrassed in his situation but certainly never betrayed the smallest sign of this. Then he said:

"Why don't I ever see you at my staff conferences?"

"Well, Sir, your Chief of Intelligence attends and of course represents all three Services."

It wasn't long before a day came when the chief of intelligence was absent visiting some distant place and a messenger appeared hot foot from Lieutenant-General Browning, the Supremo's Chief of Staff, ordering Hugh to attend the morning conference due to begin in a few minutes. Hugh dashed off and took an empty seat at a very long table around which nobody less senior than a lieutenant-general was seated. One or two of them turned and looked at him with astonishment. Presently the Supremo began asking him questions which fortunately he was able to answer, and after it was over several of these very senior officers came up to him and introduced themselves — a gesture of real courtesy to a sister Service which he greatly valued.

To mark the German capitulation in 1945, a small ceremony was held at Kandy HQ. The heads of department lined up opposite the Supremo's office over which floated nine national flags of nations whose forces had been placed under his direction. In rear of these heads a motley throng of mostly office personnel from each department stood in four-deep ranks, ill at ease and without the discipline of silence and immobility. Some robed chaplains stood to one side. At precisely two minutes before eleven, Admiral Mountbatten and his American deputy, General Wheeler, stepped out of the central doorway and the parade was called to attention. A signal gun fired and all came to the salute as a few bars were played by a military band from nine national anthems. Then we stood "at ease" while chaplains prayed and then the Supremo read a brief address suitably worded to the occasion and ending with an exhortation to get back to the work of beating the Japanese. Our war was to go on, indeed for another year.

But Hiroshima and then Nagasaki ended this hopeless resistance, leaving behind them a feeling of horror, and too, some sense of shame that we had perpetrated the worst excess that had ever been known in human conflict. The reverberations from the explosion of those two atomic bombs have not yet died down — and it will be well if they never do. This weapon is the ultimate of all weapons because its continued use can destroy mankind from off the face of the earth.

One morning Hugh received a telephone call from one of the Supremo's ADCs inviting him to lunch at the King's House where Lord Mountbatten lived at Kandy. There were about twenty guests and, as he always managed to do, the Supremo talked to every one of them while they were having a preparatory drink, during which he introduced Hugh to an American naval commander whose name he didn't catch. They sat together at table rather naturally as they were the only sailors present. After lunch the Supremo offered Hugh a lift back to Peradinya Gardens (about three miles away) where the offices were. He drove his jeep himself with its nine allied flags mounted on the radiator cap and discoursed on the frightful toll of accidents that was building up on the narrow little road. He had established a patrol of army motor cyclists in order to keep cars on their own sides of the road and some of these men had been killed. He was trying to find a remedy and the road could not be easily widened nor could the traffic be reduced. He turned to Hugh and asked:

"How did you get on with Dempsey? I saw you two chatting away at lunch. Do you know who he is?"

Hugh, mystified, said, "No, Sir, I didn't get his name when we were introduced. I liked him; he is a nice sort of modest fellow."

"It was Dempsey — the boxer."

All things considered, probably the most widely famous man Hugh ever spoke to!

At about this time a signal came in from General McArthur saying that twenty new long-range heavy bomber aircraft destined for the bombing of mainland Japan had just joined his command and he wished them to have some wartime experience while their airfields were being developed. Could Mountbatten use them during the next month or so? Hugh read this message early in the morning and plotted out the distance from Calcutta's airport to Singapore and confirmed that the two thousand mile distance was well within their range.

He was due to visit Naval HQ at Colombo that day, and the train would leave shortly. He wondered if he could sell the idea of such an air attack to the Naval C.-in-C., knowing that the naval dockyard was a particularly treasured base in Admiralty circles.

On the train about noon, an ADC came to invite him to lunch with the Supremo, who always used that sort of occasion to meet as many junior officers as space allowed. He was seated at the Supremo's table, and when opportunity occurred asked him if he had seen McArthur's signal, and adding his own idea about bombing Singapore. Mountbatten at once rejoined:

"You must know that the dockyard is the apple of the Admiralty's eye. The C.-in-C. would never approve!"

"But Sir, you don't have to get his approval. You are under the Minister of Defence only."

"If you can sell your idea to the C.-in-C. I shan't raise any objections."

And so, as soon as he reached Naval HQ at Colombo, he asked

for an interview with the C.-in-C. upon a matter concerning the Supremo. The admiral received him at once and listened to his story and then asked a number of questions. As Hugh finished answering he added:

"Anyhow, Sir, I recall that Singapore dockyard cost the country six million pounds, and in this command we spend three million a day, so that if a successful air raid seriously damaged supplies on their way to Burma and shortened the war by only two days we would break even. It can be regarded as a simple problem of arithmetic if one wishes."

The admiral's mouth opened a little.

"I've never heard of such a thing as this in all my life. Anyhow it is the Supreme Commander's responsibility — not mine! The Admiralty won't approve."

"They need not be asked, Sir. The Supreme Commander answers only to the Minister of Defence."

"You go back to him and tell him I don't agree — and that he knows perfectly well already. Good afternoon!"

So Hugh told the Supremo that evening that the Naval C.-in-C. couldn't agree and wasn't going to take any action.

The raid duly took place ten days later and air photographs showed that two cruisers and probably three destroyers had been sunk, one of the two floating docks was sunk and the other one was half submerged, forty-six assorted merchant craft were sunk, the large graving dock was heavily damaged at its entrance gates, the small graving dock was completely destroyed, and the whole workshop and power house area was absolutely flattened. A second raid was carried out a few days later and the remaining floating dock was sunk and the large graving dock suffered further destruction. In sum, there was now nothing left to bomb. The damage was the heaviest and most complete destruction achieved from the air during the whole of World War II. Hugh walked all over the area a year later and saw the devastation. The Japanese had repaired nothing except for the refloating of the smaller floating dock.

A few days after the Japanese capitulation on their mainland, Lady Mountbatten was hurriedly flown out from London to take charge on behalf of the Red Cross of the rescue of prisoners of war from the numerous Japanese camps scattered across the whole area of our command. Warships and aircraft and a small staff at HQ were placed under her direction, and the speed and competence with which the rescue proceeded saved some hundreds of lives. Lady Mountbatten had already performed a similar operation in Hungary a year earlier, and Mountbatten talking to Hugh at the time said:

"I've sent for my wife. She knows more about this sort of thing than anybody else alive, and I am making this job our top priority."

When the Japanese in Burma finally capitulated, a somewhat motley headquarters throng flew off in several aircraft to attend at the formal Japanese surrender of swords at Rangoon, which was, of course, General Slim's great day. These staff people had headed the supply effort of the Army in Burma and perhaps that was their greatest reward.

Later, Lord Mountbatten ordered Marshal Terauki, the Japanese Area Commander who was at Saigon, to appear at Singapore and hand over his sword at a public ceremony. The marshal pleaded that he had had a stroke and was not fit to travel. Mountbatten sent doctors to examine him and they reported that he was indeed a dying man and would not survive the journey (although his sword was sent), so that General Itagaki, the next in seniority, had to be accepted as a substitute. In due course outside the Supreme Court Building on Singapore Maidan, he and nearly a hundred more junior commanders were compelled to climb up the many steep steps and personally hand over their swords to Mountbatten. Some of us feared that one or another amongst them might attack him in a final gesture of *bushido*, and at least one of the ADCs was inconspicuously prepared for such an eventuality. On this great day all however went peaceably, but later Mountbatten said:

"I did rather wonder if one of them might not attack me, and when Itagaki got close and I saw his face working like a madman, I wondered if he would go for me or fall down with a stroke before he handed over his sword! But of course that didn't happen."

Hugh's intelligence empire, officially consisting of some fourteen hundred personnel, very rapidly flittered away; the majority of them were not even under Admiralty direction but civilian ministries seemed able to secure air transportation on a priority basis.

The Japanese collapse had occurred at the end of August 1945, and SEAC HQ moved to the Cathay Building, the first "tower" structure to be built in Singapore. In December the SEAC staff were flown down to Singpore and billeted in commandeered houses about five miles out of town. Hugh quickly acquired an official jeep — only because he knew the CO of the transport depot — and with it came an "official" civilian driver, and a Royal Marine as well, presumably as a sort of "military protector", who turned out to be a remarkably efficient kind of guardian and knew how to get gasoline when there wasn't any, and where to get food that nobody else could obtain.

A key clause in the written document of surrender which the Emperor of Japan was compelled by General McArthur to broadcast in person stated that the emperor henceforth renounced his hereditary claim to godhead, a claim hitherto conceded by all Japanese people, and conferring upon him a degree of authority and power obtainable by man in no other manner.

Hugh's Japanese interpreters monitored the emperor's speech, an official copy of which they had on their desk, and to their astonishment, when the emperor's voice to which Hugh was listening came to this clause, there was a momentary hesitation and then the emperor omitted the key words and went on directly to the next following paragraph.

Hugh collected the manuscript of the translated speech as soon as it was typed and walked over the short distance to the Supremo's office and showed Lord Mountbatten what had happened. He read the speech and then leant back in his chair for a moment.

"This is McArthur's business — not mine. I shan't do anything about it." Hugh rejoined:

"But Sir, this may be crucial for the future. Surely we could simply call attention to the discrepancy?"

"No. It's not my business." And there the matter ended. Hugh never felt satisfied in after years, and considered that the Japanese were left in a position to resurrect the imperial deity when and if it ever suited them.

Hugh found himself now at last in a position of leisure and independence that had never before been his lot. Several small trawlers arrived from England and one of these he shanghaied, fitted it out as a survey ship and sent it off to examine the small ports and anchorages on the west coast of Siam, about which no information existed in any official document known to him. His principal office assistant, an ex-motor torpedo-boat captain, decorated for his skilful work in the Greek Islands, was placed in command, and the little ship did some interesting surveys and spent its occasional few hours in port doing medical work amongst the sparse and neglected coastal population. Indeed, they became altogether too popular as medics for their real work to pass unnoticed.

He himself finally had a brief collapse in health and took himself off in his jeep to Cameron Highlands, the 5,000-foot hilltop health station in Central Malaya where after a few days in the army field hospital he moved to the "Green Cow" the original little hotel of the settlement, now presided over by a famous artist's model of the late Victorian age in London.

In the hospital he had met an RAF wing commander who, while out for an evening walk, had got lost in the jungle for over a week and had managed to survive almost entirely by eating young unfolding ferns. Finally some Sakai (diminutive aboriginal mountain tribesman) had found him and carried him on their backs into Cameron Highlands. He had never once been able to see the sun because of the heavy tree-top foliage almost two hundred feet above the ground, where a whole society of flowers and animals and insects have their dwelling.

Hugh, once his strength improved, walked daily in or near the camp, and as he progressed, went still further afield, until one day he sighted on a distant ridge several European bungalows which appeared to be on fire. Communist infiltrators from the north were known to be moving into Malaya and so he decided to investigate. The next day, when he sighted the buildings again, he was puzzled to see them still ablaze. An hour later, as he climbed the last ascent, he saw that brilliant flame-coloured shrubbery half smothered the stripped remains of what had once been white civil servants' summer holiday cottages. The Japanese had taken away every sort of fitting, including electric wiring and all the plumbing, and one or two owls flapped heavily away as he entered the first building, which was no more than a burnt-out shell with part of a roof remaining at one end.

A little later he took his jeep with its two-man crew up into the more distant mountains as far as the track would permit, hoping to establish how far south the Communists had penetrated and to find out what effect they were having on the sparse population that had been left on abandoned plantations. At one point the roadway ran down a long hill and a river just below it flows in the opposite direction, creating the remarkable appearance of actually running uphill — a sight well known to the white planters, of course.

A short distance beyond this the original bridge across the river had been destroyed, and when the jeep reached that point they found an East African Army Engineer company in the process of building a new timber bridge which was not yet open to traffic. Hugh spoke to the officer in charge, who promised that if he would wait for twenty minutes, the jeep would be able to go ahead. When he drove forward to the edge of the bank he saw before him just two narrow lines of planking, and down below standing waist-deep in the stream about forty Africans spread across in small groups, each one holding up a tree trunk which supported the two tracks. Hugh decided to take the wheel himself, and somehow managed to steer successfully the short distance to the far bank, and when they got there observed that the Malay driver had his two hands placed firmly over his eyes.

"I did not want to see, Sir, how I was going to die!" was his only comment. Hugh regarded this as about the most dangerous incident of his life. Next day, when they returned, the bridge appeared to be much more solid, but in fact it swayed to and fro sideways in an alarming manner. The little handful of Malay estate coolies they met on their route suffered from malnutrition and appeared cowed and spiritless after years of starvation and Japanese oppression, and were too frightened of the Communists to do more than admit that "a man had passed that way" two or three weeks ago and that he had posted up on tree trunks red printed propaganda notices at frequent intervals along the route he followed. While they stopped for a picnic lunch and a midday snooze there suddenly emerged from the jungle a Sakai family, an old man with a spear, a young man with a blowpipe, a boy with a bow, and a young girl with a bag over her shoulder wearing a woven grass triangular patch about four inches wide as the only clothing among the whole party. They froze in their tracks, taken aback by the sleeping jeep crew, and scarcely acknowledged the Malay driver's questions, and then vanished into the jungle as silently and swiftly as they had appeared. They were on a hunting expedition from their village, which probably consisted of a couple of palm-thatched shelters. Hugh saw Sakai people on another occasion when the men were persuaded to give a demonstration of their skill with the blowpipe. They unfailingly hit a mark at thirty paces distance, but at forty paces the arrow would not have penetrated a thick hide. Physically these jungle near-pygmies are the most perfectly built humans imaginable, their only equals Hugh ever saw being an occasional Fijian spear fisherman, who also lives an entirely natural existence.

On the way south back to Singapore the roads had become dangerous because of Communist infiltration from the north, and army anti-communist check-points had been established at frequent intervals which so delayed progress that Hugh left the jeep and its crew at Malacca and boarded a train which carried some protective armoured plating. Beds were made up on the floor to avoid the dangers from sporadic firing, though his train on this day did not suffer any molestation and he slept too well to hear any gun-fire there may have been through the night. The Communists had become bold and very active all over Malaya.

There followed two trips in the Supremo's personal plane. They flew first to Batavia and were housed for the night in the old Dutch Club, a sweltering airless structure dripping with damp and thick with mosquitoes. A heavy official Dutch dinner occupied most of the evening. Next day they flew to Bandoeng, a Dutch hill-station in the interior of Java, set amongst rich rice paddy-fields, but terribly run-down. A few Dutch families had lived there throughout the Japanese occupation and were now under siege from "freedom fighters" who were even more dangerous. As we had no troops available for their protection, the local Japanese garrison had been allowed to keep their arms and to act as security police. While Mountbatten and his daughter, who was acting as his WREN secretary, and his ADC, with Hugh trailing along at the end of the line, were entertained to lunch by a Dutch household, distant gun-fire broke out, and from the dining-room window they saw a column of black smoke rising from a house on fire about two miles away. Their Dutch hosts told them that this was an almost daily incident and would not prevent their hosts taking their children back to afternoon school, a school which they had staffed themselves and kept open during the entire Japanese occupation.

Later the party took off for Palembang, the great oil port in Sumatra, and flew directly over Krakatoa, the island volcano which had erupted in 1883 with the largest explosion ever recorded on earth. The black jagged broken lava walls of the crater stand glistening out of the sea and, to the astonishment of those in the plane, heavy green jungle growth was seen to occupy all the area other than sheer cliff faces. It seemed remarkable that roots of anything could have taken hold in such hard and almost new rock.

Palembang airfield is situated eleven miles from the old walled city, which is itself about eight miles distant from the large oil port. Here again "freedom fighters" had taken over control, so the Japanese were allowed to keep their arms while protecting the Dutch population, and these soldiers were positioned in force on the route. Every couple of hundred yards on either side of the road a Japanese military guard of about 100 men was drawn up in line, and as the Supremo's party in five jeeps sped along they presented arms in salute. Hugh was in the tail-end jeep and his naval uniform was of course outstandingly visible, and indeed it looked as if some of the platoon commanders had mistaken him for Mountbatten, as they shouted some sort of salute or greeting not given to the jeeps ahead.

They all went straight to a late afternoon reception held in the Dutch Club in Mountbatten's honour, and the party had not long been in progress when the British garrison commander came forward to tell Mountbatten that a force of "freedom fighters" had climbed up over the wall about half a mile away and that fierce hand-to-hand fighting with his small skeleton force was now in progress. He urged Mountbatten to get back to the airport immediately and fly out.

"Oh, no! Tell your fellows to throw them back over the wall and I'll be over there in a few minutes to lend them a hand as soon as I've said goodbye to these Dutch officials." And he did indeed set off towards the fighting, but a messenger stopped him on the way and told him that the attack had already been repelled, and that there had been only a small force involved.

Next day they flew to Medan, which lies to the northward in central Sumatra, passing over mountainous country which was never conquered nor occupied by the Dutch, and appears to be still today beyond the control of the central Indonesian government. A large part of this great central area remains unmapped and unexplored, and the untamed inhabitants apparently continue to kill or frighten off would-be explorers.

Hugh had gone to Sumatra to examine the small but potentially important and only seaport on the northern coast which was already occupied by a skeleton British force, and the naval officer in charge was at Medan airport to meet him. During the plane trip he had extracted whatever information the general in command (who was accompanying the Supremo) could supply, and later learned that a force of 500 soldiers was preparing to escort him on the 300 mile journey, which they planned to rush through in a single day. The road was dangerous and frequently cut, and there was no airstrip at the port. However, the senior naval officer had brought with him all the charts, maps, and other details which he had been collecting, so that late that evening Hugh was already in possession of all the information that existed, and he felt that the unnecessary disturbance of such a large military force was no longer justifiable, and went to the general to ask him to cancel his arrangements. The escort commander was more than grateful. He told Hugh that it was a most difficult route to protect, with narrow defiles through the mountains and sometimes a destroyed road surface. Sumatra, large and rich though it is, remains today one of the world's most uncivilised areas.

Hugh had learned from the general that a large number of Japanese officers' surrendered swords were stored at HQ at Medan and he asked if he might have one to take home as a souvenir, to which the general happily agreed, adding that he had already earmarked fifty for the supreme commander, who wanted to distribute them as souvenirs. When the trip was over and they were preparing to land at Singapore, the ADC was in the process of sorting out the swords and Hugh stretched out his hand and took one. Mountbatten was looking on, and at once remonstrated.

Hugh said: "Well, Sir, I asked the general for one as he had a large number stored at Medan and he promised to send one aboard the aircraft for me with those you had already ordered."

"I never heard anything about that!"

"Well, I suppose not, Sir. It was just fixed up between the general and myself, and evidently he hasn't put a label on my one."

"Oh, well! There seem to be plenty to go round!" And there the matter ended, but he didn't look at all pleased. When Hugh unsheathed his sword later on in England he cut his thumb as he was testing the blade and was surprised to find it razor sharp, and very much ready for instant use.

Back in Singapore a civil government was being organised by Malcolm McDonald (son of the prime minister), who had been wartime High Commissioner in Canada and had just come out to head our administration. There were about nine sultanates in the Malayan peninsula, none of them willing to surrender their positions, so that difficult and prolonged negotiations were inevitable. The Sultan of Johore, who had cunningly stood off the Japanese for five long years, was ill and had gone to England for treatment, and his palace at Johore was now occupied by the Army C.-in-C. General Dempsey. Hugh met one of the Rajah's sons who was Minister of Agriculture, a key position in the state where famine conditions were widespread, chiefly because the Japanese had commandeered all foodstuffs and had also eaten almost all the water buffalo that ploughed the fields. Touring the interior with the young minister, Hugh saw the emaciated state of the people and watched the minister encouraging them wherever he went. They found a school still operating in one village and the children took them to see the open-air theatre they had constructed — a little raised platform at one side of a grassy clearing in the jungle where they were rehearsing a Shakespeare play and attempting to build scenery with canes and paper, bubbling over with excitement as they played out one act for the visitors. Hugh had only a few dollars in his pocket and a packet of sandwiches, but they wouldn't accept the money, though they were unable to resist the sandwiches. It was a touching incident that lingers in the memory. The teacher had malaria and could hardly stand as he showed them the dog-eared grimy little book of the play — the only school book that had survived a Japanese search for "subversive literature".

As soon as Lady Mountbatten had completed her task of evacuating the several thousand sick and wounded from all Japanese war prisoner camps in the command, which took her a month, she came to Singapore to live at Government House, where the Supremo was installed. Hugh had set up his office in the Cathay Building with two reserve officers as assistants, and a second officer WRNS as secretary. A general reception was organised in the building to welcome Lady Mountbatten, and Hugh was led up to be introduced to her. She seemed to know a good deal about him as soon as she heard his name and spoke of his service in the Home Fleet. He wondered how such a thing could be possible. Thirty years later when he met a lady, who had been one of her secretaries in London, she told him that whenever someone was coming to the house her staff were instructed to find out as much as possible about the guest, and then, when the day came, the secretary would take the guest list to her and she would go through it committing to memory the details of each person.

A little later on, after Malcolm McDonald arrived in Malaya, Mountbatten asked if Hugh knew him — which he did not, but he had heard good reports of his wartime work at Ottawa. Within a

few days an invitation came to dinner at Government House, and
he soon found himself led up to McDonald and talking to him. He
seemed a quiet, serious man, taking in all that he heard, and he did
splendid work uniting the several independent states in what is
now a single country — though Singapore Island is outside that
union and wholly independent of it, perhaps because the city is in
reality almost completely in Chinese hands, and the Chinese just
do not mix with the Malays. They scarcely have any point of real
empathy.

About this time Hugh flew up to Bangkok, which everyone
hoped would be at the centre from which rice might be obtained to
relieve the famine conditions in Malaya and elsewhere. Siam
traditionally had a shaky government beset on all sides by
ambitious political generals seeking to control the public affairs.
The king, not quite twenty years old, was still inexperienced and
no match for the many practised politicians. The Siamese naval
officers welcomed Hugh warmly and made every effort to assist
his enquiries. Through them he met a notable flying man, the
young Prince "Nicky", fourth in succession to the throne, who
had been trained at Cranwell Air Force Officers' College in
England, a lively and wholly delightful person who took him off to
his little bungalow on the river-side to meet his wife. They invited
him to dinner next night and to meet the king, who would be their
guest, an invitation he was compelled to refuse because the naval
HQ staff were giving a dinner for him that evening. However
Prince Nicky urged him to come on to his party afterwards if he
possibly could.

Later he heard that the king, accompanied by his mother (who
was of mixed racial blood), decided to go home early and sent for
the Queen Mother who was in another room. When she appeared
she said that she was having a lovely time and wouldn't be ready to
leave for some while. This public rebellion infuriated the king,
who made the gesture which demands the kowtow (that the person
shall go down and place the forehead on the ground at the king's
feet), and the lady, her face working in fury, was compelled to do
this and then to follow him out to his waiting car. Gossip in
Bangkok had already made Hugh aware that the Queen Mother
was unpopular and hot-tempered, that she was often seen
quarreling with the king, and that she had a lover, some man of
low degree in the palace entourage. There was a feeling in the
upper ranks of the capital that something violent was about to

emerge in the royal palace.

Two days later the king was shot in the back of the head by an unidentified assassin. Four doctors (including a British surgeon) examined the body, and Hugh learned from him exactly how the bullet had travelled and that the pistol must have been almost touching the neck at the moment of discharge. No charge was ever laid against any person, and the late king's brother, only about seventeen years old, was publicly declared as the successor. It is curious to recall that Hugh speaking to Mountbatten on his return to Singapore a day or two before the assassination had said that he felt that the king was unlikely to survive for very long. Mountbatten had been in Bangkok himself a little earlier for a state visit and had been driven through the streets with the king and had suggested that he should bow and acknowledge the plaudits of the people and abandon the traditional attitude of immobility, looking straight ahead like an idol.

While Hugh was in Bangkok he drove out to the palace, parts of which were open to the public. He joined a group of tourists at the gate and the guide led them through one courtyard after another, but Hugh lost his group while he was gazing at the gilded ornate dome of a very beautiful pagoda. However, he spotted an open gateway and then wandered on and on through several doors until he was completely lost. Eventually a fat brilliantly-dressed man — probably a eunuch — spoke to him in English, saying that he had no business to be in that place; it was the private quarters of the royal family, and of course he apologised and explained what had happened. The eunuch took him in hand and showed him the temple he had been admiring and then led him back to the main entrance. This was one of the many occasions when Hugh suddenly felt the reality of the prestige which was accorded in so many places to the uniform of the Royal Navy. It really did appear that the Service had won for itself a particular kind of recognition, perhaps a kind of widespread trust in its integrity.

He learned here that there were about three hundred princes, sons of kings, living in Siam at that time. They received small pensions for life, but their royal status died with them. Nobody knew how many royal daughters — or widows — there might be, but such ladies could and did marry commoners as and when they pleased, and lost their royal status upon their marriage. Women were not accorded any notable public status in oriental societies in those days; any change there may be in this respect will only come in at a very gradual pace.

In Borneo, Britain held possessions in the north: British North Borneo, Sarawak, which was a protectorate on the west coast, and the small but important oil port of Labuan and the immediate territory of its hinterland. The Labour Party government in England after the war was resolved to disentangle the homeland from as many 'colonies' as it could manage, and as quickly as possible. Many of these were financial liabilities and Britain was compelled to make economies everywhere in order to stave off bankruptcy.

Accordingly a senior official was sent out to Sarawak to arrange to give that country its "freedom". About 130 years earlier a British merchant family (Brooke) had established a trading post on the Sarawak coast and, during a rebellion against the native authority, had assisted in establishing peace, and Mr Brooke was afterwards elected by the Dyak people as their hereditary rajah, and the state became a British "protectorate" which was occupied by a small Japanese force when the war began. Mountbatten in his position as the senior British authority in the area was commissioned to perform the official act of handing over the territory, and he, with a small personal staff, and also Hugh, flew off from Singapore in a Sunderland flying boat to the city of Sarawak, a five-hour journey. When they sighted the coastline the pilot went down close to the water so that the passengers could see some fishing boats. These were being harrassed by larger junks manned by pirate crews who usually seized the fish, and, if resistance were offered, would sink the boat, callously leaving the crew to fend for themselves. They were alarmed presently to see five swimmers making towards the coastline about twenty miles away, but the flying boat could not come down to rescue them because of the waves, and, as they passed low overhead, they saw the men waving and laughing and quite unconcerned about their fate. These Dyak seamen are powerful swimmers and thought nothing of the twenty mile stretch ahead of them. They looked like gold-coloured fish in the water as the sun flashed on their bodies. Their splashing would keep sharks away as long as they kept together.

The Brittania flying boat landed in the river opposite the town and Mountbatten and his staff were taken off to the rajah's palace, while Hugh went to stay with the temporary administrator of the government. That night he met the Chinese member of the

NEGRI Council, the twenty-two member body representing various groups of citizens as their "parliament". He learned that, although the Japanese had been rigorous in commandeering food and supplies, they had never been able to spread out into the countryside because every night their cordon of sentries placed round the town were almost all found each morning with their throats cut. The Dyaks had been quietly surprising them in the dark and in due course the sentries had been withdrawn into the lighted streets, but still suffered a steady toll of casualties, though in smaller numbers. He was told that the Japanese soldiers were absolutely terrified of these Dyaks.

Next day the council met at the palace where the Rajah, the Supremo and the Colonial Office official from London faced them on a little platform. The official stepped forward, made a short speech in English explaining the purpose of the meeting, and then went on to read a quite lengthy document — also in English — setting out the terms under which Britain deposed the rajah and gave up the protectorate status, the legal requirement being that the NEGRI Council assent to all this.

Then he told all those in favour to hold up their hands. A few did; others who did not know English, were asking their neighbours what was going on, but only a handful knew. Then the official began to urge those who had not raised their arms to do so and some did. He rapidly counted the uplifted hands and announced that the council had agreed to the proposition by a majority of seventeen votes to five. The document was then signed by the three on the platform; the official folded the paper, slipped it into his pocket and walked out. Bedlam broke out and eventually the puzzled council dispersed. All this was conveyed that evening to Hugh by the Chinese member, with whom he had dinner. This experienced man was shaken by the apparent trickery practised by the Colonial Office official, and asked Hugh if such a proceeding was normally to be found in British administration.

Hugh, while in Melbourne, was staying in the same hotel where Rajah Brooke was living — a broken man and a very sick one. The rajah had left Sarawak when the Japanese invaded his country, with the idea that as a prisoner he would be powerless to help his people in any way at all, whereas as a free man he would be in a position to help his country in whatever way might be open to him. Having got away and experienced the complete lack of British or any other interest in the affairs of Sarawak he now realised that he would have been far better off if he had remained at home to share whatever difficulties faced his country. He was utterly dejected at what he now came to regard as his desertion and seemed to think only of abdication in favour of a nephew who would be his nearest successor.

In the evening of "freedom day", which was an expression invented by the British government, a general reception was held at the club, attended by the ex-Rajah and his wife, the whole of the very small British community, and about a dozen of the leading Dyak chieftains, mostly coming from the mountainous hinterland. They don't wear clothes, but have a long sort of coloured scarf wound tightly round their waists and tucked between their legs. Head-dresses of beads, shells and brilliant feathers, necklaces and arm bands in all colours complete their ceremonial regalia, and they make a brilliant display. As soon as the rajah and his party arrived, the chieftains began a sort of chant, and then, one after another, advanced towards him, tears streaming down their weather-beaten faces, as they went down on their knees in homage and bent so that their foreheads touched the ground at his feet. It was an act of broken-hearted farewell. The rajah's face was an ivory mask and his eyes clouded and expressionless. How he managed to remain standing rigidly straight through the hour-long ordeal one could not imagine. Dinner was served at several long tables and then the whole company moved out to the large polo ground where a small stand with several rows of chairs had been erected. The Brookes and the Supremo and their personal staffs of course occupied the front row. The Colonial Office official from London, who had not been at the club, was nowhere to be seen.

There followed a two-hour series of displays and dances and an immense fireworks programme under the light of a full moon. Hugh found himself seated beside the Roman Catholic bishop who had spent most of his life in Borneo and was able to discourse on every item in the programme with deep knowledge and understanding of Dyak society. The main part of the entertainment was the enacting of battle and hunting scenes in a kind of ballet, wonderfully presented by superb dancers. The bishop explained that every tribe and almost every village had its own dance troupe trained from early youth to enact scenes relevant to its actual living experience, some of which represent historical events of long past times. For Hugh it was an entertainment unequalled by any other he ever witnessed — the most beautiful to look at and the most brilliantly executed. Next day the little party from Singapore flew back almost silent — and thoughtful. Hugh felt for the first time in his life ashamed of his country, yet aware that its white democratic society could not be wholly blamed for its lack of knowledge and understanding of a race of naked head-hunting savages hidden away at the other side of the world, but also aware that henceforth these people would be compelled to make what terms they could with a world about which they knew next to nothing. He longed to go back to Sarawak but never managed to revisit it.

Later SEAC Command was formally disbanded and Mountbatten left to become Viceroy of India and to organise the withdrawal of the British civil and military presence. Chaos quickly ensued as British authority vanished. In Delhi itself, multitudes clamoured to get into the Anglican Church College compound seeking protection; General Auchinlek, the Army C.-in-C., disappeared for three weeks before he eventually escaped to the coast; Lord and Lady Mountbatten and a small staff travelling by train from Simla in the far north were in great peril for three days while several attacks were launched upon the train as it passed through towns. Most of the European personnel had to lie on the floor to escape gunshot at one time or another. These included an old shipmate of Hugh's who described the journey to him as being "far more dangerous than four years of warfare at sea". It has been said that three million Indians died in the rioting.

At Singapore, Hugh became the local "Staff Officer, Intelligence", on a regular peace-time basis for a few weeks until his relief arrived from England, when in July 1946 he took off in a Liberator aircraft for home. While leaving Ceylon in a fierce thunderstorm, lightning seemed to enter the passenger compartment, brilliantly illuminating everything in sight, but without causing damage. They landed at Lyneham in Wiltshire, and were deposited at the local railway station to await a train to London. Hugh, loaded with baggage, stumbled over his Japanese sword, and barked his shins, which bled profusely, so that he arrived back from the wars at his sister's home in London looking quite like a wounded hero.

Chapter 17

The Admiralty

As we have seen, Hugh's long active participation in naval intelligence affairs at sea came to an end with the Japanese war, and his duties at Singapore amounted to winding up and closing down the business of war and to resuming the routine of naval peace-time organisation. There followed some weeks of foreign service leave and then he was appointed as Naval Assistant to the Director of Naval Intelligence, which sounded quite impressive, but in fact added up to the function of odd job man. Whatever was not routine almost automatically landed in his "In" basket and the work was interesting and sometimes involved the sweeping away of some ancient customs and practices that the years had accumulated.

Amongst such jobs was the business of managing the affairs of the sixty-two naval attachés. They all had something to talk about and several of them became good friends. The Russian group — about a dozen of them, only one being a proficient English speaker — were frequently asking questions to which answers were often enough complex.

Almost every other week there was a diplomatic function which soon became the duty of the odd job man. He would attend with the DNI or else appear in his stead. At these functions the Russian group, usually about eight men and women, invariably stood shoulder to shoulder, unable to speak any European language, and seemingly unwilling to engage in any interchange of converse, though Hugh always tried to create some contact. They drank sparingly and were the first to leave. Hugh had early on made friends with the Polish Naval Attaché (a part of this group), who was a delightful young commander, and they would meet from time to time for lunch or dinner at some restaurant. After several

471

months of this Hugh saw his friend at the other side of the room at one of these cocktail parties and walked across to speak to him. The little man went red in the face and whispered:

"You must not speak to me. I am not allowed to talk with you again. It is very serious!" And he nodded in the direction of the Russian group, all of whom were looking directly at the two men. Hugh replied with an invitation to lunch tomorrow at their favourite restaurant, and the Polish officer said he would try to get there but was not sure that it would be possible. In spite of enquiries at the Russian Embassy this officer was never seen nor heard of again, and no sort of explanation was furnished in face of repeated enquiries.

There had been in the Naval Intelligence Division a long-standing contact with the Admiralty Press Division, and Hugh had, of course, spent over six years working with pressmen at sea in the Home Fleet and had come to know quite a number of naval reporters.

Each year the Press Club gave a dinner for officers of the Admiralty Press Division and for the DNI and his personal assistant at an ancient inn in Fleet Street where steak and oyster pudding was the main dish; a visit was paid to a printing press to see tomorrow's newspapers emerging out of a chain of rollers at midnight. The guests also toured round some part of the *Daily Express* office building and followed the news articles through the reporters' work room up to the editor's desk, and from there to the typesetter's department until the paper began its journey through the printing machinery and was finally packed off to the early trains out of London.

There was, too, an annual dinner given by the Attachés for the Director of Naval Intelligence, and Hugh was invited to this, the invitation card indicating that his wife was included. To this he replied that, alas, there was no wife, but perhaps the attachés would be kind enough to remedy the deficiency. Evidently the reply was widely circulated, for when he arrived for the party he was assailed on all sides, both by attachés and their wives, with a good deal of hilarious banter. But more seriously the Mexican, Argentinian and also the Chilean attachés each separately took him aside that evening a little later on and proposed to him that he should come to their countries as British Naval Attaché, and the Argentinian definitely asked the Director that his appointment should be made. When the Director informed Hugh of this he refused to go on the ground that, as he had no private income whatever, it would be practically impossible for him to fulfil the social role that would be expected of him in Buenos Aires. In any event he had lately been earmarked for the appointment of Naval Intelligence Staff Officer in South Africa, and that he would have much preferred.

Not long after Hugh's arrival in NID, Prince Philip had been sent on a tour of the various ministries and their departments to familiarise himself with the main streams of the government of the country as part of the preparation for his forthcoming marriage. He was very interested in the Intelligence Division, and after a general briefing by the Director, Hugh was sent to conduct him through some of the more important parts of this organisation. He was full of penetrating questions, and spoke exactly like Lord Mountbatten, using familiar phrases and reacting in an almost identical manner to his mentor who had, of course, brought him up from boyhood, and evidently exerted a considerable influence over his earlier developing years. The interview, which went on all day long, was quite uncanny in the close resemblance between the two men.

During the war years Hugh had of course been prevented from skiing which was, at this period of his life, the sport which attracted him most. But now that he was able to choose leave periods to suit himself he travelled out to the Alps every winter and settled on the Austrian Tyrol as offering the most attractive snow conditions. He always chose some place above five thousand feet because one could be assured of an adequate depth of snow and, normally, an absence of thaw. He finally decided that Compatch on the very border of eastern Switzerland offered the best conditions he could find, for there, no less then five different valleys provided sunshine and shelter from wind and suitable terrain under whatever varied conditions best suited each day. He had to climb over half a dozen avalanches to reach his goal the first time he discovered this little secret village. He steadily improved his performance and finally won his silver badge — the mark set for the second-class performer. Unfortunately an injured knee cut short his prospects as a holder of the gold badge of which he was almost certain in the succeeding year. The injured knee threatened to lame him for the rest of his life. He sold all his equipment and practically went into deep mourning in this his forty-seventh year.

On the occasion of the wedding of Princess Elizabeth to Prince

Philip, London was *en fête* and the main routes were brightly decorated. The newly-married couple drove along the Mall and passed the Admiralty entrance at about thirty feet distance and naval personnel had a very close view of the young couple, and particularly of the princess' happy triumphant smile. People felt that she had obtained what she really wanted and that gave enormous public satisfaction. As she passed that point she was bending down in the open carriage trying to keep her little corgi dog out of sight and in good order.

There had been an earlier moment of excitement as the Princess, accompanied by the King, drove in the State Coach to Westminster Abbey and passed under the Admiralty Arch. Hugh was in charge of the sixty-strong group of Foreign Naval Attachés positioned on the roof above the archway from which one of the finest views in London may be obtained. Just as the royal escort began to emerge from Buckingham Palace half a mile away, a very red-faced police officer exploded on to the roof and commanded every person there to get down below — nobody is ever allowed to stand directly above the sovereign at any time, and the responsible official's head was to be delivered on a charger forthwith. Hugh shepherded the reluctant and, some few of them, angry attachés downstairs where they were found places at suitable windows in the building. The policeman was somewhat mollified when Hugh got a chance to explain to him who the spectators were and that they had moreover been invited there by the First Lord of the Admiralty, the cabinet minister who rules the Navy, and nothing further was ever heard from the police.

Another event viewed from the Admiralty was the annual Trooping of the Colour, which marks the sovereign's birthday each summer. One of the regiments of the guards parades its colours before the sovereign and some four thousand troops perform complicated marching manoeuvres on the restricted area between the Admiralty and Downing Street where the prime minister lives. It is one of the great sights of London, and Hugh's office window looked directly down upon the brilliant spectacle. Many guest spectators were always invited to view this parade.

On still another day when deep snow had recently fallen, Hugh was idly gazing out of his office window when a smartly dressed and comely young lady stepped off the pavement and decided to walk towards Whitehall across a couple of hundred yards of the Horse Guards Parade ground, now a glittering white field. Within yards she was up to her knees and her skirts were dragging in the bitterly cold snow — and of course she soon became numb and almost unable to move her feet in any direction at all. There she stood in the bright sunshine wringing her hands and firmly anchored. A mounted trooper on sentry duty jumped off his horse and waded across the deep snow, picked up the lady in his arms and carried her across the remainder of the parade ground to safety — and one hopes an experience of disaster that ended happily. Some of the Admiralty windows were almost blocked as the sailors watched the gallant soldier, and of course the lady as well.

Another memory of this period was Derby Day, 1947. Hugh had travelled from London to Tattenham Corner, which is only about two hundred yards from a turning point in the course, and walked with his packet of sandwiches right up to the rails and watched the several preliminary races only a few steps distant. When the Derby started about twenty horses came along head-on and one could just manage to distinguish Winston Churchill's racing colours in the leading rank. As they began to turn the corner they came closely packed on the near-side rails there was a loud crack like a pistol shot. Churchill's horse fell with a broken leg, for it had struck and accidently broken a wooden upright post on the rails. The horse had of course to be destroyed, and one could but admire the quick arrival of the ambulance crew who took the poor beast away.

London continued to provide an endless succession of happenings which enlivened the work-a-day life of those who lived and worked there.

But at this point we have to step back a long way in time, for Hugh had begun to devlop quite other ideas.

He felt increasingly that he was — as it were — in the wrong box. He had at an earlier date considered politics as a possible way of future life, and had joined a Conservative Party political training night school. He found it interesting and a new avenue of experience, but after a few months discovered that what his instructors really wanted was a membership who would obey in exact detail the party line on all matters. They did not want a new man with bright and possibly new ideas, and this failed to dovetail in with his personal views and, in any event, these were still in a rudimentary stage of experimental developement, and wide open to a variety of influences. Like most of the demobilised Service people he felt that there ought to be a better way than gun-fire for persuading people to live their lives in simple honesty. Politics travelled a far different road. The public, he discovered, might rightly seek some particular end, but those desires would always be in some measure conditioned by self-seeking interests, and the politicians wanted power and votes, and whatever desires they had were always subjected to a compromise where the interest of the country was concerned. The complexity of interests never ends. Democracy, he thought, was a fine ideal, but there were never enough honest men to make it work.

Twenty-six years earlier a dusky fortune-teller squatting on a boat-deck of the Blue Funnel freighter *Tiresias* in Singapore harbour had persuaded Hugh, stretched out in a deck-chair and half asleep, sweating from every pore in the humid temperature of a very hot afternoon, to have his palm read. The man was genuinely astonished to discover a marked split in the lifeline, which, he said, indicated that this drowsy client was destined in middle life to make a drastic change in his career. Hugh was only moderately interested, but never wholly forgot this prediction.

He was now in his forty-eighth year, had recently contracted a gastric ulcer which had been treated for three weeks in a naval hospital, and he felt ill and exhausted, and, after almost a year of pondering upon his future, he reached a decision to retire from the Service. When he went to the DNI to apply for permission to retire his request was at once granted, and he felt at that moment that he had really and truly shot his bolt and that no adequate naval service remained any longer within his grasp. He had carefully considered the offer of forthcoming employment in South Africa and now felt that the situation of apartheid was so distasteful a prospect that he would never be able to stomach the restrictions which must in that situation inevitably bind him to compromise between duty and politics. There was no real naval role for him in South Africa, he believed, and his actual duty would be to retain and conserve the Royal Navy presence in the republic where he would be the only remaining link with that presence.

The Admiralty was very good to him, and quickly arranged his affairs, granted a "golden bowler" by way of a one thousand pound gratuity, and arranged at his wish for him to go to Belfast to take passage to Halifax in Nova Scotia on board the recently refitted Canadian carrier *Magnificent*. He was given the captain's after cabin and officially messed in the wardroom, though most of his meals were taken in the captain's sea cabin, where he learned a great deal about Canadian naval expansion during the war — a time of extraordinary growth and of outstanding service in the toughest conditions on earth. The work of the huge fleet of small Canadian ships engaged on gruelling convoy service is a saga yet to be adequately chronicled — and advertised too.

This surely was a moment in life sought out for reflection. Hugh had seen a wide variety of peoples and places; he had inevitably acquired through personal experience at least some knowledge of the ways in which different peoples think and act. He had not only witnessed but also understood that the two world wars were not merely isolated incidents but rather that the first was a foundation for a progression towards the second, and that beyond the second came a crescendo of movement towards a third. Professor Tonybee had demonstrated his views of this situation over the whole span of Hugh's professional life, and was regarded as a pessimist by many observers. There had been a moment in Khrushchev's flamboyant journey through the United States when he said:

"Nobody but a lunatic could undertake a nuclear war!" But of course Khrushchev was removed from office and died not long afterwards.

Professor Michael Howard, the Oxford University historian, has spent thirty or more years writing about the anatomy of war, examining how it comes to pass, and Moltke, the German military architect, writing ninety years ago exclaimed: "Woe to him who is first to set fire to Europe!"

And now we, in our generation, have laid such a train of gunpowder that its ignition is actually capable of destroying certainly most — perhaps all — of humanity. To date no sign has appeared that the match cannot be actually struck, and if it is, the conflagration must inevitably occur.

The week-long calm Atlantic sea voyage came to its quiet uneventful end, and he landed at Halifax in due course to be welcomed by a niece and her Royal Canadian Naval husband, and there was finally broken the last and final strand that held Hugh to his Service. No one could have felt more utterly lost than he did on this day.

Yet there did still remain that second furrow in the lifeline on his hand and, though he firmly rejected any serious belief in the validity of palmistry, he admitted to himself a kind of nebulous wonder about where he might presently be led.

He was looking forward to seeing some of the four generations of his family, most of whom he had yet to meet. They were scattered right across the vast space of Canada. It was certain that he would learn much there and also enjoy his travels, but he realised that any life worth living must surely contain something more solid, more reliable, and more worthwhile; for he was not yet sure where or how that value would make itself felt. It was indeed a quest into the unknown, and finally resulted in him becoming a priest in the Anglican Church in 1952.

The End